*The
Grand Strategy
of the Roman
Empire*

Other Books by Edward N. Luttwak

THE ISRAELI ARMY (With Dan Horowitz)

THE POLITICAL USES OF SEA POWER

DICTIONARY OF MODERN WAR

COUP D'ETAT: A PRACTICAL HANDBOOK

Edward N. Luttwak

THE GRAND STRATEGY
OF THE ROMAN EMPIRE

From the First Century A.D. to the Third

THE JOHNS HOPKINS UNIVERSITY PRESS

BALTIMORE AND LONDON

TO MY WIFE, DALYA

The Johns Hopkins University Press, Baltimore, Maryland 21218
The Johns Hopkins Press Ltd., London

Library of Congress Catalog Card Number 76–17232
ISBN 0-8018-1863-x
Library of Congress Cataloging in Publication data will be found on the last printed page of this book.

CONTENTS

MAPS

FIGURES

TABLES

FOREWORD

The author of this book is a specialist in strategic analysis and contemporary international relations. In systematically analyzing the grand strategy of the Roman Empire during four centuries, he has done for Roman historians what they have not done for themselves. To be sure, there is no lack of books and articles on Roman military subjects; the author's substantial bibliography is only a selection. Acute and illuminating analyses of imperial strategy and policy in various sectors in one period or another exist and remain highly valuable. But the handbooks and general studies of a generation or more ago are becoming out of date and inadequate. The "Clausewitzian" approach found in some may be invalid, as Dr. Luttwak suggests. In any event, a vast amount of fruitful work has been done in the last few decades, based largely on excavations and new documents, especially inscriptions. The standards of provincial archaeologists have become more meticulous, their techniques more resourceful, and their accumulated knowledge more precise. Many scholars have concentrated on important questions with which Dr. Luttwak is not directly concerned: e.g., the army as a factor in Romanization and in administration, its internal structure, recruitment, etc. Usually they have dealt with a relatively limited period or area. To my knowledge, no study comparable to this book exists.

Its distinctive contribution consists, first, in its comprehensive and sustained character, covering as it does the entire empire and a period of several centuries, during which fundamental changes took place; secondly, in its concentration on "grand strategy"; thirdly, in the author's knowledge of contemporary strategic analysis, with which few ancient historians are at all acquainted; and, finally, in his intelligent and perceptive judgment in particular matters. He has been discriminating in his use of monographs and articles, which cannot be taken for granted when a scholar ventures into a field not his own.

It is to be hoped that this book will not be read merely by those already interested in the Roman Empire. For centuries, and even in the first decades of this nation, theorists and illustrious commanders thought that Roman military institutions and practices deserved study. This was not simply antiquarianism. Dr. Luttwak in his Preface stresses resemblances between our strategic predicament and that of the Romans. They are at least provocative and stimulating.

No one will suppose that a work of synthesis such as this, however successful, will remove the need to give further attention to the questions considered. Specialists will doubtless find errors or disagree with conclusions. New materials and studies will continue to appear. It is natural, too, for historians to react to abstract patterns by noting complexities and contradictions. But if they decide to modify or reject some of the patterns found here, they will at least find themselves concerned with significant questions lucidly presented.

J. F. Gilliam
Institute for Advanced Study

PREFACE

An investigation of the strategic statecraft of the Roman Empire scarcely requires justification. In the record of our civilization, the Roman achievement in the realm of grand strategy remains entirely unsurpassed, and even two millennia of technological change have not invalidated its lessons. In any case, the study of Roman history is its own reward.

To one accustomed to the chaotic duplication, scientistic language, and narrow parochialism of the literature of international relations, the cumulative discipline, austere elegance, and cosmopolitan character of Roman historiography came as a revelation. And these virtues are especially marked in the specialized literature on the Roman army and the military history of the empire. Nevertheless, my own work was prompted by an acute dissatisfaction with this very same literature: the archaeologists, epigraphists, numismatists, and textual critics, whose devoted labors have uncovered the information on which our knowledge rests, often applied grossly inappropriate strategic notions to their reconstruction of the evidence. It is not that these scholars were ignorant of the latest techniques of systems analysis or unaware of the content of modern strategic thought; indeed, their shortcoming was not that they were old-fashioned, but rather that they were far too modern.

From the beginning of the nineteenth century until Hiroshima, strategic thought was dominated by post-Napoleonic, "Clausewitzian " notions, and these notions have pervaded the thinking of many whose primary interests are far removed from military matters. In their crude, popularized form, these ideas stress a particular form of war, conflict between nationalities; they stress the primacy and desirability of offensive warfare in pursuit of decisive results (thus inspiring an aversion to defensive strategies); and they imply a sharp distinction between the state of peace and the state of war. Finally, these ideas accord primacy to the active use of military force, as opposed to the use of images of force, for the purposes of diplomatic coercion.

Only since 1945 has the emergence of new technologies of mass destruction invalidated the fundamental assumptions of the Clausewitzian approach to grand strategy. We, like the Romans, face the prospect not of decisive conflict, but of a permanent state of war, albeit limited. We, like the Romans, must actively protect an advanced society against a variety of threats rather than concentrate on destroying the forces of our enemies in battle. Above all, the nature of modern weapons requires that we avoid their use while nevertheless striving to exploit their full diplomatic potential. The revolutionary implications of these fundamental changes are as yet only dimly understood. It is not surprising, therefore, that even contemporary research on Roman military history is still pervaded by an anachronistic strategic outlook.

The paradoxical effect of the revolutionary change in the nature of modern war has been to bring the strategic predicament of the Romans much closer to our own. Hence this reexamination of the historical evidence from the viewpoint of modern strategic analysis.

Acknowledgments. To my teachers, colleagues, and friends, Walter Laqueur, Robert Tucker, David Abshire, James King, George Liska, Robert Osgood, Francis West, and James Schlesinger—*non tamen adeo virtutum sterile saeculum ut non et bona exempla prodidit.* Michael Aronson, JoAnn Gutin, and Shom Edmonds all variously contributed their efforts to this book, earning my gratitude and respect. Mrs. Catherine Grover typed with much care a difficult text.

*The
Grand Strategy
of the Roman
Empire*

INTRODUCTION

In our own disordered times, it is natural to look back for comfort and instruction to the experience of Roman imperial statecraft. No analogies are possible in the economic, social, or political spheres of life, but in the realm of strategy there are instructive similarities. The fundamentals of Roman strategy in the imperial age were rooted not in a technology now obsolete, but in a predicament that we share. For the Romans, as for ourselves, the two essential requirements of an evolving civilization were a sound material base and adequate security. For the Romans, as for ourselves, the elusive goal of strategic statecraft was to provide security for the civilization without prejudicing the vitality of its economic base and without compromising the stability of an evolving political order. The historic success of the Roman Empire, manifest in its unique endurance, reflected the high degree to which these conflicting imperatives were reconciled. It was certainly not battlefield achievements alone that ensured for so long the tranquillity of vast territories, lands which have been in turmoil ever since.

Had the strength of the Roman Empire derived from a tactical superiority on the battlefield, from superior generalship, or from a more advanced weapons technology, there would be little to explain, though much to describe. But this was not so. Roman tactics were almost invariably sound but not distinctly superior, and the Roman

soldier of the imperial period was not noted for his *élan*. He was not a
warrior intent on proving his manhood but a long-service professional pursuing a career; his goal and reward was not a hero's death
but a severance grant upon retirement. Roman weapons, far from
being universally more advanced, were frequently inferior to those
used by the enemies whom the empire defeated with such great
regularity. Nor could the secular survival of the empire have been
ensured by a fortunate succession of great feats of generalship: the
Roman army had a multitude of competent soldiers and some great
generals, but its strength derived from method, not from fortuitous
talent.

The superiority of the empire, and it was vast, was of an altogether more subtle order: it derived from the whole complex of ideas
and traditions that informed the organization of Roman military
power and harnessed the armed power of the empire to political
purpose. The firm subordination of tactical priorities, martial ideals,
and warlike instincts to political goals was the essential condition of
the strategic success of the empire. With rare exceptions, the misuse
of force in pursuit of purely tactical goals, or for the psychic rewards
of purposeless victories, was avoided by those who controlled the
destinies of Rome. In the imperial period at least, military force was
clearly recognized for what it is, an essentially limited instrument of
power, costly and brittle. Much better to *conserve* force and use
military power indirectly, as the instrument of political warfare.

Together with money and a manipulative diplomacy, forces visibly
ready to fight but held back from battle could serve to contrive
disunity among those who might jointly threaten the empire, to
deter those who would otherwise attack, and to control lands and
peoples by intimidation—ideally to the point where sufficient security or even an effective domination could be achieved without any
use of force at all. Having learned in the earlier republican period
how to defeat neighbors in battle by sheer tactical strength, having
later mastered the strategic complexities of large-scale warfare in
fighting the Carthaginians, the Romans finally learned that the most
desirable use of military power was not military at all, but political;
and indeed they conquered the entire Hellenistic world with few
battles and much coercive diplomacy.

The same effort to conserve force was also evident in war, at the
tactical level. The ideal Roman general was not a figure in the heroic
style, leading his troops in reckless charge to victory or death. He
would rather advance in a slow and carefully prepared march,
building supply roads behind him and fortified camps each night in
order to avoid the unpredictable risks of rapid maneuver. He preferred to let the enemy retreat into fortified positions rather than

accept the inevitable losses of open warfare, and would wait to starve out the enemy in a prolonged siege rather than suffer great casualties in taking the fortifications by storm. Overcoming the spirit of a culture still infused with Greek martial ideals (that most reckless of men, Alexander the Great, was actually an object of worship in many Roman households), the great generals of Rome were noted for their extreme caution.

It is precisely this aspect of Roman tactics (in addition to the heavy reliance on engineering warfare) that explains the relentless quality of Roman armies on the move, as well as their peculiar resilience in adversity: the Romans won their victories slowly, but they were very hard to defeat.

Just as the Romans had apparently no need of a Clausewitz to subject their military energies to the discipline of political goals, it seems that they had no need of modern analytical techniques either. Innocent of the new science of "systems analysis," the Romans nevertheless designed and built large and complex security systems that successfully integrated troop deployments, fixed defenses, road networks, and signaling links in a coherent whole. In the more abstract spheres of strategy it is evident that, whether by intellect or traditional intuition, the Romans understood all the subtleties of deterrence, and also its limitations. Above all, the Romans clearly realized that the dominant dimension of power was not physical but psychological—the product of others' perceptions of Roman strength rather than the use of this strength. And this realization alone can explain the sophistication of Roman strategy at its best.

The siege of Masada in A.D. 70–73 reveals the exceedingly subtle workings of a long-range security policy based on deterrence. Faced with the resistance of a few hundred Jews on a mountain in the Judean desert, a place of no strategic or economic importance, the Romans could have insulated the rebels by posting a few hundred men to guard them. Based at the nearby springs of Ein Geddi, a contingent of Roman cavalry could have waited patiently for the Jews to exhaust their water supply. Alternatively, the Romans could have stormed the mountain fortress. The Jewish War had essentially been won, and only Masada was still holding out; but this spark of resistance might rekindle at any time the fire of revolt. The slopes of Masada are steep, and the Jews were formidable fighters, but with several thousand men pressing from all sides the defenders could not have held back the attackers for long, though they could have killed many.

The Romans did none of these things. They did not starve out the Jews and they did not storm the mountain. Instead, at a time when the entire Roman army had a total of only twenty-nine legions to garrison the entire empire, one legion was deployed to besiege Masada, there to reduce the fortress by great works of engineering, including a huge ramp reaching the full height of the mountain. This was a vast and seemingly irrational commitment of scarce military manpower—or was it? The entire three-year operation, and the very insignificance of its objective, must have made an ominous impression on all those in the East who might otherwise have been tempted to contemplate revolt: the lesson of Masada was that the Romans would pursue rebellion even to mountain tops in remote deserts to destroy its last vestiges, regardless of cost. And as if to ensure that the message was duly heard, and duly remembered, Josephus was installed in Rome where he wrote a detailed account of the siege, which was published in Greek, the acquired language of Josephus, and that of the Roman East.

The suggestion that the Masada operation was a calculated act of psychological warfare is of course conjecture. But the alternative explanation is incredible, for a mere blind obstinacy in pursuing the siege would be utterly inconsistent with all that we know of the protagonists, especially Vespasian—that most practical of men, the emperor whose chief virtue was a shrewd common sense.

We need not rely upon conjecture to reconstruct in considerable detail the basic features of Roman imperial statecraft from the first century A.D. to the third, the subject of this enquiry. The narrative sources, indispensable to an understanding of the detailed conduct of policy and its motives, are sadly incomplete and sometimes suspect. But the labors of generations of scholars have yielded a mass of detailed evidence on the physical elements of imperial strategy: the force-structure of the army, the design of border defenses, and the layout of individual fortifications. At the same time, enough is known of the salient moments and general nature of Roman diplomacy to form a coherent picture of imperial statecraft as a whole, both the hardware and the software.

Three distinct systems of imperial security can be identified over the period. We may properly speak of *systems*, for they each integrated diplomacy, military forces, road networks, and fortifications to serve a common objective. Moreover, the design of each element reflected the logic of the whole. Each system was intended to satisfy a distinct set of priorities, themselves the reflection of changing conceptions of empire: hegemonic expansionism for the first system; territorial security for the second; and finally, in diminished circumstances, sheer survival for the imperial power itself. Each system was based on a different combination of diplomacy, direct force, and fixed infrastructures, and each entailed different operational methods; but, more fundamentally, each system reflected a different Roman world-view and self-image.

With brutal simplicity, it might be said that with the first system the Romans of the republic conquered much to serve the interests of the few, those living in the city—and in fact still fewer, those best placed to control policy. During the first century A.D. Roman ideas evolved toward a much broader and altogether more benevolent conception of empire. Under the aegis of the second system, men born in lands far from Rome could call themselves Romans and have their claim fully allowed; and the frontiers were efficiently defended to defend the growing prosperity of all, and not merely the privileged. The result was the empire of the second century A.D., which served the interests of millions rather than thousands.

Under the third system, organized in the wake of the great crisis of the third century, the provision of security became an increasingly heavy charge on society, a charge unevenly distributed, which could enrich the wealthy and ruin the poor. The machinery of empire now became increasingly self-serving, with its tax-collectors, administrators, and soldiers of much greater use to one another than to society at large. Even then the empire retained the loyalties of many, for the alternative was chaos. When this ceased to be so, when organized barbarian states capable of providing a measure of security began to emerge in lands that had once been Roman, then the last system of imperial security lost its last support, men's fear of the unknown.

One

THE JULIO-CLAUDIAN SYSTEM. *Client States and Mobile Armies from Augustus to Nero.*

The first system of imperial security was essentially that of the late republic, though it continued into the first century A.D., under that peculiar form of autocracy we know as the principate. Created by the party of Octavian, himself a master of constitutional ambiguity, the principate was republican in form but autocratic in content. The magistracies were filled as before to supervise public life, and the Senate sat as before, seemingly in charge of city and empire. But real control was now in the hands of the family and personal associates of Octavian, kinsman and heir of Julius Caesar, and the ultimate victor of the Civil War that had begun with Caesar's murder and ended in 30 B.C. with the final defeat of Anthony and Cleopatra.

Julius Caesar the dictator had overthrown the weak institutions of the republic. His heir, all-powerful after Actium, restored and immediately subverted the republic. In 27 B.C., Octavian adopted the name Augustus, redolent with semireligious authority; Rome had a new master. In theory, Augustus was only the first citizen (princeps), but this was a citizen who controlled election to all the magistracies and the command of all the armies.

7

Neither oriental despot nor living god, the princeps was in theory still bound by the laws and subject to the will of the Senate. But the direct power controlled by Augustus, the power of his legions, far outweighed the authority of the Senate, and the senators gave this power its due in their eager obedience.

Under Augustus the vast but fragmented conquests of two centuries of republican expansionism were rounded off and consolidated in a single generation. Spain was fully occupied by 25 B.C., and three provinces were organized (Baetica, Lusitania, and Tarraconensis), though the last native revolt was not suppressed until 19 B.C. The interior of Gaul, conquered by Caesar but not organized for tax collection, was formed into three new provinces—Aquitania, Lugdunensis, and Belgica. In southern Gaul, the old province of Gallia Transalpina, formed in 121 B.C., was not reorganized but merely renamed Narbonensis; this was a land already heavily Romanized and long since civilized.

Germany was another matter. It was not until ca.12 B.C. that Roman incursions reached the Elbe. Roman soldiers and traders were establishing a presence, but to establish a German province it would be necessary to eliminate all independent powers between Rhine and Elbe. This the Romans set out to do, beginning in A.D. 6 with a great pincer operation from the Upper Rhine and the Danube, which was to enclose what is now Bohemia and trap the Marcomanni, the most powerful nation in southern Germany. In the meantime, P. Quinctilius Varus was in northwest Germany with three legions and auxiliary troops, not to fight but to organize tax collection in lands already counted as conquered.

But the great offensive against the Marcomanni had to be called off just as it was about to begin: Illyricum, in the rear of the southern pincer, had erupted in a great revolt. In A.D. 9 the revolt was finally suppressed, but just then the three legions and auxiliary troops of Varus were ambushed and destroyed by the Germans of Arminius, a former auxiliary in Roman service and a chief of the Cherusci. The Varian disaster brought the Augustan conquest of Germany to an end. The lands east of the Rhine were evacuated, and two military commands, for Upper and Lower Germany, were established instead to control the lands west of the Rhine.

To the south, Roman policy had greater success. The Alpine lands stretching from the foothills in northern Italy to the upper course of the Danube were subdued by 15 B.C., partly to be incorporated into Italy, and partly to be organized into two provinces, Raetia and Noricum (roughly Bavaria, Switzerland, and western Austria). East of Noricum, the sub-Danubian lands already under Roman control encompassed the coastal tracts of Illyricum, Macedonia, and the client kingdom of Thrace. Under Augustus, Roman power conquered all the remaining riparian lands of the Danube, stretching from Croatia to Soviet Moldavia on the modern map. In A.D. 6, when the encirclement of the Marcomanni was about to begin,

Roman power was still too new to pacify these lands, not fully tranquil even in our own day. When the revolt came, it was on a grand scale; the so-called Pannonian revolt, actually centered in the roadless mountain country of Illyricum, was by far the most costly of the wars of Augustus. It took three years of hard fighting with as many troops as the empire could muster—even slaves and freedmen were recruited—to subdue Illyricum. The Varian disaster followed the end of the revolt in A.D. 9 almost immediately, and ambitious schemes of conquest beyond the Danube could no longer be contemplated. The coastal lands of Illyricum were organized into the province of Dalmatia, and the interior became the province of Pannonia. The lower course of the Danube all the way to the great delta (on the post–1945 Russo-Rumanian frontier) was fronted by the vast command of Moesia, but the client kingdom of Thrace occupied much of the hinterland, in modern Bulgaria.

In the East, there were no Augustan conquests. The western half of Anatolia had long since been provincial territory (the province of Asia [southwest Turkey] dated back to 133 B.C.). The client kingdom of Galatia was annexed in 25 B.C. and formed into a province; beyond Galatia, kingdoms subject to Rome stretched from the Black Sea right across to the province of Syria, the largest being the kingdom of Cappadocia. To the east was vast, primitive, and mountainous Armenia, almost entirely useless but nevertheless important, for beyond Armenia and south of it was the civilized Parthia of the Arsacids—the only power on the horizon that could present a serious strategic threat to the empire.

Augustus did not try to avenge the great defeat inflicted by the Parthians on the Roman army of Crassus in 53 B.C., at Carrhae. Instead, in 20 B.C. he reached a compromise settlement under which Armenia was to be ruled by a king of the Arsacid family, who would receive his investiture from Rome. Behind the neatly balanced formality there was strategy, for Parthian troops would thereby be kept out of a neutralized Armenia and far from undefended Anatolia and valuable Syria. There was also politics—domestic politics. The standards lost at Carrhae were returned to Rome and received with great ceremony; Augustus had coins issued falsely proclaiming the "capture" of Armenia.

Adjoining the client kingdoms of eastern Anatolia to the south was Syria, organized as a taxpaying province in 63 B.C. Next was Judea, a client kingdom until A.D. 6, and beyond the Sinai, Egypt. A province since 30 B.C., Egypt was most directly controlled by Augustus through a prefect who could not be of senatorial rank. A senator might always dream of becoming emperor, and control of the Egyptian grain supply could be worth many legions to a rebel.

The rest of North Africa was provincial territory: Cyrenaica (eastern Libya) had been organized since 74 B.C., and the province of Africa (western Libya and Tunisia) was still older, dating from the destruction of

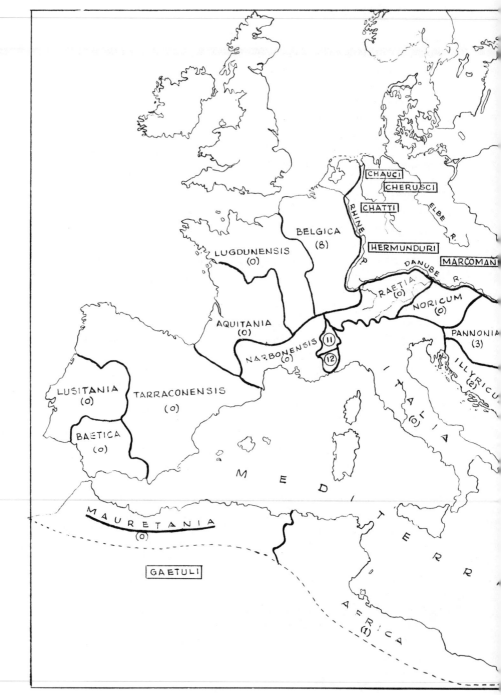

MAP 1.1. THE EMPIRE IN A.D. 23

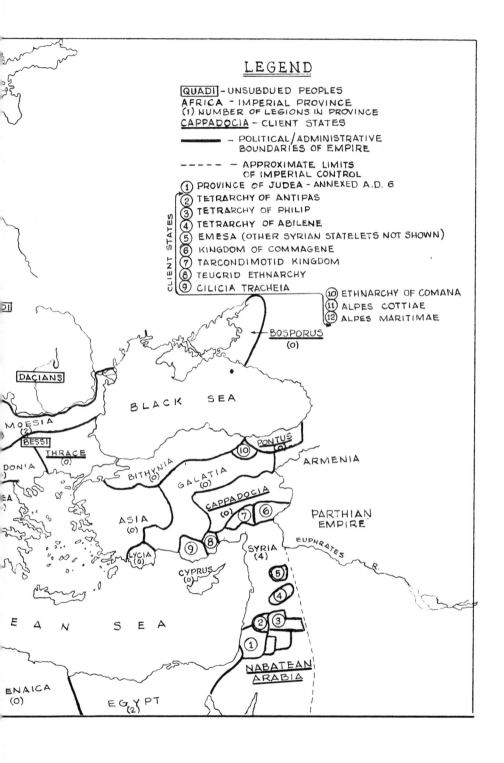

LEGEND

QUADI - UNSUBDUED PEOPLES
AFRICA - IMPERIAL PROVINCE
(1) NUMBER OF LEGIONS IN PROVINCE
CAPPADOCIA - CLIENT STATES

——— - POLITICAL/ADMINISTRATIVE
BOUNDARIES OF EMPIRE

- - - - - APPROXIMATE LIMITS
OF IMPERIAL CONTROL

CLIENT STATES

(1) PROVINCE OF JUDEA - ANNEXED A.D. 6
(2) TETRARCHY OF ANTIPAS
(3) TETRARCHY OF PHILIP
(4) TETRARCHY OF ABILENE
(5) EMESA (OTHER SYRIAN STATELETS NOT SHOWN)
(6) KINGDOM OF COMMAGENE
(7) TARCONDIMOTID KINGDOM
(8) TEUCRID ETHNARCHY
(9) CILICIA TRACHEIA
(10) ETHNARCHY OF COMANA
(11) ALPES COTTIAE
(12) ALPES MARITIMAE

→ BOSPORUS
(0)

DACIANS

BLACK   SEA

MOESIA
(2)
BESSI
THRACE
(0)

DONIA

EA

PONTUS
(0)

ARMENIA

BITHYNIA
(0)

GALATIA
(0)

ASIA
(0)

CAPPADOCIA
(0)   (7)   (6)

PARTHIAN
EMPIRE

EUPHRATES

R.

(9) (8)

LYCIA
(0)

CYPRUS
(0)

SYRIA
(4)

(5)

(4)

(2) (3)

(1)

NABATEAN
ARABIA

E A N   S E A

ENAICA
(0)

E G Y PT
(2)

Carthage in 146 B.C. But the circle was not complete, and Augustus did not seek to close it: beyond the province of Africa, in the lands of modern Algeria and Morocco, Roman control was indirect, being exercised through the client kingdom of Mauretania.

By A.D. 9 the energies of Augustan expansionism were spent, exhausted by the travails of Illyricum and Germany. The fact could not be hidden, but necessity could be presented as virtue. When Augustus died in A.D. 14, his stepson Tiberius of the Claudian family (Augustus counted himself of the Julian) received a vast empire, which he had done much to conquer, as his inheritance, but he also received the admonition that its boundaries were not to be expanded further.

Tiberius was both able and, it is said, sinister; he ruled until A.D. 37. He had to fight to subdue internal revolts, but fought no wars of conquest. Tiberius's acquisition of power was simple: a cowed Senate eagerly and fearfully proclaimed him ruler, and no army commander descended on Rome with his legions to contest the office. Another followed Tiberius by the same means—Gaius, nicknamed Caligula. Unbalanced, or perhaps merely maligned in our sources, Gaius was murdered in A.D. 41. There was talk of restoring the republic. But Claudius, uncle of the murdered emperor, was proclaimed emperor in turn, not by the Senate but by the Praetorian Guard, and not disinterestedly: each of the 4,500 Praetorians was paid 3,750 denarii as a cash bounty, more than sixteen years' worth of pay to a private serving in the legions.

A man of grotesque appearance, foolish in his dealings with women, Claudius presided over a regime noted for its progressive benevolence to the provincials, and which soon resumed the path of imperial conquest after an interval of thirty-seven years. In A.D. 43 Britain was invaded, to be conquered only in part thereafter, in gradual stages—more than 160 years later, the emperor Septimius Severus was still campaigning in Scotland.

Senators might still try to restore the republic with their daggers, but Claudius was killed, probably in A.D. 54, by poison, for pettier motives. His stepson Nero then ascended to the principate, the last of the Claudians. Nero inaugurated his rule with the first Parthian War of the principate. Tiridates, an Arsacid, had been made king of Armenia without benefit of a Roman investiture; and it was feared that Armenia might be transformed from buffer state to base of operations for Parthian armies advancing against undefended Anatolia and weakly held Syria.

Nero is known for extravagance and murder, but there was wisdom in his regime: the conduct of the Parthian War was moderate and successful, the outcome another useful compromise. In A.D. 66, after eleven years of intermittent war and almost continuous diplomacy, Tiridates was crowned king of Armenia once again, but this time in Rome.

The settlement came just in time. In A.D. 66 the Jewish revolt began and soon became a major war. It was to last until A.D. 73, if the isolated resistance of Masada is counted. Nero did not live to see its end. The last of the Julio-Claudians killed himself in A.D. 68; misfortune or excess had left him without the support of either Praetorians or Senate when his office was contested.

C. Julius Vindex, a new man, a Gaul and a governor of Lugdunensis in Gaul, was one of the many whom Nero's unsystematic terror had frightened but not fully intimidated. He declared Nero unfit for the office and proposed as princeps S. Sulpicius Galba, of venerable age, noble origin, a strict disciplinarian, and very rich. Galba could count on the aristocratic sentiments of the Senate, but as governor of Tarraconensis he had only one legion at his disposal. He began to raise another, but could not save Vindex when the governor of Upper Germany descended on Gaul with his legions.

It was one thing to destroy the Gallic levies of a Gallic upstart, but quite another to defend actively the power of Nero against Galba, a great Roman aristocrat. Thus Nero's cause triumphed, but Nero was lost. He had no support in Rome, or so he thought, possibly in petulance and panic. He did not appeal to the legions on the frontiers, where Julio-Claudian prestige might have obscured his extreme personal shortcomings. Instead, he planned an escape to Egypt, or so it is said. En route, he was deserted by his escort of Praetorians and sought refuge in the home of an ex-slave. There he heard that the Senate had declared him a public enemy, to be flogged to death by the ancient custom. With help, he managed to commit suicide on June 9, A.D. 68.

Thus ended the rule of the Julio-Claudians.

I
The System
in Outline

The most striking feature of the Julio-Claudian system of imperial security was its economy of force. At the death of Augustus, in A.D. 14, the territories subject to direct or indirect imperial control comprised the coastal lands of the entire Mediterranean basin, the whole of the Iberian peninsula, continental Europe inland to the Rhine and Danube, Anatolia, and, more loosely, the Bosporan Kingdom on the northern shores of the Black Sea. Control over this vast territory was effectively ensured by a small army, whose size was originally determined at the beginning of the principate and only slightly increased thereafter.

Twenty-five legions remained after the destruction of Varus and his three legions in A.D. 9 and throughout the rule of Tiberius (A.D. 14-37).[1] Eight new legions were raised between the accession of Gaius-Caligula in A.D. 37 and the civil war of A.D. 69-70, but four were cashiered, so that under Vespasian there were twenty-nine

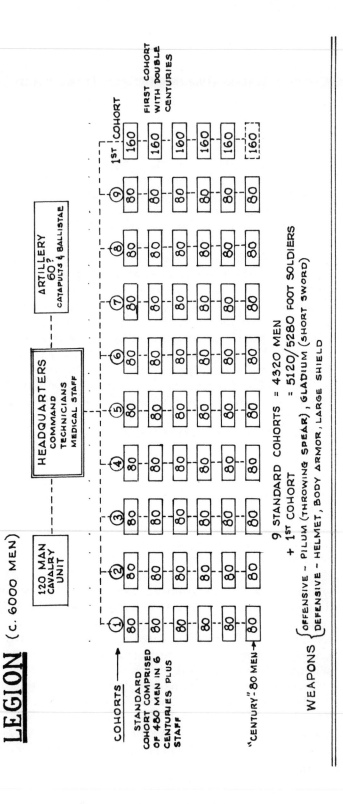

LEGION (c. 6000 MEN)

COHORTS →

STANDARD COHORT COMPRISED OF 480 MEN IN 6 CENTURIES PLUS STAFF

"CENTURY" = 80 MEN →

120 MAN CAVALRY UNIT

HEADQUARTERS
COMMAND
TECHNICIANS
MEDICAL STAFF

ARTILLERY 60?
CATAPULTS & BALLISTAE

① ② ③ ④ ⑤ ⑥ ⑦ ⑧ ⑨   1ST COHORT

FIRST COHORT WITH DOUBLE CENTURIES

9 STANDARD COHORTS = 4320 MEN
+ 1ST COHORT = 5120/5280 FOOT SOLDIERS

WEAPONS { OFFENSIVE – PILUM (THROWING SPEAR), GLADIUM (SHORT SWORD)
DEFENSIVE – HELMET, BODY ARMOR, LARGE SHIELD

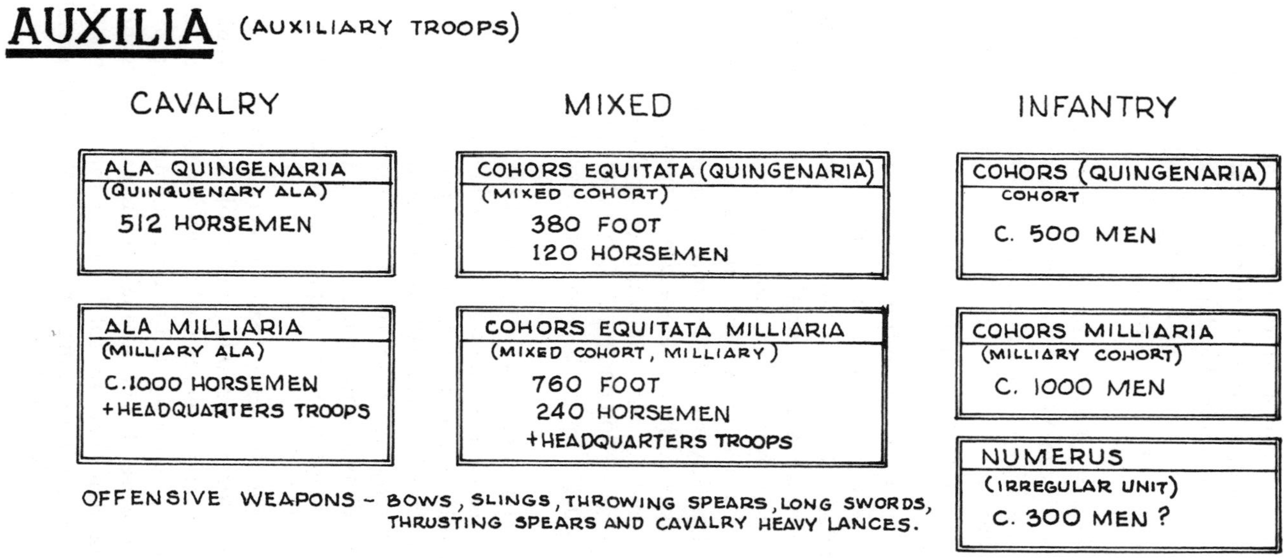

AUXILIA (AUXILIARY TROOPS)

CAVALRY

ALA QUINGENARIA
(QUINQUENARY ALA)

512 HORSEMEN

ALA MILLIARIA
(MILLIARY ALA)

C. 1000 HORSEMEN
+HEADQUARTERS TROOPS

MIXED

COHORS EQUITATA (QUINGENARIA)
(MIXED COHORT)

380 FOOT
120 HORSEMEN

COHORS EQUITATA MILLIARIA
(MIXED COHORT, MILLIARY)

760 FOOT
240 HORSEMEN
+HEADQUARTERS TROOPS

INFANTRY

COHORS (QUINGENARIA)
(COHORT)

C. 500 MEN

COHORS MILLIARIA
(MILLIARY COHORT)

C. 1000 MEN

NUMERUS
(IRREGULAR UNIT)

C. 300 MEN ?

OFFENSIVE WEAPONS – BOWS, SLINGS, THROWING SPEARS, LONG SWORDS, THRUSTING SPEARS AND CAVALRY HEAVY LANCES.

FIG. 1.1. ROMAN UNIT ESTABLISHMENTS IN THE FIRST AND SECOND CENTURIES A.D.

legions on the establishment, only one more than the original number set by Augustus.[2]

There is some small margin of uncertainty on the exact manpower strength of the legions, but the authorities agree that each consisted of about 6,000 men, including 5,120 or 5,280 foot soldiers, a cavalry contingent of 120 men, and sundry headquarters' troops.[3] On this basis, the upper limit on the number of legionary troops would be about 168,000 men until A.D. 9, 150,000 thereafter, and no more than 174,000 after A.D. 70.

In addition to the legions of heavy infantry, then still manned mostly by long-service citizen volunteers, there were the *auxilia*, generally manned by non-citizens during this period.[4] Organized into cavalry "wings" (*alae*), light infantry cohorts, or mixed cavalry/infantry units (*cohortes equitatae*), the *auxilia* were functionally complementary to the legionary forces.

There is no satisfactory evidence on the total size of the auxiliary forces for the empire as a whole, but the authorities accept the general validity of a statement in Tacitus[5] according to which, in the year A.D. 23, the aggregate number of the auxiliary forces was roughly the same as that of the "Roman," or legionary, forces.[6]

For our purposes, it suffices to know that the total number of auxiliary troops did not greatly exceed that of the legionary forces—a possibility nowhere suggested in the literature. Accepting the 1:1 ratio as a valid approximation, the total number of Roman troops would thus be on the order of 300,000 for A.D. 23, with a theoretical maximum of roughly 350,000 for the balance of the period until A.D. 70.[7]

Since Augustus claimed to have personally paid off 300,000 men on retirement with either lands or money,[8] it would seem that the total number of men in the ground forces was not particularly large by the standards of the time. However, the well-known difficulties of citizen-recruitment, already acute at this time, reflected a true demographic problem—Pliny's "shortage of youths" (*iuventutis penuria*): the total male population of military age in Italy probably numbered less than a million.[9]

It was easier to pay for the army than to recruit its members. Annual pay and upkeep for a trained legionary soldier in the ranks came to 225 *denarii* per year; the overall cost of retirement grants, set at 3,000 *denarii* in A.D. 5, was a burden not much smaller than pay and upkeep, and there were also occasional donatives.[10] Nevertheless, it has been suggested that the total cost of the army on an annual basis did not amount to more than half of the imperial revenue during the early principate.[11]

In view of this, there is no reason to believe that the reorganization of the army after the Battle of Actium was dictated by financial or even manpower constraints. It appears more likely that the number of legions was set at twenty-eight, from a total of sixty or so (some only fragments) deployed by both sides during the Civil War,[12] on the basis of a rational scheme of deployment, in which it was the desired level of forces that set the costs, rather than the other way round.

In a famous passage of the *Annals* Tacitus provides the only comprehensive survey of the deployment of the legions extant in the narrative sources.[13] Its accuracy is generally accepted by the authorities.[14] According to Tacitus, in A.D. 23, ninth year of the principate of Tiberius, there were eight legions on the Rhine, three in Spain, two in the province of Africa, two in Egypt, four in Syria, two in Moesia and two in Pannonia (for a total of four along the Danube), and finally two in Dalmatia, for a total of twenty-five. And then there were the *auxilia*, of which Tacitus refrains from giving a detailed breakdown.

From this account one may gather the impression that the legionary forces, and the auxiliary troops with them, were distributed to form a thin perimeter. The consequent lack of a strategic reserve, held uncommitted in the deep rear, is regularly remarked on and criticized.[15] It is true that the forces in Italy, nine praetorian cohorts and four urban cohorts, did not amount to much; the latter were primarily a police force and the former could provide no more than a strong escort for the rulers of Rome when they set out to campaign in person. On the other hand, Tacitus describes the two Dalmatian legions as a strategic reserve, which could cover *in situ* the northeastern invasion axes into Italy while also being available for redeployment elsewhere, since Dalmatia was not a frontier province.

In fact, the impression of a perimeter deployment is misleading. For one thing, as it has been pointed out, a key factor in the distribution of the legions was the needs of internal, rather than external, security.[16] Hence the three legions in Spain, which was not frontier territory but was in the final stages of a secular pacification effort, and the two legions of Dalmatia, in the rear of the forces holding Pannonia. As Tacitus points out, Dalmatia was a convenient location for a strategic reserve, but the province had also been the scene of the dangerous Pannonian revolt in A.D. 6–9, "the most serious of all our foreign wars since the Carthaginian ones," according to Suetonius (*gravissimum omnium externorum bellorum post Punica*).[17]

Similarly, the two legions in Egypt were obviously not required to ward off external threats, i.e., nomadic incursions. To counter or deter such elusive enemies, auxiliary units, especially if mounted, were much more effective than the solid mass of the legions. The latter, on the other hand, were very suitable for the task of maintaining internal security.

There was as yet no demarcated imperial frontier and no system of fixed frontier defenses, nor were the legions housed in permanent stone fortresses as they were to be in the future. Instead, the troops slept in leather tents or in winter quarters (*hiberna*) built of wood, in camps whose perimeter defenses were no more elaborate than those of the marching camps that legionary forces on the move would build each afternoon at the conclusion of the day's march.[18] Nor were such legionary camps sited as tactical strong points.[19] Indeed, they were not defensive positions at all.

Deployed astride major routes leading both to unconquered lands ahead and to the sometimes unsettled provinces in the rear, the legions were not there to defend the adjacent ground, but rather to serve as mobile striking forces. For practical purposes, their deployment was that of a field army, distributed, it is true, in high-threat sectors, but not tied down to territorial defense. Uninvolved in major wars of conquest between A.D. 6 and A.D. 43 (Britain), the salient function of the army was necessarily defensive, i.e., providing security against the sudden emergence of unforeseen threats.

These threats were primarily internal. Aside from the sporadic transborder incursions of Germans, Dacians, and later, Sarmatians, and the conflict with Parthia over the Armenian investiture, Rome's major security problems were the result of native revolts within the empire. Characteristically, a delay, sometimes of generations, would intervene between the initial conquest and the outbreak of revolt: while the native power structure and "nativistic atmosphere" were still largely intact (and with Rome itself having introduced concepts of leadership and cohesion through the local recruitment of auxiliary forces), the resistance to the full impact of imperial taxation and conscription was often violent, sometimes more so than resistance to the initial conquest had been.[20] Thus the revolt in Illyricum of A.D 6–9 and the intermittent revolt of Tacfarinas in Africa between A.D. 14 and 24; there were also more localized uprisings, such as that of Florus and Sacrovir in Gaul, of A.D. 21 and, as a borderline case, the Jewish War.

Since northwest Germany had been counted as conquered, and P. Quinctilius Varus, "a leading lawyer without any military qualities,"[21] was there to organize a province rather than conquer one, the Varian disaster of A.D. 9 must also be counted as an "internal" war.[22] Throughout this period, the control of internal insurgency presented a far more difficult problem than the maintenance of external security vis-à-vis Parthia—whose power was the only "systemic" threat to Rome, and then only on a regional scale.

The colonies were a second instrument of strategic control. Julius Caesar had routinely settled his veterans outside Italy, and Augustus founded twenty-eight colonies for the veterans discharged from the legions. Not primarily intended as agencies of Romanization,[23] the colonies were islands of direct Roman control in an empire still in part hegemonic; as such, they were especially important in areas like Anatolia, where legions were not ordinarily deployed. Whether located in provincial or client-state territory, the colonies provided secure observation and control bases. Their citizens were, in effect, a ready-made militia of ex-soldiers and soldiers' sons who could defend their home towns in the event of attack and hold out until imperial forces could arrive on the scene.

Neither the legions and *auxilia* deployed in their widely spaced bases nor the colonies outside Italy, scattered as they were, could provide anything resembling an all-round perimeter defense. There were no guards and patrols to prevent infiltration of the 4,000 miles of the imperial perimeter on land; there were no contingents of widely distributed mobile forces ready to intercept raiding parties or contend with localized attacks; there was no perimeter defense. In other words, there was no *limes*, in its later sense of a fortified and guarded border. At this time the word still retained its former (but not, apparently, original) meaning of an access road *perpendicular* to the border of secured imperial territory;[24] *limes* thus described a route of penetration cut through hostile territory rather than a "horizontal" frontier, and certainly not a fortified defensive perimeter.

It is the *absence* of a perimeter defense that is the key to the entire system of Roman imperial security of this period. There were neither border defenses nor local forces to guard imperial territories against the "low-intensity" threats of petty infiltration, transborder incursion, or localized attack. As we shall see, such protection was provided, but by indirect and nonmilitary means. By virtually eliminating the burden of maintaining continuous frontier defenses, the net, "disposable" military power generated by the imperial forces was maximized. Hence, the total military power that others could perceive as being available to Rome for offensive use—and that could therefore be put to political advantage by diplomatic means—was also maximized. Thus the empire's potential military power could be converted into actual political control at a high rate of exchange.

The diplomatic instruments that achieved this conversion were the client states and client tribes, whose obedience reflected both their perceptions of Roman military power and their fear of retaliation. Since clients would take care to prevent attacks against provincial territory, their obedience lessened the need to provide local security at the periphery of empire against low-intensity threats, thus increasing the empire's net disposable military power . . . and so completing the cycle.

II
The Client
States

In A.D. 14, when Tiberius succeeded Augustus to the principate, a substantial part of imperial territory was constituted by client states, which were definitely *of* the empire even if perhaps not fully within it.[25] In the West, primitive Mauretania was ruled by Juba II, a Roman creature originally established on his throne in 25 B.C. In the Levant, Judea was now a province, but in parts of Herod's former kingdom the tetrarchies of Philip and of Antipas remained autonomous. In Syria, the small kingdom of Emesa and the tetrarchy of Abilene were comparatively well-defined entities in an area that comprised a welter of lesser client cities and client tribes—Pliny's seventeen "tetrarchies with barbarous names" (*praeter tetrarchias in regna descriptas barbaris nominibus*).[26]

East of Judea was the merchant state of Nabatean Arabia. Its sparse population lived in small desert cities or roamed the desert, and its ill-defined territories stretched across Sinai and northern Arabia. Western Anatolia was organized into provinces, except for the "free league" of Lycia, but farther east there were still two large client states, Cappadocia and Pontus, as well as the smaller Teucrid principality, the Tarcondimotid kingdom, Comana, and the important kingdom of Commagene, whose territory included the southern access routes to contested Armenia, the crucial strategic back door to Parthia.

Across the Black Sea the Bosporan state (east of Crimea) had no contiguity with imperial territory but was subject to a degree of Roman control nonetheless, its chronic turbulence apparently offset in Roman eyes by its commercial value. In the Balkans, Thrace remained a client state until A.D. 46. Even in the northern extremities of the Italian peninsula the important transit point of the Cottian Alps was ruled by a local chief, albeit one who was no more than an appointed official in Roman eyes.

These constituted client states of a still partially hegemonic empire did not exhaust the full scope of the client system. Roman diplomacy, especially during the principate of Tiberius, also established an "invisible frontier" of client relationships with the more primitive peoples beyond the Rhine and Danube.[27] Lacking the cultural base that a more advanced material culture and Greek ideas provided in the east, these clients were not as satisfactory as those of Anatolia or the Levant. Specifically, diplomatic relationships were less stable, partly because the power of those who dealt with Rome was itself less stable; moreover, these clients, who were migratory if not nomadic, had a last resort that the territorial client states of the East never had—migration beyond the reach of Roman power.

Conditions were thus unfavorable, but the Romans were persistent. In A.D. 16 Tiberius called off the series of reprisal offensives against the Germans beyond the Rhine that had followed the destruction of the three legions under Varus. As soon as the Roman threat was removed, the two strongest powers remaining in Germany, the Cherusci of Arminius and the Marcomannic kingdom of Maroboduus, naturally began to fight one another, and the way was opened for a Roman diplomatic offensive.[28] During the balance of Tiberius's principate this resulted in the creation of a chain of clients from Lower Germany to the middle Danube. The Frisii, Batavi, Hermunduri, Marcomanni, Quadi, and the Sarmatian Iazyges (whose settlement between Tsiza and Danube had been procured by Rome) all became client tribes.[29] Even in Britain, client relationships had been established in the wake of Julius Caesar's *reconnaissance en force*,[30] though Strabo's description (an "intimate union"[31]) was no doubt an exercise in Augustan public relations: Britain remained unconquered and only very partially subjected to Roman desires.

These important diplomatic instruments were maintained by the successors of Tiberius, as some had been developed before him. The territories of these tribal clients could not be thought of as being within the perimeter of imperial security; nor were they destined for ultimate annexation, as the eastern client states were. Sometimes dependent and therefore obedient, and sometimes hostile, client tribes and tribal kingdoms required constant management with the full range of Roman diplomatic techniques, from subsidies to punitive warfare.

Roman notions of foreign client polities and the Roman view of the relationship between empire and client were rooted in the traditional pattern of patron-client relationships in Roman municipal life.[32] The essential transaction of these unequal relationships was the exchange of rewards (*beneficia*)—accorded by the patron—for services (*officia*) performed by the client. Discrete gradations of the inequality between empire and client were recognized, though with the continuing increase in Roman power a divergence often developed between the formal and the actual relationship. By the later stages of the process, a client king whose formal status was that of a "friend of the Roman people" (*amicus populi Romani*)—a title suggesting recognition for services rendered "with a lively sense of favours still

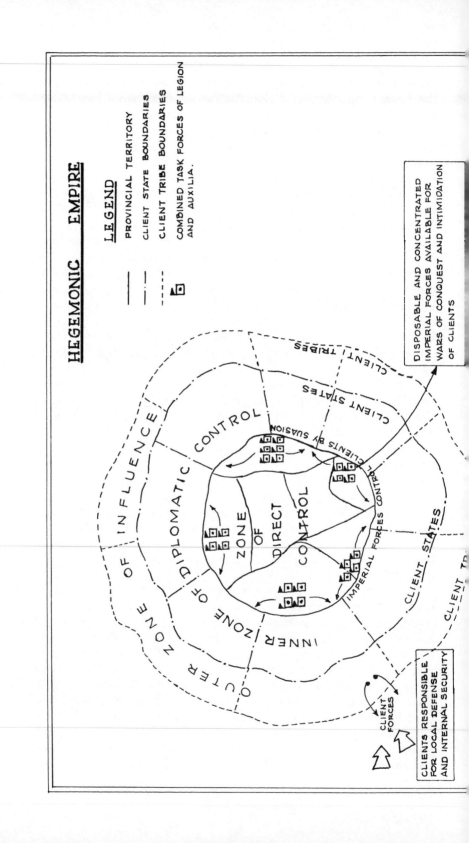

HEGEMONIC EMPIRE

LEGEND

——— PROVINCIAL TERRITORY

—·—·— CLIENT STATE BOUNDARIES

– – – CLIENT TRIBE BOUNDARIES

[□] COMBINED TASK FORCES OF LEGION AND AUXILIA.

DISPOSABLE AND CONCENTRATED IMPERIAL FORCES AVAILABLE FOR WARS OF CONQUEST AND INTIMIDATION OF CLIENTS

CLIENTS RESPONSIBLE FOR LOCAL DEFENSE AND INTERNAL SECURITY

OUTER ZONE OF INFLUENCE

ZONE OF DIPLOMATIC CONTROL

INNER ZONE OF DIPLOMATIC CONTROL

ZONE OF DIRECT CONTROL

CLIENT TRIBES

CLIENT STATES

CLIENTS BY SUASION

IMPERIAL FORCES CONTROL

CLIENT STATES

CLIENT TRIBES

CLIENT FORCES

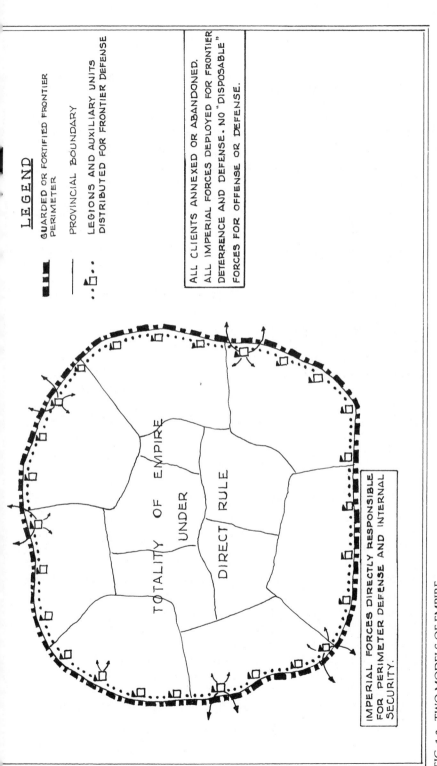

FIG. 1.2. TWO MODELS OF EMPIRE

to come," but with no connotation of subservience—[33]was generally no more than a vehicle of Roman control. This applied not only to foreign and security policies but also to dynastic and domestic matters. In fact, no clear areas of authority were left as the client ruler's prerogative.[34]

The conventional characterization of the client kingdoms as "buffer states" does not correctly define their complex role in the system of imperial security. Only Armenia was a true buffer state, serving as a physical neutral zone between the greater powers of Rome and Parthia, and providing them with a device that would serve to avoid conflict as long as they desired to avoid conflict. But Armenia was *sui generis*, acting as a true client state only intermittently.[35] The security *officia* provided by the client states amounted to much more than the passivity of a true buffer state. There were positive acts (including the provision of local troops to serve as auxiliaries for the Roman army and for purely Roman purposes[36]), but the most important function of the client states in the system of imperial security was not formally recognized as an *officium* at all: by virtue of their very existence, the client states absorbed the burden of providing peripheral security against border infiltration and other low-intensity threats.

There was at this time no truly empire-wide threat, though some lesser threats may have been seen as such: for example, in A.D. 9 there was momentary fear of a Germanic invasion of Gaul and even Italy in the aftermath of Varus's defeat.[37] The only great power that counted was Parthia. Always recognized as a potentially formidable rival, under the Arsacids Parthia was chronically weakened by internal struggles and does not appear to have been viewed as a menace. In Tacitus's later view, at any rate, the "free" Germans were deemed to be more formidable antagonists than the Arsacid despots.[38]

Partly because of the very nature of the threats faced by Rome, the value of the client states in the security system as a whole far exceeded their actual military effort, because their contribution was not merely additive to Roman military power, but complementary. Efficient client states could provide for their own internal security and for their own perimeter defense against low-intensity threats, absolving the empire from that responsibility. Thus, no legions had to be committed to Judea while Herod's regime lasted. By contrast, after Herod that turbulent province required the presence of at least one legion (X *Fretensis*) and sometimes more: three legions from A.D. 67 until the Jewish revolt was finally suppressed three years later (V

Macedonica, X *Fretensis*, XV *Apollinaris*), and the X *Fretensis* alone thereafter; two legions following the outbreak of Bar-Kokba's revolt of A.D. 132, and the same two legions (VI *Ferrata*, X *Fretensis*) thereafter.[39]

The provision of internal security was of course the most obvious function of client states, and the one most commonly recognized.[40] In addition, however, efficient client states would also shield adjacent provincial territories from low-intensity threats emanating from their own territory or from the far side of the client state periphery.[41] Often approximated but not always achieved even by the most successful client states, this level of efficiency required a delicate balance between strength and weakness, such as that supposedly achieved by Deiotarus, client king of Galatia (d. 25 B.C.), who was described in Cicero's special pleading as strong enough to guard his borders but not strong enough to threaten Roman interests.[42]

More commonly perhaps, the client states could *not* ensure high standards of internal and perimeter security comparable to those of provincial territory. Sometimes there were major disorders that threatened adjacent provincial lands or important strategic routes and therefore required the direct intervention of imperial forces. In King Juba's Mauretania, for example, thirty years of intermittent warfare were needed to subdue the Gaetuli; the fighting continued until A.D. 6. Soon thereafter, the revolt of Tacfarinas broke out in north Africa, not to be finally suppressed until A.D. 24, with the eventual commitment of two legions, III *Augusta* and IX *Hispana*.[43] (The center of the revolt was the province of Africa, but Juba's Mauretania and its chronically unruly tribes were also involved.) Another client state with severe internal and external security problems was Thrace, whose ruler, Rhoemetalces I (and later his quarreling successors), had to be repeatedly assisted against the Bessi.[44] But even in such cases, the *status* of the territories involved made an important difference. If direct Roman intervention did become necessary, its goal could be limited to the essential minimum of protecting local Roman assets and keeping the client ruler in control of his people, in contrast to the much greater military effort ordinarily required for suppressing insurgencies fully and bringing the affected areas up to provincial standards of tranquillity. In other words, the direct intervention of Rome in the affairs of a client state would not mean that every rebel band would have to be pursued into deep forest or remote desert as the Roman system of deterrence and Roman prestige required in provincial territory.[45]

Thus, where client forces were inadequate, the locals could at least *absorb* the resultant insecurity, and the Romans were content to let them do so.[46] To censure Rome for such attitudes, as Mommsen did in commenting that the client states enjoyed neither "peace nor independence," reveals a lack of historical perspective.[47] As we shall see, it was only much later that the systemic goals of the empire changed, requiring a change in the fundamental strategy toward provision of high standards of security even at the peripheries of empire.

Against high-intensity threats, such as invasions on a provincial or even a regional scale, client states and client tribes could contribute both their own interposed forces and their capacity to absorb the threat—in other words, they could provide geographic depth. Any system of troop deployment that achieves high levels of economy of force does so by avoiding the diffusion of strength entailed by the distribution of forces along the full length of a defensive perimeter. Consequently, if high-intensity threats *do* materialize, they can usually be dealt with only after the fact. In the event of an invasion, enemy penetrations can only be countered and reversed after forces have been redeployed to the scene; at Roman rates of strategic mobility this might be long after the damage had been done.[48]

Given the relationship between the system's economy of force and its inability to defend all frontier sectors all of the time, the damage that invasions could inflict until repelled was a critical variable. If the damage were great, the costs of such penetrations could exceed the benefits achieved by the centralized deployment of forces. The client states were very important in reducing these costs: even if their own forces could *not* maintain a defense until imperial troops arrived on the scene, the resultant damage would be inflicted not on Rome, but on what was not yet Roman territory in the full sense. This would considerably reduce the loss of prestige and the domestic political costs of enemy invasions to the rulers of Rome. Thus, during this period no Roman forces were ordinarily deployed to guard the entire Anatolian sector (from Zeugma in northeast Syria to the Black Sea), which faced Armenia and the major invasion axes from Parthia. Instead, at the time of Tiberius's accession to the principate in A.D. 14, it was the client rulers of Pontus, Cappadocia, and Commagene who themselves guarded the entire sector with their own forces, and it was their territories that would have absorbed the first impact of an invasion. In a typical failure to appreciate the strategic significance of the Augustan arrangement, whose very essence was the avoidance of perimeter deployment, the absence of permanent Roman garrisons has been described as a "grave military defect."[49] By A.D. 72, in the principate of Vespasian, all three states had been annexed, and annexation required that a permanent garrison of two legions (stationed in the reorganized province of Cappadocia) be deployed on the Anatolian-Armenian border.[50] Thus, instead of an "invisible" border guarded by others at no direct cost to Rome, a new defended sector had to be created, and a supporting road infrastructure had to be built. When the "defect" was duly corrected, the defense of eastern Anatolia permanently reduced the empire's disposable military power, and therefore reduced the system's economy of force.

Another obvious contribution of client states and client tribes to Roman security was the supply of local forces to augment Roman field armies on campaign. Naturally, these troops would fall into the Roman category of *auxilia*, i.e., cavalry and light infantry, rather than legionary forces of heavy infantry. (Though one legion, the XXII *Deiotariana*, originated, as its *cognomen* indicates, in a formation raised by Deiotarus of Galatia, which had been trained and equipped as heavy infantry in the legionary manner.)[51] In fact, many of the *auxilia* organic to the imperial army started out as tribal levies, which were then absorbed in the regular establishment, or in client-state troops, which were incorporated into the Roman army when their home states were absorbed.[52] Auxiliary troops contributed by clients had played an important part in the campaigns of the republic, not least because they could provide military specialties missing from the regular Roman arsenal, such as archers, and especially mounted archers.[53]

The complementarity between *auxilia* and legionary forces was an important feature of the Roman military establishment; moreover, the forces maintained by the client states were substantial. Even in A.D. 67, when the clients of the East had been much reduced by annexation, the three legions deployed under Vespasian to subdue the Jewish revolt were augmented, according to Josephus, by 15,000 men contributed by Antiochus IV of Commagene, Agrippa II, Sohaemus of Emesa, and the Arab ruler Malchus.[54] Forces supplied by client princes or tribes relieved the pressure on the available pool of citizen manpower (as did the regular non-citizen *auxilia*) and reduced the financial burden on the Roman military treasury (*aerarium militare*). Even if they received pay and upkeep (as the tribal levies must have done), the auxiliaries would not have to be paid the very generous retirement grants due legionary troops.

Weighed against these benefits, however, was the corresponding loss of fiscal revenue that the client system entailed: once duly annexed as provinces, client states would of course bear the full burden of imperial taxation. (Tribal clients—which would not, one

MAP 1.2. THE EAST UNDER THE JULIO-CLAUDIANS

COLCHI

DARIAL
PASS

IBERI

ALBANI

• SATALA

R.

ARMENIA
MINOR

ARMENIA

• ARTAXATA

UPHRATES

OPHENE)

LAKE
VAN

• TIGRANOCERTA

PARTHIAN EMPIRE

ADIABENE

DESSA

• NISIBIS

•CARRHAE

KHABUR

MESOPOTAMIA

R.

EUPHRATES

R.

TIGRIS

R.

LEGEND

ASIA - PROVINCES
PONTUS - ROMAN CLIENT-STATES
(SOPHENE) - PARTHIAN CLIENT-STATES
COLCHI - FRIENDLY NATIVES
FRETENSIS - LEGIONARY DEPLOYMENT (A.D. 23)

imagines, have been easy to tax in any case—already seem to have contributed fighting manpower to the empire in lieu of tribute, as the Batavi certainly did.)[55]

III
The Management
of the Clients

The value of state and tribal clients in the system of imperial security was a commonplace of Roman statecraft.[56] In his survey of the distribution of imperial forces, Tacitus introduces the client kingdoms of Mauretania and Thrace, and the Iberian, Albanian, and other kings of the Caucasus in his listing of the legions, obviously viewing the clients as equivalents to Roman forces.[57] In the same passage, Tacitus carefully distinguishes the status rankings of the various clients he mentions: Mauretania is described as "a gift from the Roman people" to Juba II, while the Caucasian clients are viewed more or less as protectorates, "to whom our greatness was a protection against any foreign power." Thrace, ruled as it was by native clients subjected but not created by Rome, is simply said to be "held" by the Romans.[58]

What contemporary observers like Tacitus may not have fully realized was that the clients were not merely additive but complementary to Roman military power, and that this complementarity was crucial to the preservation of Rome's economy of military force. In fact, the system presupposed a hegemonic rather than a territorial structure of empire, as the republican empire clearly had been and as the principate eventually ceased to be.[59] Octavian had clearly appreciated the value of the system,[60] so much so that after his victory at Actium he had no compunction about confirming the rule of six of the major clients who had faithfully served his rival Anthony.[61] It was only with minor clients that Octavian allowed himself the luxury of punishing his enemy's friends and rewarding his own; for example, he removed the Tarcondimotid rulers of Hierapolis-Castabala (in Cilicia) who had been faithful to Anthony until the end. Even there, however, he eventually reversed himself and reinstated the Tarcondimotid Philopator a decade after Actium, a battle in which Philopator's father had lost his life on Anthony's side.[62] Octavian evidently discovered (and Augustus remembered) that efficient and reliable client rulers were very valuable instruments, and that not every associate deserving of reward could master the exacting techniques of client statecraft.

Inherently dynamic and unstable, client states and client tribes required the constant management of a specialized diplomacy: Roman control and surveillance had to be continuous. In the East, the dynasts who operated the client system were sufficiently aware of their own weakness (and of the inevitability of Roman retribution) to remain strictly loyal. Even so, internal dynastic rivalries and the complications of interdynastic family relations could threaten the stability of the system. Thus Herod's troubles with his sons—or his senile paranoia—upset the internal equilibrium of his own important client state. Worse, these factors had repercussions on Cappadocia, since Glaphyra, daughter of Archelaus, ruler of Cappadocia, was married to Alexander, one of Herod's executed sons.[63]

The vagaries of individual character, inevitable in dynastic arrangements, were all-important. For example, Eurycles, who inherited the small state of Sparta from a canny father, turned out to be an inveterate and dangerous intriguer; having left his own mean lands, Eurycles sowed discord between Cappadocia and Judea for his own personal advantage, and also seemingly caused unrest in Achea. While the important rulers of important states, such as Herod and Archelaus, were guided with great tact and patience by Augustus, Eurycles, petty ruler of a village-state of no strategic importance, was simply removed from office.[64]

Augustus was personally well-suited for the task of controlling the clients, and his own firm but gentle paternalism was very much in evidence. But Roman dealings with client states had long since coalesced into a tradition and a set of rules, which no doubt served to guide policy. For example, it was understood that no client could aggrandize himself at the expense of a fellow-client without explicit sanction from Rome.[65] When Herod broke this cardinal rule by sending his forces into the adjacent client state of Nabatean Arabia, then in turmoil, Augustus promptly ordered him to stop. By way of punishment, Augustus wrote to Herod that henceforth he could no longer regard him as a friend and would have to treat him as a subject; given the style of the man, this was equivalent to a harsh reprimand.[66]

In order to contend with the inevitable counter-charges that attackers could level at their victims in order to justify their own aggression (a feature of controlled international systems then as now), the rule established by Rome under the republic specified that a client could only respond to attacks by strictly defensive measures, until a Roman ruling settled the issue.[67]

It was understood that Roman interests were best served by maintaining local balances of power between nearby clients, so that the system could keep itself in equilibrium without recourse to direct Roman intervention. Unfortunately, as rulers and circumstances changed over time, so did the power balances at the local level. Client rulers had their own military forces, their own ambitions, and their own temptations. Those in the East, moreover, could at times have invoked the countervailing power of Parthia, as Archelaus of Cappadocia (in A.D. 17) and Antiochus IV of Commagene (in A.D. 72) were accused of having done.[68]

Loyal and efficient client rulers were rewarded by personal honors, ordinarily receiving Roman citizenship (which Augustus's highly restrictive citizenship policy made an important privilege); but no honor or title could confer genuine equality in a world where none could equal Roman power.[69] More tangible rewards were also given, primarily territorial. That model client, Polemo I, king of Pontus, received Lesser Armenia from Anthony, and when Augustus detached that territory from Pontus, Polemo received instead the important (but, as it turned out, ungovernable) Bosporan state.[70] Similarly, when Herod—a very efficient client ruler indeed—was still in Augustus's good graces, he was granted in 24–23 B.C. part of the plateau country of Ituraea (Golan-Hauran), at the expense of another client, Zenodorus, who had failed to control the nomadic raiding of his subjects.[71]

Relationships with the client tribes and barbaric kingdoms of continental Europe were of a different order. For one thing, these peoples were at least potentially migratory, even if not at all nomadic. They could flee into the remote interior, as Maroboduus did by taking his Marcomanni to Bohemia to escape the pressure of Roman military power on the upper Rhine.[72] This option had its costs: the abandonment of good lands for the uncertain prospect of others possibly inferior and also perhaps the loss of valued commercial contacts with Roman merchants. Peoples migrating away from Roman power could still hope to remain within the sphere of Roman commerce, whose reach was much greater, but they could no longer play a profitable middleman role.[73]

The major difference between these two groups was cultural. The client rulers of the East and their subjects were, as a rule, sufficiently sophisticated to understand the full potential of Roman military power in the abstract, while the peoples of continental Europe often were not. The rulers of eastern client states and their subjects did not actually have to *see* Roman legions marching toward their cities in order to respond to Rome's commands, for they could imagine what the consequences of disobedience would be. (Perhaps for this reason, the Romans promoted education for the sons of European tribal chiefs.)[74] Further, the client rulers of the east normally enjoyed secure political control over their subjects. Only this could ensure that their own perceptions of Roman power—and the restraints that this perception imposed—would be shared by their subjects. By contrast, in the less structured polities of Europe, the prudence of the well-informed (e.g., Maroboduus in A.D. 9) would not necessarily restrain all those capable of acting against Roman interests.[75]

Since the forceful suasion of Roman military power could only function through the medium of others' perceptions (and through the internal processes of decision and control of other polities), the primitive character of the peoples of continental Europe could negate such suasion, or at least weaken its impact.[76] To the extent that the processes of suasion were negated by the inability or refusal of its objects to give Roman power its due, the actual political control generated by the military strength of the empire was correspondingly reduced. As a heroic generalization—for there were numerous exceptions—one can therefore say that while Roman military power was freely converted into political power vis-à-vis the sophisticated polities of the East, when employed against the primitive peoples of Europe its main use was the direct application of force. The distinction is, of course, quite basic. For power born of *potential* force is not expended when used, nor is it a finite quantity. Force, on the other hand, is just that: if directed to one purpose, it cannot simultaneously be directed at another, and if used, it is *ipso facto* consumed.

To be sure, Roman reprisals would soon educate their victims, making it more likely that the same group would in future respond to Roman orders. But as a practical matter, such induced propensities to respond to potential force would apply only to direct threats; further, they could be counteracted by tribal relocations; and their impact could still be attenuated by loose structures of internal control. In the strategic ambush by the German Cherusci against the three unfortunate legions serving beyond the Rhine under P. Quinctilius Varus, these three negative factors were all in evidence.[77]

Nevertheless, Roman diplomacy persisted in trying to transform the northern border peoples into clients, and not without success. Direct political ties between the empire and selected chiefs were fostered by systematic policy.[78] As already noted, citizenship was a common reward for chiefs; some received the equestrian rank. Where sanctions were ineffective, positive incentives of a more tangible sort could take their place. The payment of subsidies to the border peoples, often popularly associated with the era of Roman decline, was already an established policy even before the principate.[79] In a disordered, barbaric world, however, even relationships cemented with money and honors were unstable. Arminius, the betrayer and destroyer of Varus, had himself been given the citizenship and had served as the commander of an auxiliary force of Cherusci. His father-in-law, Segestes, and his own brother, Flavus,

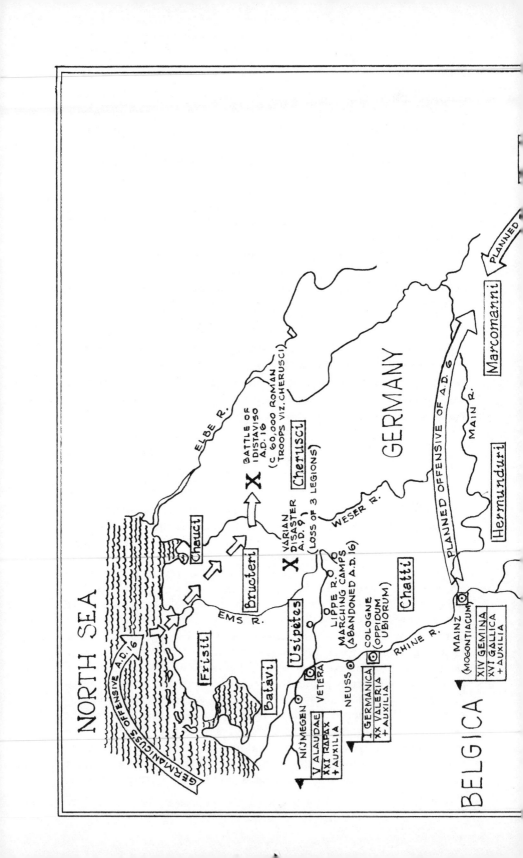

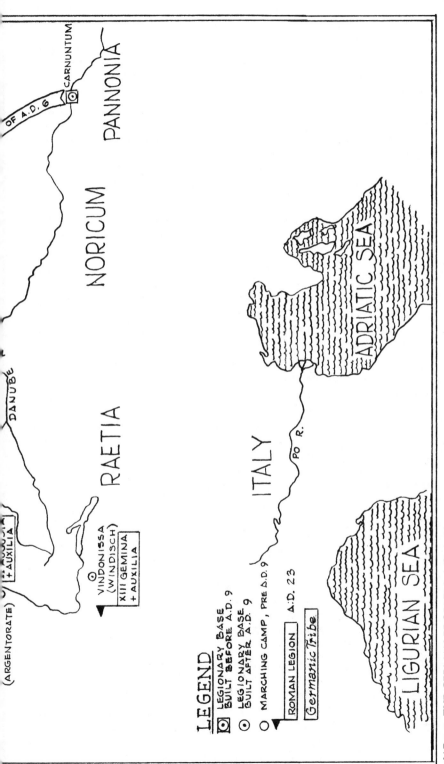

MAP 1.3. THE GERMAN PROBLEM, A.D. 6–16

both remained loyal to Rome (Segestes reportedly tried to warn
Varus of the ambush), or so the sources say.[80] This did not help to
save Varus and his men; the incident makes clear that the patterns of
authority in a native society disintegrating under Roman pressure
were too weak to support a satisfactory client relationship. Segestes
was evidently a chief in his own right, but he lacked the degree of
control over his Cherusci that any self-respecting dynast of the East
would have had.

In spite of the terrible experience of the *clades Variana*, the Romans
did not despair of the policy, nor even of the family: during the
principate of Claudius, the Cherusci asked that a king be appointed
for them, and they received as their ruler a son of Flavus and nephew
of Arminius, a Roman citizen educated in Rome—whose name was
Italicus.[81] By then the client system had taken hold, after a full
generation of ceaseless effort. When Tiberius decided to withdraw
Germanicus and his forces from beyond the Rhine in A.D. 16, thus
suspending the reprisal operations that had followed the crisis of
A.D. 9, the new diplomatic policy was launched. Even if these lands
were not to be conquered, the Romans could not simply ignore the
peoples living beyond the Rhine and Danube. These peoples, both
great and little, represented too powerful a force to be left uncon-
trolled on the long and vulnerable perimeter of the empire, which still
had no border defenses.

By A.D. 16, then, a coherent policy of diplomatic control was
emerging for the first time, though most of its elements had long
since been present. The first instrument of this policy was a manipulative and divisive diplomacy, intended to keep the Germanic peoples
divided and, if possible, occupied in fighting one another.[82] But the
Romans needed to do more than that. Once they became aware of
the magnitude of the threat that the Germans represented, they
could not be satisfied with attempts to weaken them by diplomatic
intrigues. Much as they enjoyed the thought of barbarians killing one
another,[83] the Romans clearly realized that it was far more practical
to make *positive use* of German energies through the creation of a
chain of client tribes, which would form an active barrier between
the perimeters of the empire and the possibly still more dangerous
barbarians deeper inland.

The control mechanism was complex. It was necessary to manipu-
late the tribes through their chiefs, while controlling the chiefs by
means of personal threats and personal inducements; always there
was the latent threat of force against the tribe as a whole. By
channeling money and favors through chosen client chiefs, the
Romans helped the latter gain power over their subjects, while the
Romans gained power over them.[84] Some of the chiefs were ap-

pointed by Rome, while others rose on their own; but in either case the task of diplomacy was to maintain the two lines of control, internal and external, in working order. This must have required a good deal of petty border diplomacy of which we know little. What is certain is that the policy was successful over a prolonged period: speaking of the once formidable Marcomanni and Quadi, Tacitus describes both as ruled by client rulers maintained in power—and controlled—by a combination of occasional armed assistance and financial support.[85]

The major active instrument of client management among the primitive peoples of continental Europe was a systematic policy of subsidization.[86] The passive instrument, on the other hand, was the latent threat of Roman reprisals. The satisfactory state of affairs recorded by Tacitus in *Germania,* published in A.D. 98, was the final product of this integrated policy. The sequence of events leading to the situation Tacitus describes can be reconstructed as follows: first, when the outbreak of the Pannonian revolt in A.D. 6 forced the Romans to cancel the planned invasion of Bohemia, an accommodation was reached with Maroboduus and his Marcomanni; whether they were simply bought off or conciliated by treaty, it is certain that they remained peacefully passive during the three years of the revolt. In A.D. 9, after the Varian disaster, Maroboduus refused to cooperate with Arminius in a concerted attack on the empire.[87] Following the Roman withdrawal, in A.D. 17 war broke out between the two greatest chiefs of Germany. Maroboduus was the loser, and though he asked for help under a claim of alliance reciprocity, his appeal was refused by the Romans.[88] Overthrown and driven out in A.D. 18, Maroboduus merely received refuge in the empire, living out the last eighteen years of his life in comfortable exile in Ravenna.[89] Shortly afterward, the Hermunduri fought and defeated Catualda, who had succeeded Maroboduus through Roman intrigue. Tiberius finally stepped in to appoint Vannius, chief of the Quadi, ruler over the Marcomanni as well ("Suevi" being the generic name for both), thus creating a full-fledged client state on the middle Danube.[90] Vannius naturally received a regular subsidy[91] but, again, no guarantee of protection. He was left to his fate when attacked in turn by the Hermunduri, though he, too, was given personal refuge.[92]

Tiberius's successor, Gaius (Caligula), may have intended to renew the attempt to conquer Germany in his own erratic way, and in A.D. 39 forces were seemingly assembled on the Rhine for the purpose. Suetonius's diverting account of the episode is amusing but incredible; in any case no move was made.[93] Claudius, who succeeded Gaius, clearly reverted to the policy of Tiberius: in A.D. 47 the great general Cn. Domitius Corbulo (who was to win fame under Nero) was ordered to stop his attacks on the Chauci in northern Germany. In the eternal pattern of imperial expansion, the attack had originated in a *counter*offensive against the sea-raiding Canninefates, but it was apparently developing into a general invasion of northern Germany. On orders from Claudius, the legions were withdrawn from the right bank of the Rhine.[94] Inevitably, some petty border warfare persisted (e.g. in A.D. 50, against the Chatti), but this was clearly of a defensive nature—punitive responses to transborder raiding. Roman strategy in Germany under Claudius and Nero, as under Tiberius, was to rely on clients, unstable as these clients might be.[95]

More is known of Roman client management in the East. In A.D. 17 Tiberius made a drastic reduction in the client state structure of eastern Anatolia: Archelaus of Cappadocia (whose son-in-law Herod had executed) was tried and removed from office on the grounds of treasonable relations with Parthia; at about the same time, both Antiochus III of Commagene and Philopator of Hierapolis-Castabala died.[96] Tiberius decided to annex the three states. Cappadocia was by far the largest, but Commagene was also of particular strategic importance since its territory included one of the three crossings of the middle course of the Euphrates leading to Parthian lands.[97] Tiberius organized Cappadocia into a new province and attached Commagene to Syria, assigning the detached territory of Cilicia Tracheia and Lycaonia to Archelaus II, son of the deposed ruler of Cappadocia. (These moves have been explained as a strategic response to the breakdown of the Armenian settlement in A.D. 16, when the Roman client king Vonones was expelled from Armenia.[98])

Gaius substantially reversed Tiberius's annexationist policy. Antiochus IV was restored to Commagene, which became a client state once more with the addition of Cilicia Tracheia. The sons of Cotys II, the murdered king of Thrace, who had been brought up in Rome as Gaius's playmates, all received kingdoms: Polemo II was given Pontus and—in theory—the Bosporan state (whose *de facto* ruler was Mithridates); Cotys III was given Lesser Armenia; and Rhoemetalces was given half of Thrace (the other half being under the rule of another Rhoemetalces, son of Rhescuporis, the killer of Cotys); a further creation was Sohaemus, appointed to a tetrarchy in Ituraea (Hauran).[99]

A more important beneficiary of Gaius's generosity was C. Julius Agrippa I, "an oriental adventurer," nephew of Herod the Great. Agrippa, who had been imprisoned by Tiberius, was freed and amply rewarded by Gaius: in A.D. 37 he was given a small principality east of the Jordan; a year later he was granted further parts of Ituraea, lands actually detached from the provincial territory of Syria; in A.D. 40 he also received Abilene and finally Galilee and Peraea, thus in effect virtually reconstituting the northern half of Herod's kingdom under his rule.[100]

Both ancient and modern historians attribute Gaius's generosity to his personal emotion and to his madness. So also do they account for his deposition and execution of Ptolemy, king of Mauretania, in A.D. 40, which was followed by the annexation of that country.[101] But Gaius's successor, Claudius, who was neither mad nor improvident with the empire's resources, did not undo what Gaius had done. On the contrary, his policy was clearly intended to stabilize the settlement left by Gaius: Mithridates was recognized as ruler of the Bosporan state that Polemo II had been unable to control, and the latter was compensated in Cilicia; Antiochus IV of Commagene, whom Gaius had removed in A.D. 40, reversing himself, was restored to his throne in Commagene; and Julius Agrippa (Gaius's favorite) received Judea and Samaria as further additions to his kingdom. These lands, it should be noted, had been under direct imperial rule since the removal of Archelaus, son of Herod, in A.D. 6.[102]

The client states needed constant management: unsatisfactory rulers had to be replaced (as in the case of the Spartan Eurycles) and successors had to be found for rulers who died. But the method of indirect rule endured. If there were further annexations (Judea again, in A.D. 44, Thrace in A.D. 46, and, under Nero, Pontus in A.D. 64), there were also retrocessions, such as those which gradually enlarged the territories of C. Julius Agrippa II, worthier follower of his father and namesake.[103] (There is evidence indicating that Claudius actually appointed a special diplomatic agent charged with the management of client relations *in situ*.)[104] In the absence of an organized foreign office, the work must have entailed a considerable burden on the office of the emperor; but this was a burden that the Julio-Claudian emperors were obviously willing to accept, together with all the ambiguities and complexities of the client system. Much depended on who the client rulers were. Men like Polemo I of Pontus and C. Julius Agrippa II (who remained in power until A.D. 93) were obviously specialists in the techniques of indirect rule, reliable and effective.

In the simpler lands to the west, the reality of imperial service was not concealed behind the screen of a false independence. A British chieftain mentioned by Tacitus, Cogidubnus, described himself as "King and Legate of the Emperor in Britain" (*Rex et Legatus Augusti in Britannia*) according to an epigraphical reconstruction.[105] Cottius, son of Donnus, was also in this position—he was prefect of the Cottian Alps to the Romans and king to the locals.[106] It has been suggested that such dual status was a Claudian invention;[107] if so, it would confirm the impression that Claudius or his policy-makers understood the virtues of indirect rule particularly well.

IV
The Tactical Organization
of the Army

The legions of the second century B.C. described by Polybius[108] were complex formations with a balanced structure: in addition to the core of heavy infantry, they included a significant contingent of cavalry and a substantial proportion of light infantry.[109] There were three classes of heavy infantry: *hastati, principes,* and *triarii;* the first two classes, each consisting of 1,200 men, were armed with composite oval shields, swords, and the *pilum,* a heavy throwing spear nine feet long which was to emerge as the characteristic missile weapon of the legionary infantry.[110] The 600 or so *triarii* were still armed with the *hasta,* the long thrusting spear.

What made these legions balanced forces, as opposed to the legions of the principate, was their contingent of 1,200 light infantry (*velites*) armed with swords, small shields (*parmae*), and the *hasta velitaris* (a short, light javelin), and their ten small squadrons of cavalry amounting to 300 horse in all.[111] To be sure, these legions with neither archers nor slingers were obviously weak in missile weapons; while the organic cavalry contingent was rather small as well, too small to be employed independently.

But when Gaius Marius (157–86 B.C.) reformed the legions, he made them much *more* unbalanced than before. The *velites* were abolished and the cavalry contingent was apparently withdrawn gradually: there is no mention of organic legionary cavalry in the wars of Julius Caesar.[112] Also, the *triarii* were eliminated (though not their weapon) in the shift to a new tactical organization based on the 480-man standard cohort, whose men were armed with the two-foot, double-edged, "Spanish" sword, the *gladius,* as well as *pila.*[113]

The legions of the principate were essentially similar in structure, except that a small (120 horse) cavalry contingent was apparently reintroduced.[114] This meant that the legions became narrowly specialized forces of heavy infantry. In fact, as has been pointed out, legionary troops were actually dual-purpose infantry and combat engineers.[115] Each legion had engineering specialists in its headquarters, men who could survey a canal, design a circus, plan roads, and above all, build or demolish walls and fortifications.[116] The troops must have been trained as skilled or semiskilled workers, and their personal kits included basic construction tools, notably a carefully designed multi-purpose pickaxe, the *dolabra*. (Cn. Domitius Corbulo, the leading Roman general of the Claudian period, was fond of saying that victory was to be won by using the *dolabra*.)[117] The legions of the principate also included another "heavy" element: organic artillery in the shape of stone-throwing *ballistae* and catapults that shot arrows or bolts. These weapons feature prominently in the recorded accounts of sieges, but were also used for fire-support in the field.

Under the right conditions, this unbalanced structure produced the highest degree of tactical effectiveness in the most reliable element of the Roman army, the legions. The "right conditions," however, were those of high-intensity warfare: close combat to hold ground under attack, or to seize ground against *concentrated* enemy forces, including forces manning elaborate fortifications. By the same token, the relatively slow-moving legionary infantry was unsuited for guerrilla (or counter-guerrilla) warfare, and indeed for all mobile warfare against elusive enemies, particularly the cavalry armies of western and central Asia. Purely legionary forces would perform rather poorly in such low intensity warfare, which required small units, dispersal, much more missile power than shock capability, and as much cavalry as possible, except in dense forest or high mountain terrain. Such warfare, moreover, did not ordinarily require the engineering skills so highly developed in the legions.

The legion was trained to fight as a solid mass, in concentration; it had very little missile power, since there were few *pila*, and the range of the hand-thrown *pilum* would not normally exceed 100 feet.[118] Moreover, the legionary cavalry could only provide scouts and pickets; it was inadequate for proper screening against hostile cavalry and utterly inadequate for independent use as heavy "shock" cavalry or for harrassing tactics against enemy infantry, in the manner of the mounted bowmen of the East. While lighter or otherwise more mobile forces could mount hit-and-run attacks against them, legionary forces could only advance slowly but relentlessly toward the centers of the enemy's power to reduce them by siege or assault.

Given the degree of specialization of the legionary forces and their tactical limitations, it is clear that the *auxilia* were not merely additive but complementary to the legions, as it was long ago pointed out.[119] Thanks to the *auxilia*, the Romans could avoid a dilution of their citizen manpower into the kinds of forces for which it was unsuited, such as the cavalry[120] and missile troops, archers and slingers.[121] At the same time, the particular capabilities of the legionary forces gave them "escalation dominance" over both enemies and unreliable allies—for in the last analysis they could always prevail over the *auxilia* in high-intensity warfare. Legionary forces could not prevent *auxilia* from running away, but they could be fairly certain of defeating them in open battle or siege warfare, unless conditions were exceedingly unfavorable. Unfavorable conditions did prevail during the revolt of Civilis (A.D. 69-70), when two legions (V *Alaudae* and XV *Primigenia*), depleted and short of food, were besieged and massacred by dissident Batavian auxiliaries in the ill-situated camp of Vetera in Lower Germany; four legions (I *Germanica*, XVI *Gallica*, IV *Macedonica*, and XV *Primigenia*) were later forced to surrender or went over to the rebels.[122]

The revolt of Civilis had the general character of a war between legions and *auxilia*: eight Batavian auxiliary cohorts revolted, and Civilis himself, while an officer of the *auxilia*, was also a tribal chief (as two other famous rebels, Arminius and Tacfarinas, had also been). The dissidence of the *auxilia* under conditions of stress was not a unique episode, even though the subsequent treason of Roman legions certainly was. In the narrative sources, the inherent unreliability of auxiliaries emerges repeatedly under both empire and Republic: Sulla was concerned with preserving their loyalty, according to Frontinus,[123] and Plutarch records the unreliable conduct of Crassus's auxiliary cavalry at Carrhae.[124] In A.D. 70, when Q. Petilius Cerialis reached the zone of operations during the suppression of Civilis's revolt, he thought it prudent to send his Gallic auxiliaries back to their homes before entering the fight, with the message that the legions alone were adequate to restore order.[125]

In the two-level structure of the Roman army, the citizen forces of the legions, ordinarily highly disciplined and reliable, tacitly served to keep the *auxilia* under control, by means of their tactical superiority in high-intensity warfare, if necessary. This was a *latent* function of the legions, but it was one of obvious importance. Once the reliability of the *auxilia* was secured—and later reforms were to ensure it more fully[126]—the combination of the legionary infantry/combat engineers with the cavalry, light infantry, and missile troops of the *auxilia* gave the Romans tactical superiority in most terrains and against most enemies, as well as "escalation dominance" against virtually all.

Tacitus records that when Germanicus crossed the Rhine to search for the remains of the lost legions of Varus, and more important, to reestablish Roman prestige by reprisal operations meant to redeem the deterrent capability of Roman arms, he did so with two legions, eight *alae* of auxiliary cavalry, and no fewer than twenty-six cohorts of auxiliary infantry.[127] Apparently, there was no standard allotment of *auxilia:* Varus had brought only three *alae* of cavalry and six cohorts of auxiliary infantry with his three legions.[128]

The most obvious deficiency of Roman arms was in the cavalry. As early as 202 B.C. the Romans had relied on mercenary Numidian cavalry to help fight the cavalry armies of Hannibal,[129] and although a Roman citizen cavalry did exist (as did the cavalry of the Italian *socii* until the "social war"[130]), the pattern of reliance on non-citizen cavalry was maintained consistently. In the army of the principate the auxiliary cavalry appeared in two guises, as the *alae* of cavalry proper and as the *cohortes equitatae*, mixed units of infantry and cavalry. Both, like the normal infantry auxiliary cohorts, came in two classes of formation: the *ala quingenaria* with 512 men, and the *ala milliaria* with roughly twice as many. The *cohors equitata* apparently had 380 or 760 infantry for the two classes of unit and 120 or 240 cavalry.[131] (Milliary units, however, did not become significant until the Flavian era.[132])

Since the cavalry of antiquity had no stirrup (or, at any rate, the cavalry available to the Romans had none), it has sometimes been assumed that all Roman mounted troops were in fact "light" cavalry, i.e., horsemen trained and armed to attack from a distance with bow or javelin, or else to harass the enemy in close quarters with spear or sword—as opposed to "heavy," but not necessarily armored, cavalry, who were armed with the long lance and trained to fight as a shock force intended to press home the charge.[133] Without stirrups, it has been argued, the cavalry could not charge solid infantry, for no horseman could keep his balance once contact took place. It is certainly true that the development of closed-rank infantry tactics from Sparta onwards made the simple cavalry charge virtually obsolete against *disciplined* foot soldiers, since even the best shock cavalry would be defeated by infantrymen dressed in close order who presented a wall of shields and spearpoints in the direction of attack. In fact, the Romans used heavy (though unarmored) cavalry as well as light, because the cavalry charge could still be very effective against undisciplined infantry.[134] Moreover, the lack of stirrups would not prevent cavalry charges against enemy cavalry, especially unarmored "light" horsemen.

In addition, it is virtually certain that a cavalry tactic that could defeat even disciplined infantry had in fact been devised: this was the combined use of heavy cavalry armed with lances and mounted bowmen (i.e., light cavalry). This technique was used by the Parthian cavalry army that annihilated the seven legions Crassus took to the field of Carrhae in 53 B.C.[135] A classic combination of fire and shock, this tactic employed high volumes of arrow fire from mounted bowmen to attack the ranks of the Romans, while the lancers forced them to remain in closed ranks by the threat of a charge (or actual attack)—thus ensuring their vulnerability to arrow fire. In this manner, the infantry could neither come to grips with the bowmen nor march away to shelter—even if suitable terrain were close at hand. Once it is realized that even without the stirrup, horsemen could and did press the charge, the value of the auxiliary cavalry of the *alae* can be seen in proper perspective: they added not only a scouting and counter-scouting as well as a pursuit force to the legions, but also a shock element—very useful in breaking concentrations of light cavalry and quite lethal against undisciplined warriors on foot.

In relying on auxiliary cavalry, the Romans were merely compensating for the poor quality of their citizen horsemen (and horses?). On the other hand, their reliance on auxiliary missile infantry (archers, slingers, and javelin-throwers) served a positive purpose: it preserved the *comparative advantage* the Romans enjoyed in the superior arm of the heavy infantry. Given their chronic manpower shortage, it would have been inefficient to dilute scarce citizen manpower by deploying it as light infantry, a commodity easily obtained outside Italy. Here, too, there were very old precedents: Livy records the recruitment of a thousand archers and slingers from Syracuse in 217 B.C.,[136] and during Caesar's wars in Gaul, the "classic trio"—Cretan archers, Balearic slingers, and Numidian infantry (spearmen?)—already appears, to remain a fixture of the auxiliaries of the principate.[137]

According to a nineteenth-century experiment sponsored by Napoleon III, the maximum practical range of the Roman throwing-spear (*pilum*) in the hands of a strong and trained man was about 100 feet.[138] According to the same experiment, the maximum *effective* range of the composite bow made of a wooden core with sinew on the outside and bone keratin on the inside[139] was between 175 and 190 yards.[140] (Much longer ranges have been cited, but these probably refer to special bows, special bowmen, *and* special [i.e., light] arrows.) In fact, however, the maximum accurate *and* effective range of the composite bow of antiquity was closer to 55–65 yards.[141] The most important advantage of the bow over the *pilum* was thus its greater *volume* of fire rather than its superior range: soldiers on the march could carry only a few *pila* (two being the probable standard), while bowmen would have many arrows.

Slingers and bowmen performed the same function—giving cover and support with their missile fire to advancing (or retreating) infantry. In siege warfare, and in mobile warfare as well if conditions allowed, light missile fire was supplemented by the artillery. Since well-built fortifications would withstand the shot of all but the very largest stone-throwers (*ballistae*), the more common mission of the artillery in siege warfare must have been to give covering fire for the advance of battering rams and other shock engines.

The artillery was sufficiently mobile for field use, too, at least on firm and level ground: in A.D. 14 Germanicus used arrow-firers (*tormenta*) to drive the Chatti from the opposite bank while his troops made a contested river-crossing; in another episode two years later, he used artillery to cover the assault of Roman troops against an earthwork manned by Cherusci warriors—forcing the Cherusci to keep their heads down and suspend their missile fire.[142]

We do not know the standard number of artillery weapons organic to the legions, but there were probably six pieces per cohort (i.e., at least sixty per legion)—mostly arrow-shooting catapults, the rest heavier, stone-throwing *ballistae*. The *auxilia* ordinarily had no artillery or siege engines.[143] For one thing, allowing them such weapons would have contradicted the principle of "escalation dominance." (A contemporary parallel: one of the precautions taken by the British in India in the aftermath of the Mutiny was to deny artillery to most Indian regiments.)

Although the skills of the *auxilia* complemented those of the legions, so that mixed legionary/auxiliary task forces were in fact "balanced" multi-purpose field armies, the overall comparative advantage of the Roman army was still in high intensity warfare: the slow but relentless strategic penetration of enemy territory in depth, secured by road construction and *en route* fortifications; full-scale battles against dense troop concentrations; and, above all, offensive and defensive siege warfare.[144] As the degree of force concentration and combat-intensity increased, so did the tactical superiority of the Romans.[145]

This tactical-structural factor had strategic implications of great significance: the Roman army was clearly best equipped to serve as an instrument of warfare against enemies with *fixed* assets to protect—primarily cities, but also such things as arable lands or even irrigation systems. Conversely, Roman capabilities were less useful in fighting enemies whose assets and sources of strength were not fixed, or at any rate, not concentrated. It was pointless for the Romans to cut a path through forest and swamp to reach the primitive townships of the Germans, since the real sources of German strength were rural and diffuse: even the loss of all their towns would not be a serious blow. By the same token, Roman capabilities were not suited to fighting the Parthians (or later the Sassanids) in the East, since, although the Iranians did have large and important cities, their major sources of strength were diffused in the small seminomadic settlements of the remote Iranian plateau. Even when the Romans conquered and sacked Parthian cities, including Ctesiphon, the capital, as they first did under Trajan, the power of the Arsacids was not broken.

So it was with Dacians, Sarmatians, and the nomads of Arabia and North Africa as well: none could resist the relentless advance of Roman invasion columns, but neither could the Romans apply their strength effectively against the widely dispersed rural base of warrior nations whose life and whose strength did not depend on the survival of a city-based economic and social structure. Consequently, if the Romans persisted in their efforts, their only real alternative was to attack the population base itself, in a war of extermination. In the absence of a settled pattern of life that the army could control and reorganize under Roman rule, peace required that first a desert be made. Thus at the conclusion of Domitian's campaign against the Nasamones of North Africa, he reported to the Senate that the war had been won, and that the Nasamones had ceased to exist.[146]

If this analysis of Roman military capacities is correct, a technico-military reason for the geographic limits of imperial expansion suggests itself. A function not of sheer space, distance, or even demography, these limits were of a qualitative nature and—most important—*they applied to coercive diplomacy as well as to war.* Environmental factors that conditioned the effectiveness of the Roman army as an instrument of war also determined its utility as an instrument of diplomatic control. The "armed suasion" generated by Roman military power was effective against polities with fixed assets to protect, for these were the values that Roman power threatened, if only implicitly. Since the Romans *could* destroy or appropriate these assets, they could also subjugate their owners without doing either, thus converting them into clients.

The conditions for which the training, weaponry, and techniques of the Roman army were most effective, whether for war or for diplomatic coercion in the absence of war, were absent in the North African semidesert, in the uncleared forest lands of Central Europe, in the plains of what is now the Ukraine, in the arid plateau of Iran, and in the deserts of Arabia. Roman power could still penetrate these areas, but only at a disproportionate cost.

V
The Strategic Deployment of Forces

Until Domitian forbade the practice,[147] the large-unit structure of the Roman army, organized as it was around legions of roughly 6,000 men, was accentuated still further by the habit of deploying the forces in multi-legion camps like Mogontiacum (Mainz), Vetera

(Xanten), and Oppidum Obiorum (Cologne) on the Rhine frontier. Since the *auxilia* were with the legions, the forces of the Roman army were concentrated on a few points around the periphery of the empire, leaving little or nothing for the interior and with a very uneven distribution on the perimeter itself.

Thus, in A.D. 6, out of a total of twenty-eight legions, four were in Spain, five on the Rhine or beyond, two in Raetia, five in Illyricum, three in Moesia, and nine in the whole of North Africa, Egypt, and Syria.[148] After the ambush of Varus's legion in A.D. 9, the Spanish garrison was reduced to three legions, the German increased to eight, the Raetian eliminated, the Illyrian left unchanged, and the Moesian reduced to two. One legion remained in North Africa, two in Egypt, and four in Syria.[149] This distribution was maintained until the invasion of Britain in A.D. 43.[150]

Clearly, then, the uneven development of client states in East and West had military implications: in the East, where client states were highly developed (and where the Armenian settlement of 20 B.C. left a deep buffer zone between Rome and Parthia), Roman security was ensured by a few mediocre legions, powerfully supplemented by the obedience of clients aware of the much greater potential of Roman forces elsewhere. In the West, on the other hand, the day-to-day security of the imperial periphery could only be ensured by immediate and visible legionary presence. What the sophisticated populations and leaders of the civilized East could readily visualize, Germans and Dacians had to see with their own eyes.

By absorbing the burden of providing internal and perimeter security, the client states of the East allowed the Romans to keep their striking power concentrated—and it was, of course, this same concentrated strength that generated the powerful "armed suasion" that kept the client states in subjection in the first place. Small though it was, the four-legion garrison in Syria had this quality of concentrated strength which, paradoxically, would have been dissipated by the attempt at *military* control of vast territories of Asia Minor. Moreover, with Parthia to the east still the only great power on Rome's horizon, a dispersion of strength would have entailed grave dangers. It is in this light that the deployment policy of the period must be seen. Both the lack of central reserves and the chosen deployment of the legions on the perimeter must be viewed in the perspective of a security structure that was still anchored on the complex, fragile, but supremely efficient client system. There *was* a strategic reserve, but it was deployed on the line. Located near zones of expected threat or opportunity (i.e., opportunity for conquest), the legions were not actually committed to the territorial defense of their segment of the perimeter, as was later the case. If a threat materialized in any one sector, forces could ordinarily be withdrawn from the others; there was no real danger that Germans, Dacians, and Parthians would coordinate their attacks on the empire.[151]

Under these political circumstances, the defense strategy of the empire had to cope with two kinds of threats: "endemic" threats, which were more or less stable in intensity over prolonged periods of time (such as the German threat between A.D. 9 and the crisis of A.D. 69–70), and "sporadic" threats, which were inherently unpredictable (such as native revolts). It would therefore have been wasteful to retain substantial forces in a central strategic reserve. Such a reserve is preferable to the use of *ad hoc* forces drawn from the line only if it can be redeployed in time to reinforce sectors under attack, and quick redeployment could rarely be accomplished in the Roman Empire. Where the threat was endemic and stable, it was not the availability of a reserve that was needed, but permanently deployed forces; where the threat was sporadic and unpredictable, reserves could hardly ever hope to arrive on the scene in good time, and the damage done was likely to be inflicted very early, in any case. It was much more efficient to keep all forces on the perimeter, where their presence was continuously useful either militarily or diplomatically, and not in an interior reserve.

The peculiar geography of the empire—a hollow ring around the Mediterranean—deprived the Romans of the defender's usual advantage, shorter inner lines of communication, except when sea transport was feasible. In the absence of early warning of emerging threats, Roman forces could only march at three miles an hour toward an enemy whose offensive was already under way. This meant that a strategic reserve could not make a great deal of difference, for it would not matter much if enemy incursions within imperial territory lasted one month rather than two; with or without a centralized reserve, the Roman response could rarely be rapid enough to reinforce a sector while it was still succesfully containing enemy attacks.

The system did, however, entail additional risks. For one thing, there was always the possibility that major threats—even if uncoordinated—would materialize simultaneously on different segments of the perimeter. Moreover, there was one danger that was more than a contingency: when legions were withdrawn from one sector to meet a threat on another (or to build a concentration of offensive forces), unsubdued provincial populations and enemies beyond the border were liable to take the opportunity to rebel against Roman rule or to raid imperial territory. This was more than a contingency since there was obviously a causal relationship between the removal of Roman troops from a given sector and the emergence of threats previously latent. And there was the further risk of a chain reaction, such as that which materialized in A.D. 6. In that year, the Pannonian revolt broke out when Illyricum was stripped of its legions to augment the forces being concentrated for the two-pronged offensive against Maroboduus and for the strategic encirclement of Bohemia. Tiberius, in charge of five legions, had actually crossed the Danube on his northwest line of advance from Carnuntum,[152] when the revolt broke out to his rear.[153] The small Roman force left in the base of Siscia (now Sisak, in Croatia) was besieged by the rebels, who seem to have gained control of most of the province. The provincial legate of Moesia, A. Caecina Severus, who was bringing his forces north to join Tiberius for the planned offensive against Maroboduus, instead set out to quell the revolt. But the Danubian frontier of his own province had now been stripped of its two legions, and Dacian raiders crossed the river and penetrated Moesia. Just as Tiberius was forced to cancel the invasion of Bohemia in order to return to fight in Illyricum, so Severus was forced to cut short his own rescue effort in order to return to Moesia. In the end, it took three years and all the forces the Romans could muster to subdue Illyricum.[154]

Viewed in the context of the sporadic and widely separated threats the Romans had to face, the chain reaction brought about by the planned offensive against Maroboduus was only an exception, even if a very important one. The normal experience of the early principate was the successful maintenance of imperial security on a very narrow and very economical base of military power.

VI
Conclusion
Under the republic, the Romans generally solved the security problems of their growing empire by further expansion, but this expansion was mostly hegemonic rather than territorial. The usual outcome of Roman wars and Roman victories was a minimum of territorial aggrandizement and an altogether more far-reaching extension of Rome's diplomatic control by means of the client system. In the late republic, however, new policies were formed by new forces in Roman political life, and the rhythm of territorial expansion accelerated perceptibly, reaching a climax under Augustus.

Augustus obviously did not practice in his own lifetime what he preached in his famous posthumous injunction against further conquest recorded by Tacitus (and to which Tacitus strongly objected).[155] Under his direction, wars of conquest were fought in all directions, resulting in the annexation of vast teritories: the future provinces of Moesia, Pannonia, Noricum, and Raetia, as well as the Alpes Cottiae and Maritimae. These last annexations were long overdue security measures against the depredation of the Salassi upon transalpine traffic, but the security motive was less compelling elsewhere. The annexation of manageable and efficient client states was not, however, Augustan policy, except as a last resort: Judea was annexed in A.D. 6, but only because no adequate successor to Herod was to be found in his family—and Judea was not a province to be lightly entrusted to one of the entrepreneurial client princes of Asia Minor.

Due to the system's economy of force, the Augustan military establishment was sufficient not only to defend the empire but also to sustain expansion; at any one moment large troop concentrations could be assembled for wars of conquest by drawing down the forces ordinarily deployed on the line, albeit at some risk. In A.D. 6, for example, out of a total legionary establishment of only twenty-eight legions, no fewer than twelve could be concentrated for the offensive into Bohemia that was to take Roman power to the Elbe.[156] Admittedly, this proportion proved to be too high and entailed grave risks, but the system was undoubtedly highly elastic.

The accepted view is that Augustus's goal, even before the great crises of A.D. 6-9 in Illyricum and Germany, was limited to the establishment of a "scientific" frontier on the Elbe—a "Hamburg-Prague-Vienna" line.[157] More recently, it has been argued convincingly that Augustus had set himself no such limit, being still in full pursuit of the Alexandrian—and Roman—dream of world conquest. It has also been pointed out that Roman geographic (and demographic) knowledge was still so undeveloped that even the conquest of China could seem feasible.[158]

In any case, the system was well-suited to the support of further expansion, and it was so employed by Claudius in the conquest of Britain. As long as there were peoples and cultures susceptible to the "armed suasion" radiated by Rome's military power, and thus turned into dependable clients who would themselves absorb the security burdens resulting from past expansion, further expansion remained possible.

Two

FROM THE FLAVIANS TO THE SEVERI. *"Scientific"* Frontiers and Preclusive Defense from Vespasian to Marcus Aurelius.

When Nero died in A.D. 68, another had already claimed his place. But the emperor Galba did not arrive in Rome until October and did not live beyond January, A.D. 69. M. Salvius Otho, ex-governor of Lusitania, though in Rome as Galba's follower, procured his murder at the hands of the Praetorians and was acclaimed emperor in turn. By then yet another had risen to claim the office, Aulus Vitellius, governor of Lower Germany and master of its four legions. So far, contention had been resolved in suicide and murder; now there was to be civil war also.

In the two Germanies there were seven legions in all: forty thousand men and at least as many auxiliaries. Vitellius could count on most, enough to seize Rome and the imperial power. Otho did not command such power in his own right; no legion was bound to his person, for his former province of Lusitania had none. In Rome there were the Praetorians, 4,500 men at most, a legion of ex-marines newly raised by Nero (I Adiutrix), some detachments from the frontier armies of the Danube, and some auxiliaries. These were not enough; Otho also paid two thousand gladiators to serve him.

His real hope was the five legions of the Danubian armies and the two legions close at hand in Dalmatia. The men were willing. If the legions on the Rhine had a candidate in Vitellius, the legions on the Danube would have Otho. The cause of Vitellius was denuding the German frontiers, as soldiers were removed to Italy to fight for the imperial power; now the cause of Otho would expose the Danubian frontiers as well. But Otho's plans, and Otho's men, were slow. At Bedriacum, near Cremona, in northern Italy the two gathering armies met; the more numerous Vitellians won. By April, A.D. 69, Rome had its third emperor of the year, gross and bloodthirsty, according to the sources, but successful—or so it seemed.

Vitellius had defeated Otho by bold and rapid maneuver. He was to be defeated in turn by cautious and wide-ranging preparation. When Vitellius entered Rome in July, A.D. 69, the two legions in Egypt, at the instigation of the prefect-governor, had already proclaimed another emperor, T. Flavius Vespasianus.

Vespasian had been successfully fighting the Jewish War with an army of three legions, supported by auxiliaries and the troops of client states. He had the support of Egypt, Syria, and all the eastern client princes—and their money was as useful as their troops. There was no danger that his rear would be subverted the way his own agents were subverting the West. His son Titus remained in command in Judea, still the scene of operations and power base of the Flavian cause: the fighting legions in Judea could always overawe both Syria and Egypt to keep allegiances firm.

Vespasian remained in Egypt and left the bloody business of civil war to others. His agents fomented unrest among the Batavian auxiliaries on the Rhine to draw and pin down Vitellian legionary troops; and the grain supply from Egypt was cut off—perhaps this alone would force Vitellius to capitulate. In the meantime, 20,000 troops set out from Syria on the long road to Rome. By October, A.D. 69, Vitellians and Flavians were fighting, once again at Bedriacum. The Syrian troops had not yet reached Italy, and Vespasian was still in Egypt; but the Danubian armies, who had lost their Otho, could expect no favors from Vitellius, and they had rallied to the Flavian cause. It was troops from Pannonia who won the second battle of Bedriacum. Horror followed. Those who fought in the name of Vespasian were not controlled by him. Cremona, near the scene of battle, was sacked as if it were a foreign city, and as the wild men from wild Pannonia marched on Rome, disorder followed in their wake. In December, A.D. 69, Vitellius was killed in Rome, and the Senate voted the imperial powers to Vespasian. He did not enter the city until October, A.D. 70.

The civil war was to exact one more penalty. To occupy the Vitellian troops in Lower Germany, the formidable Batavians, led by their chief, Civilis, had been instigated to revolt in the name of the Flavian cause. Civilis, client chief of a client tribe, could count on eight auxiliary cohorts manned by his tribesmen in the Roman service, and he augmented their strength with free Germans. By the end of A.D. 69 Vitellius was dead, and Romans no longer needed help to fight other Romans. But Civilis now continued to fight in his own cause and rallied some Gauls to his side: the rebels spoke of creating a Gallic empire.

Four legions on the Rhine, depleted, starved, and demoralized, were overcome by siege or subversion. Civilis had won control of the lower Rhine. But the provincial Gauls on one side of the river did not abandon the Roman allegiance, and the free Germans on the other did not invade the defenseless empire en masse. Both were wise in their restraint. Nine sound legions under sound Flavian commanders moved against the renegade legions and the auxiliaries, leaving their own auxiliaries prudently aside. Such force could not be resisted. The revolt of Civilis was suppressed, but the Rhine frontier had disintegrated: its troops evacuated or lost, its winter camps burned, and Roman prestige—and Roman deterrence—severely damaged.

Vespasian's dynastic ambition was overt. He had two sons, and he was determined that the empire would be ruled by a Flavian or not at all. His first, Titus, duly followed him in the office when Vespasian died in A.D. 79, but Titus died in A.D. 81. A younger son, Domitian, succeeded him. The sources are kind to the first two Flavians, but not to the third. His power threatened, Domitian reacted with repression. The ancient autocrat lacked the scientific devices of the modern dictator, however, and repression, while provocative, could not be fully reliable. In A.D. 96 Domitian was murdered.

Between the end of civil war in A.D. 70 and Domitian's death twenty-six year later, there had been no spectacular wars of conquest. In Britain, the area of Roman control had been pushed to the north, but the island had not been fully conquered; nor had a settled frontier been established across the narrow neck of land below savage Scotland. In Germany, a Rhine frontier had been systematically reestablished and equally systematically abandoned as Roman control advanced and left the river behind. In a long series of frontier-rectification campaigns, roads, camps, and forts were built east of the Rhine and north of the Danube to drive back hostile peoples and to enclose the fertile salient between the rivers. Not recognizable as wars of conquest in the grand manner, the engineering campaigns of the Flavians failed to generate enthusiasm in the sedentary martial spirits in Rome. Domitian's very useful frontier war with the German Chatti in A.D. 83 was ridiculed by contemporary commentators.

In A.D. 85 the well-organized Dacians of the middle Danube, ruled by Decebalus, a formidable figure in our sources, crossed the frontier to attack Moesia. Domitian's subsequent war against the Dacians ended neither in victory and triumph nor in disgrace. There were tactical defeats and tactical victories, but the combination of invasion threats from Germans and

Sarmatians upstream from Dacia and the attempted usurpation of L. Antonius Saturninus, governor of Upper Germany, in A.D. 89, distracted Domitian from a decisive war against Decebalus, if indeed one had been planned.

Domitian's murder in A.D. 96 left the office vacant, but no civil war ensued. Equilibrium between the power of Praetorians and that of legions (which we may infer but cannot prove), or possibly the bitter memories of civil war, left the Senate free to choose the next emperor. Its choice set a pattern. M. Cocceius Nerva was old, unmilitary, respected, and noble, but chiefly old. In the future, whenever rare circumstances left this choice to the Senate, old aristocrats would be chosen, as if the senators wanted to ensure that the privilege of choice could soon be exercised again.

Elderly and unmilitary nobles were generally defenseless against active army commanders with legions at their call, and the Senate's subsequent nominees soon lost their offices and their lives. But Nerva or his advisers were wise. After news of mutiny reached Rome, after unruly Praetorians had publicly humiliated the new emperor, Nerva chose to adopt M. Ulpius Trajanus, a distinguished soldier and popular governor of Upper Germany, as his son and successor. Even before Nerva died in A.D. 98, Trajan was the new ruler of the empire. Adoption created the useful fiction of a family succession, an orderly transfer of power that simple soldiers and dynasty-minded provincials could readily accept; the deliberate act was safer than the genetic gamble of natural succession, and the result could be acceptable to the Senate.

Trajan was a soldier, and a good one; wars of conquest were feverishly anticipated, and this time there was no disappointment. A limited war against the Dacians in A.D. 101–2 resulted in a compromise settlement, but one which marked a victory: Dacia was to be a client state with Decebalus as the client king. But the protagonist did not fit the part. In A.D. 105–6 war had to be renewed, for Decebalus was disobedient and Trajan's patience was exhausted. Hard fighting and a great victory followed. A large new Dacian province across the Danube was added to the empire.

But the natural arena for a Roman conqueror was the East. The Armenian settlement had broken down once more: once again an Arsacid occupied the throne of Armenia without the sanction of Rome. Anatolia now had an organized frontier, but with only two legions in Cappadocia and only three in Syria itself, it could not be a safe frontier. If Parthian forces could assemble freely in Armenia they might strike with greater force either due west or due south at their choosing, and to the south was Syria, a core province of the empire. Both strategic necessity and personal ambition required war. Between A.D. 114 and 117 Trajan's army conquered not merely Armenia but much of Mesopotamia down to the Parthian capital of

Ctesiphon. *Trajan had conquered more than any ruler of Rome since Augustus. Then came disaster. Insurrection in the rear and a Parthian counteroffensive from the hinterland of Iran forced the rapid evacuation of all the conquered lands. Trajan did not outlive his ultimate defeat. In A.D. 117 he fell ill and died in Cilicia, on his way back to Rome.*

P. Aelius Hadrianus, Trajan's supposedly adopted successor, followed a policy of consolidation, not conquest. Dacia was retained, but all the eastern conquests were abandoned. Hadrian continued the chain of adoptions with Antoninus Pius (138–61), who in turn adopted two sons as co-emperors, Lucius Verus (161–69) and Marcus Aurelius (161–80). The Antonine era, as it became known, was a period of stability and consolidation, of secure frontiers and systematized defenses; it was the climax of imperial success, the result of a sequence of good and long-lived emperors and of favorable circumstances. Having weathered the great crisis of A.D. 69—when it had seemed on the verge of dissolution—the empire of the Flavians, Trajan, Hadrian, and the Antonines had seemingly achieved a system of everlasting security, a pax Roman and eternal. By the later years of the great stoic emperor Marcus Aurelius, however, wars, invasions, and the plague shattered the Antonine peace. From then until the end, with only relatively brief intervals of respite, the survival of the empire was to be a bitter struggle.

I
The System
in Outline

The most characteristic device of the Roman art of war under the republic and early principate was the marching camp. At the conclusion of the day's march, legionary troops on the move were assembled at a site, carefully selected in advance, where they were put to work for three hours or more[1] to dig a perimeter obstacle ditch, erect a rampart, assemble a palisade with prefabricated elements (*pila muralia*),[2] and pitch tents. Although archeological evidence shows a wide variety of perimeters in the surviving sites,[3] the internal layout apparently followed a standard scheme: tent sites were neatly grouped by units around a broad T-shaped roadway at the center of the camp, which faced the headquarters area, and a broad gap was left between the inner edge of the rampart and the first line of tents.[4]

Modern commentators often point out that the strength of the camp defenses was not commensurate with the elaborate effort needed to build them after a day on the march.[5] The strategic mobility of Roman forces was undoubtedly reduced by this tiring and time-consuming camp-building routine.[6] However, though the flimsy palisade made of portable two-pointed stakes, the shallow ditch three Roman feet deep, and the rampart only six feet high[7] would not do much to stem a major assault, it would be a mistake to underestimate the tactical utility of standard marching camp defenses.

Even modest earthworks (and pointed stakes) would be sufficient to break the impetus of a cavalry charge; indeed, no cavalry would normally attempt to charge against such obstacles. Furthermore, the margin of sixty Roman feet[8] between the outer perimeter and the first line of tents on the inside would afford considerable protection against arrows or throwing-spears. Moreover, the broad roadways would ensure that if the camp came under attack, the troops could be mustered in an orderly manner, avoiding the certain confusion and possible panic easily caused by men rushing about in a small space strewn with impedimenta.

Nevertheless, modern commentators are undoubtedly right in stressing the tactical shortcomings of the camp defenses. It was certainly no part of Roman practice to man a beleaguered camp in the manner of a fortress: once assembled, the troops would march out to fight the enemy in the open, where the shock force of disciplined infantry could be brought to bear with full effect. (Only auxiliaries armed with missile weapons could fight at all usefully from behind the camp fence.) But it was the *nontactical* functions that made the Roman marching camp much more than a mere defensive perimeter and that gave it "a degree of importance without parallel in modern warfare."[9] The marching camp was, in effect, a powerful psychological device.[10]

For troops venturing into hostile territory and possibly exotic surroundings, the familiar context of the camp defenses would provide a welcome sense of security. With stray natives and wild beasts firmly separated from the soldiers' vicinity by ditch, rampart, and palisade, the troops could wash, care for their equipment, converse, and play in a relaxed atmosphere. This same sense of security would allow them to sleep soundly and so be fit for march or battle on the next day. Thus, the physical brutalization and cumulative exhaustion of troops living in field conditions would be mitigated by a nightly opportunity for recuperation.

The marching camp was also a labor-saving device. It is true that much labor was needed to build it, but once the camp was ready for the night, the protected perimeter would allow a proper watch with a minimum of men. A standard objective of night operations is to deny sleep to the enemy; even if little damage is inflicted, noisy hit-and-run attacks night after night can cause a progressive deterioration in the physical and mental condition of the troops under attack, partly by forcing more and more men to be assigned to guard duties at the expense of sleep. Here again the marching camp was of great value in preserving the energies of the troops, since, if our source is reliable, only sixteen men in each eighty-man legionary century were posted to guard and picket duties for the night watch at any one time.[11]

It is sometimes claimed that the marching camp also provided an element of tactical insurance, since if Roman troops were defeated in the field they could take refuge in the camp and prepare to fight another day.[12] But this could only be so if the defeated troops had an intact marching camp within easy reach, which was unlikely: it was standard practice to slight the defenses once the site was left. In a more subtle sense, however, the observation has merit. Nothing is more difficult than to canalize defeat into orderly retreat and avoid a rout. The campsite could provide a natural rallying point and a ready-made framework for redeployment.

The Roman marching camp thus combined the tactical advantages of a bivouac with the convenience of billets,[13] and had the added benefit of a guarded perimeter that could always be turned into a heavily fortified earthwork, given more time and labor. The characteristically Roman institution of the marching camp was a crucial factor in the strength of an army whose peculiar quality was always resilience under stress.

The security policies of Vespasian and his successors, which reached a logical culmination under Hadrian and his successors, may be seen as an attempt to transform the empire into a marching camp writ large. The metaphor is perfectly applicable: the network of imperial border defenses created under these policies, like those of the marching camp, were intended to serve not as total barriers but rather as the one fixed element in a mobile strategy of imperial defense.

The first step was the demarcation of imperial frontiers. Although major natural barriers had in some cases provided reasonably clear borders for the Julio-Claudian empire, in many places its borders would have been difficult to determine with any precision. The zone of direct control and provincial organization gave way to areas of political control, and the latter in turn merged into areas of greater, and then lesser, influence.

Where no ocean or broad desert gave visible definition to the limits of empire, only an exercise in subjective political judgment could

MAP 2.1. THE FRONTIERS IN THE SECOND CENTURY

LIMES
POROLISSENSIS

DATIAE

BLACK SEA

PER
SIA

LOWER MOESIA

ARMENIA

THRACIA

PONTUS ET BITHYNIA

ACEDONIA

CAPPADOCIA

PARTHIA

ASIA

GALATIA

PIRUS

LYCIA
ET
PAMPHYLIA

CILICIA

SYRIA

ACHAEA

CYPRUS

SYRIA
PALAESTINA

CRETE

SEA

ARABIA

CYRENE

EGYPT

RED SEA

determine just where the sphere of imperial control finally came to an end. An understandable psychic satisfaction could be derived from claiming some vague form of suzerainty over remote peoples whom Rome did not really control, and these empty claims are not always easy to distinguish from the genuine client relationships that broadened the real scope of imperial power so considerably. It may be easy to discount Augustan bombast as far as India (and perhaps the Scythians) is concerned,[14] but these false claims of suzerainty were paired with very similar claims that were altogether more valid, as in the case of Juba's Mauretania or Herod's Judea.

All this had changed by the time of Hadrian. The limits of empire were by then demarcated very precisely, on the ground, so that all could tell exactly what was Roman and what was not. The established client states had been absorbed, and with several significant exceptions that illuminate the purpose of the rest, the land borders of the empire were guarded by defended perimeters that complemented the natural barriers of river and ocean. The invisible borders of imperial power had given way to physical frontier defenses: in Britain, the complex of fortifications of "Hadrian's Wall" defined Roman territory from sea to sea on the Tyne-Solway line; in Germany, a much less elaborate trench-and-palisade or fence barrier cut across the base of the salient formed by the converging upstream courses of the Rhine and Danube; in North Africa, segments of a trench-and-wall system, the *Fossatum Africae*, have been identified over a distance of 750 kilometers along the edge of the Sahara in modern Algeria. In the Dobruja (in modern Romania) a continuous wall of less certain attribution formed a short perimeter from Axiopolis (Raşova) on the Danube to the sea at Tomis (near Costanta). This is a typical "scientific" frontier and may have been the first continuous perimeter of imperial times—if it was indeed built under Domitian.[15]

No such continuous wall systems have been identified on the long eastern borders of the empire in Asia, from the Black Sea to the Red, with one interesting exception;[16] nor has evidence come to light indicating an eastward extension of the *Fossatum Africae* of Numidia into Tripolitania, Cyrenaica, or Egypt (or westward to Mauretania). As we shall see, the sections of the *limes* (i.e., defended border) that remained "open" illuminate the true military purpose of those that *were* provided with an unbroken perimeter barrier. For the absence of such barriers does not mean that there was no *limes*, in the sense of a linear perimeter:[17] the essential element of the *limes* was not the wall, palisade, or fence, but rather the network of roads linking the frontier garrisons with one another and the frontier zone as a whole with the interior.[18]

II
Border Defense: The
Tactical Dimension

The new strategy of perimeter defense inaugurated by the Flavians required an investment of colossal proportions over the course of three centuries: on every segment of *limes*, whether provided with a continuous barrier or not, road networks, forts large and small, and towers for observation and signaling were built and repeatedly rebuilt according to changing schemes of defense and in response to variations in the nature of the threat. Thanks to the devoted labors of generations of scholars, the physical elements of Roman frontier policy have been uncovered in a coherent, if incomplete, manner. But while the archeological, epigraphical, numismatic, and literary evidence has been augmented and assiduously collated by these labors, the meaning and purpose of Roman frontier defense during this phase of empire remains controversial.

The Romans are not otherwise held to have been irrational or timid, yet the fixed defenses built by them are often said to have been both useless[19] and demoralizing, owing to the supposedly fatal "Maginot Line" mentality that the mere presence of these fixed defenses allegedly engendered.[20] These judgments reflect not only a modern awareness of the third-century breakdown of the system, but also a seemingly ineradicable Clausewitzian prejudice against defensive strategies and defensive construction—a prejudice as common among historians writing of Hadrian and his policies as among contemporary military analysts discussing today's ballistic missile defenses.

The most common fallacy of such analyses is the tendency to evaluate defensive systems in absolute terms. If a defense can be penetrated, it is said to be "useless"; and only an impenetrable defense is conceded to be of value. This appraisal is highly misleading: its equivalent, for the offense, would be to regard as useless any offensive system that cannot prevail against all forms of resistance, under all circumstances. Defensive systems should instead be evaluated in relative terms: their cost in resources should be compared to their military "output." Further, the value of defensive systems must be assessed in terms of the type of threat they are intended to counter. One system may be most effective against "low-intensity" threats (infiltration, hit-and-run raids, etc.), another against the maximal threat of invasion. Each should be evaluated accordingly, for defensive systems are normally intended to provide a *finite* barrier only against a particular kind of threat, while absorbing, deflecting, or at least filtering other threats greater or lesser in intensity than those against which the system is designed.

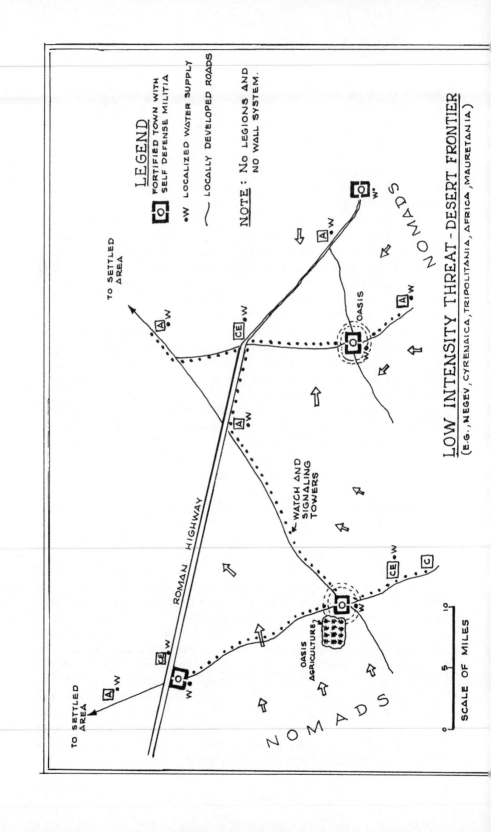

LEGEND

⊡ FORTIFIED TOWN WITH SELF DEFENSE MILITIA

•W LOCALIZED WATER SUPPLY

～ LOCALLY DEVELOPED ROADS

NOTE : No legions and no wall system.

LOW INTENSITY THREAT – DESERT FRONTIER
(E.G., NEGEV, CYRENAICA, TRIPOLITANIA, AFRICA, MAURETANIA)

NOMADS

TO SETTLED AREA

OASIS

ROMAN HIGHWAY

← WATCH AND SIGNALING TOWERS

TO SETTLED AREA

OASIS AGRICULTURE

N O M A D S

SCALE OF MILES

0   5   10

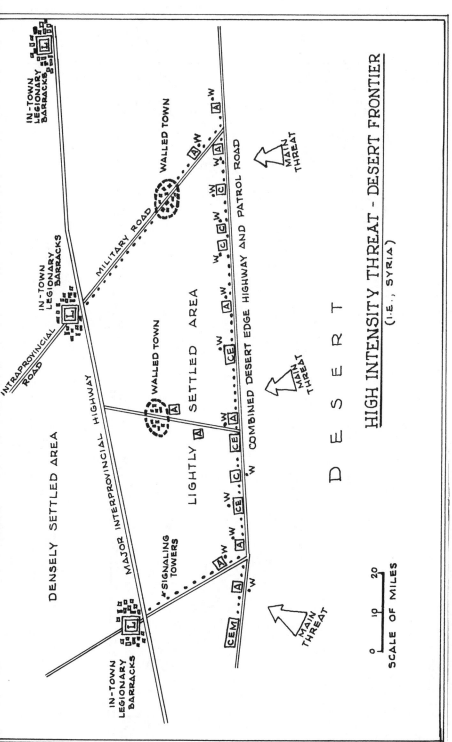

FIG. 2.1. MODELS OF FRONTIER ORGANIZATION I

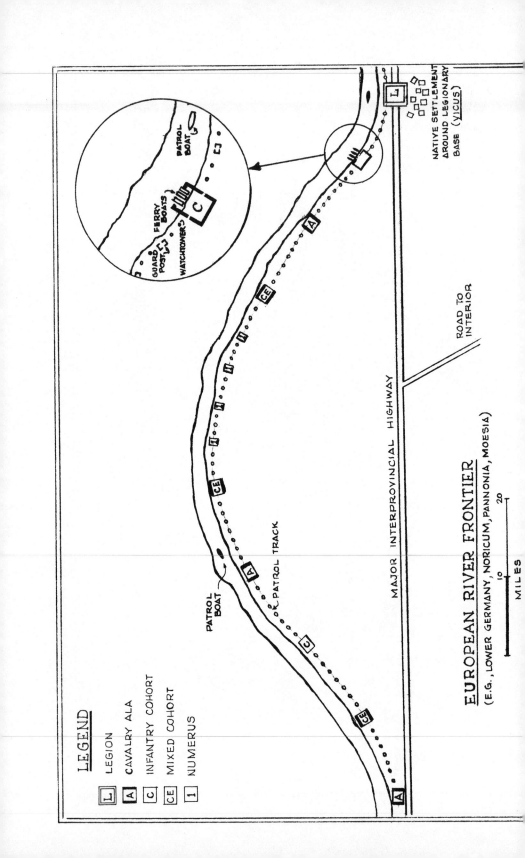

LEGEND

L	LEGION
A	CAVALRY ALA
C	INFANTRY COHORT
CE	MIXED COHORT
1	NUMERUS

GUARD POST
FERRY BOATS
WATCHTOWER?
PATROL BOAT

PATROL BOAT
PATROL TRACK

MAJOR INTERPROVINCIAL HIGHWAY

NATIVE SETTLEMENT AROUND LEGIONARY BASE (VICUS)

ROAD TO INTERIOR

EUROPEAN RIVER FRONTIER
(E.G., LOWER GERMANY, NORICUM, PANNONIA, MOESIA)

0   10   20
MILES

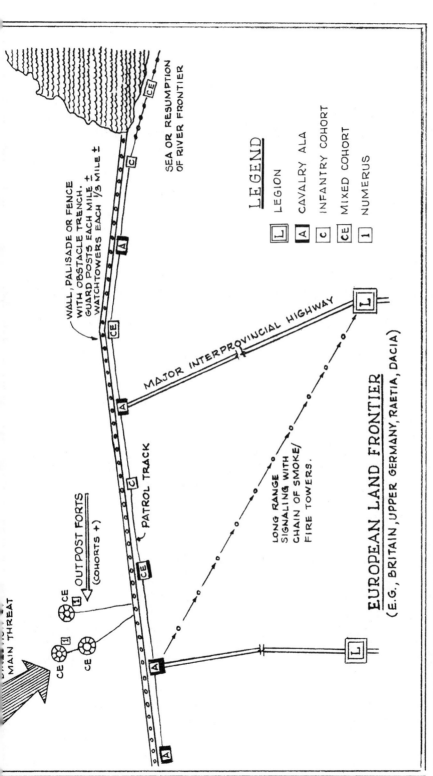

FIG. 2.2. MODELS OF FRONTIER ORGANIZATION II

Roman frontier defenses in sectors provided with linear barriers, whether walls, palisades, fences, or earthworks, were in fact designed to combat low-intensity threats—primarily transborder infiltration and peripheral incursions. These barriers were *not* intended to provide the total defense against large-scale attack. Instead, both types of *limes*, whether "open" or "closed" (i.e., provided with continuous barriers), served as base lines for mobile striking forces, which operated against large-scale attacks in a tactically offensive manner, but within the framework of a defensive strategy. While minor, endemic threats were countered by the fixed defenses and a minimum of manpower (the ordinary guard force), more serious threats were met by concentrated mobile forces sent forward for interception or for "spoiling" attacks.

During this phase of empire, the operational method of border defense against high-intensity threats was mobile and offensive, not static: combat was to take place *beyond* the border rather than within it. In other words, the complex of fixed defenses built along the *limes* served only as a *supporting infrastructure* for offensive operations in the event of major attacks, and it should be evaluated as such. There was no question, at this time, of using the frontier defense infrastructures to shelter the garrisons serving on the sector. To validate these statements, we must first set the barrier elements (walls, palisades, fences, and earthworks) in the context of the other components of the defenses, which were present in every tract of *limes*, whether open or closed.

Watchtowers and outpost forts. Their function was to provide surveillance against infiltration and early warning of impending large-scale attacks. Watchtowers were usually built directly into the barrier element, if there was one, as in the case of the turrets spaced out at intervals of 540 feet along Hadrian's Wall in Britain; these provided dense surveillance coverage, but little in the way of early warning.[21] Outpost forts, on the other hand, were located well outside the border. Such forts have been identified on the major routes north of Hadrian's Wall, and three of them (Birrens, Netherby, and Bewcastle) have been given a securely Hadrianic dating.[22] In the case of the *Fossatum Africae* in modern Algeria, the dating of the elements in the system is less certain, but an outer zone of surveillance and active defense has been identified with reasonable certainty to a depth of sixty to eighty kilometers beyond the border line.[23]

Communications. This second functional element (partly based on the same physical structures) was a simple two-way signaling system that linked the outposts and surveillance towers with the auxiliary forts in the rear and with the legionary fortresses of the sector, the latter sometimes located deep in the rear. Communications, by crude fire and smoke signals, required that perimeter forts or towers have a clear view to the rear, though not necessarily to either side.[24] (It has been observed that on the Antonine Wall in Scotland, where the irregularities of the ground sometimes preclude a line-of-sight alignment, semicircular extensions of the wall appear to have served as the base of signaling towers.)[25] A communication network is present even where there is no trace of a perimeter barrier: a scene on Trajan's column shows a regular pattern of signaling stations along the Danube where there was no wall or other barrier.[26] In Britain, where the two legionary fortresses (York-Erburacum, Chester-Deva) remained over 100 and 140 miles behind Hadrian's Wall, respectively, a vertical axis of signaling towers has been identified linking the Carlisle sector of Hadrian's Wall with the fortress of the legion VI *Victrix* at York.[27]

Troop basing. The third indispensable element in the system was the guards, patrol units, auxiliary forces, and—though not always—legions, which were housed in an ascending hierarchy of guardposts, auxiliary forts, and legionary fortresses. The latter term is used conventionally to describe legionary *bases*, but during this phase of empire no elaborate defenses were built around the complex of barracks and service buildings that made up each legionary "fortress."

Roads. These were the essential elements of the system: each defended sector was served by a network of "horizontal" and "vertical" roads, the latter providing axes of penetration beyond the border as well as rearward routes for communication, reinforcement, troop circulation, and supply. Where the *limes* was not guarded by linear barriers (as, most importantly, on the Syrian frontier[28]), horizontal perimeter roads also served as patrol routes against infiltration and small-scale incursions. When the outer lines of the perimeter were shorter than the inner ones, as was case with the trans-Danubian *limes* of Raetia, the horizontal frontier roads also served as interprovincial highways. Based as it was on the rapid concentration of mobile forces, the frontier defense of this phase of empire was critically dependent on the density and quality of the road network. Characteristically, the first step in the Flavian reorganization of the frontiers of eastern Anatolia was the construction of west-east "vertical" highways, linking the approaches to the frontier zone with western Anatolia.[29]

The physical elements of Roman *limites* were only the skeleton of the system; they did not delimit its scope, which was defined rather by "the whole moving complex of patrolling, trafficking, and diplomacy which grew up around these structural lines and . . . extended far beyond the areas covered by them. . . ."[30] Their layout makes it quite clear that the walls, palisades, fences, or earthworks that formed the linear barriers in Europe and Numidia during this phase of the empire were *not* intended to provide fighting platforms in the manner of medieval castle walls. For one thing, their physical design would have precluded such use. In the case of Hadrian's Wall, for example, the rampart walk was no more than six feet wide, too narrow to be a satisfactory fighting platform.[31] In the case of the palisades, fences, and walls of Upper Germany and Raetia, as well as in the "curtain" element of the *Fossatum Africae*, there was of course no rampart or parapet at all.

The obvious unsuitability of the linear barriers as fighting platforms against large-scale attacks has sometimes resulted in description of them as merely "symbolic."[32] This reduces their function to that of mere boundary markers. If that were so, their construction would have been wildly irrational, given the vast effort needed to build them. In fact, however, Roman linear barriers, by no means the first known to antiquity,[33] had at least two separate tactical functions. First, they enhanced the *reliability* of surveillance and decreased the quantity of manpower needed for protection against infiltration. By presenting an obstacle that could be crossed, but not very quickly, the walls, palisades, or fences increased the effectiveness of surveillance, especially at night when the visual observation range of the sentries in their turrets or watchtowers would be drastically reduced. The barriers also provided security for small patrols by posing an effective obstacle to ambush; this meant that the size of patrol units could safely be kept very small.

The second tactical function of the linear barriers was directed at much graver threats, such as mass incursions by mounted raiders or even outright invasions. For cavalry forces, the barriers were a formidable obstacle. Hadrian's Wall was fronted by a V-shaped ditch thirty feet wide and at least nine feet deep; beyond the ditch and past a berm from six to twenty feet wide[34] stood the wall, twenty feet high including the parapet.[35] The palisades and fences of Upper Germany and Raetia were generally lower (twelve to thirteen feet), while the reconstructed segments of the *Fossatum Africae* show a wide degree of variance: the obstacle ditch ranged from 4.0 to 6.0 meters wide and 2.30 to 3.40 meters deep, and the wall from 2.0 to 2.50 meters high.[36]

It might appear that the low wall of the *Fossatum Africae*, not much higher than a reasonably tall man, would not present much of an obstacle to marauders. But as an authority on Roman desert frontiers has pointed out, even a relatively shallow ditch and a low wall could suffice to discourage mounted raiders:[37] instead of being able to penetrate settled areas at will, relying on surprise and shock tactics, mounted raiders would be forced to stop in order to breach the wall and fill in the ditch, so their mounts could pass. And once inside the barrier, the raiders could not be certain of a rapid exit—unless they returned to the original entry point. By posting a detachment to close the original breach and sending patrols to locate the raiding party, the defenders could trap the raiders inside the perimeter, counting on the barrier to slow down their escape. The principal tactical problem in countering such threats was always the elusiveness[38] of the enemy, and even if wall systems could not keep them out, they could certainly help to keep them in.[39]

Attempts have been made to relate the linear elements of frontier systems to tactics of border defense against high-intensity threats also, but these have not been very convincing.[40] The linear elements worked best against *low-intensity* threats; they could be of little use in fighting large enemy concentrations, which were to be intercepted well beyond the curtain whenever possible. Against large-scale attack, the walls, palisades, fences, or perimeter roads (e.g., on the Syrian *limes*) were not the first line of defense, but rather the last.[41] As such, their function was only to provide a jumping-off place for mobile operations, and "rear-area security" behind the zone of active combat.[42]

Roman frontier policy during this phase of empire has been criticized on the grounds that the deployment of forces along the *limites* amounted to an inelastic "cordon," bound to be penetrated. Napoleon (*"le système de cordons est des plus nuisibles"*) and Clausewitz have been quoted to this effect.[43] The essence of cordon deployments is the *even* distribution of available defensive forces all along the line of interception, in order to cover the full frontage equally. It is certainly true that the attackers of a cordon have the full advantage of concentration against a dispersed defense, as do all mobile columns against all *tactically static* lines: even if the offense is numerically inferior overall, and perhaps grossly so, it can still attain crushing local superiority at the chosen points of penetration. It is for this reason that all capable practitioners of war and all progressive theoreticians have always regarded evenly distributed cordon deployments as inherently inferior, in *large-scale warfare against mobile forces*. Indeed, in such warfare it is only rational to choose a cordon deployment if the

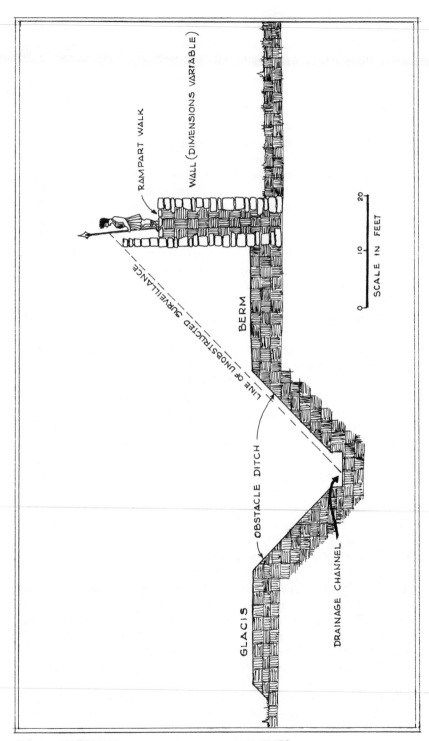

FIG. 2.3. HADRIAN'S WALL: THE BARRIER ELEMENTS

defense suffers from inferiorities that cannot be overcome. For example, an army composed solely of infantry, opposed by cavalry forces, can have no hope of successful maneuver in any case, so the *only* feasible defense may be the formation of a continuous interception line. Similarly, the cordon may be the best form of deployment for defensive forces that are grossly inferior to the attackers in command and control (or in their means of communication); again, such forces would be outmaneuvered in mobile warfare in any case, and by adopting cordon tactics they can at least hope to delay the enemy. When such deficiencies are *not* present, the voluntary adoption of a cordon with its resultant dispersal of strength can only signify a failure of generalship—or so goes the argument.

None of these organic inferiorities affected the Roman army during this phase of the empire. There was no inferiority in the overall level of mobility: although the core of the army was still very much the heavy infantry of the legions, it also contained large cavalry forces. In the second half of the second century, the Roman army included at least ten milliary and ninety quingenary *alae*, a total of some 55,000 horsemen at full establishment.[44] There was, moreover, the light cavalry of the mixed *cohortes equitatae*, at the rate of 240 horsemen for each milliary and 120 for each quingenary cohort. (There is no precise data on the number of *cohortes equitatae* out of the total of 40 to 50 milliary cohorts and 270 quingenary cohorts estimated for the second half of the second century, but the proportion may have been quite large.)[45] In all, it has been estimated that in the second century the Roman army had a total of 80,000 mounted auxiliary troops of all types.[46]

Clearly, there was no overall lack of mobility. It has been calculated that in the second century, the front headquarters for Hadrian's Wall (in the milliary cavalry fort of Stanwix) could deploy some 5,500 cavalry of *alae* and perhaps 3,000 light cavalry of *cohortes equitatae*[47]—a very large force indeed for a sector 73½ miles wide. In Lower Germany, on the other hand, in the period A.D. 104–20 the units attested on the sector included a total of 3,700 horsemen.[48]

What matters, of course, is not the absolute mobility of part of the frontier troops, but the *relative* mobility of all. In some sectors, the Romans did face primarily the threat of mounted raiders (or cavalry armies, in the case of the eastern sector), but elsewhere loosely organized tribal communities of farmers could hardly have supported a large number of horsemen. In the Balkans, the Sarmatians fought primarily on horseback, as heavy cavalry armed with the *contus*, a heavy lance, (i.e., a shock weapon);[49] but all the Germanic tribes fought primarily on foot until well into the fourth century.[50] The only sector where the Romans always faced an enemy capable of fielding large cavalry armies was, of course, the Parthian.

It would be misleading to evaluate the mobility of Roman forces purely in terms of the auxiliary cavalry; but it is equally misleading to compare the legionary troops burdened with their notoriously heavy kit to lightly armed barbarians.[51] Day-to-day security functions were, in any case, the province of the auxiliary troops, who were not equipped with heavy shields or provided with weighty kits. Furthermore, Roman commanders were perfectly capable of exercising "load discipline"—essential then as now to preserve the mobility of field units against the universal tendency of soldiers to gather and keep. (Suetonius's account of Tiberius personally inspecting the kit of the troops setting out across the Rhine is a vivid picture of a great general in action.)[52]

Nor was there any question of an inherent inferiority in command, control, and communications. The disciplined division of authority within the Roman army must have produced a much more flexible system of command and control than that of loosely organized warrior bands. As far as communications are concerned, there can be no comparison between Roman signaling methods and whatever improvised pool of runners their enemies could put together.

In the absence of the intrinsic inferiorities that alone can justify the adoption of cordon tactics, why, then, did the Romans adopt them all the same, as some authorities assert? Actually, they did not. Roman troops were *not* evenly distributed along a line of interception in the manner of "frontier guards"; rather, they retained the character of mobile striking forces. Sometimes deployed in depth behind the sector defenses and sometimes deployed along the line itself, Roman troops remained concentrated within the ascending hierarchy of guard posts, auxiliary forts, and legionary "fortresses." Along Hadrian's Wall, for example, the original structure of forces was as follows:

a) The legions VI *Victrix* at Erburacum (York) and XX *Valeria Victrix* at Deva (Chester).[53] Far from being deployed along the line as a static cordon, these forces were concentrated in the deep rear (between 100 and 140 miles from the wall). It should be noted, incidentally, that the legion at Chester was deployed in a classic economy-of-force hinge position: it was equally available to support the auxiliary forces distributed in forts throughout Wales (together with the third legion in Britain, the II *Augusta* at Isca Silurum [Caerleon]) or to backstop the northern sector, together with the VI *Victrix*.[54]

b) The auxiliary *alae* and cohorts deployed in the three (Hadrianic) outpost forts and in sixteen wall forts, totaling some 5,500 cavalry and 10,000 infantry.[55] These forces, though on the line itself (unlike the legions), were nevertheless deployed as concentrated striking forces, not evenly dispersed along the line. (It is believed that all these *auxilia* were under the command of the headquarters unit on the wall, the milliary *Ala Petriana* stationed at Stanwix,[56] which was no mean force even on its own.)

c) Guards and lookouts, fewer than 3,000 men in all.[57] This was the only troop element that *was* thinly distributed and therefore operationally static. These troops manned the "milecastles" (small forts built into the wall at intervals of one Roman mile) and provided the lookouts for the turrets, two of which were spaced out between each pair of milecastles. (Since the turrets had an internal area of only fourteen square feet, they must have been manned in rotation, by guards drawn from the adjacent milecastles.)[58]

This breakdown reveals the true nature of the deployment. Of a grand total of almost 30,000 troops deployed on the sector, no more than 10 percent at most were committed to static defense,[59] and this is by no means a large proportion. In fact, it is comparable to the proportion of manpower that a mobile field army would allocate for security duties in the rear.

On other segments of the imperial perimeter there was a similar articulation of forces. On the trans-Danubian *limes* in Raetia, for example, the late-second-century structure of forces consisted of five elements in an ascending hierarchy of concentration: on or very near the palisade or fence small towers were strung out, each housing a handful of men (*Wachposten* or *Blockhäuser*); also on the line, larger guard posts (*Feldwache*) were spaced at less frequent intervals; then still larger "fortlets" (*ZwischenKastelle*) at longer intervals; and finally, entire *alae* and *cohorts* were deployed in standard auxiliary *castella*, located mostly also on the line but sometimes well behind the "curtain."[60] In addition, as of A.D. 179–80, the sector was backstopped by the legion III *Italica* deployed at Castra Regina (Regensburg), constituting the only striking force of major proportions.

The structure of forces described above was not that of the original (i.e., Flavian) scheme of border defense in Britain, Upper Germany, or Raetia. In that scheme, the auxiliary forts had frequently been located well behind the perimeter, itself only marked by watchtowers and outpost forts, since there were no linear barriers as yet. In both cases, the post-Flavian trend was to move the forts right up to the perimeter itself, usually abandoning the older forts behind the line. The change was once associated specifically with Hadrianic frontier policy, and much was made of it: the defense had supposedly been made "inelastic" by being deprived of the second "line" formed by the chain of auxiliary forts. But recent archaeological evidence suggests that this change was only one of degree.[61] In any case, the tactical criticism is not valid, for at that time it was no part of Roman tactics to *allow* penetrations of the line, in the manner of a defense-in-depth, where the enemy is to be trapped between outer and inner lines in a combat zone *within* the perimeter. Instead, the scheme called for a forward defense: the aim was to intercept the enemy *beyond* the perimeter. Hence the "Hadrianic" reorganization merely meant that auxiliary interception forces were already based at jumping-off positions, instead of having to march forward to them from forts several hours away.

It is now possible to reconstruct the outlines of the operational method of border defense. Instead of playing the role of the passive "line" to the dynamic mobile column of the offense (which could thus attain crushing numerical superiority at the chosen points of penetration), the forces deployed on each sector were obviously intended to sally out of their forts to intercept major bands of attackers, i.e., *intermediate-level* threats. For threats below and above this threshold, tactics differed: against small-scale incursions and solitary attempts at infiltration, the guards in the fortlets (milecastles or their equivalents) would suffice; in the case of large-scale invasions, the *auxilia* would sally forth to contain the threat while legionary forces marched forward to backstop their defense.

The only troops *not* normally available for massed mobile deployments were that small proportion assigned to guard duty on the line. And these provided a "rear-area security" function, which mobile forces in the field would need in any case. One cannot therefore speak of an "inelastic frontier cordon"[62]—not, at any rate, at the tactical or operational (i.e., provincial) level. For the essence of a cordon defense is the low degree of concentration imposed by the attenuated line of deployment, while at this time Roman frontier forces were still essentially mobile and could mass as quickly as any field army. The Romans, whose forces still retained their core of legionary heavy infantry, must have systematically tried to escalate the level of battlefield concentration on *both* sides: all else being equal, concentration would favor the Romans, for their forces fought most efficiently at the higher levels of combat intensity.[63]

The great difference between the post-Flavian system of frontier defense and that of the Julio-Claudian era was in the provision of day-to-day security against low-intensity threats. While Roman forces fully retained their ability to fight large-scale wars, since their capacity for mobility and concentration remained high (though legions were no longer deployed in multiple camps),[64] they now had another type of military capability: they could provide a "preclusive" defense against low-intensity threats. Both force-structures could ensure ultimate superiority in the field, the *sine qua non* of the empire's survival. But only the second could also ensure a high level of *civil* security, even in frontier zones.

These two dimensions of security were, and are, functionally very different and entail contradictory requirements. Isolated infiltrators and small bands of raiders cannot be reliably intercepted by large striking forces marching or riding across the countryside. On the other hand, a thinly distributed interception line that provides a preclusive defense over the full length of the frontier cannot also stop *large-scale* attacks. The conflicting demands of battlefield superiority, which requires concentration, and preclusive security, which requires linear dispersion, cannot be resolved unless a third element is introduced into the equation. This was the role of the *limes* infrastructure, with its roads, watchtowers, guard posts, walls, palisades, and fences systematically built on the frontiers. These infrastructures resolved the contradiction between concentration and dispersion by serving as highly effective labor-saving devices. They enabled the army to provide preclusive security against low-intensity threats with a small fraction of its total force, while preserving the army's ability to fight in large-scale combat with the bulk of its forces.

Battlefield superiority was and is indispensable for strategic survival; any power that survives in a hostile environment does so by defeating the highest-intensity threats with which it is confronted from time to time. But strategic superiority does not automatically entail preclusive security. A state may retain control over its territory even if it does not repel each and every small-scale penetration. Under the Julio-Claudians, there were no linear defense infrastructures, so high levels of day-to-day security for exposed frontier areas could not have been attained without fragmenting the Roman army into a very large number of small guard detachments. Actually, the legions and the *auxilia* were deployed in compact masses, often in multilegionary camps. Between the widely separated legionary bases there was often no active defense at all. Instead, it was the client states and client tribes beyond the frontier who were to provide security within it, by themselves suppressing transborder infiltration at its source. Given the level of political organization and control within these states and tribes kept in awe by the legions, fully effective preclusive defense was out of the question. Few clients could be expected to control every would-be infiltrator and warrior-raider among their populations.

Notwithstanding the endemic insecurity of its unguarded frontiers, the Julio-Claudian system was highly efficient—efficient, that is, in terms of the goals of the empire at that time. But by the second

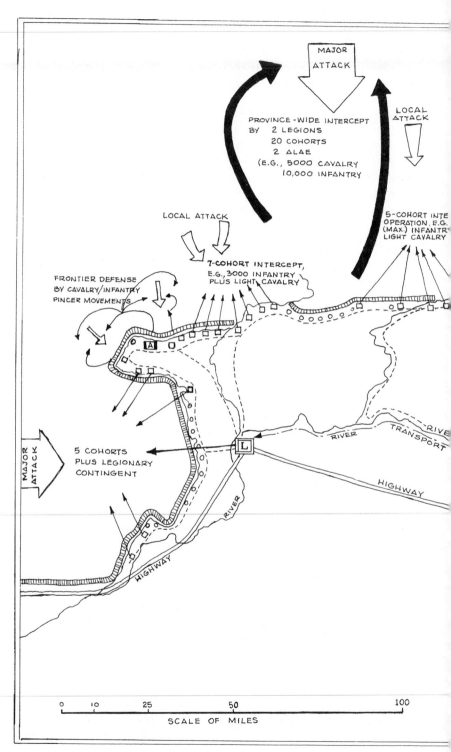

FIG. 2.4. THE TACTICS OF FORWARD DEFENSE

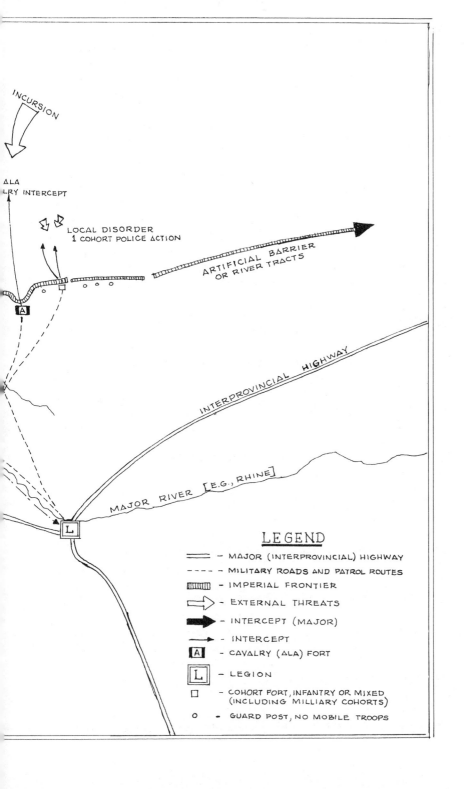

INCURSION

ALA
LRY INTERCEPT

LOCAL DISORDER
1 COHORT POLICE ACTION

ARTIFICIAL BARRIER
OR RIVER TRACTS

A

INTERPROVINCIAL HIGHWAY

MAJOR RIVER [E.G., RHINE]

L

LEGEND

═════ – MAJOR (INTERPROVINCIAL) HIGHWAY

----- – MILITARY ROADS AND PATROL ROUTES

▭▭▭▭ – IMPERIAL FRONTIER

⇨ – EXTERNAL THREATS

➤ – INTERCEPT (MAJOR)

→ – INTERCEPT

🄰 – CAVALRY (ALA) FORT

L – LEGION

▢ – COHORT FORT, INFANTRY OR MIXED
    (INCLUDING MILIARY COHORTS)

O – GUARD POST, NO MOBILE TROOPS

century the goals had changed. Ultimate strategic security remained
essential, but now there was a further requirement and a new goal:
providing *continuous* security for civilian life and property, and insulat-
ing provincials from barbarians. In particular, the purpose of the
linear barriers was to divide the barbarians beyond from the barbarians within, who were in the process of becoming Romans.[65] Economic development, urbanization, and political integration—the
ultimate goal—all required regular, day-to-day security and also the
insulation of provincials from their kin, living nearby in freedom and
savagery.

How, then, does one explain the "open" *limites* of eastern Anatolia,
Syria, Palestine, Arabia, Egypt, Cyrenaica, Tripolitania, and Mauretania, where there were neither walls nor palisades? Why was the
goal of preclusive security for civilian life pursued so consistently in
Numidia and the West and seemingly not at all in the rest of the
empire? In answer, we must note, first of all, that in Europe the river
frontiers of the Rhine and Danube were not protected by linear
barriers. Instead, watchtowers and signal stations were complemented by riverine patrol fleets (*Classis Germanica, Classis Pannonica,*
and *Classis Moesica*).[66] A similar adaptation to circumstances is found
in the case of the desert frontiers of Asia and Africa. There, too, no
continuous barrier was needed against low-intensity threats. There
were, of course, numerous nomadic tribes who would raid the
frontier zones, given the opportunity (into the twentieth century the
predatory *razzia* was the major cottage industry of the desert). But
this did not mean that *linear* defenses were needed, since there were
no broad cultivated zones to be protected. On the Syrian, Arabian,
Palestinian, and Saharan frontiers there were only isolated towns
and small islands of oasis agriculture, and it was much more efficient
to protect these points individually than to protect the whole area. In
the Negev Desert of Israel, for example, towns like Nitzana, Haluza,
Rehovot, and Shivta were fortified islands in a sea of desert that
needed no protection because it held nothing of value for the Romans
and no targets for the nomads.[67] Houses were built close to one
another on the periphery of these settlements, an all-round perimeter was formed, and mounted raiders would not venture into the
gaps; hence, these towns did not need walls. Towers for early
warning of impending attack, communications to summon mobile
troops, plus a road network, sufficed to ensure security for the desert
towns. Their mere existence proves that the towns *were* secure, for
no settled life can survive within raiding range of desert nomads
unless provided with a reliable defense.

Scattered sources of water dictated a scattered agriculture across
the entire desert belt from Mauretania to Syria; thus all these areas

could be protected by systems of "point" defense, echelonned in depth. On the Syrian *limes*, this meant further that the system could be effective against the high-intensity Parthian threat, which required good roads and a substantial body of troops but no linear barrier.[68]

The modern security problems of Israel provide a very exact parallel: in the post-1967 period, Israel faced a high-intensity invasion threat on the Suez Canal-Sinai sector, but only a low-intensity infiltration threat on the Jordan river border with the Hashemite kingdom. Accordingly, two very different defensive systems were employed. The Israelis stationed a large mobile force deep in the Sinai with only a picket line of small and widely separated observation strongholds (the so-called Bar-Lev line) on the canal itself; there was no attempt to preclude infiltration on this sector, since inside the canal frontier there was no civilian life, only empty desert. But on the Jordanian frontier, against the much less significant threat posed by the Palestinian guerrillas, the Israelis were forced to construct an uninterrupted barrier of fences, surveillance devices, and mined strips to prevent infiltrators from penetrating the settled areas of the West Bank, which are within walking range of the river Jordan.

Since the southern edge of Numidia also faced the desert, why was the linear barrier of the *Fossatum Africae* built? This, the longest of all Roman barriers, is a huge exception to the pattern of "point" defenses found on other desert frontiers. Here again, the military factor was conditioned by the hydraulic: the *fossatum* coexisted with *linear* water-management schemes that allowed the development of oasis agriculture not in scattered water points but across long stretches of what would otherwise have been desert.[69] Both the linear defenses and the extensive water-management infrastructures of Numidia were based on the same scheme of frontier settlement and defense: then as now, the two indispensable requirements of desert survival were water and security. Since the establishment of the settlements was concurrent with that of their defenses, the system as a whole must have had a purpose beyond the creation of a closed loop of irrigation and defense in the frontier zone itself. This purpose, which had to be external to *both* aspects of the *fossatum* if it were to be rational, was surely provision of high levels of security for the territory *behind* the frontier zone, between the frontier and the Mediterranean coast, an area that would otherwise have been vulnerable to seasonal nomadic raiding.

Without dependable security for civilian life and property, there could be no economic development to generate surpluses and thus sustain towns. Without the *fossatum* to contain the chronic threat of nomadic raiding, Numidia would have remained undeveloped; there would have been neither extensive urbanization nor its political concomitant, Romanization. Here more than elsewhere the purpose of *continuous* frontier barriers is apparent: they were designed, not to shelter an army afflicted by a Maginot-Line mentality, but rather to allow civilian life to develop in ways calculated to facilitate the long-term survival of the empire, by creating a social environment receptive to Roman ideals and responsive to imperial authority.

III
Border Defense: The
Strategic Dimension

Even though frontier security tactics were offensive, there is no doubt that at the empire-wide, strategic level, the pattern of deployment was that of a thin linear perimeter, and that the military power of Rome *was* fragmented into regional armies. By the time of Hadrian these armies were already acquiring separate identities (*exercitus Germanicus, Raeticus, Norici, Dalmaticus, Moesicus, Dacicus, Britannicus, Hispanicus, Mauretanicus, Cappadocicus,* and *Syriacus.*[70]) Each of these armies, organized around the core of legions stationed permanently in each region, provided with fleets where appropriate to give waterborne support to the land forces (there was almost no naval warfare),[71] was deployed in response to centralized assessments of the *regional* threat. Given hindsight of the concentrated threat that was to materialize in the second half of the second century on the Rhine and Danube, and which was to threaten the very survival of the empire two generations later, critics have censured this deployment on the grounds that it was inelastic and inherently fragile. But at the time of Hadrian there was *no* systemic threat, and thus no reason to sacrifice the long-term political priority of a preclusive frontier defense for the sake of a more "elastic" deployment directed at nonexistent regional or systemic threats.

The only alternative to the regional distribution of the army would have been a centralized deployment, with large troop concentrations based at key transit points on the inner lines of communication rather than deployed on the outer perimeter of the frontiers. There was, of course, no possibility of adopting a fully centralized deployment strategy, using only a thin deployment of border guards on the frontier and keeping all other forces in a single and undivided strategic reserve. Such a deployment can only be as effective as the means of transport are rapid.

Even today, certain precautionary deployments *in situ* are deemed to be necessary to contend with threats that are liable, if they emerge, to do so very rapidly. For example, even possessing airborne mobility at speeds of 600 m.p.h., the U.S. Department of Defense considers both Germany and South Korea too remote to permit the efficient device of allocating centrally located but "earmarked" forces. It is for this reason that American troops must be stationed in the theater itself, with the resultant diseconomy of force, regardless of the obvious political functions that these deployments also serve.

It is only when the defended area is small (in relation to the speed of transport) that the problem of troop deployment does not arise, since the inter-sector redeployments needed to match enemy concentrations against any one sector of the perimeter will not present any difficulty. Indeed, redeployments within the perimeter may then actually anticipate the emergence of the threat. For example, troops holding a small fort under siege will ordinarily be able to redeploy from rampart to rampart by moving on shorter, internal lines, even before the offense can complete *its* concentration of forces by moving around the longer exterior lines. But the Roman empire was not a small fort under siege. It cannot be visualized as a fort at all, however large: for any fort will always have the advantage of shorter inner lines. (The more the perimeter approximates a circle, the greater is this advantage; the more the perimeter approximates a thin rectangle, in which "long-axis" inter-sector distances on the inside will be virtually the same as those on the outside, the smaller the advantage.) In fact, the geographic shape of the empire was most unfavorable: its center was the hollow oblong of the Mediterranean, and the Mediterranean could be as much a barrier as a highway.

Seaborne transport could, of course, be much faster than transport on land, but it was subject to the vagaries of the weather. From November to March navigation was virtually suspended; even the largest vessels available to the Romans, the Alexandrine grain ships, waited until April to set out on their first voyage of the season.[72] Two-day voyages between Ostia and the nearest point in North Africa (Cape Bon), six-day voyages between Sicily (Messina) and Alexandria, and seven-day voyages between Ostia and the straits of Gibraltar are recorded; but these speeds, averaging 6, 5.8, and 5.6 knots respectively, are all exceptional—which is, no doubt, why they were recorded.[73] It has been calculated that *normal* speeds for fleets, with favorable winds, were of the order of 2 to 3 knots, slowing to only 1 or 1.5 knots with unfavorable winds.[74] Compared to the speed of troops marching on land, even these speeds are high: with normal kit, over level ground—and paved roads—Roman troops would march for roughly 15 Roman miles (or 13.8 statute miles) per day over long distances,[75] while ships could carry them over a distance of 27 miles in twenty-four hours for each knot of speed. Moreover,

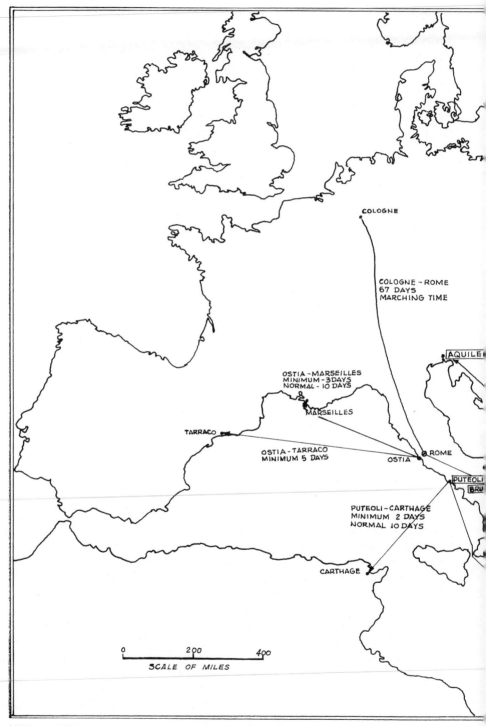

COLOGNE

COLOGNE ~ ROME
67 DAYS
MARCHING TIME

AQUILE

OSTIA ~ MARSEILLES
MINIMUM - 3 DAYS
NORMAL - 10 DAYS

MARSEILLES

TARRACO

OSTIA ~ TARRACO
MINIMUM 5 DAYS

OSTIA

ROME

PUTEOLI

BRU

PUTEOLI ~ CARTHAGE
MINIMUM 2 DAYS
NORMAL 10 DAYS

CARTHAGE

0   200   400

SCALE OF MILES

MAP 2.2. STRATEGIC MOBILITY IN THE ROMAN EMPIRE

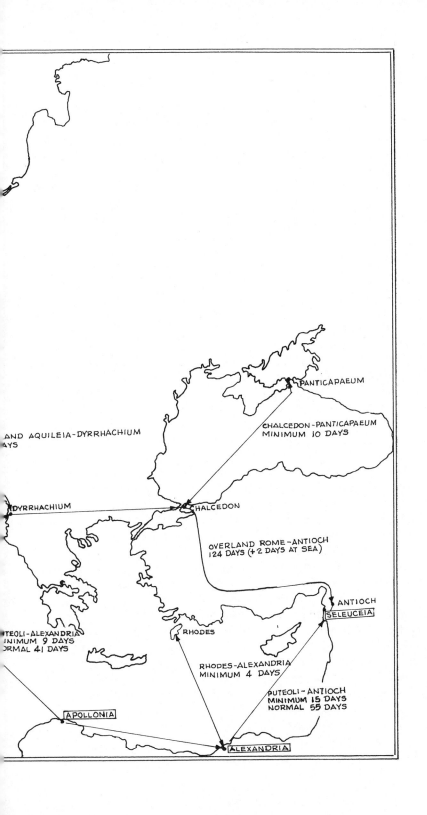

AND AQUILEIA-DYRRHACHIUM
AYS

DYRRHACHIUM

CHALCEDON-PANTICAPAEUM
MINIMUM 10 DAYS

PANTICAPAEUM

CHALCEDON

OVERLAND ROME-ANTIOCH
124 DAYS (+2 DAYS AT SEA)

ANTIOCH

SELEUCEIA

TEOLI-ALEXANDRIA
INIMUM 9 DAYS
ORMAL 41 DAYS

RHODES

RHODES-ALEXANDRIA
MINIMUM 4 DAYS

PUTEOLI-ANTIOCH
MINIMUM 15 DAYS
NORMAL 55 DAYS

APOLLONIA

ALEXANDRIA

distances were often shorter by sea than on land, and sometimes much shorter.

For example, the voyage between the naval base of Puteoli (near Naples) and Alexandria would take under forty-two days at sea, even at the minimal speed of one knot. On land, however, the journey would take roughly 180 days of uninterrupted marching, plus two days at sea; and the full overland route by way of Aquileia (near Trieste) at the head of the Adriatic would require no less than 210 days. But this is a comparison of extremes, the straight-line journey by sea against a half-circuit of the Mediterranean. On the Rome-Antioch route, for example, a distance of 1,860 miles on land plus two days at sea (between Brindisi and the landfall on the *Via Egnatia*), the sea voyage would take roughly fifty-five days at 1 knot, plus two days on land (Seleuceia-Antioch), while the land march would take roughly 124 days on land plus two days at sea, a ratio of 1:2.2 as opposed to the 1:4.3 ratio between land and sea journeys on the Rome-Alexandria route.

As soon as the ratio narrowed any further, the sea voyage often became the less desirable alternative. Ancient sailors could not contend with rough weather, and ships might be delayed unpredictably even in the sailing season, having to wait for weeks in order to sail. Moreover, long sea journeys were liable to impair the health of the troops.[76] Nevertheless, troops were frequently transported at sea, and special transports were also available for horses.[77]

Unlike the ancient empires centered on Mesopotamia or the Iranian plateau, the Roman empire had no real inner lines. With Cologne roughly sixty-seven days' march from Rome, and Antioch, gateway to the critical Parthian sector, still more remote, the delay between the emergence of a new threat on the frontier and the response of a fully centralized system would have been unacceptably long. Had the Romans deployed their forces in a single centralized strategic reserve in the modern manner, their enemies would have been able to invade and ravage the provinces at will, and then retreat before relief forces arrived on the scene. There is thus little point in criticizing the deployment policy associated with Hadrian—though it spanned the entire Flavio-Antonine era. The great inter-sector distances, and the severe limitations on Roman strategic mobility, made the choice of a regional deployment policy inevitable. Since, as we have seen, it mattered little whether the troops were actually on the frontier or echelonned in depth, the only question that remains is whether the chosen distribution of forces was fortunate in the light of the threats that unpredictably emerged.

The outlines of this deployment strategy during the second century, corresponding more or less to the second phase of empire under the present analysis, may be discerned in the distribution of the legions.[78] These outlines must be deduced cautiously, however, since no exact correlation can be assumed between legionary and auxiliary deployments—the latter equally important if not more so, at least numerically.

As Table 2.1 indicates, the variation in legionary deployments during the second century was very small, in spite of the upheavals of Trajan's wars and the still greater turbulence of the wars of Marcus Aurelius two generations later. The original number of Augustan legions, twenty-eight prior to the Varian disaster, had grown only to thirty by the end of the period, and the change in regional distributions reflected more the resilience of the system than the dramatic vicissitudes of the second century.

Table 2.1
Legionary Deployments, A.D. 23 to A.D. 192

	23	ca. 106	ca. 138	ca. 161	ca. 192
Britain	0	3	3	3	3
Northern Front	8	4	4	4	6
Lower Germany	4	2	2	2	2
Upper Germany	4	2	2	2	2
Raetia/Noricum	0	0	0	0	2
Central Front	7	12–13	10	10	10
Upper Pannonia	3	3	3	3	3
Lower Pannonia	0	1	1	1	1
Dalmatia	2	0	0	0	0
Upper Moesia	0	3–4	2	2	2
Dacia	2	2	1	1	2
Lower Moesia	0	3	3	3	2
Eastern Front	4	6	8	8	8
Cappadocia	0	2	2	2	2
Syria	4	3	3	3	3
Judea	0	1	2	2	2
Arabia	0	0	1	1	1
Garrisons	6	4	3	3	3
Egypt	2	2	1	1	1
Africa	1	1	1	1	1
Spain	3	1	1	1	1
Other	0	1–0[1]	0–1[2]		
Total	25	30	28–29	28	30

[1]The XXI *Rapax*, if still in existence, possibly in Upper Moesia.
[2]The IX *Hispana*, whose location, if the legion was still in existence, is unknown.

In Britain, there was no change at all, even though during this period the frontier moved forward from Hadrian's Wall to the Antonine Wall, the latter to be abandoned again by the end of the century. The "northern front" remained static at four legions until after the Marcomannic War, when the legions II *Italica* and III *Italica* raised in A.D. 165 were posted to Noricum and Raetia, respectively.[79] On the "central front," the reorganization of sector defenses in the wake of Trajan's conquest of Dacia (and the establishment of what was perhaps the most scientific of all scientific frontiers) resulted in the consolidation of the Danube armies at the level of ten legions, after the surge of Trajan's second Dacian war.[80]

On the "eastern front," the two-unit increase in the legionary deployment reflected the annexation of Nabatean Arabia in A.D. 106, which, as a province, received a legionary garrison. (It was the VI *Ferrata* or the III *Gallica*, replaced under Hadrian by the III *Cyrenaica*, stationed at Bostra, where it remained in permanence.)[81] The other additional legion (VI *Ferrata*) was deployed in Judea, in the wake of the last of the Jewish revolts, which was finally suppressed in A.D. 135, not before the destruction of one (or possibly two) legions.[82] The legionary garrison was thus doubled, since the X *Fretensis* (stationed in Judea since the time of Nero) also remained there, in permanence.

The obvious change from the deployments of A.D. 23 recorded by Tacitus[83] is the transfer of legions from the consolidated inner zones of the empire, where their function had been to maintain *internal* security, to the periphery, where they faced a primarily external threat. Dalmatia, a difficult country then as now, divided by mountains crossed by few roads, had its garrison reduced to one legion during the rule of Nero;[84] and the IV *Flavia Felix*, the last Dalmatian legion, was withdrawn by Domitian (ca. A.D. 86) to serve in the Dacian war.[85] The scene of the great rebellion of A.D. 6–9, Dalmatia appears to have been thoroughly pacified thereafter. Similarly, the legionary establishments of Egypt and Spain were reduced drastically from a total of ten legions at the beginning of the principate to only three by the end of the Julio-Claudian era, until the further involuntary reduction brought about by the nonreplacement of the XXII *Deiotariana*, which was destroyed or cashiered during the Jewish revolt of A.D. 132–35.[86]

While the core provinces of the empire were now securely held by a handful of legions, the periphery needed stronger forces: as we shall see, this reflected a change in the *instrumentalities* of Roman security policy, from the client system to a seemingly more secure but ultimately more fragile reliance on direct military force.

Since Britain had needed four legions from the inception of the Roman conquest (A.D. 43) until Domitian, and three thereafter, neither the four-unit increase in the legionary establishment achieved under the Flavians[87] nor the redeployments from Egypt, Spain, and Dalmatia sufficed to provide the additional forces required on the Danube frontier and for the reorganized "eastern front." Accordingly, the armies deployed on the Rhine were substantially reduced. In the case of Lower Germany, for example, the number of legions was halved to two, and the auxiliary forces were reduced also, as Table 2.2 illustrates.[88]

Table 2.2
Auxiliary Troops in Lower Germany

	A.D. 70–83	A.D. 104–120	Third Century
Alae	6	6	7
Milliary cohorts	2	1	1
Milliary cohorts (*equitatae*)	1	0	0
Quingenary cohorts (*equitatae*)	11	6	5
Quingenary cohorts	8	6	7–8
Numeri	0	0	4

Thus the legionary garrison of Lower Germany decreased from about 22,000 combat troops to about 11,000, while the auxiliary establishment decreased from about 15,500 to about 10,000 (increasing again only slightly, to about 10,500 men, in the third century). Notice the absence of any milliary *alae* throughout this period, the reduction in the milliary cohorts, and the withdrawal of the only milliary *cohors equitata* on the sector. Milliary *alae* were probably premium forces allocated to high-threat zones and always deployed at key points.[89] Obviously, Lower Germany was not one of these points—unlike Upper Germany, which had the milliary *Ala II Flavia*, or Britain, which had the *Ala Petriana*.

On all fronts the changes in the pattern of legionary deployment reflected not merely the course of local events but also the advent of a new strategy of preclusive frontier defense. The security policy initiated by the Flavians had clearly matured, its major feature being the deliberate choice of optimal regional perimeters, chosen not merely for their tactical and topographic convenience but also for strategic reasons in the broadest sense—in other words, "scientific" frontiers.

If one compares the borders of the Roman Empire under Hadrian with those of the short-lived empire of Alexander the Great—or, for that matter, with Napoleon's empire at its height, the first immediately reveals the workings of a rational administrative policy, not an undirected expansionism. In Britain, with any idea of total conquest abandoned,[90] the frontier was fixed on the Solway-Tyne line, that of Hadrian's Wall. Earlier, under Cn. Julius Agricola, governor of Britain from A.D. 79 to 84, the Romans had penetrated much farther to the north, beyond the Clyde-Forth line.[91] This not only enclosed much more territory than the Solway-Tyne line but was also much shorter. However, scientific frontiers are designed not to encompass as much territory as possible, but to encompass the *optimal* amount of territory—in other words, the area that it is profitable to enclose on political, economic, or strategic grounds. The shortest line will not necessarily be the best frontier if it happens to enclose difficult terrain, inhabited by difficult peoples—as the Clyde-Forth line certainly did.

Two decades after Hadrian's Wall and its infrastructures were built, the Clyde-Forth line was reoccupied, and in A.D. 142 the Antonine Wall was built to demarcate and secure the new frontier. On the basis of the fragmentary evidence available, it has been argued that the advance was precipitated by the breakdown of the tribal *clientelae* that had constituted the diplomatic glacis of Hadrian's Wall.[92] The new system was much simpler and, in a way, more functional: closely spaced forts at intervals of roughly two miles made the "milecastles" and turrets of Hadrian's Wall unnecessary; there was, instead, a simple wall roughly ten feet high with a six-foot patrol track screened by a timber breastwork. No equivalent to the *vallum* was built in its rear, but there was the indispensable obstacle ditch (here roughly forty feet wide and twelve feet deep), as well as a perimeter road running behind the wall.[93]

Seen as lines on the map, and especially on a small-scale map which does not show the topography but only the geography, the Antonine Wall seems much more "scientific" than the Hadrianic; for one thing, it was much shorter, only 37 miles in length as opposed to 73 1/3. The Antonine Wall, however, had a very significant disadvantage: Roman methods of pacification in frontier zones required that the inhabitants and the terrain be suitable for settlement and development, so that "self-Romanization" could emerge as the voluntary response to the Roman ideas and Roman artifacts of a prosperous population. Diplomacy, on the other hand, required that those who lived beyond the frontier be responsive to the threats and inducements of the system of indirect control. The men and terrain on both sides of the Clyde-Forth line fulfilled none of these conditions. As a result, the rear of the Antonine Wall was never fully pacified, and its front remained unsecured, for no glacis of dependent clients was formed. By A.D. 158 restoration work was underway on Hadrian's Wall,[94] and the Clyde-Forth line collapsed then or shortly thereafter, when the peoples divided by the barrier rose up in revolt.[95] The forces in

Britain were already badly overextended,[96] and by A.D. 162 the onset of the Parthian War made reinforcement of the British garrisons impossible.

Although the Antonine Wall was briefly reoccupied and restored, Hadrian's original scheme of frontier defense was vindicated by the end of the century when his Wall became the frontier once again, as it would remain until the end but for the short-lived attempt (A.D. 208–11) of Septimius Severus to occupy lowland Scotland.[97]

In Germany, the original goal of conquest beyond the Rhine was abandoned in the aftermath of the Varian disaster, but the post–A.D. 16 withdrawal did not lead to retreat to a "scientific" frontier, for the Rhine was certainly not that. It is true that in places where the banks were steep and high, the Rhine was topographically convenient for surveillance and defense, and moreover, the Rhine river fleet (*Classis Germanica*) could give useful waterborne support to the forces on land, being particularly efficient for frontier patrols against low-intensity threats.[98] But as a strategic frontier, the river had a grave defect: the L-shaped Rhine-Danube line that hinged on Vindonissa (Windisch) formed a wedge roughly 180 miles long at the base (Mainz-Regensburg), and 170 miles long to the apex, cutting a deep salient into imperial territory.

As a result, the imperial perimeter between Castra Regina (Regensburg) and Mongontiacum (Mainz) was lengthened by more than 250 miles, not counting the twists and turns of the two rivers. This added ten days or so to the time needed for strategic redeployments between the German and Pannonian frontiers on the shortest route by way of Augusta Vindelicorum (Augsburg). Worse, the deep wedge of the Neckar valley and Black Forest formed a ready-made invasion axis, which endangered lateral communications north of the Alps and was only a week's march away from the northern edge of Italy.

Nothing illustrates the systematic strategic policy of the period better than the long series of frontier rectification campaigns that gradually transformed the Rhine-Danube perimeter. On this sector, at any rate, it is quite clear from the map of archaeological investigations that the emperors' individual differences of temperament and orientation, so strongly stressed in the narrative sources, did not affect the continuity of imperial policy.[99]

There was also continuity in method. Roads and forts were built in sets, by means of "engineering offensives" in the Roman style, based on the three critical hinge-points of the region: the legionary bases at Mainz (I *Adiutrix* and XIV *Gemina* under Vespasian), Strasbourg (VIII *Augusta*), and Windisch (XI *Claudia*).[100] First, under Vespasian, and

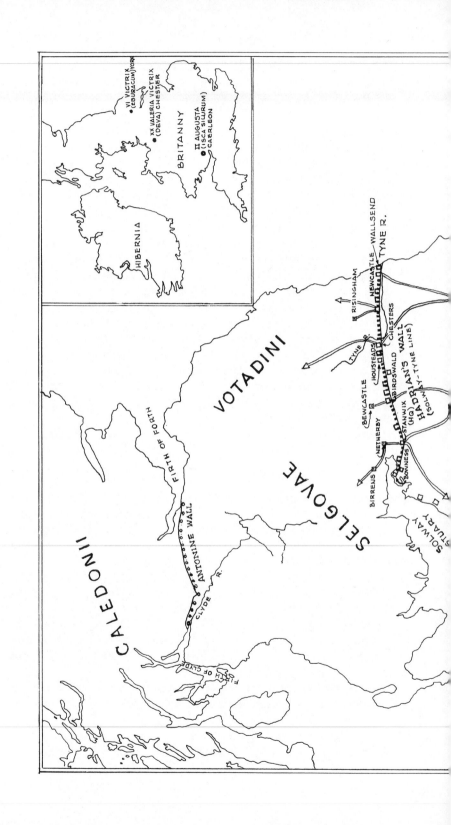

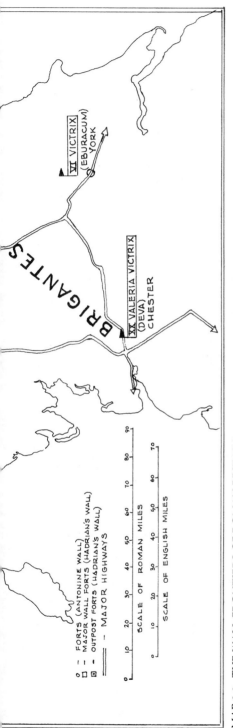

MAP 2.3. THE WALL FRONTIERS OF ROMAN BRITAIN

indeed as soon as order was reestablished in Germany after the revolt of Civilis (ca. A.D. 70), old fort sites in the Wetterau bridgehead (e.g., Wiesbaden and Hofheim) on the right bank of the Rhine opposite Mainz were rebuilt and reoccupied. Other forts were established on the right bank of the Rhine as far south as Heidelberg-Neuenheim; at the same time, the old forts on the left bank of the Rhine may have been evacuated, as Rheingönheim was.[101] So far, these moves would have been consistent with either a limited bridgehead strategy (cf. the outpost forts beyond Hadrian's Wall) or with a more ambitious attempt to open a Mainz-Augsburg axis, across the apex of the Rhine-Danube salient. Around A.D. 74, however, a further line of penetration was opened on the Windisch-Rottweil axis; this bisected the point of the salient and would have made possible an improved—if still indirect—connection from Rhine to Danube on the Strasbourg-Tuttlingen axis. It would also have provided flank security for the more drastic surgery of a Mainz-Augsburg axis (together with the Vespasianic forts built, or rebuilt, along the Danube, from Linz to Oberstimm and further west to Emerkingen).[102]

Domitian's German campaign of A.D. 83–85, on which Frontinus provides some precise but abstruse data,[103] established a frontier on the crest of the Taunus Mountains, which dominate—and could now protect—the fertile Wetterau. This was Domitian's war against the Chatti, ridiculed by Tacitus.[104] Another "engineering" campaign, featuring the construction of forts, roads, and watchtowers from the confluence of the Lahn and Rhine along the crest of the Taunus and southeast to the Main, this offensive featured a coherent plan and systematic organization. It left behind an organized frontier manned by patrols and secured by a series of small road forts, watchtowers, and auxiliary forts.[105]

One benefit of the new *limes* was to deny access to the Neuwied basin and Wetterau. The latter was the territory of the Mattiaci, a people already under Roman diplomatic control but until then vulnerable to harassment by the Chatti.[106] After a break imposed by the Dacian troubles on the Danube and the attempted usurpation of the legate of Upper Germany, L. Antonius Saturninus, Domitian's frontier rectification offensive resumed on a large scale ca. A.D. 90. It was at this stage that the salient was finally cut and the *agri decumates* enclosed. New forts were built on the Main from Seligenstadt to Obernburg and to the Neckar River; along the edge of the Odenwald, a chain of small forts and watchtowers secured a connecting *limes* road. On the approaches to the river the larger cohort forts begin to appear again, from that of Oberscheidental to Wimpfen, on the

Neckar, continuing with a series of cohort forts to Köngen. The nature of the connection between the Neckar line at Köngen and the Danube *limes* is unclear; it is certain, however, that a much shorter route from Pannonia to Germany was now available by way of Köngen; a Heidenheim-Faimingen route to the Danube seems probable.[107]

The final perimeter between the Rhine and Danube was not established until the Antonine era, when the line from Miltenberg-Ost, Welzheim, and Schirenhof to Eining was established and fortified in the "Hadrianic" manner, with a palisade screening the usual patrol tracks and linking watchtowers, small forts, and auxiliary bases.[108] Because of the cumulative nature of this vast enterprise, the new frontier in its final form was actually laid out in depth, with forts and roads behind the rough triangle of the *limes* between the Rhine and Danube that had its apex at Schirenhof. There the Raetian segment of the perimeter joined the Upper German segment, at a point roughly thirty-one miles north of the Danube and sixty-four miles due east from the Rhine. This ultimate perimeter line was systematically consolidated over a period of more than a century by the addition of obstacle ditches, walls, and improved surveillance towers; and stone walls eventually replaced the palisades on the Raetian segment of the *limes*.[109]

From a purely geographic standpoint, the Eining-Taunus frontier was a great improvement over the old Rhine-Danube line, but the logic of its design is by no means apparent on the map. Domitian's *limes* on the Taunus Mountains was anything but the shortest line between points: rather, it formed an awkward bulge that came to a narrow point in the area of Arnsburg. Yet while the southern segment of his *limes*, below the Main, was eventually left behind when the Antonine perimeter (hinged on Lorch further to the east) was established, the curious hook-shaped line north of the Main was *not* replaced, but was retained as the permanent frontier.

Domitian's *limes* on the Taunus reveals the higher priority of the strategic over the tactical and the clear precedence given to the goal of Romanization-through-economic-development over the attractions of a straight perimeter line. At the *strategic* level, the Taunus frontier had the effect of closing the natural lines of communication on a major invasion axis between northern Germany west of the Elbe and the upper Rhine region.[110] At the same time, as an outward salient rather than an inward wedge, the line did not prolong the strategic redeployment route across the sector.

At the *operational* level, the Taunus frontier, though itself costly to man owing to the dense network of forts, roads, and watchtowers,

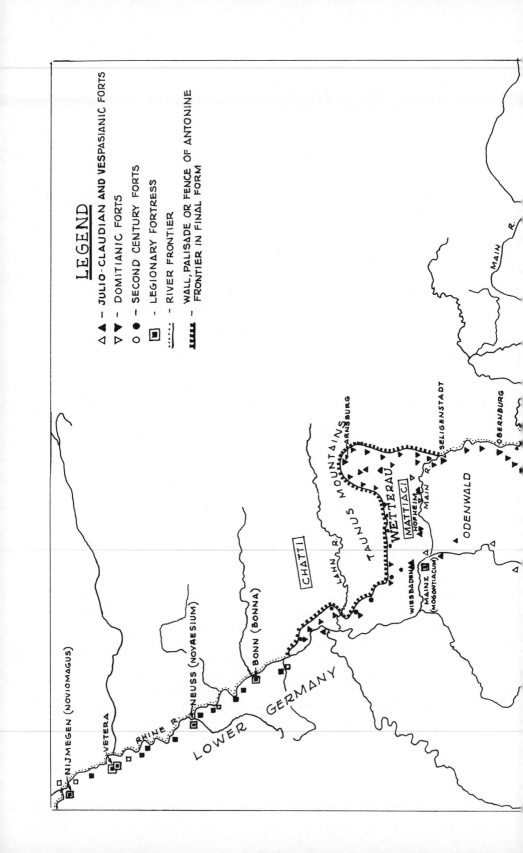

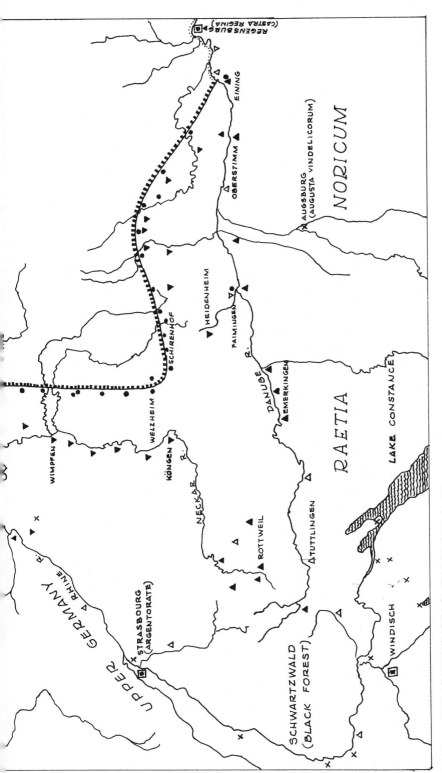

MAP 2.4. THE ADVANCING FRONTIER IN GERMANY

had the effect of simplifying the problem of frontier defense for the whole of Upper Germany, since it pushed back the Chatti—apparently the most dangerous neighbors of the empire in the entire region—from the Rhine Valley and the Wetterau. This, in turn, allowed an eventual reduction in the provincial garrison. The legionary forces in Mainz (consisting of two legions until A.D. 89) and the auxiliary forces distributed within the salient could concentrate to fight off the Chatti whether the invaders advanced due south toward the Neckar or due west toward the Rhine. In order to concentrate in the right places, the Romans needed early warning of impending attacks, and the new frontier was obviously intended to provide such advance warning, as well as to canalize major attacks and contain minor ones.

The role of the politico-economic goal of Romanization in determining the shape of the frontier can only be hypothesized by inference: the area enclosed by the Taunus-Main frontier, the Wetterau, is highly productive, arable land. (The forests had been cleared and the land opened for farming long before the Romans arrived.)[111] Here a productive agriculture could generate prosperity, *if* day-to-day security against infiltrators' threats were provided. Agriculture, in turn, could provide the material basis of urbanization, and the latter would then facilitate the processes of Romanization. Precisely because it neglects the obvious military advantages of straight lines, this particular segment of the *limes* corroborates the "society-building" explanation of Roman frontier policy better than most.

There is, therefore, a consistent pattern in Roman frontier policy, and a hierarchy of priorities: first, the frontier must facilitate strategic transit between the continental regions of the empire; second, it should *not* include areas inherently difficult to settle, urbanize, and Romanize (such as Scotland); third, it *should* include lands suited for settlement—lands that would enhance the strength of the empire in men and resources. Finally, as a distinctly secondary priority, the frontier should be as short as possible, in order to reduce the manpower required for outposts and patrols. (Since the Romans at this time would fight against large-scale threats with *mobile* troop concentrations, the length of the perimeter was not important vis-à-vis such threats.)

Another major consideration, which may well have been important in the case of the Taunus-Main frontier, was more or less the reverse of the strategic-transit requirement: where the Romans faced several particularly powerful enemies across the *limes*, it was useful to separate these enemies from one another by forming a salient between them. This salient would also provide an added layer of security for the roads and populations at its base. Here, too, the mere length of the frontier became a secondary priority.

What Domitian's *limes* on the Taunus achieved tactically, Trajan's *limes* in Dacia was to achieve on a strategic scale. Until Trajan's conquest of Dacia, the imperial perimeter followed the course of the Danube all the way to the delta on the Black Sea.[112] A series of legionary bases stretched from Raetia to what is now Bulgaria, and the intervals between bases were covered by a somewhat denser network of auxiliary forts that reached into the modern Dobruja, in Romania. The two Danube fleets, the *Classis Pannonica*, which operated upstream from the Iron Gates, and the *Classis Moesica* below, complemented the watchtowers, signal stations, and patrols on the left bank of the river.

The most important single threat to this long frontier, which spanned the territories of six important provinces, was constituted by the Dacians. Their power was centered in the high ground of Transylvania, and they had already formed a centralized state under a ruler named Burebista in the first century B.C. Their expansionism had put them in violent contact with Roman armies even earlier.[113] This propensity for centralization, rare among the peoples in the area, made them dangerous enemies for any power whose lands reached the Danube: Dacian raids were directed at the entire vast arc from what is now Vienna to the Black Sea. Under Augustus, the Dacian problem was alleviated, but not solved, by punitive expeditions and reprisal operations.[114] Under Tiberius diplomacy was tried, but the Dacians could not be turned into reliable clients (perhaps because they had gold of their own[115]). The Romans therefore used the Sarmatian Iazyges, installed between the Tisza (Theiss) and Danube, to keep Dacian power away from that stretch of the river.[116] By the time of the Flavians, the Roxolani, another Sarmatian people (i.e., of Iranian stock), occupied the plains along the lower course of the Danube. Tacitus records their ill-fated raid of A.D. 69 across the Danube and into Moesia, in which 9,000 mounted warriors were intercepted by the legion III *Gallica* and cut to pieces as they were retreating, laden with booty.[117]

In A.D. 85/86, under Domitian, the Romans again had to fight the Dacians, who had recentralized under the rule of Decebalus. After driving the Dacians back across the Danube following yet another incursion into Moesia, the Romans pursued them, but suffered a serious defeat; in A.D. 88 this was avenged by a successful strategic offensive, which culminated in a great victory at Tapae, in the plain beyond Turnu Severin.[118] Perhaps Domitian intended to follow up

MAP 2.5. THE SECOND-CENTURY FRONTIERS
IN EUROPE

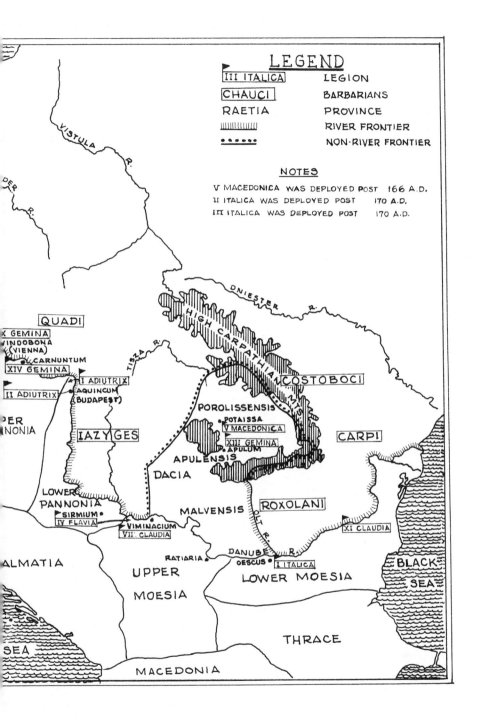

LEGEND

III ITALICA	LEGION
CHAUCI	BARBARIANS
RAETIA	PROVINCE
⊞⊞⊞⊞⊞	RIVER FRONTIER
••••••	NON-RIVER FRONTIER

NOTES

V MACEDONICA WAS DEPLOYED POST 166 A.D.
II ITALICA WAS DEPLOYED POST 170 A.D.
III ITALICA WAS DEPLOYED POST 170 A.D.

this victory in the field with an advance on Sarmizegethusa, the seat of Decebalus and his court, but the revolt of Antonius Saturninus, legate of upper Germany, intervened in January, A.D. 89. By then, however, the client system on the Danube sector was crumbling, and this drastically restricted the strategic options open to the Romans.

The Romans faced three major tribal agglomerations in the region, which had been under a loose but effective form of diplomatic control since the time of Tiberius: the Marcomanni, the Quadi (centered in the general area opposite Vienna), and the Iazyges. There is no evidence that these peoples had helped Domitian's forces in the campaigns of A.D. 85 and A.D. 88 against Decebalus. But neither had they hindered it, for the Romans could not have mounted simultaneous offensives across the 600 miles of the Danube border from Dacia to the Marcomannic territory west of the Elbe. The acquiescence of these powerful neighbors was essential for any strategic offensive against Dacia, just as the acquiescence of the Dacians was essential for any strategic offensive against the Marcomanni, Quadi, or Iazyges. Thus, when the Marcomanni, Quadi, and Iazyges all threatened war,[119] Domitian was forced to make peace with Decebalus on the basis of the *status quo ante* (and a technical aid program);[120] for the next several years there was inconclusive war against Germans and Sarmatians upstream from Dacian territory, which itself remained at peace.[121]

It is in this context that Trajan's wars with Decebalus and his ultimate conquest of Dacia must be seen. It once was *de rigueur* to contrast Trajan's heedless adventurism with Hadrian's peaceful disposition. Across the Danube, as across the Euphrates, Trajan supposedly left deep salients that marked his grandiose conquests but lengthened the imperial perimeter needlessly. Trajan's annexation of Dacia has also been explained as a throwback to the days of predatory imperialism and unlimited expansionism.[122]

It is certainly true that once Dacia was conquered, after Trajan's second war against Decebalus in A.D. 106, the frontiers of the new province of Dacia formed a deep wedge centered on the Sarmizegethusa-Apulum axis, eventually adding more than 370 miles to the length of the imperial perimeter.[123] In fact, on the map the new province presents a classic profile of vulnerability. This impression is strengthened by the nature of the military deployment left in place once the campaigns were over. The salient's center of gravity was not at its base, but toward the apex, since the legionary base at Apulum in the Maros valley was nearer to the northern edge of the Carpathians than to the Danube. Neither then nor later was the Dacian *limes* as a whole enclosed with a wall system; it remained organized as a network of independent strong-points astride the main invasion routes, guarding the major lines of communication.[124]

This new frontier, which makes so little sense in the light of the superficial strategy of small-scale maps, becomes highly rational in the light of the hierarchy of priorities of Roman policy: the elimination of Dacia's independent power provided the necessary conditions for a restoration of Roman diplomatic control over the Germans and Sarmatians of the entire region. Both deterrence and positive inducements (i.e., subsidies) would be needed to keep Marcomanni, Iazyges, and Roxolani from raiding the Danube lands; and as long as Decebalus remained in defiant independence, the deterrent arm of the policy would be fatally weakened. As a province, Dacia was not worth having, but as a strategic shield for the region as a whole it was very valuable indeed.

Following Sarmatian attacks of A.D. 116–19, the flanks of Dacian salient were narrowed through the evacuation of the western Banat to the north and Muntenia to the south. By A.D. 124–26 Dacia had been divided into three provinces (Malvensis, Porolissensis, and Apulensis), and at least sixty-five separate outposts were built to provide a defense-in-depth of Dacia Porolissensis. This *Limes Porolissensis* formed the outer shield of the entire system of Danubian defense, with rear support provided by the legion XIII *Gemina*, stationed in Apulum. On either side of the Dacian salient were the plains occupied by the subsidized Sarmatians: Iazyges to the west and Roxolani to the east. Had Rome been weak and the Sarmatians strong, the Dacian provinces would have been vulnerable to encirclement (across the neck of the peninsula of Roman territory on the Danube); but with Rome as strong as it then was, the Dacian frontier effectively separated the Sarmatians on either side and weakened their combined power. Though subsidies might still be required, the strong auxiliary garrisons of Dacia Malvensis (on the Danube) and Dacia Porolissensis (on the Carpathians) as well as the legion in Dacia Apulensis would suffice to complement the inducements with the threat of retaliation for any transborder raiding.[125]

The elimination of the Dacian threat provided security for the Dobruja and all the Danube lands up to Vienna; with security there came, first, agricultural prosperity and, then, urbanization: the coastal Greek cities of the Dobruja recovered swiftly from the effects of insecurity, while new cities emerged in the entire region, from Thrace to Carnuntum (Deutschaltenburg). The legionary bases at Ratiaria and Oescus on the lower Danube were left in the deep rear by the conquest of Dacia, and the legions were withdrawn since the sector was no longer of military significance. But the two localities

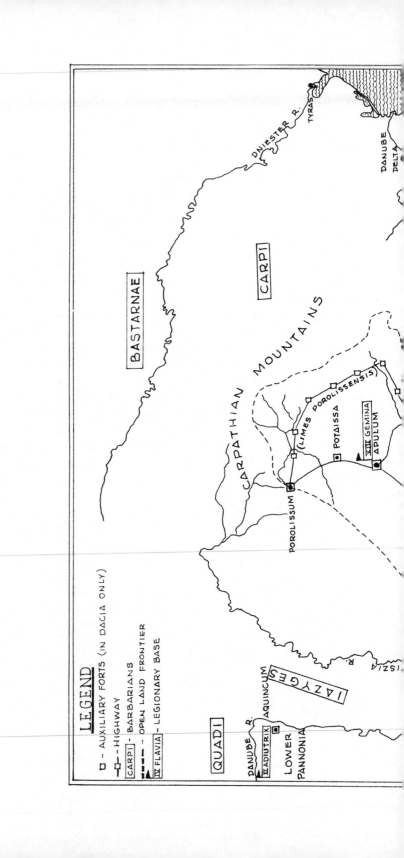

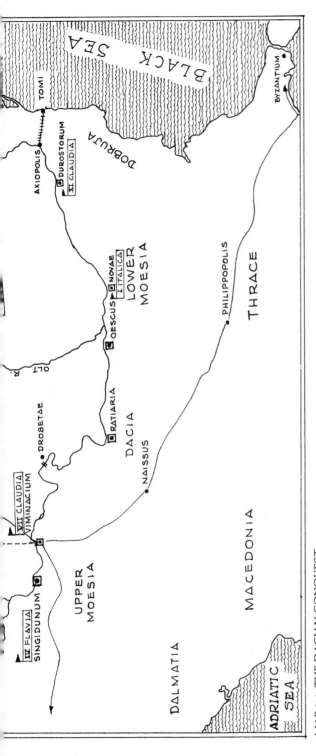

MAP 2.6. THE DACIAN CONQUEST

did not wither away. Instead, they became civilian settlements, with the high status of *coloniae*.[126] Once the scene of raid and counter-raid, the Danube valley could begin after Trajan's conquest to contribute to the human and material resources of the empire, augmenting its fundamental strength.

The only priority of Roman frontier policy that the Dacian frontier did not satisfy was the lowest tactical priority, since the perimeter was lengthened rather than shortened. This did not, of course, affect imperial communications, which could now follow routes just as short but much more secure. Nor is the impression of vulnerability given by the map of the Dacian frontier justified. Aside from its obvious topographic advantage, the *Limes Porolissensis* was a salient only in purely military terms: its flanks east and west were not open invasion axes, for they were occupied by peoples under Roman diplomatic control.[127]

Though the conquest of Dacia thus reinforced Rome's strategic and diplomatic control of the entire Danube frontier, the *Limes Porolissensis* was still something of an outpost, or rather a whole series of outposts centered on the XIII *Gemina* at Apulum, the only legion left in place once the frontier was organized.[128] As is true of any outpost, as long as the sector as a whole was securely held, the Dacian salient added to this security. Far from being vulnerable to encirclement, the salient itself could be used as a base to encircle the Iazyges to the west or the Roxolani to the east: Roman forces could advance on the Drobeta-Apulum highway and then turn to attack the Sarmatians in the rear.[129]

But the military worth of an outpost declines and finally becomes a liability as the security of the baseline diminishes. Thus, in the great crisis of the third century, when Rome lost control of the Sarmatians on either side of the salient, the *Limes Porolissensis* did become a vulnerable salient liable to be cut off, as well as a drain on the resources of the sector as a whole. It was finally abandoned during (or just after) the reign of Aurelian (A.D. 270–75).[130] Until then, however, the Dacian *limes* had been the highly cost-effective military instrument that ensured Rome's military and diplomatic control over the entire region.

In the Julio-Claudian era, the system of imperial security on the "eastern front," from eastern Anatolia through Syria to the Red Sea, was based on three elements: the chain of client states, which absorbed the burdens of day-to-day security against internal disorder and low-intensity external threats; the buffer of Armenia; and the army of Syria, four legions strong until the Armenian crisis of A.D. 55.[131]

Of these three elements, only Armenia's status as a buffer state was not wholly within Roman control. From the time of the Augustan settlement until the Flavian era, the Armenian question required constant management, for it was crucial to Roman security in the sector and equally crucial for the security of the Arsacid state of Parthia. If Armenia were under some form of Roman suzerainty, or even a condominium such as that established under the Neronian compromise ("Arsacid secondgeniture and Roman investiture"),[132] then Syria's army could defend Cappadocia and Pontus as well as Syria from Parthian attack. If, on the other hand, the Arsacids were free to station armies in Armenia, then each of the two sectors would require a frontier army of its own, independently capable of containing Parthian attacks until the arrival of strategic reinforcements. Without an advanced base, Parthian forces advancing toward Pontus and Cappadocia by way of the difficult routes across Armenia could move no faster than the legions of Syria advancing to intercept them up the Euphrates. Hence the Parthians could not hope to surprise or outmaneuver the Romans in launching an attack against *either* sector.

This was the precise meaning of Armenia's status as a buffer zone, and it is this factor that explains the rationality of Nero's diplomatic and military offensives of A.D. 55–66. The Parthian ruler Vologaeses I had driven Radamistus, a usurper, from the throne of Armenia, giving his throne to his fellow-Arsacid, Tiridates.[133] This act suggested the possibility that Arsacid armies would now have free use of Armenian territory, and therefore that Cappadocia and Pontus could no longer be secure without armies of their own.[134] In A.D. 55 Nero's great general, Cn. Domitius Corbulo, was appointed legate to Cappadocia and provided with powerful expeditionary forces. (These included the legions III *Gallica* and VI *Ferrata* from the army of Syria, IV *Scythica* from Moesia, and the usual complement of auxiliary forces.)[135]

Corbulo engaged in diplomacy while organizing a fighting army, and in A.D. 58 he successfully launched a difficult campaign in the difficult terrain of Armenia, conquering the two major centers in the country, Artaxata and Tigranocerta. The *status quo ante* having been restored, a reliable client prince, Tigranes, was duly appointed king of Armenia and provided with a small 2,000-man guard force.[136] But following an Armenian raid into Arsacid territory, Vologaeses resumed the war, after the terms he offered were rejected by Rome.[137] Earlier, the Romans had offered to recognize the Arsacid Tiridates as king of Armenia, provided he accepted a Roman investiture, but this offer had been rejected by Vologaeses.[138] After Corbulo's victory, the balance of power had shifted, and this naturally curtailed the scope of

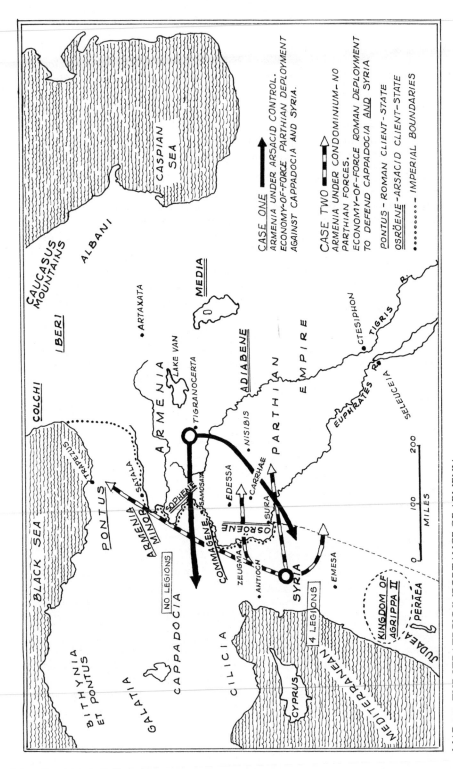

MAP 2.7. THE STRATEGIC IMPORTANCE OF ARMENIA

diplomacy: it may also have induced the Romans to contemplate annexation.[139] It took the defeat of L. Caesennius Paetus, sent out to take charge in Cappadocia when Corbulo left to take over the Syrian sector, to restore a balance of power. After a successful show-of-force invasion by Corbulo, now in supreme command and provided with a high-grade legion drawn from Pannonia (the XV *Apollinaris*),[140] a diplomatic settlement was finally concluded. In A.D. 66 Tiridates was crowned in Rome as king of Armenia, in a lavish ceremony whose cost scandalized Suetonius.[141]

It was no great victory that Rome won in the Armenian settlement; indeed, it may have seemed that after five years of desultory war, the situation had merely reverted to the position of A.D. 54, when Vologaeses had originally placed his brother on the Armenian throne.[142] But strategic gains need not be the product of grandiose victory. The nominal condominium sufficed to ensure the security of the Pontic-Cappadocian sector, thus obviating the very great cost of deploying a counterpart to the Syrian army along the upper Euphrates.[143]

As we shall see, the Flavians eventually abolished what was left of the client-state system on the "eastern front," and this naturally required for the first time the deployment of permanent legionary garrisons in eastern Anatolia. The legion XII *Fulminata* was permanently stationed at Melitene in Cappadocia, on the central route between Armenia and Cappadocia, and the legion XVI *Flavia Firma* was probably in Satala (near a more northerly crossing of the Euphrates) in the territory of the former client state of Lesser Armenia.[144]

The eastern frontier that Trajan inherited, though neater than the confused patchwork of client states of the Julio-Claudian era, was still highly unsatisfactory.[145] From the ill-defined borders of the Nabatean client state (east of Judea and south into northwest Arabia), the frontier cut across the desert by way of Damascus and Palmyra to the Euphrates, probably reaching the river above Sura. From there it followed the river through Zeugma to the north until its eastward turn into Armenia, then overland to the Black Sea, to a point east of Trapezus (Trabzon).

In fact, as drawn on the map of the empire at the accession of Trajan, this frontier was scarcely tenable. Largely as a result of the distribution of rainfall, Roman territory in the Levant was limited for all practical purposes to a narrow strip almost five hundred miles long (from Petra to Zeugma), much of it less than sixty miles wide. Though theoretically in Roman hands, the lands to the east of this fertile strip were mostly desert, which required no security force for border defense against low-intensity threats ("point" defenses would suffice) but which, on the other hand, could not support the substantial forces which would be needed to meet any high-intensity threats. The Romans were in the uncomfortable position of holding a long and narrow strip with the sea to the west and a vulnerable flank to the east. Opposite Antioch, the greatest city of the region, the depth of the territory controlled by Rome was scarcely more than a hundred miles—not enough if Parthian armies were to be contained until forces more numerous and better than the Syrian legions could arrive from Europe.

These geographic factors, which every power in the Levant has had to contend with, made the Euphrates frontier inadequate; Trajan's Parthian war (A.D. 114–17) has been explained as an attempt to establish a "scientific" frontier beyond the river. The only possible line that would satisfy the requirements of strategic depth, rear-area security, and economy of deployment was a perimeter that would follow the course of the river Khabur to the western edge of the Jebel Sinjar, then continue east along the high ground toward the Tigris and north again into Armenia.[146]

Though by no means straight, this frontier would have had advantages far greater than mere geographic simplicity. If strongly manned, the Khabur-Jebel Sinjar-Tigris line would provide a reliable defense-in-depth from south-north attacks for both the Antioch region to the west and Armenia to the north. This line would cover the major east-west invasion axes from Parthia leading to northern Syria and southern Cappadocia. Moreover, this double L-shaped frontier would also interdict the advance of armies moving westward, whether above or below the Euphrates, and it would automatically outflank any westward advance into southern Armenia. Finally, the frontier zones would have adequate rainfall (200 mm. or more per year), so that long-term deployments could be maintained economically, while the consolidation of the frontier through the development of civilian settlements would also be feasible.[147] The only real alternative to this line would have been a frontier running along the edge of the Armenian plateau, but this would have left Roman forces too far from Ctesiphon to intimidate its rulers.

Trajan's Parthian war was not, however, a limited border-rectification offensive, nor is it usually considered to have been a purely rational enterprise entirely motivated by strategic considerations. The origins of the conflict conform to the stereotyped pattern of Roman-Parthian relations: the Arsacid Osroes (king of Parthia since A.D. 110) replaced a fellow-Arsacid, Axidares, king of Armenia by Roman approval, with another, Parthamasiris, who had not been

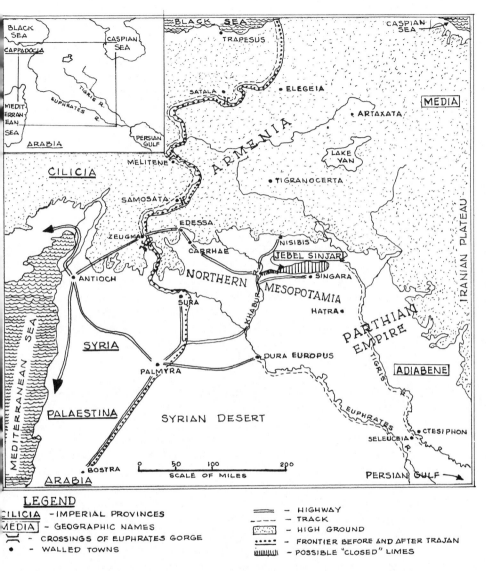

LEGEND

CILICIA – IMPERIAL PROVINCES

MEDIA – GEOGRAPHIC NAMES

)(– CROSSINGS OF EUPHRATES GORGE

• – WALLED TOWNS

═══ – HIGHWAY

──── – TRACK

▓▓▓ – HIGH GROUND

••••• – FRONTIER BEFORE AND AFTER TRAJAN

ıllılılı – POSSIBLE "CLOSED" LIMES

MAP 2.8. THE PARTHIAN EMPIRE AND THE ROMAN EAST

approved by Rome as required by the terms of the agreement of A.D. 63.[148] By the end of A.D. 113, Trajan was in Antioch "to review the situation."[149] Between A.D. 113 and 117—diplomacy having failed (and it is uncertain to what extent each side seriously attempted to resolve the crisis peacefully)[150]—Trajan's armies conquered Armenia and Mesopotamia, captured Ctesiphon and the golden throne of the Parthian kings (Osroes himself having fled), visited the Persian Gulf, and advanced across the Tigris into remote Adiabene, which seems to have then become the short-lived province of Assyria.[151]

Provinces were being organized, client kings were being enrolled into allegiance to Rome in place of older Parthian loyalties, and a fiscal administration for the India trade was apparently being organized, when disaster struck. Since A.D. 114, Trajan had advanced farther and conquered more than any Roman since Augustus, but by the late summer of A.D. 117 he was dead in Cilicia, and little remained of his conquests. The new provinces had risen in revolt, and so had the Jews in a vast arc from Cyrene to Mesopotamia, with catastrophic results in Cyrene, Egypt, and Cyprus. Parthamaspates, placed in Ctesiphon as the Roman client king of a diminished and dependent Parthia, was losing control, and the lesser client kings were losing either their thrones or their imposed Roman allegiance.[152]

Hadrian, new ruler of Rome and Trajan's former lieutenant in the East, completed the strategic withdrawal that Trajan had begun: the new provinces were abandoned, and by the end of A.D. 117 all that remained of Trajan's vast conquests was a confirmed claim of suzerainty over Armenia and Osrhoëne.[153] A fragmented narrative source of prime importance explains the motivation for Trajan's Parthian war as no sounder a reason that an irrational love of glory,[154] and this interpretation has been accepted by most modern historians.[155] Other explanations are cast in terms of a rational but nonmilitary goal, the control of the trade routes to India.[156] A strategic purpose, the establishment of the Khabur-Jebel Sinjar-Tigris frontier, has also been adduced as Trajan's dominating motive, and to this writer at least it seems the most convincing.

What is certain is that until his further conquests across the Tigris, down to Ctesiphon and beyond, Trajan's policy in the East had been consistent with that of the Flavians. Like them, he continued the process of political consolidation, with the annexation of Nabatean Arabia in A.D. 106. Like them, he placed a legionary deployment to secure the new province (at Bostra, renamed Nova Traiana); and like them, he extended the road infrastructure, building a major new highway across eastern Syria and down to the Red Sea by way of

Bostra and Petra.[157] The establishment of a defended salient down the Euphrates, up the Khabur River, and across the ridge of the Jebel Sinjar would not have been inconsistent with the established methods of frontier reorganization—if, that is, Armenia north of the Nisibis-Zeugma axis were left as a client kingdom.

For an empire whose resources of trained military manpower had hardly increased since the days of Augustus, the conquests of Trajan were obviously too extensive to be successfully consolidated. Nor did the entrenched cultures of the region offer much scope for long-term Roman policies of cultural-political integration (though there were major exceptions in the Greek cities). Above all, the further conquests of Trajan could not be *efficient*: the vast investment of effort—which would inevitably result in diminished security elsewhere—could only be compensated by added security against Parthia or by the acquisition of added resources in place. And Parthia was not strong enough to merit such a vast military effort, but it was resilient enough to prevent the profitable incorporation of the new provinces.

IV
The Decline of the
Client System

When Vespasian concentrated his forces at Ptolemais in the winter of A.D. 67 while preparing to advance into Judea, then in full revolt, four client rulers, Antiochus IV of Commagene, M. Julius Agrippa II, Sohaemus of Emesa, and the Arab chieftain Malchus, contributed a total of 15,000 men to his army.[158] Aside from Vespasian's three legions (XV *Apollinaris*, V *Macedonica*, and X *Fretensis*[159]), which were to be fully engaged in the sieges and guerrilla warfare of the Jewish War, there were only four legions in the entire Levant. One of these (the III *Gallica*) was redeployed to Moesia in A.D. 68, so that only the three Syrian legions remained to cover the entire vast eastern sector from the Red Sea to the Black, and one of these (XII *Fulminata*) was also committed to the Jewish War for a time.[160]

Although there was peace between Rome and Parthia at the time (as a result of Nero's compromise of A.D. 63), and although there were some *auxilia* free from the Judean commitment in the region, the concentration of forces against the Jews was rendered possible only by the glacis of client states and client tribes that shielded the eastern borders of the empire. Without this support, it would have been highly imprudent to commit very nearly the full disposable legionary reserve of the empire to the Jewish War (three legions out of twenty-eight), with no security for the long exposed flanks other than that provided by three Syrian legions of indifferent quality.[161]

Indeed, the client system of the East was then revealed at its most efficient. To the south in Sinai, and on the eastern borders of Judea, the Nabatean kingdom of Arabia absorbed and contained the endemic petty attacks of the nomads,[162] and several smaller clients remained in Syria. On the Euphrates, Osrhoëne was a buffer state essentially Parthian in orientation but unlikely to cooperate in hostility to Rome. Across the river, Osrhoëne faced not Roman territory but the key client state of Commagene, whose loyalty was as yet unquestioned. Farther north, near the Black Sea, was Lesser Armenia, under Aristobolus; it, too, was paired across the Euphrates with another client state, Sophene, ruled by another Sohaemus.[163]

In practice, this meant that the chronically sensitive borders with Parthia and the avenues of nomadic raiding were shielded by powers beholden to the empire, but not of it in a full sense. The client states deployed their own forces to contain minor attacks, and their resistance to *major* attacks, whether successful or not, would allow time for an eventual disengagement from Judea to free the army of Vespasian for action elsewhere.

By A.D. 69 Nero was dead, Vespasian had been proclaimed emperor, and a civil war was under way. Again the client states stood Vespasian in good stead: Tacitus records that Sohaemus of Sophene, Antiochus IV of Commagene (who had great wealth to contribute), and other client rulers extended their support to the Flavian cause; there is no record of any client state opposition or even unfriendly neutrality.[164] Later, in A.D. 70, when Titus set out for the final campaign of the Jewish War, Tacitus once again recorded the troop contributions of the client rulers; the list included a large number of Arabs, motivated by neighborly hatred.[165]

And yet it was none other than Vespasian, the direct beneficiary of the client-state system, who presided over its substantial dismantling. Pontus, ruled by Polemo II, had already been annexed under Nero in A.D. 64;[166] nevertheless, the regional structure of indirect control was still essentially intact. But within four years of Vespasian's accession, Lesser Armenia, Sophene, and Commagene had all been annexed.[167] The fate of the lesser clients is unknown, but the only survivals of any importance were the state of Agrippa II, Nabatean Arabia (not annexed until after A.D. 92 and A.D. 106, respectively),[168] the petty kingdoms of the Caucasus,[169] Palmyra, and the Bosporan state.[170]

Scholars have explained Vespasian's annexationist policy as one facet of his more general policy of centralization.[171] In his overall attempt to restructure the empire on a new basis, administrative centralization and the territorialization of what was still in part a hegemonic empire were mutually complementary. The strategic goals of the Flavians and the survival of the client-state system were, in fact, mutually exclusive. It is true that there were still some minor client states in the East when Trajan came to hold court at Satala in A.D. 114: the Arsacid ruler of Armenia did not present himself, but the petty kings of the Albani, Iberi, and Colchi, among others, did.[172] Moreover, in the wake of the retreat that followed his Parthian war, Osrhoëne was left behind as a new client state, under Parthamaspates, who had been Trajan's candidate for the Parthian throne.[173] But although the terminology is unchanged, the client states that survived annexation into the second century were not like the old. Though difficult to define in legal terms, the change in the relationship between Rome and the client states had important strategic implications.[174]

The annexation of the major clients of Anatolia and Syria had substituted the presence of Roman legions for the "leisurely processes of diplomacy"[175] from the Black Sea to the Red. With the deployment of direct military force where before there had been only a perception of Rome's potential for ultimate victory, there came the need to provide new administrative and communications infrastructures. Under the Flavians, a network of highways was constructed in Anatolia; also, very likely, a frontier-delimiting road from Palmyra to Sura on the Euphrates was built (under the supervision of Marcus Ulpius Traianus, father of the future emperor).[176] Behind the highways a chain of legionary bases spanned the entire sector, from Bostra in the new province of Arabia, to Satala, only seventy miles south of the Black Sea.

Under Vespasian, the territories of Galatia, Pontus, Cappadocia, and Lesser Armenia were at first amalgamated into an enormously enlarged Galatian province of 112,000 square miles. Cilicia Aspera, formerly part of Antiochus IV's possessions, was combined with Cilicia Campestris (until then part of Syria) to form a new province of Cilicia. When in A.D. 106 Rabbel II, last of the Nabatean rulers, was deposed, Arabia too became a very large province, stretching from modern Der'a in southern Syria to Medain Salih, deep in the Hejaz, and comprising also the Sinai peninsula. Trajan obviously found the greater Galatia of Vespasian far too unwieldy: by A.D. 113 at the latest, it had been divided into its major constituent elements, Galatia and Cappadocia.[177]

The reorganization of the eastern sector of the empire required a sharp increase in legionary deployments: the number rose from the Julio-Claudian norm of four legions, all in Syria, to an eventual total of eight by the time of Hadrian.[178] Thus the needs of the eastern front had doubled, while the total number of legions in the Roman army had increased—at most—by only one unit. The built-in reserve afforded by the previous pattern of legionary deployments was therefore virtually exhausted: when entire legions were removed for short-term redeployments, insufficient forces remained. It is this, much more than the *tactical* reorganization of frontier defenses, which deprived the imperial army of its inherent elasticity.

In the absence of client-state forces ready to suppress low-intensity threats, and of client-state territories apt to absorb high-intensity attacks, it was the central forces of the empire itself that had to meet both kinds of threat. Vespasian himself already had to deal with "frequent barbarian raids" in Cappadocia (i.e., greater Galatia), and in A.D. 75 the king of Iberia (in the Caucasus) had to be helped to fortify the approaches to the Dariel Pass ("The Caucasian Gates").[179] The processes of client-state diplomacy may have been "leisurely," and perhaps disturbingly intangible for a soldier who had risen to become emperor through the highly tangible power of his legions, but the ultimate consequence of annexation was the substitution of an enfeebling dispersion of forces for the virtually costless projection of Rome's remote but dynamic military power.[180] (Eventually, some Roman troops—a sub-unit of the legion XII *Fulminata* —were even stationed in the remote mountains of the Caucasus.)[181]

It is clear that a client state such as Hadrian's Osrhoëne was in a definite sense outside the empire, just as the old-style client states had been of it, even if not in a legal sense. The difference was intangible but all-important—a matter of expectations. The old-style clients understood that the client-state system was a temporary instrument of imperial control. Now it became a permanent substitute for that control. The ultimate intention—and capacity for annexation—was visibly gone, and with it went the principal incentive to obedience on the part of client rulers intent on delaying the evil day.

Under the Julio-Claudians, the stronger a client state was, the better it could fulfill its diverse security functions. An empire that was perceived as capable of further expansion was also an empire that could keep even powerful clients in subjection. Not so under the new system, in which the only satisfactory clients were those weak enough to be kept in awe by the forces deployed in direct proximity to them. In the absence of the ultimate sanction of annexation, only weak clients were safe clients. But their very weakness rendered them unsatisfactory as providers of free military services. Strong client states, on the other hand, had now become dangerous, since the bonds of dependence had been weakened.

Under the earlier system, even Decebalus, ruler of Dacia, could have been transformed into a highly useful client in the wake of Trajan's first and victorious Dacian war (A.D. 101–2).[182] Defeated but still powerful, a Dacian client state could have assumed responsibility for preventing infiltration and raids on the Daco-Roman frontier and for interdicting Sarmatian attacks. The relationship between a client Decebalus and Rome under the earlier system of empire would have been shaped by the realities of power: Decebalus, kept in subjection by the ultimate threat of war and deposition, could have complied overtly with Roman security *desiderata* without fear of domestic opposition. Confronted with the worse alternative of direct imperial rule, the Dacians would have had a powerful incentive to obey a ruler who himself obeyed Rome. Not so in the new strategic environment. Faced with an empire that could concentrate superior forces on the Dacian sector only with visible difficulty,[183] and more important, which was obviously reluctant to expand (as shown to all by the failure to annex Dacia in the wake of Trajan's first war), Decebalus was insufficiently intimidated to act as a satisfactory client.[184] And even if he personally had been willing to obey Rome, it is likely that others in Dacia would have demanded a more independent policy. Thus it can be argued that Dacia had to be annexed, paradoxically enough, *because* the empire had become visibly defencist, and its rulers reluctant to annex. In other words, Trajan had to destroy Dacian independence because the option of indirect rule was no longer open to the empire.[185]

Although tribal and state clients did not everywhere disappear, in the presence of a system of preclusive defense they were either redundant (if weak) or inherently unstable (if strong). In Britain, the breakdown of the client relationship with the Brigantians of Cartimandua may have been the prime cause of the campaigns of Agricola and later of the establishment of the Solway-Tyne frontier.[186] In Lower Germany, a client structure of sorts did survive, based on the repentant Batavi, the Frisii, Tencteri, and Usipetes.[187] But there, too, the relationship had changed: in place of the unpaid tribal militias provided for local defense at no direct cost to the empire,[188] regular regiments of auxiliary troops had to be deployed to guard the frontiers.

As for the vulnerable sector of the lower Danube, the Roxolani had already acquired the dangerous status of neighbors who were both fully independent and subsidized.[189] Foreshadowing the ironic reversal of the client system that was to take place a century later, the nature of the subsidy relationship between clients and empire began to change in character. From its beginnings as a donation given to reward deserving chieftains, the subsidy became a short-term rental of good behavior, which could not be suspended without undermining the security of the border zone. The ultimate ability of the empire to crush the peoples it chose to subsidize was not yet in question, but without a credible threat of annexation, the incentives naturally had to be augmented—in order to maintain the equilibrium between threats and incentives on which the system was based.[190]

In the new system of empire, neighbors were no longer automatically classified either as targets of conquest or as clients. Instead, they tended to function in the manner of "buffer states," of which Armenia had long been the prototype. The buffer state performs only one military function: it serves as a physical neutral zone between greater powers, providing them with a means of avoiding conflict for as long as they want to avoid it. A buffer state cannot constitute an active obstacle to high-intensity threats, nor will it normally assume responsibility for containing low-intensity threats as client states would; for the buffer state cannot be freely disciplined by one side or the other without provoking the intervention of the rival greater power.

Although the Parthian sector of the empire was *sui generis*, because Parthia was the only civilized state adjacent to Roman territory, Armenia was not unique in being a buffer state. Osrhoëne, just east of the Euphrates, also played this role through many vicissitudes, until the interventions of Romans and Parthians finally destroyed its quality as an instrument of conflict-avoidance and made it instead one more focus of conflict—featuring, as usual, the installation and deposition of rival candidates to the kingship. In A.D. 123 Hadrian replaced the Parthian appointee, Pacorus II, with one of his own, the Parthamaspates whom Trajan had earlier left at Ctesiphon in precarious control of a short-lived Parthian client state. With this, Osrhoëne became a new-style client state (i.e., a buffer state) until a Parthian intervention removed the Roman appointee; in A.D. 164, under Marcus Aurelius, Rome intervened once more and continued to do so in rivalry with Parthia until Osrhoëne was finally annexed under Septimius Severus in A.D. 195.[191]

The multiple military services provided by the old-style clients had been a crucial factor in preserving the concentrated flexibility of the Roman army. But the system was by no means costless: lands that *could* have been brought within the sphere of the cultural-commercial processes of Romanization were not; peoples that could have been subjected to the full weight of imperial taxation were not. These costs were worth paying as long as the resultant economy of Roman military power was being put to use, however infrequently, to secure further expansion. But once "scientific" borders were everywhere set in final form, the dynamic combination of hegemonic control and offensive military power became redundant, and with it the entire system of client-state peripheries.

V
The Army and
the System

"For their nation does not wait for the outbreak of war to give men their first lesson in arms; they do not sit with folded hands in peacetime only to put them in motion in the hour of need . . . they never have a truce from training, never wait for emergencies to arise. Moreover, their peace manoeuvers are no less strenuous than veritable warfare; each soldier daily throws all his energy into his drill, as though he were in action. . . . Indeed, it would not be wrong to describe their manoeuvres as bloodless combats and their combats as sanguinary manoeuvres."[192] Thus wrote Josephus, on the preparedness of the Roman army—in theory. His primary audience of fellow Jews by then needed no instruction in the matter.

Once the empire was mobilized to fight, with first-class leaders in charge of first-class legions brought from Europe, it was invincible. Then the solid infantry of the legions would move into action, complemented by the variegated panoply of auxiliary light infantry, cavalry, and missile troops. Then, even if the enemy could not be drawn out to fight in close combat, or outmaneuvered in field operations, it would still be defeated by the relentless methods of Roman "engineering" warfare. To fight the Chatti in the Taunus Mountains of Germany, assault roads leading to their fortified high places were cut in the forest; to fight the last handful of Jewish warriors in the remote desert fortress of Masada, the Romans built an assault embankment 675 feet long and 275 feet high, surmounted by a stone platform another 75 feet high and equally wide.[193]

The ability to bring large numbers of men on the scene of combat, to construct the required infrastructures, to provide a steady supply of food and equipment in remote and sometimes desolate places—all this reflected the high standards of Roman military organization.[194] But once the overall strategy of the empire was transformed from hegemonic expansionism to territorial defense, and a preclusive defense at that, the qualities needed by the Roman army changed also. The empire and its armies still needed the ability to deploy large forces under good generals to fight large-scale wars, but now this "surge" capability was not enough. Under the new system, the army also needed a *sustained* defensive capability over the full length of a land perimeter that was 6,000 miles long even before the conquest of Dacia.[195]

The physical requirement was for forces able both to guard the borders against infiltration and to serve in war. The moral requirement was to preserve the fighting skill and *élan* of troops assigned to routine guard and patrol duties, or merely residing in legionary fortresses, year after year. These troops had no ready prospect of war and booty, and little chance of exposure to the leadership of fighting generals or to the natural discipline of battle. For the Roman army as for any other, it was much easier to elicit a short-term "surge" response for battle than to maintain adequate standards of preparedness on a permanent basis. Where troops remained for long inactive, in a hospitable environment, they would cease to be soldiers. Tacitus recounts the harsh expedients used by Cn. Domitius Corbulo in A.D. 55–58 to turn the men of his two Syrian legions (III *Gallica* and VI *Ferrata*) into fighting soldiers for Nero's Parthian war: after weeding out the old and unfit who had been kept on the rolls—men who had never been on guard, who knew nothing of the simplest drills, and who lacked even helmets and breastplates—Corbulo kept the rest under canvas for their training in the harsh winter of the Anatolian Mountains. Even so, there were reverses in the first engagements of the following spring.[196] Aside from whatever delays may have been caused by the continued attempts to reach a diplomatic settlement, it appears that Corbulo's army was in training for three years before the start of the victorious campaign in Armenia.

Subsequently appointed governor of Syria, Corbulo must have employed all his famous severity on, and set a personal example of self-discipline for, the two remaining Syrian legions as well (X *Fretensis* and XII *Fulminata*). And yet, when in A.D. 66, C. Cestius Gallus, next governor of Syria, marched into Judea to quell what was still a small uprising, he was soundly defeated. Built around the XII *Fulminata* and comprising 2,000-man detachments from two other Syrian legions, the expeditionary force also included six cohorts of auxiliary infantry, four cavalry *alae*, almost 14,000 client-state troops, and large numbers of irregulars who had volunteered to join in what must have seemed sure to be a quick and certain victory.[197]

The Jews (or rather, the Zealots) could only muster untrained men, armed with spears and bows. Gallus soon reached Jerusalem, but failed to take the Temple Mount by storm; he was then maneuvered into retreat.[198] His army suffered heavy losses as it withdrew. The XII *Fulminata* lost its eagle standard[199]—an ignominy sufficiently rare to warrant disbandment in most cases—and the imperial forces made good their escape only after abandoning their baggage, losing their artillery and siege engines, and suffering 5,780 casualties, according to Josephus.[200] The defeat of Gallus turned the uprising into a more serious affair. Eventually it took a full-scale war to defeat the Jews, a war fought with an army that included two legions brought from Europe, fit for serious warfare, unlike the Syrian.

The circumstances that undermined the strength of the Syrian legions had been peculiar to the East during the Julio-Claudian era: a pattern of local recruitment, infrequent war, and prolonged stationing; moreover, it seems that the Syrians were deployed in city barracks rather than rural camps, a practice always frowned upon.[201] These circumstances were no longer limited to the East in the post-Flavian era. They were found throughout the empire.

The danger was obvious: all the legions might deteriorate as the Syrian had done. Large-scale offensive warfare would everywhere cease once "scientific" frontiers were attained, and local recruitment was rapidly becoming the norm, while the supposedly bracing rural camps gave way to stone fortresses, which rapidly acquired an urban atmosphere.[202]

It is against this background, as well as that of the Civil War, that the army policies of Vespasian and his successors must be seen. First, in the wake of Civilis's revolt, Vespasian restored order to the legionary forces: four legions (I *Germanica*, IV *Macedonica*, XV *Primigenia*, and XVI *Gallica*) were disbanded for having surrendered or lost their eagles. At the same time, two legions manned by transferred sailors from the fleets (I and II *Adiutrix*) and a legion raised by the short-lived emperor Galba (VII *Gemina* ex *Galbiana*) were placed on the regular establishment, together with two newly created legions (IV *Flavia felix* and XVI *Flavia firma*).[203]

Vespasian's accession had divulged the secret of empire, so to the problem of maintaining ordinary discipline was now added the problem of political security. Both the success and the shortcomings of Flavian army policy in the wake of the Civil War[204] are illustrated by the attempted *putsch* of L. Antonius Saturninus, legate of Upper Germany, against Domitian in A.D. 88–89.[205] While Saturninus was able to persuade the two legions under his command (XIV *Gemina* and XXI *Rapax*) to support his cause by appropriating the treasure chests of their saving banks, the legate and army of Lower Germany remained loyal to Domitian, and the *putsch* collapsed. This episode, incidentally, showed that diplomatic penetration could be a two-way street: Saturninus had apparently purchased the support of the German Chatti from across the Rhine. But the Rhine thawed prematurely, the Chatti could not cross the ice, and the attempt to use client-state manipulation for private aims failed.[206]

When the reformed legions were reestablished on the Rhine in the wake of the Civil War, their fairly rudimentary earth and wood *hiberna* (winter camps) gave way to bases built of stone; subsequently, permanent bases were built for the legions in Britain and throughout the empire.[207] This is perhaps the clearest expression of the long-term strategy: having attained "scientific" frontiers, no further movement is expected; not, at any rate, beyond the reach of fixed base points.[208]

While attempts were made to prohibit unseemly entertainments for the troops,[209] the spacious and well-equipped legionary fortresses provided standards of comfort and hygiene that soldiers (or, for that matter, most civilians) were not to experience again until the nineteenth century, if then. Even in the torrid and bleak North African desert, the fortress of the legion III *Augusta* at Gemellae (built in A.D. 126–33) was provided with a fully equipped bath in the Roman manner, built on an area of more than 6,700 square feet.[210] Elaborate measures were needed to supply the baths with fuel (desert tamarisk) and water.

Integral to the design of legionary fortresses and auxiliary forts was a hospital, with five-cot rooms for bedridden patients and separate lavatories for each pair of rooms.[211] The legions and some auxiliary units had doctors (*medici*) on the regular establishment, as well as orderlies and medical specialists (*medici chirugi, medici clinici*).[212] The narrative sources suggest that the military doctors were highly regarded in the medical profession. The authorities had to make special efforts to ensure the health of troops in fixed bases; the liberties that men can take in the field, so long as they change campsites frequently, would have resulted in chronic illness in permanent sites.

More subtle measures were needed to cope with the more serious problem of preserving the fighting skill and *élan* of troops who faced the prospect of a lifetime in the army without ever seeing action. (From the conclusion of Trajan's Parthian war [A.D. 117] to the wars of Marcus Aurelius in the 160s, there was almost half a century of tranquillity, with only sporadic and localized warfare in the remote northern frontiers of Britain and in Mauretania [A.D. 141–52].) The answer was an increased emphasis on troop selection,[213] training, [214] and professional specialization.[215] Epigraphic evidence of unique value gives us a glimpse of army exercises under Hadrian. Albeit an official speech, the professionalism[216] evident in Hadrian's remarks to the troops in Africa gives authenticity to the evidence.[217]

Only constant training could preserve the combat capabilities of an army that had settled down to an indefinite term of peacetime soldiering. Moreover, as the savage mutinies of A.D. 14 had shown, and as the sack of Cremona during the Civil War was to show again, the concentration of large numbers of men into legions fully conscious of their inherent power as the empire's major fighting force entailed grave risks for civil society. It is not surprising, therefore, that the major emphasis in army policy was not innovation but rather the maintenance of discipline. Even Hadrian, the man of broad conceptions and great expertise in military matters, was no innovator.[218] Instead, his major concern was the restoration of routine and discipline in the wake of the disruptions caused by Trajan's wars.

Under Hadrian the legions were deployed at fixed bases which, in most cases, they were never to leave again; and soldiers soon acquired unofficial families in the settlements (*vici*) that grew spontaneously around the legionary bases. It is sometimes assumed that this domestication diminished the army's combat capabilities by undermining its fighting spirit.[219] Had the Roman army structured its capabilities on the raw courage of the troops, the observation would have merit. But in fact a preference for methodical and cautious warfare had been the hallmark of the Roman army long before Hadrian. According to Frontinus, Scipio Africanus once replied to a critic of his prudence by saying that his mother had given birth to a general, not a warrior (*"imperatorem me mater, non bellatorem, peperit"*).[220] So, also, were the armies of Hadrian and his successors. As in the past, the Roman army would fight and win by relying on sound tactics, strategic method, and superior logistics. It did not need to emulate the savage spirit of barbarian warriors in order to prevail. These were soldiers who received regular pay (increased to 300 *denarii* by Domitian),[221] retirement benefits, and occasional donatives in lieu of the uncertain prospect of booty, and they could be kept in fighting trim by administrative means: regulation, inspection, and the detailed execution of prescribed exercises.

In the course of the second century there were only minor changes in the equipment of the legions,[222] with one major exception: the introduction of the *carroballista*, a powerful arrow- or bolt-shooting machine as mobile as any cart.[223] Already present in Trajan's army and shown on Trajan's column,[224] the *carroballista* appears to have become the most important type of artillery in the legionary establishment, used alongside a small number of heavier and altogether less mobile stone-throwing machines. The introduction of the *carroballista* must have increased even further the Roman advantage in the high-intensity warfare at which the legions were already so adept.

But the maintenance of frontier security against low-intensity threats, the major business of the Roman army during much of the second century, called for lighter forces trained and equipped for guard, patrol, and escort duties as well as highly mobile but small-scale warfare. It is not surprising, therefore, that the proportion of auxiliary troops in the army seems to have increased during the second century.[225] There was, moreover, a trend toward increased diversification in both structure and function. For example, milliary *alae* and cohorts were either introduced or greatly increased in numbers during the post-Flavian period (the first authenticated appearance at a milliary *ala* occurs in A.D. 85).[226] The new formations were clearly useful in bridging the gap between the legions and the quingenary *auxilia*, less than a tenth as large in manpower: given the inevitable friction that the brigading of different units would cause, the milliary units resulted in a sounder overall force-structure.

There was also structural innovation in the opposite direction: the introduction of a new kind of force, the *numeri*, commonly associated with Hadrian but possibly already in existence under Domitian.[227] The *numeri* are far less familiar to historians than either legions or the *alae* and cohorts. They can be recognized primarily by the structure of their names: an ethnic designation followed in most cases by a functional one.[228] It is likely that the *numeri* were smaller units than the quingenary auxilia (300 men?), and that as newly raised ethnic units they retained a pronounced national character, which most of the *auxilia* had lost long before.[229] It is recorded that they were allowed to retain their native war cries, and it is sometimes said that their introduction was motivated by the need to renew the fighting spirit of the now-staid *auxilia*.[230]

A more important consideration was the fact that the military manpower of the *numeri* was readily available, and probably cheap.[231] Further, unlike the manpower of the regular *auxilia*, the manpower of the *numeri* was self-renewing instead of self-extinguishing: discharged auxiliaries received the citizenship, so their sons were candidates for legionary rather than auxiliary recruitment,[232] but soldiers who served in the *numeri* did not, and their sons were thus available for service outside the legions.[233] This was important: while the recruitment problem was chronic for all formations, it must always have been less intractable for the better-paid legions. From a structural point of view, the *numeri*, being smaller units, were better suited for the fragmented deployments required on the "closed" frontiers—as in Germany, where the western Taunus and Odenwald segments of the Hadrianic frontier were guarded by small forts manned by *numeri*.[234] It is also possible that the troops who manned the milecastles of Hadrian's Wall in Britain belonged to *numeri*. In both cases, the undesirable alternative to the use of *numeri* would have been to split *alae* or cohorts into many small subunits. The *numeri*, moreover, contributed to the *functional* diversification of the Roman army; they cannot simply be regarded as "low-category" troops.

The first requirement for diversification was for additional cavalry and missile troops to balance the legionary infantry. Irregular North African horsemen (*Mauri gentiles*) were prominent among the troops who fought in Trajan's wars, and so were oriental archers; both were considered irregulars (*symmachiarii*) then and appeared as *numeri* later.[235] While it seems improbable that the Romans looked to the *numeri* to infuse the troops with barbarian energy, mounted archery was very much an eastern specialty, and it is natural to find *numeri* of mounted archers from Palmyra and Sura side by side with regular auxiliaries such as those of Ituraea. Mounted missile troops were obviously suitable as border forces, since they could deal with elusive infiltrators and skirmishers; it is not surprising that they are prominent in the garrison of the Dacian *Limes Porolissensis* on the Carpathians, which had no continuous wall barrier.[236]

Outside the *numeri* there was some specialization of a more recondite sort: under Trajan, for example, both a milliary *ala* of lancers (*Ala I Ulpia Contariorum*) and one of dromedary troops (*Ala I Ulpia Dromadariorum*) were raised.[237] The first may have been something of an experimental unit of heavy shock cavalry; the second was obviously a case of terrain specialization. Clearly, since the Roman army was no longer an undifferentiated force apt to fight anywhere, regional patterns of deployment had become useful: dromedary troops for the desert, mounted archers for "open" frontiers such as those of Dacia and above all the Euphrates, light spearmen (*Raeti Gaesati?*) for mountain country, and so on.

Most borders required a combination of static troops, to man forts, watchtowers, and guardposts, and mobile troops, i.e., cavalry, for patrol and escort duties. At the provincial level, the force-mix could easily be obtained by combining cavalry *alae* with auxiliary, or even legionary, infantry; but at the strictly local level, the frictions of brigading could be avoided by the deployment of the *cohortes equitatae*. The latter appear to have had 120 cavalry to 480 infantry if quingenary, and 240 cavalry to 800 infantry if milliary.[238] Sometimes dismissed as low-grade mounted infantry, the traditional bane of true cavalrymen,[239] it seems that the *cohortes equitatae* were, on the contrary, organic combinations of normal infantry with *light* cavalry, that is, cavalry that relies on harrassment (as opposed to shock) tactics. In the event of large-scale warfare, the cavalry and infantry would fight with their respective branches, and not in combination,[240] but for normal frontier security duties it is clear that the cavalry-infantry mix of the *cohortes equitatae* would be employed organically, with the infantry holding the fixed points of the system while cavalry patrols covered the intervening perimeter zones.

The territorialization of the legions, arising from their deployment in permanent bases, raises the basic question of flexibility for large-scale warfare. If the legions could no longer leave their bases, where did the troops of expeditionary forces come from? For part of the answer (for warfare at an intermediate level of intensity) we can look to the expeditionary corps based on *auxilia*, as in the case of the operations in Mauretania under Antoninus Pius in the mid-second century, when the only legion in Africa (III *Augusta*) was reinforced by auxiliary cavalry forces sent into the coastal staging bases of Portus Magnus, Cartennae, and Tipasa.[241] (In the last, a circuit of walls 2,400 meters long has been excavated; this provided base security for forces shipped in from Europe, the *Ala Flavia Brittanica* [a milliary cavalry unit], the *Ala I Ituraeorum Sagitarriorum* [mounted archers], *Ala I Ulpia Contariorum* [lancers, heavy cavalry] and an *Ala I Cananefatium*.)[242] Such troops would have to acclimatized prior to engaging in serious warfare, and the provision of a secure base at the landing point was obviously a sound move.

But the Roman army could not dispense with legionary troops for large-scale warfare. Three entire legions appear to have been sent to the East for the Parthian war of Marcus Aurelius. (They were the I *Minervia* from Bonna [Bonn] in Lower Germany, the II *Adiutrix* from Aquincum [Budapest] in Pannonia, and the V *Macedonica* from Troesmis [near Galați] in Lower Moesia.)[243] Much more frequent was the use of *vexillationes*, detachments drawn from the legions, ranging in size from very small units under the command of centurions to the large formations commanded by legionary legates.[244] Long an established practice, the use of *vexillationes* increased considerably in the post-Trajanic era. The legions as a whole developed local attachments and could not be easily moved—for soldiers were not likely to countenance indefinite separation from their (as yet unofficial) families. But it was still feasible to find one or two thousand troops in each legion freely available for large-scale warfare far from their bases.

There was a much stronger disincentive and a much stronger reason for not redeploying entire legions than the reluctance of the troops to leave their homes. With frontier security now reliant on the stationing of forces *in situ* (rather than on others' perceptions of their remote power), the removal of legions was liable to cause an immediate breakdown in the diplomatic structure of transborder control at the local level. This, in turn, was liable to precipitate attacks against imperial lands. It is true that on a day-to-day basis, peoples across the border dealt mostly with the auxiliary forces in their perimeter forts; but the integrity of imperial territory was ultimately secured by the "deterrent suasion" emanating from the concentrated power of the legions. Their removal was bound to upset the local balance of power and neutralize deterrence, thus forcing a total reliance on the "war-fighting" capabilities of the forces left in place.

When under Marcus Aurelius three entire legions (as well as several *vexillationes*) were sent to fight against Parthia, the governors of the affected provinces were told to compensate for their transfer by "diplomacy." Not surprisingly, without a deterrent the structure of diplomatic control broke down, precipitating the northern wars of Marcus Aurelius immediately after the victorious conclusion of the Parthian war.[245] Using *vexillationes* on a strategic scale was much more effective, as had already been shown in A.D. 83–85 under Domitian, when C. Velius Rufus in Germany had a force drawn from nine separate legions under his command.[246] The support elements and headquarters of the legions could then be left in place, together with older, married soldiers—precisely those troops that were less likely to be useful on remote fronts and more likely to do their very best on the defensive, and for the same reason: the frontier had become their home and that of their families. Further, legionary officers and N.C.O.s expert in dealing with the locals across the border would also remain in place, and so would the psychologic "presence" of the legion as a deterrent. This was likely to be less-than-proportionally affected by the departure of *vexillationes* of moderate size. In any case, the development of civil and military infrastructures, roads, and supply depots on all sectors of the empire would make the support and logistic elements of the legions redundant for expeditionary purposes: local support elements, and base infrastructures already in the combat zone, could no doubt be "stretched" to accommodate *vexillationes* consisting only of legionary combat echelons, i.e., the cohorts. This, incidentally, would also alleviate the transportation problem.

Finally, there was the element of troop selection. Unless extruded by their home units, rather than picked by detachment commanders, the men of the *vexillationes* were liable to be younger and fitter than the average legionary. They were also likely to be unattached—as suitable for mobile and offensive warfare as the older family men left behind would be resilient on the defensive.

VI

Conclusion

It cannot be pretended that expeditionary units extracted from an army which was everywhere based on static frontier positions could have as much combat power as the strategically mobile armies of the early principate. A strategy optimized for preclusive defense—even though by no means a "cordon" strategy—could not enjoy the very high ratio of net "disposable" military power of the earlier system of hegemonic control and mobile armies. While under Nero three legions could be deployed to Judea in A.D. 66 with no apparent strain on the system, Trajan's army was obviously stretched nearly to the breaking point by A.D. 116, and that of Marcus Aurelius even more so by A.D. 166. Ultimately, the decreased elasticity of the system had to be compensated for by the recruitment of two new legions (II and III *Italicae*).[247] The margin upon which the safety of the system depended had become dangerously thin.

Three

DEFENSE-IN-DEPTH. *The Great Crisis of the Third Century and the New Strategies.*

The outstanding virtue of the constitutional device invented by Augustus, the principate, was its reconciliation of republican traditions with autocratic efficiency. Its outstanding defect was that the succession was neither dynastic nor truly elective. When a tolerable emperor chose a capable successor and made him a son by adoption, all was well. Adoption satisfied the dynastic sentiment of the army and the common people without offending the anti-dynastic prejudice of the Senate. But if there were no adequate son and none was adopted, he became emperor who could make himself emperor, usually by force.

During the fortunate second century, Trajan (98–117) was adopted by Nerva and himself adopted Hadrian, who lived till A.D. 138. Hadrian, in turn, adopted Antoninus Pius (138–61), who adopted two sons: Lucius Verus, who died in 169, and Marcus Aurelius, who ruled the empire until 180.

Then the chain of successful adoptions was fatally broken. Marcus Aurelius did not adopt a son, for one was born to him, Commodus, wholly unfit for the office he inherited. Commodus was murdered in 192. Three months later, his successor by proclamation, the elderly Pertinax, was murdered also. The Praetorian Guard, as the strongest military force actually in Rome, were the immediate arbiters of the succession, and they

127

chose to sell the office. The buyer, Didius Julianus, did not last the year. Septimius Severus, legate of Pannonia, brought the superior force of the Danube frontier legions to bear by marching on Rome and claimed the throne. But if one legate could make himself emperor, so might another. For five years Severus had to fight destructive internal wars: other legates with other legions contested the office, just as Severus himself had done.

Having defeated his rivals, Severus engaged in successful external war until his death at York in 211, on campaign. His two natural sons, Caracalla and Geta, then jointly inherited the imperial power as Commodus had done, and with equal merit. Having murdered his brother in 212, Caracalla was murdered in 217. Succession by murder and civil war now became the norm.

Between the natural death of Septimius Severus in 211 and the accession of Diocletian in 284, there were twenty-four more-or-less legitimate emperors and many more usurpers; that is, rulers who could not control Rome. Most were short-lived, but some usurpers ruled substantial parts of the empire for several years. In fact, the longest reign of the period was that of a usurper, Postumus, who controlled Gaul for nine years. The average reign of the "legitimate" emperors was only three years. One emperor, Decius (249–51) died in battle fighting the Goths; another, Valerian (253–60), was captured by the Persians and died in captivity; Claudius II (268–70) died of the plague. All other emperors and most usurpers were murdered or they perished in civil war.

Sanguinary turmoil at the very core of the imperial system was bound to invite aggression from without. But there is also reason to believe that the magnitude of the external threat had increased independently. On the Rhine and upper Danube, the old and fragmented neighbors of the empire had begun federating into much larger and more dangerous agglomerations during the second century, even before the domestic upheavals began. Instead of the many peoples recorded in the first and second centuries—Frisii, Bructeri, Tencteri, Usipi, Chatti, Hermunduri and so on—the empire now confronted the larger federations of the Franks and the Alamanni, who could concentrate much more manpower in attacking the frontiers. Having for so long confronted a single adversary whose single culture had infiltrated all their separate lives, different barbarians found a common cultural basis for action against the empire. It became much harder for Roman diplomacy to contrive divisions among men who now had much in common.

In the East, the weak Arsacid regime of Parthia was overthrown ca. 224 by the Persian dynasty of the Sassanids, and the new enemy immediately proved to be altogether more formidable than the old. For the empire this change had catastrophic consequences, for its entire strategy of containment was thereby unbalanced. Septimius Severus had fought Parthia more successfully than any Roman before him, and his success had been consolidated by the establishment of a "scientific" frontier in Northern Mesopotamia, on the Khabur River-Jebel Sinjar line. But this did not suffice to contain the Persian attack of a generation later.

Domestic strife and foreign aggression were not merely parallel; they interacted perversely with one another. It was fortunate for Rome that the territorialization of the army (which most modern historians like to deplore) was already far advanced: it must have acted as a brake on eager pretenders, for soldiers were less likely to be enticed into leaving the frontiers to fight internal wars if their own families and their own lands would thereby be exposed to foreign invaders. Nevertheless, troops were all too frequently removed from frontiers already under attack to fight in private wars between emperors and usurpers. There was also a more subtle connection between external attack and domestic instability: regional usurpations were in part a reaction to the failure of the central government to provide security for border regions.

This interaction between internal disorder and foreign invasion had disastrous results: the history of the third century is largely a history of invasions, many made possible by domestic strife, and some so deep that Rome itself had to be provided with walls. Much that had been built and achieved since Augustus was irreparably destroyed. Destroyed as well was an entire conception of empire.

Much of the time, the emperor of the hour had to devote his attention to the threat from within even when attacks were underway from without: it was more important to protect the office than to ensure the tranquillity of remote frontiers. Sometimes external security was sacrificed directly for internal: Philip the Arab (244–49) abandoned the Persian campaign of his predecessor and victim Gordian III (238–44) to seek a prompt and unfavorable peace treaty, in order to return to Rome to claim the imperial power before another could do so in his place.

That the ideal of a unitary empire was still dominant, that a form of cultural patriotism had become prevalent, and that an anxious longing for order remained universal, are all proven by the rapid success of Diocletian's efforts to restore the political stability and territorial security of the empire. Diocletian (284–305) had risen from peasant to emperor through the ranks of the army, but he was neither a peasant nor a simple-minded soldier by the time he attained the purple. Schooled in the chaos and insecurity of half a century, Diocletian relentlessly pursued a policy of internal regimentation and systematic frontier consolidation; the one exemplified by his celebrated edict on prices, the other by stout forts built all around the imperial perimeter.

Himself the beneficiary of a wholly unregulated system of succession, Diocletian invented, or at least applied, a scheme of great constitutional ingenuity that was to abolish the danger of civil war. The tetrarchy, the joint *rule of four, was to produce future rulers for the empire with the assured regularity of a machine. There were to be two equal co-emperors, an Augustus for the West and one for the East; in 286 Diocletian made Maximian the Augustus for the West, himself retaining the East. Then came a refinement: each Augustus would have a junior emperor, with the title of Caesar; in 293 Diocletian made Galerius his own Caesar and chose Constantius I Chlorus to be Maximian's. Each Caesar would marry the daughter of his Augustus, and eventually succeed him, then choosing a Caesar in turn as his own junior associate. The four rulers, the tetrarchs, could campaign simultaneously in as many sectors, and no vast areas of the empire would ever again be left unattended, to breed usurpers. In 305 Diocletian (and Maximian, his fellow Augustus) abdicated, and he retired to a splendid palace in Dalmatia, the only emperor ever to retire voluntarily. By 309 the machine of the tetrarchy had already broken down. No predictable and automatic succession ensued, for six Augusti disputed the title. Nevertheless, the institution of dual control endured until the very end of the western empire, and the chaotic succession struggles of the third century did not recur.*

A magnificent palace falling into ruin, the empire was restored under the tetrarchy, but it was restored as a solid and austere fortress. The agency of this transformation was a perfected system of taxation-in-kind, which ruthlessly extracted the food, fodder, clothing, arms, and money needed for imperial defense from an empire which became one vast logistic base. In the military realm, the reforms of the tetrarchy marked a critical stage in the secular transformation of the assured territorial defense of the second century into the defense-in-depth of the late declining empire. The age of the tetrarchy was a time of grim and painful innovation, presided over by a man whose qualities even the most hostile sources cannot fully obscure. In the stern rule of Diocletian lay the key to a difficult salvation for the empire and its civilization, while in the seemingly happier age of Constantine were the beginnings of the final disaster.

I
The System
in Outline

Faced with an enemy sufficiently mobile and sufficiently strong to pierce a defensive perimeter on any selected axis of penetration, the defense has, in principle, two alternatives open to it. The first, usually described as "elastic defense," entails the complete abandonment of the perimeter with its fortifications and associated infrastructures. Instead, the defense is to rely exclusively on mobile forces, which should be at least as mobile as those of the offense. The two sides then fight on an equal footing: the defense can be as concentrated as the offense, since it need not assign troops to hold any fixed positions nor detach forces to protect territory; on the other hand, the defense thereby sacrifices all the tactical advantages normally inherent in its role (except knowledge of the terrain) since neither side can choose its ground, let alone fortify it in advance.

The second operational method is the defense-in-depth, based on the combination of *self-contained* strongholds with mobile forces deployed between or behind them. Under this method, which has many variants, both ancient and modern, warfare is no longer a symmetrical contest between structurally similar forces. While only the offense has the advantage of full freedom of concentration, the defense has the advantage of mutual support between self-contained strongholds and mobile forces in the field. If the strongholds are sufficiently resilient to survive attack *without* requiring the direct support of the mobile elements, if the mobile elements in turn can resist or evade concentrated attacks in the field without needing the shelter of the strongholds, and finally, if the offense must eventually reduce the strongholds in order to prevail,[1] then the conditions are present for a successful defense-in-depth. Sooner or later, the offense will be faced by the superior strength of both fixed and mobile elements acting in combination.

These, then, are the two broad alternative responses to the challenge of strategic penetrations that perimeter defenses can no longer reliably contain. Neither offers the preclusive security of a dense perimeter defense, but both are more resilient. At the *tactical* level, the two methods lead to very different patterns of deployment and operational conduct. But at the *strategic* level, the qualitative difference between the two methods is less significant than the *scale* of their application, for both can be applied either across all of the defended territory, on a regional basis, or on a purely local level. As the scale of application increases, so does the short-term resilience of the system, but the depth of the territory that is allowed to become a battlefield must increase also, and this entails obvious costs to society.

Because the Romans had developed a comprehensive system of perimeter defense in the second century, their response to the first serious penetrations of the imperial perimeter, which took place under Marcus Aurelius (ca. 166), was incremental and remedial. Neither a system of elastic defense nor one of defense-in-depth was adopted. Instead, on the most vulnerable tracts of the perimeter, border fortifications were strengthened and garrisons were augmented; two new legions (II *Italica* and III *Italica*) were raised and deployed in Noricum and Raetia, respectively, which were provinces hitherto ungarrisoned by legions.[2] The basic perimeter-defense strategy was not abandoned even when the first nucleus of a strategic reserve was formed a generation later, under Septimius Severus. Instead, further attempts were made to remedy local inadequacies in the frontier system by constructing additional fortifications and augmenting garrisons.

It was only after the chaotic breakdown of imperial defenses in the great crisis of the mid-third century that definite action was taken to adopt a new strategy. When and where frontier defenses were totally overrun, remedial strategies could only take the form of elastic defense, but to the extent that deliberate choice was possible, the strategy that emerged had the character of a defense-in-depth based on a combination of static frontier forces and mobile field armies. The adoption of a defense-in-depth strategy in the later third century was, however, neither total nor definitive. *Whenever the strategy showed signs of enduring success, it was promptly abandoned.* As soon as Roman arms were able to force the enemy to revert to the defensive, or better yet, to resume a dependent client status, every attempt was made to restore the former system of preclusive security. This was the essence of Diocletian's military policy at the end of the third century and that of the more fortunate of his successors until Valentinian I (364–75), when the last sustained attempt to provide a preclusive defense of the imperial territory was made.

Long-term reliance on a defense-in-depth strategy entailed the maintenance of a stable equilibrium between the incursions of the enemy and the eventual counteroffensives of the defense. Incursions would inevitably take place, and, unless very feeble, could no longer be prevented by interception on the frontier line itself, for its garrisons were thinned out. Meeting only static guardposts and weak patrol forces on the frontier, the enemy could frequently cross the line virtually unopposed, but in the context of defense-in-depth, this no longer meant that the defense system had been "turned" and overrun. Instead, the enemy would find itself in a peripheral combat zone of varying depth, within which strongholds large and small as well as walled cities, fortified farmhouses, fortified granaries, and fortified refuges would remain, each capable of sustained resistance against enemies unequipped with siege-machines. Within and beyond this zone were the mobile forces of the defense, deployed to fight in the open but with the support of the fortified places.

Such support could take several distinct forms.[3] First, the fortified islands could serve as supply depots. Under the later empire, the most important remaining advantage of Roman forces over their enemies was their logistic superiority; Roman victories were frequently the outcome of confrontations between well-fed Roman troops and starving invaders, who had failed to find undefended food stores in the areas they had overrun.[4] Food and fodder stores in fortified strongholds were at once denied to the enemy and readily available to the forces of the defense when the latter advanced to recover territory temporarily overrun. The location of frontier-line food storehouses was ideal from a logistic point of view, since resupply was then available where it was needed most, at the troops' destination. Cavalry forces can move across country at the rate of fifty miles per day, but no logistic transport available to the Romans could keep up with them. Even in the case of infantry marching on good roads, terminal resupply would be vastly superior to baseline supply, since men can march at three m.p.h. while heavy carts cannot achieve much more than one m.p.h.[5]

A second function of fortified positions is more purely tactical. Fixed defenses on the frontier could usefully serve as obstacles even where the perimeter as a whole was not manned in sufficient strength to deny passage absolutely. Under the later empire, both old-style bases rebuilt as "hard" fortifications for sustained resistance and entirely new forts served to deny passage at accessible river crossings and preferred mountain passes. In a rational scheme of selective fortification in depth, the goal is to *equalize* the barrier effect of terrain across the sector as a whole by denying free use of the easier passage points. This is the rationale of the river forts opposite fords that characterized the Rhine and Danube frontiers under the later empire.

A third function of self-contained fortifications in a scheme of defense-in-depth is provision of rear-area security and rear-area intelligence. Imperial forces had to move as quickly as possible to achieve the rapid concentration of forces required by the new strategy, so they could not afford to interdict their own communications in order to slow enemy incursions.[6] In order to secure safe passage for gathering concentrations of imperial troops and supply trains as well as for civilian traffic, while denying unimpeded use of the roads to enemy bands, road forts were built at intervals along the highways. Road forts manned by small detachments could not effectively oppose the passage of large enemy forces, but they could at least intercept stray groups and foraging parties or impose time-consuming detours. And delay was the object, in anticipation of the relief columns that would be on their way to the sectors under attack. During the third-century invasions, prior to the construction of road forts, quite small barbarian bands had been able to penetrate rapidly for hundreds of miles into the interior, using the highways built precisely to facilitate movements within the empire.

A fourth function of self-contained strongholds is only of importance when effective mobile troops remain in their garrisons. These troops could sally out to attack an invading enemy from the rear, returning to the safety of their walls once the enemy responded in strength. Such operations would not only wear down the opposition but would also expose the enemy to a higher-than-preferred degree of force concentration. This could be critical, since the principal tactical problem facing the mobile field forces of the Romans was to come to grips with elusive and dispersed invasion forces.

A fifth function of self-contained strongholds is the conservation of the strength of *mobile* forces under stress by offering them temporary refuge. Under a pure elastic defense strategy, outnumbered defensive forces faced a stark choice: escape or defeat. But if strongholds were available, outnumbered or defeated mobile contingents need not be lost, or even widely dispersed in flight. For the empire it was always essential to conserve the scarce supply of trained military manpower, and the strongholds did so doubly, by maximizing the defense strength of garrisons within walls and by offering temporary shelter for mobile forces that would otherwise have been destroyed or driven from the field.

These strongholds did have a potential drawback: stout walls and high ramparts could eventually erode the offensive drive of the forces they contained by underlining the difference between the relative insecurity of open combat and the safety of fixed positions. This, however, was not inevitable. As is the case today, the demoralizing effect of fortifications could be counteracted by appropriate training and adequate leadership. "Maginot Line" syndromes are avoidable: poorly led troops who *do* succumb are just as likely to be driven from the field if they are unprovided with fortifications.

I have assumed throughout that fortified strongholds would *normally* be capable of sustained resistance against direct attack, given normal manning and provisioning. This was not the case with the Roman forts of the first and second centuries, however. The legionary "fortresses" and auxiliary "forts" were then no more than residential complexes, with none of the features of fortified strongholds except for walls. This was entirely consistent with their role, which was to serve as bases for tactically *offensive* operations even if they did so within the framework of a defensive strategy of territorial defense. With their spacious ground protected only by thin, low walls, and their narrow perimeter ditches designed to do no more than keep out infiltrators (or at most to break the impetus of a sudden onslaught), these "fortresses" and "forts" were incapable of withstanding determined attackers. Even the most primitive enemies[7] could contrive simple battering rams to breach the walls, only five feet or so in width.[8] Nor were the troop bases on the frontiers situated for tactical defense; they were merely set astride lines of communications, with a view to logistic and residential convenience. Wall circuits were long in proportion to the garrison strengths, owing to the spacious internal layout and the shape of the perimeter (typically a rectangle, instead of a minimum-perimeter circular or oval circuit).[9] Further, the walls commonly lacked fighting ramparts and projecting towers, from which intervening wall segments could be kept under fire. If there were towers, these were commonly decorative (i.e., non-projecting), as in the Trajanic fortress at York (Eburacum), where towers thirty square feet at the base projected only two feet from the circuit.[10] Finally, the first- and second-century bases lacked wide berms and ditches (to keep siege machines at a distance), raised internal floors (to defeat mining attempts), defensible gates, and sally ports. All of these devices became common in the Roman fortifications of the third century and after, integrated in a variety of designs that would remain models of military architecture for half a millenium and more.

It is sometimes suggested that this transformation of Roman military construction was prompted by a sudden improvement in the siege technology of the enemies of Rome.[11] This seems very unlikely. Technology is not an independent phenomenon, but a reflection of the cultural and economic base of society, and barbarian society had not changed significantly. It is true that there are references to the use of "engines" by the Goths at the third siege of Philippopolis (in Macedonia) in 267 and at the siege of Side (in Lycia) in 269, but it is doubtful that these machines were anything more than simple battering rams or scaling towers. In fact, the evidence indicates that the improvement in barbarian siege technology between the first century and the sixth was marginal.[12] Sassanid-Persian siege technology, on the other hand, had obviously advanced.

Such "tactical" explanations of the revolution in Roman military architecture are implausible, but there is a clear strategic explanation, inherent in any strategy of defense-in-depth. Roman bases were rebuilt as fortified strongholds not because the barbarians had now learned how to breach simple walls—which they must always have been capable of doing—but because the enemy had *not* acquired significant siege capabilities. Unless the strongholds could resist close investment, the defense-in-depth would quickly collapse into an "elastic defense" of the worst kind. On the other hand, facing barbarians unequipped to breach serious defenses adequately manned and incapable of starving out the well-fed defenders, the strongholds could resist while relief was on its way, then carry out their several supporting functions.

The general character of Roman defense-in-depth strategies was that of a "rearward" defense, as opposed to the "forward" defense characteristic of the earlier frontier strategy. In both, the enemy must ultimately be intercepted, but while forward defense demands that he be intercepted *in advance* of the frontier so that peaceful life may continue unimpaired within, rearward defense provides for his interception only inside imperial territory, his ravages being meanwhile contained by the point defenses of forts, towns, cities, and even individual farmhouses. The earlier system of preclusive security had been obviously superior in its benefits to society, but it was impossibly costly to maintain against enemies who had become capable of concentrating overwhelming forces on any narrow segment of the frontier. Moreover, the system was not resilient, since there was nothing behind the linear defense of the frontier. A defense-in-depth, in contrast, could survive even serious and prolonged penetrations without utterly collapsing. And this resilience added to the flexibility of imperial strategy as a whole: in the presence of multiple threats on different sectors, field armies could be redeployed to deal with them *seriatim*, for no irreparable damage would be suffered in the meantime.

Strategic rationality for the central authorities of the empire and the best interests of the provincials were two very different things, however, and this disparity was to have grave political consequences. The nexus between the multiple invasions of the third century and the multiple successions in Britain, Gaul, Egypt, and North Africa was direct. Provincial security had been sacrificed for the security of the empire as a whole, and the provincials can be excused for their failure to accept the logic of the system.

The equilibrium characteristic of successful defense-in-depth strategies was not usually maintained for very long. There was a built-in tendency for the successful defense-in-depth to give way to a temporary restoration of the earlier strategy of forward defense; if the strategy proved unsuccessful, it gave way to an imposed "elastic defense." The goal of a successful defense-in-depth, ensuring the *ultimate* possession of imperial territory, was upgraded to the Antonine goal of preclusive protection for *all* imperial territory against threats at *all* levels of intensity. The goal of an unsuccessful defense-in-depth was of necessity downgraded to the minimum of ensuring the survival of the mobile forces in the field, which were frequently headed by the emperor himself. Sometimes, for all the tactical flexibility of an "elastic defense" (in which safety could always be sought in retreat), imperial armies could not even ensure that minimum goal: thus we find the emperor Decius killed by the Goths in 251 while campaigning in the modern Dobruja; Valerian captured in 260 by the Sassanid ruler of Persia, Shapur I, before the walls of Edessa; and, in the gravest defeat of all, Valens killed with an entire field army by the Visigoths at Adrianople in the great disaster of 378.

Even when there was neither a full reversion to a preclusive defense nor a decline into a deep elastic defense, the dynamics of the strategy were inherently unstable, primarily because the defended area that became a combat zone was simultaneously part of the empire-wide logistic base. The Romans did not face a single enemy, or even a fixed group of enemies, whose ultimate defeat would ensure permanent security. Regardless of the amplitude of Roman victories, the frontiers of the empire would always remain under attack, since they were barriers in the path of secular migration flows from north to south and from east to west. Hence Roman strategy could not usefully aim at total victory at any cost, for the threat was not temporary but endless. The only rational goal was the mainte- nance of a minimally adequate level of security at the lowest feasible cost to society.

Under a successful strategy of preclusive defense, the total cost of security consisted of money spent on troop maintenance and the hidden costs of compulsory purchase and compulsory service. A defense-in-depth strategy, on the other hand, also entailed additional costs to society, which were paid by the people directly, and not through the medium of the tax-collector or recruiting sergeant: these were the losses inflicted by enemy incursions. In the short run these societal costs had no direct impact on the army, which would be fighting with men already in the ranks, fed by food already har- vested. In the very long run, on the other hand, the level of these costs would determine popular and elite attitudes toward the very idea of unitary empire, it would decisively affect the morale of autochthonous troops, and it would ultimately determine the value of the imperial structure to its inhabitants. But in the medium term there was a direct relationship between the logistic support available to the army (and therefore its capabilities) on the other hand, and the geographic depth of the defense-in-depth on the other.

If the peripheral zone that became the scene of combat in a sequence of enemy incursions and successful counteroffensives was kept thin, the damage inflicted to the army's logistic base would be

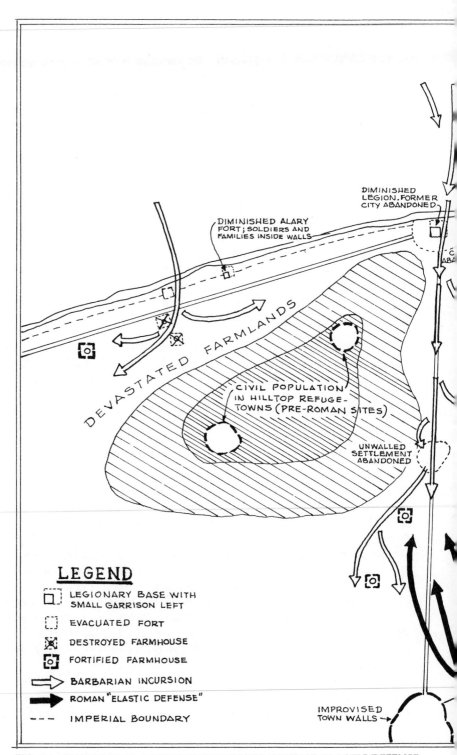

DIMINISHED
LEGION. FORMER
CITY ABANDONED

DIMINISHED ALARY
FORT; SOLDIERS AND
FAMILIES INSIDE WALLS

C
ABA

DEVASTATED FARMLANDS

CIVIL POPULATION
IN HILLTOP REFUGE-
TOWNS (PRE-ROMAN SITES)

UNWALLED
SETTLEMENT
ABANDONED

LEGEND

▢ LEGIONARY BASE WITH
SMALL GARRISON LEFT

▢ EVACUATED FORT

▨ DESTROYED FARMHOUSE

▣ FORTIFIED FARMHOUSE

⇨ BARBARIAN INCURSION

➡ ROMAN "ELASTIC DEFENSE"

--- IMPERIAL BOUNDARY

IMPROVISED
TOWN WALLS →

FIG. 3.1. OPERATIONAL METHODS OF BORDER DEFENSE: ELASTIC DEFENSE

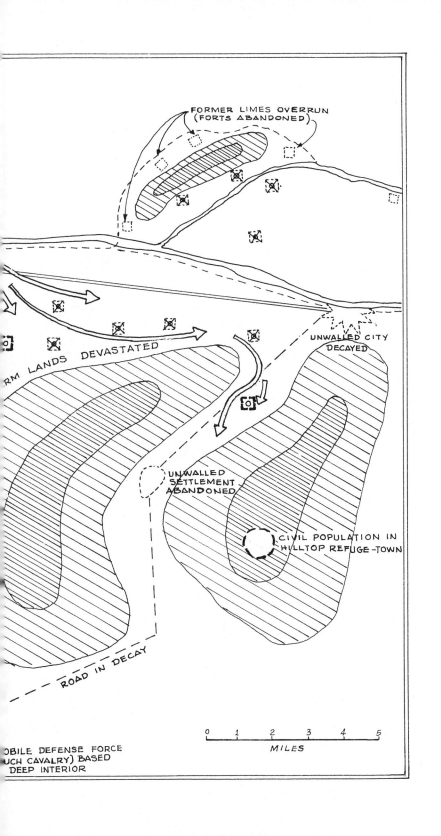

FORMER LIMES OVERRUN
(FORTS ABANDONED)

FARM LANDS DEVASTATED

UNWALLED CITY
DECAYED

UNWALLED
SETTLEMENT
ABANDONED

CIVIL POPULATION IN
HILLTOP REFUGE-TOWN

ROAD IN DECAY

MOBILE DEFENSE FORCE
(SUCH CAVALRY) BASED
DEEP INTERIOR

0   1   2   3   4   5

MILES

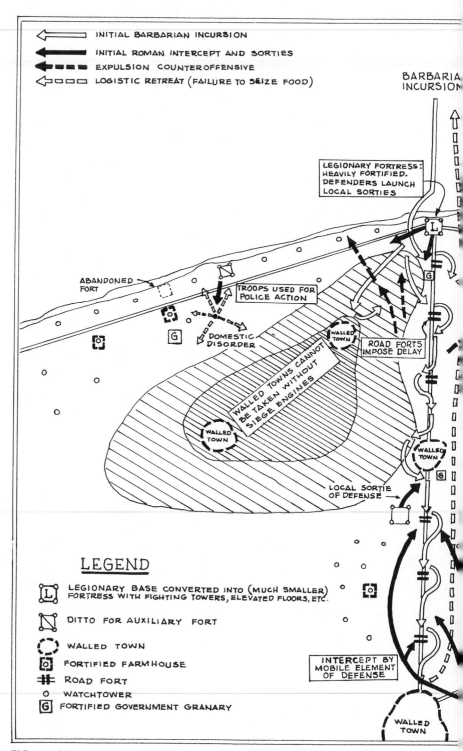

FIG. 3.2. OPERATIONAL METHODS OF BORDER DEFENSE: DEFENSE-IN-DEPTH

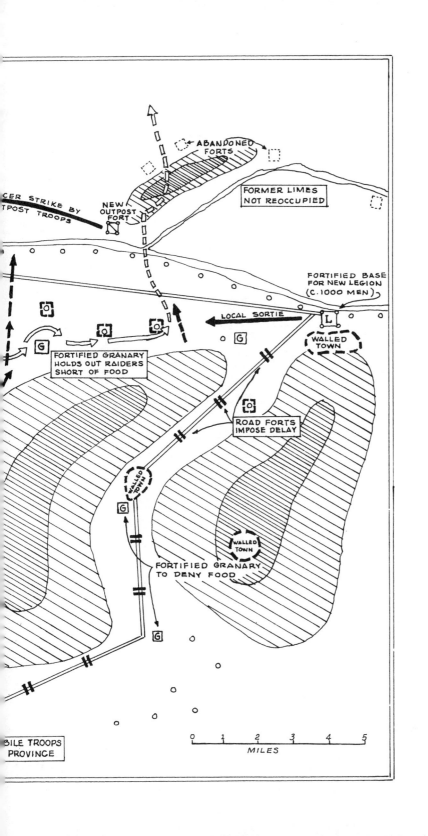

ABANDONED FORTS

FORMER LIMES
NOT REOCCUPIED

CER STRIKE BY
TPOST TROOPS

NEW
OUTPOST
FORT

FORTIFIED BASE
FOR NEW LEGION
(C. 1000 MEN)

LOCAL SORTIE

L

WALLED
TOWN

G

FORTIFIED GRANARY
HOLDS OUT RAIDERS
SHORT OF FOOD

G

ROAD FORTS
IMPOSE DELAY

WALLED
TOWN

G

WALLED
TOWN

FORTIFIED GRANARY
TO DENY FOOD

G

BILE TROOPS
PROVINCE

0   1   2   3   4   5
MILES

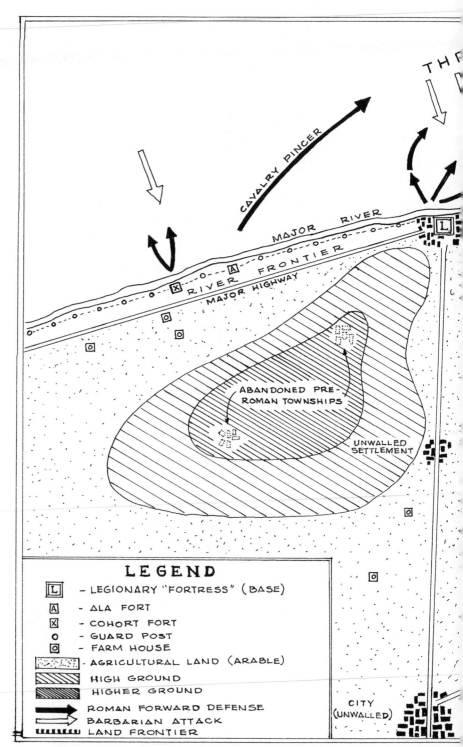

FIG. 3.3. OPERATIONAL METHODS OF BORDER DEFENSE: FORWARD DEFENSE

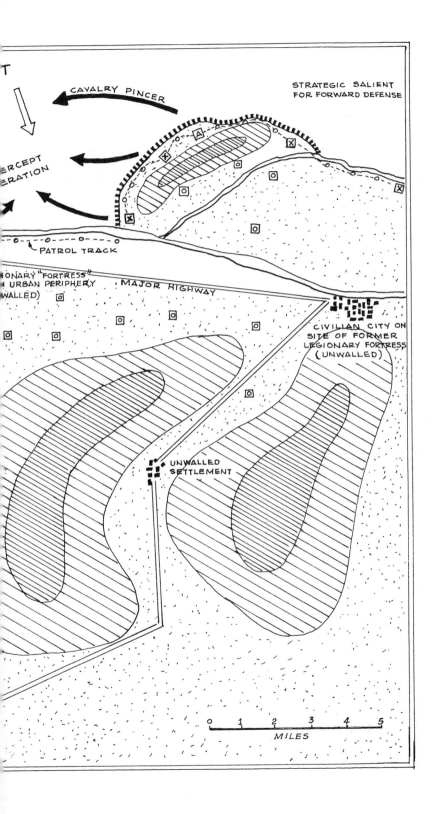

T

CAVALRY PINCER

STRATEGIC SALIENT
FOR FORWARD DEFENSE

A

ERCEPT
ERATION

PATROL TRACK

ONARY "FORTRESS"
URBAN PERIPHERY
WALLED)

MAJOR HIGHWAY

CIVILIAN CITY ON
SITE OF FORMER
LEGIONARY FORTRESS
(UNWALLED)

UNWALLED
SETTLEMENT

0   1   2   3   4   5
MILES

correspondingly limited. But this zone could only remain thin if the reaction of the defenders was prompt, and speed in reaction conflicted with the need for time in which to assemble the strongest possible force for the counteroffensive. Conversely, the greater the degree of troop concentration—other things being equal—the longer the time needed to deploy forces prior to interception, and the deeper the enemy penetration. There was, in other words, a proportional relationship between the resilience of the system and the degree of damage sustained by the empire's logistic base before the enemy was repelled

It was this conflict of priorities between the societal and logistic costs of delayed interception on the one hand and the strategic advantages of the greatest feasible preliminary concentration of forces on the other, that resulted in the cyclical nature of imperial strategy. If successful, imperial armies would suppress major threats and then go on to defeat successive incursions with shorter and shorter interception delays. At each stage, the damage done to the logistic base by each incursion would be less and less, and the imperial armies supported by the affected areas would be gradually strengthened; this in turn would tend to ensure—other things being equal—that the interception delays would be shorter still . . . and so on. On the other hand, if the imperial armies were *not* successful, incursions would become deeper and deeper, the damage done to the logistic base would be greater and greater, and the imperial forces supported by the sector would be correspondingly weakened. The mobile forces gathered to drive out the enemy would then have to come from farther and farther afield, thus delaying interception to a greater and greater extent and correspondingly increasing the damage inflicted on the logistic base . . . and so on.

Able leaders and good fortune in battle could and did reverse the downward cycle of a deteriorating defense-in-depth. In the West there were several major reversals, from the third century to the later fourth century, each time culminating in a temporary return to a preclusive border defense. Thus, in the eastern half of the empire, was the great crisis of the fifth century overcome, as were many crises thereafter. But the downward cycle that began in the West after the reign of Valentinian (364–75) was only partially reversed thereafter. Following the death of Theodosius I (in 395), the cycle became irreversible. Much of the western empire then became the scene of combat between barbarian armies that ravaged the land either in the name of an increasingly shadowy imperial authority, or simply their own. The goal of a defense-in-depth strategy, i.e., the ultimate restoration of full territorial security, had deteriorated into the goal of maintaining an elastic defense that became increasingly elastic, and that was only of value to the individuals thereby protected and made powerful. The losses of logistic base areas now acquired a permanent character, since imperial authority was devolving to warrior nations that no longer raided, but rather occupied, what had once been part of the empire.

II
The Changing Threat

The Antonine system of preclusive security had always been vulnerable to simultaneous attacks from different directions, and in 162 the Parthian invasion of Armenia initiated a whole series of conflicts that were to last, with short intervals, until the death of Marcus Aurelius, in 180.[13] The threat on the Danubian and (to a lesser extent) the Rhine sectors was permanent. The Parthian threat, on the other hand, was sporadic; Rome's eastern wars, being fought with an organized state, had a beginning and an end. Parthia and Rome remained adversaries, but there was no warfare between them from 117 to 162. When the eastern front became active in 162, *vexillationes* drawn from the legions, auxiliaries, and even complete legions were sent east, and the European frontiers were correspondingly weakened. It appears that even earlier there had been incursions by the Chatti against the Taunus *limes*, resulting in the attested destruction of frontier forts.[14] At the same time, trouble was expected on the Danubian frontiers.[15] The Romans constantly watched the barbarians, but the barbarians also watched the Romans: with the frontier garrisons visibly depleted, they naturally saw new opportunities for profitable raiding.

By 166 the armies of Marcus Aurelius had repeated Trajan's feat: they had defeated the Parthians, taken Ctesiphon, and overrun the intervening lands, but no new frontier was established.[16] Victory in the east was followed by an inconclusive war in the west. As the expeditionary forces were returning from the east, bringing a devastating plague with them, Quadi, Marcomanni, and Iazyges crossed the Danube over much of its length, evaded or defeated the weak frontier garrisons, and advanced in bands large and small deep into the empire.[17] The *SHA* speaks of a barbarian "conspiracy," but even without coordination the opportunity must have been simultaneously apparent to all.[18] By 167 Quadi and Marcomanni were at Aquileia, the northeastern gateway to Italy.[19] It was the empire's gravest military crisis since the inception of the principate. In spite of a severe fiscal crisis,[20] and in spite of the chronic shortage of manpower, two new legions, the II and III *Italicae*, were raised, ca. 165.[21] Desperate expedients were employed to find recruits.[22] In addition, strong forces of auxiliaries and *vexillationes* detached from the frontier legions were also deployed as field forces to counter the new threat.[23]

With an undefended interior, enemy penetrations could and did reach far and wide, but the threat was not particularly intense. The damage inflicted by fleeting barbarian incursions was in most places superficial. Aquileia, though devoid of troops and without a proper wall circuit, was hurriedly provided with improvised defenses, and it did not fall. The Quadi and Marcomanni were not equipped or organized for siege operations; their attack was only a large-scale raid, and their aim was probably not conquest, but booty. Since they had not seriously damaged the empire's logistic base, its eventual victory was only a question of time. By 172 the Marcomanni had been driven out of the empire, and a peace was imposed on them; two years later the Quadi were suppressed, and in 175 it was the turn of the Sarmatians.[24] When Quadi and Marcomanni renewed hostilities in 177, the outcome was a great Roman victory on the Danube in 179.[25] Marcus Aurelius had supposedly planned a trans-Danubian operation to conquer the homeland of the Marcomanni, and much else besides, but this project, if it was in fact seriously contemplated, was abandoned by his son Commodus upon the emperor's death in 180.[26]

It is impossible to quantify the magnitude of the endemic threat on the Danube that became manifest after 166. In the fragmentary sources describing the period, there is, for example, a reference to 6,000 Langobardi and Obii who broke into Pannonia, having breached the Danubian *limes*.[27] A legion with its auxiliaries could easily defeat such a force, if only the enemy could be located and constrained to battle. But the significance of the number is unclear: was 6,000 a large number or an average invading wave?

Fortunately, there is no need to quantify the change in order to establish that the overall threat faced by the empire during and after the third century was much greater than that of the two preceding centuries. The narrative sources provide enough evidence to show that the East German Goths, whose westward attacks had reached Tyras on the Dniester by 238, and who crossed the Danube delta four years later, were a much more formidable enemy than the Carpi and Sarmatians, who had been until then the major enemy in Lower Moesia.[28] Similarly, the Alamanni, whose attacks forced the evacuation of the Antonine *limes* beyond the Rhine and Danube by 260,[29] and the Franks on the Lower Rhine, who broke through the frontier *en masse* following the collapse of the Gallic empire in 275,[30] were clearly more menacing than their predecessors on those same sectors. Rome also faced the new seaborne threat of Saxon raiders against southern England and the Gallic coasts, whose depredations, based on the evidence of their coin hoards, seem to have become intense over the years 268–82.[31]

Sea raids were not unknown in the first and second centuries, but they had been limited and localized. The new seaborne incursions of Franks and Saxons in the Channel and of Goths, Heruli, and associated peoples in the Black Sea and the eastern Mediterranean were qualitatively different: from about 253 until about 269 Goths and Heruli ravaged, first, the Black Sea coasts and, later, the Aegean in a crescendo of raiding expeditions, often leaving their boats to penetrate deep inland.[32] In the process, productive lands were devastated, and many important cities were attacked, sacked, and sometimes utterly destroyed: Pityus in the first wave of sea raids in 253, Trapezus and other Pontic cities in 254 or 255, Chalcedon and Nicomedia as well as other Bithynian cities in 256, when the raiders sailed through the Hellespont into the Aegean.[33] After almost a decade of lesser attacks in 266 and 267, Goths, Heruli, and their allies again raided Thrace, Macedonia, Greece, and Asia Minor in large combined expeditions at sea, while attacks also continued on land.[34] Among many cities large and small, Athens, still a place of importance but, like the others, virtually undefended, fell to Herulian sea raiders in 267. In one of the famous episodes of both history and historiography, Dexippus rallied 2,000 Athenians to fight the Heruli,[35] but the city had already fallen; it was not to recover until the fifth century.[36]

From the strategic point of view, the security problem presented by the new seaborne threat was immense. The incremental cost to the empire of providing a *land*-based defense of 3,000 miles of coastline against sea raids was disproportionate to the magnitude of the threat.[37] Moreover, while in the Black Sea or the Mediterranean naval supremacy could ensure security on land, this was not true of the open sea north of the Channel. A few thousand sea raiders could inflict more damage, and cause more costly countermeasures to be adopted, than could twice or several times their number on land. An entirely new coastal defense organization had to be created for the "Saxon shore" in Britain and northwest Gaul. (A *Comes Litoris Saxonici per Britanniam* is found in charge of sector defenses in the *Notitia Dignitatum*.)[38]

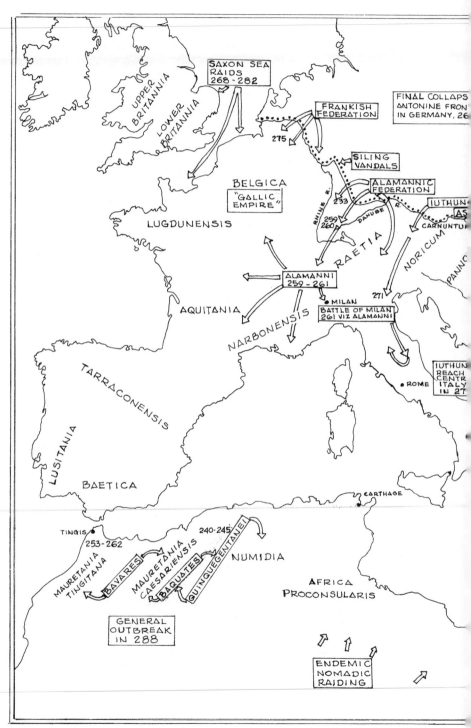

MAP 3.1. THE GREAT CRISIS OF THE THIRD CENTURY

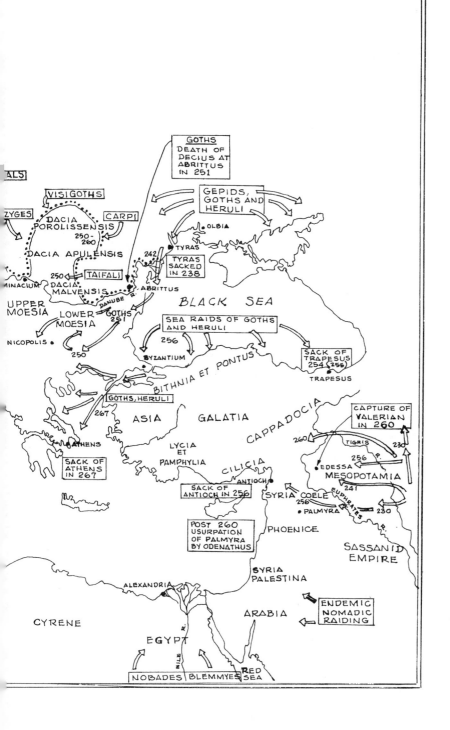

GOTHS
DEATH OF
DECIUS AT
ABRITTUS
IN 251

VISIGOTHS

GEPIDS,
GOTHS AND
HERULI

ALS

ZYGES

DACIA
POROLISSENSIS

CARPI

250-
260

DACIA APULENSIS

OLBIA

242

TYRAS

250

TAIFALI

DACIA
MALVENSIS

MINACIUM

ABRITTUS

TYRAS
SACKED
IN 238

UPPER
MOESIA

DANUBE R.

BLACK   SEA

LOWER
MOESIA

GOTHS
251

NICOPOLIS

250

SEA RAIDS OF GOTHS
AND HERULI

256

BYZANTIUM

SACK OF
TRAPESUS
254 (256)

TRAPESUS

BITHNIA ET PONTUS

GOTHS, HERULI

267

ASIA

GALATIA

CAPPADOCIA

CAPTURE OF
VALERIAN
IN 260

ATHENS

LYCIA
ET
PAMPHYLIA

260

TIGRIS R.

230

256

SACK OF
ATHENS
IN 267

CILICIA

ANTIOCH

EDESSA

MESOPOTAMIA

SACK OF
ANTIOCH IN 256

SYRIA COELE

241

EUPHRATES R.

256

PALMYRA

230

POST 260
USURPATION
OF PALMYRA
BY ODENATHUS

PHOENICE

SASSANID
EMPIRE

SYRIA
PALESTINA

ALEXANDRIA

CYRENE

ARABIA

ENDEMIC
NOMADIC
RAIDING

EGYPT

NILE R.

NOBADES

BLEMMYES

RED
SEA

The narrative sources give inordinately high figures for the size of the raiding armadas and warrior armies of the Goths and their allies. We hear of 2,000 ships in the Goth expedition of 267 and of 320,000 warriors advancing on land (across the modern Dobruja).[39] Naturally, modern historiography does not accept the accuracy of such estimates, though it is usually conceded that the dimensions of the threat were unusually large—much the largest facing Rome in the third century.[40] Only statistics that we do not have could *prove* that the threat had become stronger, and not the empire weaker. After all, acute political disarray is evident in the multiple and chronic usurpations that repeatedly disrupted the central power between the death of Alexander Severus in 235 and the accession of Diocletian in 284. There is also incontrovertible evidence of economic weakness and fiscal inadequacy. But the fundamental change in the external environment of the empire took place in the East, and its crucial significance is unequivocal. In 224–26 the Parthian state of the Arsacids was overthrown by the Sassanids, who founded the new empire of Persia.[41]

In a sense, the entire system of preclusive defense of the second century had been based on the implicit assumption that an essentially weak Parthia would remain the only power of significance in the East. Parthia was apt to contest Roman control of Armenia, but the threat it presented was sporadic: Trajan fought his Parthian war, and so did Marcus Aurelius almost half a century later; Septimius Severus fought Parthia in 195 and again in 197–99; like his predecessors, he won. Once Roman expeditionary forces were mustered and deployed in concentration, the Parthians invariably lost. Severus had, in fact, concluded his campaigns with the organization of a permanent *limes* on the line of the Khabur River, Jebel Singar, and east to the Tigris, garrisoned by his new legions, I and III *Parthicae*.[42]

In addition to being sporadic, the Parthian threat had also been limited in its geographic scope; there is no sign of an Arsacid program of conquest extending to Syria or Cappadocia, core areas of the empire. The strategic weakness of the Parthian state was organic: organized as an assemblage of semi-autonomous vassal states under Arsacid suzerainty, Parthia was inherently vulnerable to the divisive manipulations of Roman diplomacy and visibly incapable of fully mobilizing the considerable military resources of the Iranian plateau and the adjacent lands.

All this changed with the rise of the Sassanids. First, the new state was much more centralized than the old, having both administrative and ideological instrumentalities of control that the Arsacids had lacked—most importantly, a state religion.[43] Second, almost from the start Sassanid expansionism transcended the scope of Arsacid ambitions, which had been limited to Armenia. The first of the Sassanid emperors, Ardashir, like the more vigorous of his successors (notably his son, Shapur I, 241–72), was already aiming at the conquest of northern Mesopotamia and much else beyond. Until the final collapse of the Sassanid power in the seventh century, it was Syria itself that the Romans had to defend from the "Kings of Kings of Iran and non-Iran,"[44] as the rulers styled themselves after the title of Shapur I, the conqueror. A third and important difference between the Arsacid and Sassanid threats was tactical. It is apparent that under the Sassanids, the combined light and heavy cavalry tactics of the Arsacids were generally improved, but the real difference was that the Sassanids, unlike the Arsacids, developed an adequate siege-warfare technology.[45] Given the character of war in the East, which essentially amounted to cavalry skirmishing and rare cavalry battles followed by siege operations, the new siege capabilities of the Sassanid armies were of obvious importance.

A bare chronology suffices to illustrate the continuity of the Sassanid threat. In 230 Ardashir attacked imperial territory in northern Mesopotamia after an unsuccessful offensive against Armenia (then ruled by an Arsacid client king of the empire). Severus Alexander responded by taking an army to the East that won some battles and lost more, but succeeded nevertheless in restoring the *status quo ante* by 233.[46] In 241 the Sassanids were more succesful, overrunning northern Mesopotamia, including both Nisibis and Carrhae, and conquering territory as far west as Antioch.[47] The Romans launched a counteroffensive (nominally under the command of Gordian III) in 242–43, but this did not result in a restoration of the *status quo*. In the peace treaty of 244, concluded by Gordian's successor, Philip the Arab, Edessa and the entire client state of Osrhoëne around it were lost; its vassal king, Abgar XI, took refuge in Rome. The Persian threat remained quiescent until 252, when Shapur I launched the first of his great offensives; warfare was thereafter intermittent. Roman fortunes reached their nadir in 260, when Valerian was captured at Edessa, to remain until death in Persian captivity.[48]

Ultimately, the third-century Sassanid attempt to drive the frontier of the empire back into Syria failed. The campaigns of the great soldier-emperors, Aurelian and Carus, and later Galerius, reestablished Roman predominance in the region decisively by the end of the century. The peace agreement of 298 confirmed Roman suzerainty over Armenia and set the border on the Khabur River-Singara-Lake Van line. There the frontier was to remain in peace and war until

Jovian's treaty with Shapur II in 363, whereby northern Mesopotamia, including Nisibis, was finally ceded to the Persians.[49]

But the total effect of Sassanid pressure upon the empire was altogether more disastrous than these territorial changes would suggest. In fact, once the heightened threat in the East became manifest, the entire system of preclusive defense became unbalanced. Because of the system's limited supply of *disposable* mobile forces, it was essential that threats on any given sector be successfully dealt with before new ones emerged elsewhere. Legionary *vexillationes* and auxiliary troops concentrated on the Rhine could be redeployed on the middle Danube in a matter of weeks; assuming an eight-hour marching day at three m.p.h., unburdened infantry could march from the Channel coast to the Black Sea in less than fifty days. This meant that during the summer and autumn months, when organized tribal raiding was most likely, the same units could fight at opposite ends of the empire's European frontier during the same campaign season. Not so for troops committed to northern Mesopotamia, regardless of how successful their campaigning might be. Due to the greater distance, the systemic costs of warfare against Persia were out of proportion to the size of the forces involved, large though these numbers must have been.

The threat on the Rhine and Danube was endemic, but it was not until the emergence of an equally endemic threat in the East that the overall burden on the disposable forces of the empire became overwhelming. From then on, simultaneous pressures on distant sectors ceased to be a rare contingency and became normal. Thus, major Alammanic attacks on the Upper German-Raetian frontiers in 233 (the destruction of several frontier forts is attested)[50] coincided with the conclusion of the Roman counteroffensive against Ardashir, first of the Sassanids. Similarly, the final collapse of the overland frontier between the Rhine and the Danube took place (by 260)[51] at a time of maximal pressure in the East: Shapur's forces had taken Antioch itself in 256, while the sea raids of Goths and Heruli were at their height in Asia Minor.

There was a perceptible two-way interaction, intentional or otherwise, between the rhythm of Gothic attacks on land and at sea and the intensification of Persian pressures in the East. In 250 the emperor Decius set out to reestablish the lower Danubian frontier, and after driving the Carpi from Dacia Malvensis, his forces engaged the Goths who had penetrated into Thrace and forced them to raise the siege of Nicopolis.[52] A war of strategic maneuver followed, in which the Goths were eventually forced to withdraw northward into the Dobruja. It seems that a catastrophic tactical defeat then reversed an apparent strategic victory: the Roman field army under Decius was destroyed at Abrittus (in the central Dobruja) in 251.[53] In 252 Shapur opened a major offensive in the East. In the next four years came the deluge: Dacia was submerged by invaders, the Goths reached Salonika, sea raiders ravaged the coasts, and Shapur's armies conquered territory as far away as Antioch, while in the West, Franks and Alamanni were subjecting the entire Rhine frontier and the upper Danube to almost constant pressure. The attacks in the West culminated in 260—the year of Valerian's disaster, when Shapur's advance threatened even Cilicia and Cappadocia.[54]

New federations of old neighbors of the empire, like the Franks and Alamanni, relatively new arrivals in the immediate vicinity of the *limites,* like Gepids, Goths, Heruli, and Vandals (the Asdings opposite Pannonia, the Silings on the Main), and old established enemies like the Carpi and Sarmatians may have jointly constituted a threat greater than that of their predecessors; this cannot be proved. But in addition to the qualitative shift in the nature of the eastern threat, a qualitative deterioration in the integrity of the imperial leadership is also apparent. While some usurpations *reflected* breakdowns in security and did not cause them—since they were the acts of men who competed as security providers (or else were regional affirmations of the *regional* security interest)—others demonstrably *caused* the weakening of the frontiers. Frontier forces could be removed to fight in domestic struggles for power. Thus we find the stripping of the Rhine defenses in 253 when Trebonianus Gallus sent troops to fight Aemilianus; the campaign of Gallienus against Ingenuus in 258; and the redeployment of frontier troops to Italy by Postumus, the Gallic emperor, in 269.[55]

Owing to the repeated removal of *vexillationes,* legionary bases by the later third century probably contained for the most part old soldiers and those men otherwise unfit for duty in the field. It was not the Hadrianic system of preclusive security through a "forward defense" that was tested in the crisis of the third century, but only the empty shell of that system, stripped of its indispensable element of *tactical* mobility and deprived of its strategic elasticity. The Alamanni who broke through the Neckar valley and overran the overland *limes* of Upper Germany and Raetia by 260 were probably stronger than the Chatti whom Domitian had successfully driven beyond the Taunus, but it is certain that the imperial frontiers they attacked had become much weaker.

In addition to the diminution of the troops and the general lowering of their quality, there was now a functional dissonance between the infrastructure of fortifications, the strategy, and the

nature of the troops left to implement it. Static troops personally
attached to their sectors by virtue of their own local interests could
have been very useful indeed if they had been deployed in a system of
border defense organized to take advantage of their peculiar qualities. The frontiers, however, were still organized to support primarily *offensive* tactics, and were thus quite unsuited to their defenders.
The reorganization of frontier defenses during and after the third
century was therefore a realistic adaptation of system to resources.
Static and increasingly militia-like troops could not be expected to
serve effectively in mobile striking forces, but if provided with stout
walls and high towers they could be expected to hold out just as long
as the finest mobile troops. At the same time, of course, the quality of
the border troops was a function of the strategy, which now tended
to allocate the better fighting material to the mobile field armies.
Once the strategic change was accomplished, frontier defense tactics
had to be changed also: third-century border troops could not
successfully execute second-century "forward defense" tactics, but
they could be perfectly satisfactory in manning the *fixed* elements of a
defense-in-depth.

III
The New Borders
of the Empire

In the year 298, the great victory of Galerius (Diocletian's junior
emperor, or Caesar) enabled Diocletian to make a peace agreement
with Persia that was to last for thirty years. The terms were very
advantageous: the Roman frontier was advanced beyond Singara,
running due northeast of the Tigris and then west again, just south
of Lake Van.[56] This was a line both more advanced and more easily
defensible than the old frontier, which had been under Sassanid
pressure ever since 230 and which had repeatedly been overrun in
the troubled years thereafter.

In the East, and only there, the empire emerged from the tempest
of the third century with an enhanced strategic position and even
some territorial gain. The entire coastal strip running from Egypt to
Anatolia was once again protected by a broad wedge of imperial
territory hinged on the Khabur River-Jebel Sinjar-Tigris line in
northern Mesopotamia. As before, the Syrian desert to the south and
the Armenian highlands to the north were outside the frontier: if
held in strength, the northern Mesopotamian salient alone could
protect the eastern provinces from Persian attack and would also
ensure the subjection of the thinly scattered Arabs to the south and
the Armenian mountain folk to the north.[57]

Elsewhere, the reorganization of imperial defenses under Diocletian and the tetrarchy saw the formalization of losses rather than gains. The Dacian provinces beyond the Danube had been lost in stages, and under Aurelian (270–75) the frontier had reverted to the pre-Trajanic line of the river.[58] This was true in Germany as well, where the lands east of the Rhine and north of the Danube in Upper Germany and western Raetia had been abandoned and the frontier brought back to the Rhine-Iller-Danube line, by 260.[59] At the extremities of the empire, a similar retreat had taken place in Mauretania Tingitana, which was reduced to a semicircular bridgehead south of Tingis (Tangier) through the abandonment of the southern *limes* of Volubilis and of the wedge of territory due east. (The latter may have served to connect Tingitana with Mauretania Caesariensis and the rest of Roman North Africa.)[60] In Egypt also, the southern glacis of the Dodecachoinos in Nubia was abandoned, and the Roman frontier was brought back to Elephantine on the first cataract.[61]

Although these territorial losses reflected in large measure the force of circumstances, the tetrarchic reorganization of the frontiers also presents the unmistakable signs of a deliberate policy. It may well be that the Alamanni, Burgundi, and Iuthungi were simply too strong to be dislodged from the *agri decumates* and the entire Rhine-Danube salient, but it is also apparent that given a strategy of defense-in-depth, the Romans no longer found it advantageous to hold the Antonine *limes* that had cut across the base of the salient. The Taunus ridge, if securely held, could provide a strategic base for southward attacks on enemies pressing into the *agri decumates*, but it would no longer be very useful if the strategy involved meeting major attacks *within* imperial territory.

The same conditions prevailed in Dacia. There, with Carpi and Visigoths established in the Transylvanian highlands and in Wallachia, the Taifali in Oltenia, and the Sarmatians still in the Banat (but under pressure from the Asding Vandals established in what is now eastern Hungary),[62] it would undoubtedly have been very difficult to reestablish Roman control over Dacia (i.e., Transylvania and the Oltenia land bridge). But a strategic disincentive was operating here: the tetrarchic form of defense-in-depth was, as we shall see, shallow, and it did not require advanced salients. The legions and cavalry units of each province, reinforced, if need be, by expeditionary forces, were to defend provincial territory on a *provincial* scale. In contrast, the earlier "forward defense" system hinged on Dacia had been *regional* in scale, with the Dacian provinces forming a defended salient from which *lateral* counteroffensives into the Banat to the west and

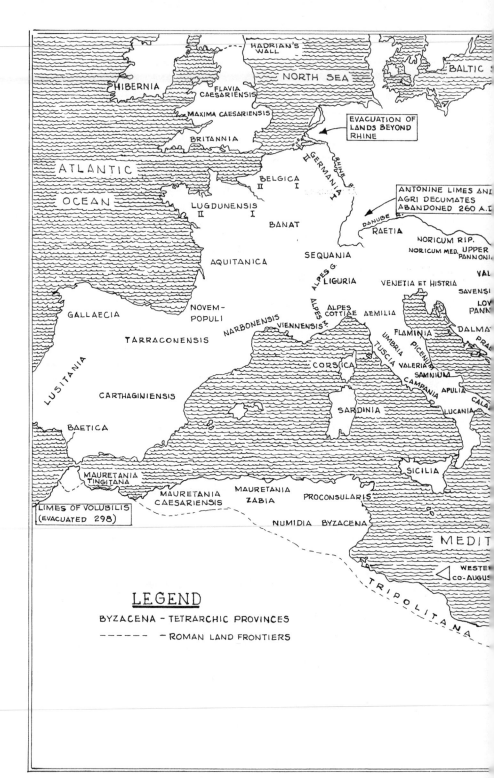

MAP 3.2. THE FRONTIERS OF THE TETRARCHY AND THE NEW PROVINCES

DACIA TOTALLY
ABANDONED—
POST 270

DANUBE R.
DACIA

SCYTHIA

BLACK SEA

LOWER
MOESIA

MAEMIMONTUS

PAPHLAGONIA

DIOS-
PONTUS

PONTUS POLEMONIACUS

ARMENIA

ARDANIA

THRACIA

RHODOPE

LOWER
ARMENIA

LAKE
VAN

MESOPOTAMIA

MEDIA

MACEDONIA

BITHYNIA

CAPPADOCIA

S
ETUS

HELLESPONTUS

GALATIA

TIGRIS

ADIABENE

THESSALIA

PHRYGIA I

ACHAIA

LYDIA

PHRYGIA II

ASIA

PISIDIA

CILICIA

OSRHOENE

CARIA

LYCIA
ET
PAMPHYLIA

ISAURIA

AUGUSTA
EUPHRATENSIS

EUPHRATES

CRETA

CYPRUS

SYRIA COELE

PHOENICE

AUGUSTA
LIBANENSIS

MESOPOTAMIA
RECONQUERED
TREATY OF 298

NEAN

SEA

ARABIA
BOSTRENSIS

RN
GUSTUS

PALAESTINA

UPPER
LIBYA

LOWER
LIBYA

IOVIA

ARABIA
PETRAEA

AEGYPTUS

HERCULEA

THEBAIS

RED SEA

CASPIAN SEA

DODECACHOINOS
EVACUATED—POST 297

Wallachia to the east were possible. Whether or not the new strategy was the right one to adopt from a conceptual standpoint, it is clear that its adoption would considerably reduce the military value of the Dacian salient.[63]

Such strategic conjecture can be validated with conclusive evidence in the case of the retreat in Tingitana. In North Africa, the recurrent attacks of the Mauri and the attacks of the Baquates in 240–45 culminated in a general attack by nomads and montagnards in 253–62, which affected Mauretania Caesarensis, Sitifensis, and Numidia—and perhaps Africa Proconsularis (modern Tunisia) as well.[64] Local punitive campaigns reestablished Roman control each time, but in 288 there was another outbreak affecting the region as a whole, and this time the empire could respond at last with large-scale measures.

Landing in Tingitania, directly across the narrow straits from Spain, Diocletian's junior Augustus, Maximian, brought an expeditionary army to North Africa, composed of Praetorian cohorts, *vexillationes* of the XI *Claudia* (from Aquileia), II *Herculia* (from Lower Moesia), and II *Traiana* (from Egypt), as well as German and Gallic *numeri*, Thracian recruits, and perhaps recalled veterans.[65] Operating in the grand manner, Maximian advanced across the full width of North Africa from Tingis to Carthage. There on March 10, 298, Maximian made a triumphal entry, after having defeated the Baquates, Bavares, and Quinquegentanei, pursued the Berbers of the Rif, Aurès, and Kabylie into their mountains,[66] and driven the nomad tribesmen back into the Sahara.[67]

Maximian's pacification offensive had been very successful, yet it was then that Volubilis and its *limes* were evacuated.[68] Here as on other sectors, there was logic in the unlikely combination of victory and retreat: victory had created the right conditions for the frontier reorganization dictated by empire-wide strategic considerations. Defeated, the barbarians could no doubt be reduced to dependence, and a buffer zone controlled by clients could be reestablished in front of the new *limites*. With so many tribesmen dead, the Romans might hope that the rest would respect the inviolability of Roman lands, at least for a time.

The retreat from the southern extremity of Egypt further substantiates the conjecture. In that sector, there *is* evidence that the new frontier line (hinged on the Elephantine) was protected by a client structure: the sedentary Nobades were established on the Nile in order to contain the pressure of the nomadic Blemmyes.[69] As before, a sound frontier was one strong enough to ensure the subjection of *strong* clients beyond it, clients who could reinforce the frontier by relieving Roman troops of the burden of day-to-day defense against low-intensity threats. The new strategy no longer aimed at providing a forward defense, and it did not even absolutely require a glacis of reliable clients; it certainly no longer required forward positions and offensive salients.

In the language of modern commerce, the frontiers of the empire that emerged from the near shipwreck of the third century had been "rationalized": exposed salients, topographically weak but strategically useful, had given way to simpler river lines in Europe and shorter desert frontiers in North Africa. It was only in the East that a forward defense frontier was reestablished, once again with obvious deliberation. Although, after a poor beginning, Galerius had outmaneuvered and thoroughly defeated the Sassanid army in 297, Diocletian contented himself with the old frontier established by Septimius Severus, except for the addition of some minor satrapies across the Tigris (for which the pro-Roman king of Armenia, Tiridates III, was compensated at Persian expense, in Media Atropatene.)[70] Notably, Diocletian refrained from claiming land due east of Singara across the Tigris and south of the Jebel Sinjar line, lands that Rome had briefly held in the wake of Trajan's conquests after 115 and that were the very embodiment of that fateful overextension. Here, too, the frontier was complemented by client relationships: with Armenia, of course, and with the Iberian kingdom in the Caucasus, which was already strategically important and was destined to be still more so, as the danger emanating from Transcaucasia became more grave.

IV
Walled Towns and Hard-point
Defenses

Rationalization was a necessary but insufficient condition for the implementation of the new strategy. Once Diocletian and his colleagues had restored the strength of the empire to the point that a *shallow* defense-in-depth on a provincial scale could be substituted for the deep "elastic defense" of the later third century, the fortifications of the frontier zones had to be changed. It was not enough to repair the fortresses, forts, and watchtowers of the Principate; mere bases for offensive forces were no longer adequate. Now it became necessary to build forts capable of sustained resistance, and these fortifications had to be built in depth, in order to protect internal lines of communication. Instead of a thin perimeter line on the edges of provincial territory, broad zones of military control had to be created to frame the territory in which civilians could live in security, as civilians.

An extreme example of this pattern was the province of Palaestina III (Salutaris), which included the Negev and the southern half of the former province of Arabia, and which was organized essentially as a military zone. There, the *limes* did not exist to protect a province, but rather the province existed to sustain the *limes*, which served a broad *regional* function in protecting the southern Levant from nomad attacks. Articulated in depth on the inner line (Gaza-Beersheba-Arava) and the outer perimeter (Nitzana-Petra), and extending south from Petra to the Red Sea, the defenses of Palaestina Salutaris were "studded with fortifications," all defensible "hard-points" built in the new style.[71] At Mesad Boqeq, for example, a typical Diocletianic *quadriburgium* has been found: it is small (22 × 22 meters) and has four massive, square towers projecting outward.[72] Water sources and signal stations were also fortified in the province-wide defended zone, and the few roads were also carefully protected. For example, the critical Scorpion Pass, which provided the main westerly link between Aila (Elat) on the Red Sea (where the legion X *Fretensis* was stationed ca. 300) and the north, was guarded by road forts at either end, a halfway station in the middle, lookout towers at the approaches, and a control point at the highest elevation.[73]

At the opposite end of the imperial perimeter, in northwest Europe, equal care was taken to fortify important highways leading from the frontiers to the interior. Under the principate, important highways had been lightly guarded by soldiers detached from their legions for these police duties (*beneficiarii consularis*).[74] But from the second half of the third century onward, both normal forts and small road forts (*burgi*) began to be built on the highways in the rear of the frontiers, as was the case on the Cologne-Tongres-Bavay road (which continued to the Channel coast at Boulogne),[75] and the highways from Trier to Cologne and from Reims to Strasbourg.[76] In the wake of the great Alammanic invasion of Italy in 259–60, which the emperor Gallienus finally defeated at Milan, and the invasion of the Iuthungi a decade later, which Aurelian crushed in the Po valley, the defense of the transalpine roads became an important priority. Its goal was erection of multiple barriers across the invasion corridors leading to northern Italy.

The effort, which may have begun in a systematic manner under the tetrarchy, was continued thereafter whenever there was sufficient stability for long-term investments to be made, as late as the latter half of the fourth century.[77] The barriers were designed to impede the very deep penetrations that had characterized the third-century attacks, such as those of the Alamanni in 259, which had reached as far as southern France and Spain as well as northern Italy.[78] Bands of pillaging Alamanni had then reached as far as Lyon and even Clermont-Ferrand in France, and down the Rhone valley and across into Spain. (Coin hoards of the period have been found in northeastern Spain.)[79]

At the initial breaching point the barbarians would have been concentrated and, therefore, formidable, but in subsequent forays they must have been dispersed. Hence the logic of the small road forts (and small civilian refuges), which could have been of little use in the face of a concentrated mass of barbarians like the one defeated by Gallienus near Milan in 260.[80] These road forts and refuges also provided some security from a new internal threat: bands of brigands (*bagaudae*), the product of a society oppressive and exploitative even in near-collapse.[81]

At the tactical level, there is a striking difference between the forts and fortresses of the principate and the strongholds of the latter empire. The latter are far from homogeneous, and within the period from Diocletian to the fifth century there are major differences in pattern. (The inadequacy of dating methods makes chronological distinctions difficult.) For our purposes, however, the entire period of late-Roman fortification, from the second half of the third century to the last sustained effort of Valentinian a century later, may be treated as a whole.

First, there is a difference in siting. While some fortifications were still built for residential and logistic convenience, i.e., in close proximity to highways and on flat ground, most late-Roman fortifications were positioned, whenever possible, for tactical dominance. The reason for the change was, of course, that the concentrated forces of the principate could deal with the enemy by taking the offensive, but the smaller frontier garrisons of the late empire would often be obliged to resist in place, awaiting the arrival of provincial, regional, or even empire-wide reinforcement. Accordingly, naturally strong positions were of prime importance. Examples of this positioning may be found in Basel, Zurzach, Burg near Stein am Rhein, Arbon, Kostanz, Kempten and Isny on the Upper Rhine and in Raetia. On the Lower Rhine, where the ground is mostly flat, forts were built on the few available hills—even if these locations were not otherwise suitable—as at Qualburg and Nijmegen.[82] This concern for easily defensible terrain is further manifest in the siting of the fortifications of the tetrarchic road fort and patrol system on the Syrian sector, based on the forward line of the *Strata Diocletiana* running from Palmyra all the way south towards the Gulf of Elat on the Red Sea.[83]

A second clear-cut difference is in the ground plans of late Roman fortifications. Old-style rectangles with rounded ditch defenses naturally persisted, since in many cases old fortifications remained in

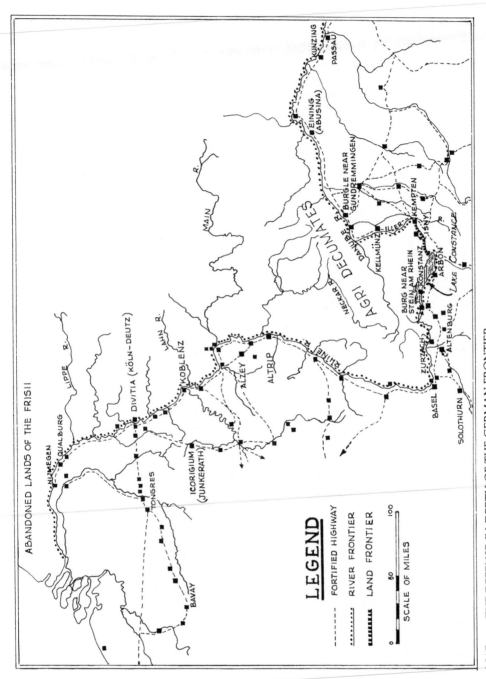

MAP 3.3. THE DEFENSE-IN-DEPTH OF THE GERMAN FRONTIER

use, but the square layout became predominant, together with irregular quadrilaterals (Yverdon), rough circles (Jünkerath) and bell-shapes—where the broader side rested on a river or the sea (Koblenz, Altenburg, Solothurn, Altrip).[84] The advantage of proximate circles and proximate squares over the older rectangular pattern is, as noted before, the shorter length of the wall circuit for any given internal area. The perfect circle—theoretically optimal—was normally avoided because it was difficult to build. The irregular wall circuits that were to become characteristic of medieval structures began to appear in places where the walls followed the irregularities of the ground—high, defensible ground, that is (as in Vemania-Isny, Pevensey, and Pilismarót on the Danube, among others).[85] This pattern also occurs where irregular river lines were used as part of the circuit.[86]

Another important difference is in the outer defense structures, the perimeter ditches and berms. Instead of the narrow, V-shaped ditches with narrow berms—only seven or eight feet wide—characteristic of first and second century structures, we find much wider berms, from twenty-five to as much as ninety feet wide; while the ditches, single or double and often flat-bottomed, were also much wider, ranging from twenty-five to forty-five feet or more.[87] Wide ditches served to keep the rams and siege engines of the attackers away from the wall. The Sassanid armies, unlike those of the Arsacids, were equipped with siege engines,[88] but the more important strategic change was on the Roman side: small garrisons were now to hold out on their own, and even the common run of barbarians who had never mastered sophisticated siege techniques were no doubt capable of using improvised rams. The wide ditches, then, were intended to impede the close approach of battering devices to the walls. These walls were made thicker, as well: instead of the standard five feet, late-Roman fort walls were commonly ten Roman feet thick, or more.[89] When older forts remained in use, the walls were simply thickened.[90]

The wide berms, on the other hand, reflected a significant tactical change. Research has shown that in the fortifications that Aurelian built around Rome, and in the late-Roman walls of Roman towns in Britain, Gaul, and elsewhere in the empire, the fire power of the defenders was now augmented with static artillery, both stone-throwers and arrow (or bolt) shooters.[91] By the fourth century, the legions had lost their organic complement of artillery, and aside from the separate artillery legions (mentioned in the *Notitia Dignitatum*), the artillery seems to have been used in large numbers only for fixed defenses (*tormenta muralia*).[92] Since these weapons, positioned on

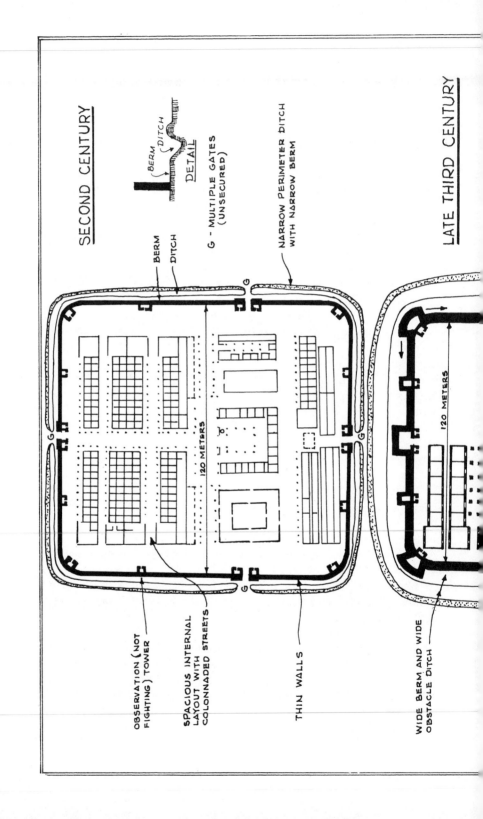

SECOND CENTURY

DETAIL

BERM
DITCH

G – MULTIPLE GATES (UNSECURED)

NARROW PERIMETER DITCH WITH NARROW BERM

120 METERS

OBSERVATION (NOT FIGHTING) TOWER

SPACIOUS INTERNAL LAYOUT WITH COLONNADED STREETS

THIN WALLS

LATE THIRD CENTURY

120 METERS

WIDE BERM AND WIDE OBSTACLE DITCH

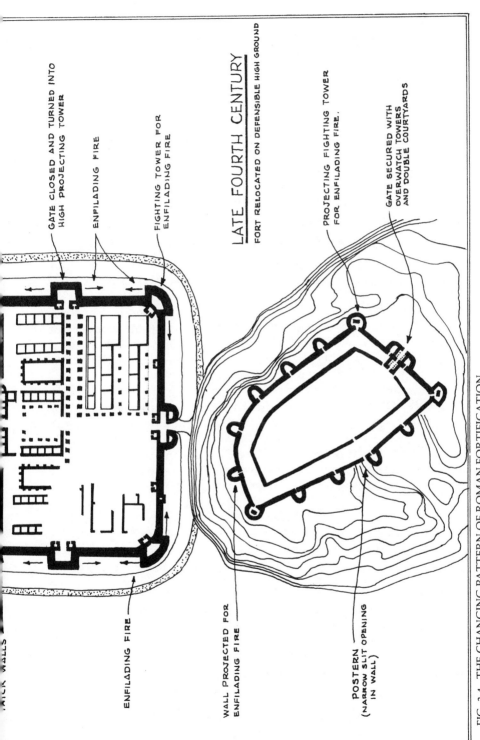

GATE CLOSED AND TURNED INTO
HIGH PROJECTING TOWER

ENFILADING FIRE

FIGHTING TOWER FOR
ENFILADING FIRE

ENFILADING FIRE

LATE FOURTH CENTURY

FORT RELOCATED ON DEFENSIBLE HIGH GROUND

PROJECTING FIGHTING TOWER
FOR ENFILADING FIRE.

GATE SECURED WITH
OVERWATCH TOWERS
AND DOUBLE COURTYARDS

WALL PROJECTED FOR
ENFILADING FIRE

POSTERN
(NARROW SLIT OPENING
IN WALL)

FIG. 3.4. THE CHANGING PATTERN OF ROMAN FORTIFICATION

towers and ramparts, could not be sharply angled, their fire could not
be directed down at attackers close to the walls. The broad berms
were designed to hold the attackers in an outer zone that could be
covered by overlapping missile fire.[93]

A more sophisticated device was an elevated floor-level inside the
fort; this was intended to counter mining, a technique that attackers
were apt to use when they lacked siege engines and when the defense
lacked the fire power needed to keep them away from the wall. Found
in forts at Bavay, Alzey, and Altrip, among others,[94] this device
suggests combat conditions akin to those of medieval sieges: an
offense incapable of breaching walls and a defense equally incapable
of striking at the besiegers, even when they closely invested the
walls.

From the third century to the fifth, the deployment of forces
evolved through several distinct phases, but it is clear that the large
and strategically concentrated frontier garrisons typical of the linear
strategy of the Principate were thinned out even while the size of the
Roman army was increasing. There were more troops than before,
but these were no longer deployed exclusively on the frontier line
itself. Hence late-Roman forts and fortresses frequently housed far
fewer men than their first- and second-century predecessors (the
outpost forts on Hadrian's wall being a notable exception). In any
case, when these fortifications came to serve as defensible hard-
points rather than as bases, the length of the wall circuits and the
internal area were reduced to a minimum. For example, Vindonissa,
first-century base of the legion XI *Claudia*, was abandoned ca. 100 and
subsequently dwindled into a village; ca. 260 an attempt was apparently made to recondition the walls of the spacious legionary fortress, but they were much too long, and the attempt was abandoned.
Finally, ca. 300 a new fort, small and strong, surrounded by a broad
triple ditch, was built within the old perimeter. At Abusina (now
Eining) on the Danube, near the eastern terminus of the Antonine
artificial *limes*, a small fort (37 × 48 meters) was built within the
spacious perimeter of an old cohort fort. And the evolution of the
fort of Drobeta is an even more striking example of this secular
transformation.[95]

Fighting towers, built high to enhance missile fire, located not on
the wall line itself but projecting outward, are typical of hard-point
defenses. Accordingly, the surveillance and decorative towers of first
and second century structures gave way in late-Roman times to
towers that took various shapes but almost invariably projected out
from the wall, in order to offer lateral fields of fire to cover
intervening wall segments. Fan-shaped towers, like those at Intercisa

(Dunapentele) on the Danube, and polygonal projecting towers, like those at Eburacum (York), were built, but round and square towers were more common.[96]

Under the principate, the gates of towns and fortresses were only meant to impress; in late-Roman conditions, however, gates became weak points that required special protection. Since forts were often held by small garrisons, and since static forces (which must often have failed to patrol aggressively) were vulnerable to surprise, strongholds were susceptible to sudden attacks, especially in places where barbarians were allowed to congregate for markets in times of apparent peace. Such considerations led to innovations in gate design: double sets of guard-towers (e.g., at Divitia, opposite Cologne); reentrant courtyards, where access to the fort proper is by way of a guarded internal yard (Bürgle, near Gundremmingen); masked gates, concealed by circular ramparts (e.g., near Kellmünz); and finally posterns, i.e., narrow slits at the base of towers or walls designed to allow the defenders to sally out unobserved; since the slits were quite narrow, they could easily be blocked by even a handful of defenders (Icorigium-Jünkerath).[97]

In comparing the ground plans of Roman and medieval fortifications, one finds the most obvious difference in the siting of the internal buildings. The standard Roman practice (well into the fourth century, it seems) was to separate the living quarters from the outer walls with a broad roadway (*via sagularis*). As in the classic marching-camp layout, the purpose was to protect the men on the inside from missiles fired from beyond the perimeter ditch. Although leaving room for a *via sagularis* would make the fort, and the all-important wall circuit, larger, this practice continued until the reign of Constantine, if not longer. (The fort at Divitia, mentioned above, features a *via sagularis*.) But from the mid-fourth century onward, barracks began to be built on the inner face of the walls, for added protection to both. This made for less well-lighted and comfortable quarters, but it was an economical way of thickening the walls. Thus we find the fort of Alzey, spacious but with built-up walls; the late Valentinian fort at Altrip, which is more compact; and the fort at Bürgle near Gundremmingen, which already has the internal layout, external circuit, and hilltop siting typical of medieval castles.[98]

The cramped quarters and irregular shapes of the new structures suggest that it was not only the tactics but the entire lifestyle of the soldiers within that had undergone a vast transformation since the days of the principate. This need not necessarily imply a decline in tactical effectiveness, for in the new defense system the functions of static and mobile troops were complementary. In fact, some static elements of the system survived in isolation long after the collapse of the whole: St. Severinus encountered the forts of Künzing and Passau when traveling across Raetia in 450.[99]

Once the frontiers were no longer defended preclusively, it became necessary to defend assets of value *in situ*, on a local scale and with local efforts. Just as the roads were secured by constructing road forts, everything else of value had to be secured also, or else it would be exposed to attack and destruction during the inevitable interval between the hostile penetration and successful interception of the defense-in-depth sequence. No volunteer civilian militia was organized systematically,[100] for obvious political reasons, and local defense essentially meant local fortification. Roving barbarian bands and home-grown marauders (*bagaudae*), unskilled and unequipped for siege warfare, could be kept at bay by stout walls manned by whatever stray soldiers were at hand, or by the citizenry armed with improvised weapons.[101]

Along with the undefended cities of the West, whose lack of wall circuits until the third century was evidence of both prosperity and security,[102] there had always been walled cities. In the East, wall defenses were the norm, since the *limites* were "open." Even in the West some cities did have walls long before any were needed. In Gaul, for example, the walls of Autun were Augustan; Cologne received a wall circuit ca. 50, and Xanten (Vetera) ca. 110, in the secure days of Trajan's principate.[103] But these walls were built either for decorative purposes, for the sake of civic dignity, or, at most, for police purposes; they were certainly not built for military reasons, and they were not meant to cope with determined attacks.[104] Hence the wall circuits were long and therefore difficult to defend; their purpose being what it was, they naturally enclosed the entire city and not merely its more defensible parts. The walls were generally thin, five feet or so in width; the towers were primarily decorative; and berms and ditches were narrow.[105]

After the catastrophic invasions of the mid-third century, all this changed. In northwestern Europe, in the wake of the breakdown of the Rhine defenses in 254 (when both Alamanni and Franks broke through the *limes*), and especially after the great Alamannic incursion of 259–60,[106] the cities of the Germanies, Raetia, and Gaul hurriedly acquired walls. These were very different from the previous enceintes. The enclosed areas were drastically reduced in an effort to achieve reasonable densities with the available military manpower: in Gaul, both Paris and Perigueux had walls enclosing less than twenty acres.[107] In addition, the walls became functional, i.e., thick and heavily protected. All available masonry was used: in the forty-acre enceinte of Athens, built in the wake of the Herulian attack of 267, a thickness of more than ten feet was achieved by filling in two wall facings with broken pieces of statues, inscribed slabs, and blocks removed from former public buildings.[108]

The civic structures built in former times of prosperity and security were sometimes incorporated in the new wall perimeters as complete units: a temple at Beauvais was used as part of the circuit, as was an amphitheatre in Paris and the main public baths at Sens.[109] In some cases even the cannibalization of the city infrastructures did not suffice to protect its core. At Augst (Augusta Raurica), which had developed as an open city with "fine public buildings—forum, basil-ica, temple of Jupiter, theatre, baths, industrial quarters, [and] public water-supply,"[110] an attempt was made at first to protect the entire city; but after 260, in the wake of the Alamannic incursions, the city was largely abandoned. A further attempt was made to defend the highest part of the plateau on which the city was built by cutting it off with ditches from the lower slopes and turning terraces into walls with cannibalized blocks, but this failed also. By the end of the third century Augst no longer existed, and only a small river fort on the Rhine remained.

Elsewhere relocation was more successful, but it entailed the abandonment of large fixed investments; the change sometimes reduced the civil population to its earlier, savage state. Fortified hilltop villages (*oppida*) had housed the barbarians before Roman power had arrived on the scene, and similar structures now housed the Romanized provincials. In the case of the Horn (near Wittnau) in Raetia, a prehistoric rampart across a narrow neck of high ground was refortified in the late third century as a refuge,[111] and numerous examples of private refuges can be found in Gaul, the Germanies, Raetia, Noricum, Pannonia, and Dalmatia.[112] Where the lack of time or of suitable defensible ground precluded the relocation of even a diminished city life, extinction followed. This was particularly true in the case of port cities like Leptis Magna, which obviously could not have abandoned the sea-coast even if suitable refuge terrain had been available.[113]

In some cases, cities were so reduced in size, and defenses became so elaborate, that they gradually became forts—or at least became indistinguishable from forts. In the East, garrisons had long been housed in cities, or rather, in specific areas of cities. Now the pattern became more general, extending from London to Chersonesus on the Black Sea, and from Regensburg on the Rhine to Tiaret in the Sahara.[114] Since some troops were simultaneously becoming part-time urban militiamen or static farmer-soldiers, there was an obvious and regressive convergence between civilian and military life: cities were becoming forts, and their inhabitants, involuntary soldiers on occasion; and forts were becoming towns inhabited by artisan-soldiers, merchant-soldiers, or farmer-soldiers. In the case of the *Limes Tripolitanus* (in modern Libya) with its *centenaria*—small fortlike farmhouses (or agriculturally self-supporting fortlets?)—the mixing of roles is complete.[115]

In arid areas, concentration was imposed on rural life by the water supply, so the conversion of rural settlements into defensible, fortified hard-points presented no real difficulty. On the other hand, where water is easily available as is the case in most of Europe, rural life was not naturally concentrated, but widely diffused. Its local protection, therefore, presented a problem that could not be solved economically. The emperor might have a wall built to enclose an estate 220 kilometers square,[116] but the ordinary farmer could not hope to enclose his fields with walls, and if he did, he would not be able to defend them. Private landlords were in a middle position. If rich enough, they could afford to build watchtowers to provide early warning of attack, and they could fortify farmhouses and granaries; if they had enough field hands, they could even organize private armies.[117]

The empire was primarily a supplier of security. Circumstances forced it to exact a higher price for this commodity after the second century, but the price need not have undermined the empire's worth to its subjects had it been able to continue to provide standards of security as high as the cost. The walled cities and the defended farmhouses of the late empire illustrate the kind of security that could be provided by a defense-in-depth, even a successful one. But in order to measure the true societal costs of the system, we should have to count the unknown number of small holdings in the open countryside that had to be abandoned. Cities, though walled and diminished, could survive, and so could the farmhouses and villas of the men of substance; it was the independent small farmer and the small estate that the invasions swept away in vast tracts of the empire.

V
Border Troops

Under the principate, the primary frontier-defense forces were the *alae* of auxiliary cavalry and the cohorts of infantry, later supplemented by the ethnic *numeri*. Lower in status than the legionary infantry, and less well paid, these troops were the principal active element in the system of frontier defense. The legions could not have played a major role in the forward interceptions and minor skirmishing that characterized border warfare, since they were not mobile enough for such tasks. The sort of mobility that border fighting required would have been a most inefficient attribute in the legions, whose chief functions were to stabilize the borders *politically*, by virtue of their commanding presence, and to guarantee the security of their sectors against the rare contingency of large-scale enemy offensives.

Units described as legions continued to serve in the imperial army until the fifth century and even later, but from the third century onward their importance in the army as a whole steadily declined. At the same time, the *alae* and *cohortes* as well as the *numeri* either underwent a gradual transformation into static forces or else disappeared suddenly in places where the frontiers were utterly overrun. There is much controversy over the timing and nature of this transformation[118] and its results.[119] One thing, however, is certain: in the course of the fourth century,[120] the full-time troops that had guarded the borders using mobile and offensive tactics gave way to part-time peasant-soldiers (*limitanei*) who farmed their own assigned lands and provided a purely local and static defense.

Since the thin line of auxiliary "forts" and legionary "fortresses" along the perimeter had gradually been replaced by a much broader network of small, fortified hard-points in order to support an evolving strategy of defense-in-depth, the fact that mobile *alae* and *cohortes* had given way to scattered groups of static *limitanei*[121] need not have resulted in a decline in the effectiveness of the troops. For the new strategy required, above all, soldiers who would hold out in their positions; only if these positions were held could a collapse of the system into an elastic defense be avoided. And men who have their own families and possessions to protect *in situ* should make capable defenders.

In modern times, military-agricultural colonies have proved to be useful and economical agents of border defense in places and times as diverse as the Transylvania of the eighteenth century, the Volga steppe of the nineteenth, and the Israeli Negev of today. In each case, self-reliant farmer-soldiers could be counted upon to deal independently with localized infiltration and other low-intensity threats, while being ready to provide *points d'appui* for mobile field armies of regular full-time troops in the event of large-scale war. In principle, therefore, there is no reason to assume that the emergence in the Roman Empire of frontier forces consisting of farmer-soldiers reflected either local degeneration, official neglect, or a politically motivated relaxation of discipline that went so far as to require of soldiers neither discipline nor training, but only their oath.[122]

Much would depend on the general state of society and on the overall security situation. Much would also depend on the quality of the supervision exercised over these farmer-soldiers, the *limitanei*. It is possible that under the tetrarchy, provincial troops (as opposed to the central field armies) came under a system of dual control, with the *limitanei* under the supervision of the provincial governor (*praeses*) and the mobile elements of each frontier province (legions and cavalry units) under the control of the *dux*, the senior military official (though both posts were sometimes filled by one man). This supposedly facilitated the localized supervision of frontier security and freed the *dux* from the burden of supervising immobile forces that could not, in any case, play a useful role in mobile warfare.[123] The state of the evidence is such that controversy persists over the entire notion of dual command.[124] *A priori*, it would seem that separating administration of the *limitanei* from that of the mobile cavalry *equites* and legions would be calculated to encourage the localization of the *limitanei* and the further degeneration of their military role. In order to maintain the efficiency of small groups of isolated farmer-soldiers, a system of regular and detailed inspection, as well as the frequent supervision of elementary training, would have been essential. Soldiers must regularly repeat fighting drills, not because they are apt to forget them, but because otherwise they will not use them in actual combat. But it is unlikely that the officials in charge, whether civilian *praesides* or military *duces* (or even a post-Constantinian *dux limitis*, whose duties concerned frontier defenses exclusively[125]) were adequately staffed to inspect the scattered outposts of the *limitanei* regularly.

The quality of the *limitanei* is also likely to have been influenced by the quality of the full-time troops stationed in their sectors. If these were well-regarded mobile forces who were always apt to be called away on campaign and were capable of fighting effectively, it is likely that some of their skills and even some of their spirit would be transmitted to the part-time farmer-soldiers in the sector. If, on the other hand, even the nominally full-time units had deteriorated into a territorial militia or simply into a static mass of pensioners unfit for serious campaigning, then the degeneration of the *limitanei* would probably be accelerated.

It is impossible to assess the quality of static border troops at different times and in different parts of the empire. Some *limitanei* may indeed have "spent most of their time on their little estates . . . and fought . . . like amateurs,"[126] and yet the particular *limitanei* so characterized successfully ensured the defense of a broad sector of Tripolitania (where no other forces were deployed) until the middle of the fourth century.[127] To say that the *limitanei* were useless implies *a fortiori* that the fixed defenses they manned must have been useless as well; this would apply particularly to the great complex of trenches, walls, towers, and irrigation works of the *Fossatum Africae*. Yet the records of imperial legislation testify to the great concern of the central authorities for the maintenance of the *Fossatum* as late as 409,[128] and only powerful memories of its effectiveness can explain the fact that in 534, following the reconquest of North Africa, Justinian ordered that the ancient *Fossatum* be rehabilitated and that *limitanei* be recruited and deployed once again to man the system.[129]

If one compares the part-time *limitanei* of the fourth century with the legionary infantry of the best days of the principate, the former may indeed appear grossly inferior and even useless. But such a comparison overlooks the fundamental change in the overall strategy of the empire, which now *required* that troops be static to hold fixed points in support of the mobile forces that were to maneuver between them. Training, discipline, and mobility were certainly required of the latter, while only stubborn resilience was required of the former. Their endurance obviously impressed Justinian, and it should impress us: remnants of a local defense network survived, even in much-ravaged Raetia, into the fifth century.[130]

VI
Provincial
Forces

Under the principate, all the forces of the army but for the 7,000 men of the Praetorian and Urban cohorts were "provincial" in the sense that they were ordinarily deployed for the defense of particular provinces. These forces consisted exclusively of full-time units, legions, *alae* of cavalry, *cohortes* of infantry, and mixed *cohortes equitatae*. There was neither a part-time border force of *limitanei* nor a regular mobile reserve, either regional or empire-wide.

By the time of Constantine in the fourth century the pattern of provincial troop deployments had been transformed: the *limitanei* had appeared and the auxiliary *alae* and *cohortes* had disappeared. Units described as legions remained, but these were evidently much smaller; they were no longer deployed in single vast bases but were fragmented into permanent detachments.[131] New types of units, cavalry *cunei* and infantry *auxilia*, made their appearance, both perhaps 500 strong.[132] Like the *limitanei*, all these provincial forces came under the sector commander, the *dux limitis*, but they remained full-time regular soldiers with a status between that of the peasant *limitanei* and the élite empire-wide field forces, the *comitatenses*.[133] This evolution, which was to result during the fourth century in a further stratification of the forces, itself began with a series of transformations originating in the third century.

Until the deluge of the third-century invasions, the legions had been the backbone of the Roman army, and their deployment had hardly changed since the Hadrianic era. At the beginning of the third century, the II *Trajana* was still in Egypt; the X *Fretensis* and VI *Ferrata* still in Palestine; the III *Cyrenaica* was in Arabia; the old III *Gallica* in the new Syrian province of Phoenice; IV *Scythica* and XVI *Flavia firma* remained in Syria proper; the new Severan legions, I and III *Parthica* (and possibly IV *Italica*) were on the new Severan frontier in Mesopotamia. XV *Apollinaris* and XII *Fulminata* were in Cappadocia. On the Danube, I *Italica* and XI *Claudia* held Lower Moesia; IV *Flavia* and VII *Claudia* were based in Upper Moesia; V *Macedonica* and XIII *Gemina* were in Dacia and I and II *Adiutrix* in Lower Pannonia; X *Gemina* and XIV *Gemina* held Upper Pannonia, while the two legions raised by Marcus Aurelius held the rest of the Danubian frontier, with II *Italica* in Noricum and III *Italica* in Raetia. The I *Minervia* and XXX *Ulpia* were in Upper Germany, and the VIII *Augusta* and XXII *Primigenia* in Lower Germany. Britain, now divided into two provinces, had II *Augusta* in *superior* and XX *Valeria Victrix* and VI *Victrix* in *inferior*; VII *Gemina* was still in Spain, and the III *Augusta* remained the only legion in North Africa deployed in Numidia.

The deployment of the legions had thus changed remarkably little from the time of Hadrian: the II and III *Italicae* had been sent after 165 to Noricum and Raetia, respectively, and the three Severan legions, I, II, and III *Parthicae*, had been added. These additions brought the legionary force to thirty-three units—possibly thirty-four, if the uncertain IV *Italica* supposedly raised by Severus Alexander in 231 is counted. One of these new legions, the II *Parthica*, was deployed in Rome, of which more below, and the rest were, logically enough, deployed in the newly conquered province of Mesopotamia—new legions for new frontiers.

This, then, is the structure that was submerged by the tempest of the third century. Given the multiple military disasters that ensued after the defeat of Decius in 251, we may presume that by then the legions had lost their legendary efficiency.[134] This must remain no more than a presumption, however, since we have no evidence on the magnitude of the threat, which may well have been far greater than that to which the second-century legions and their predecessors had been exposed. As we have seen, the *qualitative* change in the threat had certainly been most adverse.

Of the legions of the Severan army, only the VI *Ferrata* of Palestine and possibly the III *Parthica* of Mesopotamia seem to have utterly disappeared during the half century of travails that intervened between the death of Severus Alexander in 235 and the accession of Diocletian in 284.[135] More than a century after Diocletian, 188 "legions" of all types were listed in the *Notitia Dignitatum*, but this bureaucratic survival is deceptive. The large combat units of the principate had ceased to exist. The "legions" of the late empire consisted of perhaps 1,000 men in the mobile field legions and 3,000 or so in the territorial legions, and possibly fewer.[136] Moreover, their men were not the select and highly trained heavy infantry that the original legionnaires had been, and they did not have the equipment, training, or discipline to function as combat engineers[137]—by far the most successful role of the legions of the principate. Nor was artillery any longer organic.[138] In other words, these were not legions. Instead, the units were essentially light infantry formations, equipped as the *auxilia* had been, with spears, bows, slings, darts and, above all, the *spatha*, the barbarian long sword suited for undisciplined open-order fighting.[139] Clearly, such forces were not the superior troops that the legionary forces of the principate had been.

This decline did not occur suddenly during the late fourth century, though most of our evidence dates from that time. The legions that survived the deluge of the third century must have done so more in form than in content. Depleted through the successive withdrawal of *vexillationes* that never returned to their parent units, weakened by breakdowns in supply and command, repeatedly overrun along with adjacent tracts of the *limes* (and sometimes destroyed in the process), the legions must have been drastically diminished and greatly weakened by the time of Diocletian. Additionally, many of the auxiliary units, both *alae* and *cohortes*, either disappeared or survived only as *limitanei*, that is, purely territorial forces incapable of mobile field operations.

As a result of these changes, until Diocletian reformed the legions, the strategy based on forward defense could no longer be implemented (for it required a net tactical superiority at the local level), while a proper defense-in-depth strategy could not be implemented either, since the latter required a deep, secure network of fortified outposts, self-contained strongholds, and road forts. Inevitably, the only kind of defense that could be provided during the crisis years (ca. 250–ca. 284), was an elastic defense. While it would allow the enemy to penetrate, sometimes deeply, it would at least ensure the ultimate security of the imperial power (though not of imperial *territory*) if sufficiently powerful field armies could eventually be assembled to defeat the enemy, wherever he had reached. This could entail fighting Alamanni before Milan and Iuthungi after they had threatened even Rome. Powerful field armies including much cavalry were indeed assembled, and the imperial power thereby survived, but it survived only at the cost of abandoning civilian life and property to the prolonged ravages of the barbarians.

Diocletian was not content with this: his goal was to reestablish a *territorial* defense. This defense was certainly not to be *preclusive*, but it was to be at least a *shallow* defense-in-depth, in which only the outer frontier zones, not the imperial territory as a whole, would be ordinarily exposed to the ebb and flow of warfare. In his attempt to attain this end, Diocletian tried to curtail the dynamics of incursion and *post facto* interception (within imperial territory) by maintaining fortified bridgeheads intended to support the early interception of enemy attacks on the far side of the frontier.[140]

As already established, there were two preconditions for a successful defense-in-depth strategy: first, the organization of a resilient network of fortifications laid out in depth; and second, the deployment of sectoral forces sufficiently powerful to deal effectively with *local* threats. These preconditions were satisfied by a vast fortification-building effort that spanned the continents. "Quid ego alarum et cohortium castra percenseam toto Rheni et Histri et Eufratae limite restituita," cried the panegyrist, while the chronicler Malalas in the sixth century retained a memory of Diocletian's fortification-building effort in the East, a line of forts from "Egypt" (Arabia?) to the Persian frontier.[141] Modern archeology has substantiated the claims that the ancients made on Diocletian's behalf.[142] On three sectors the resulting structures are of particular interest.

The fortified *Strata Diocletiana*, built after the Persian war, between 293 and 305, reached the Euphrates from the southwest by way of Palmyra and provided a patrolled frontier between the Bostra-Damascus axis and the desert.[143] Upon this road frontier, the positions of three infantry cohorts (out of five) and of two *alae* (out of seven) have been identified.[144] Since this frontier had always been an "open" one, with no continuous barrier, the difference between the tetrarchic scheme of frontier defense and that of the principate is not readily apparent. There was, however, a basic difference, and, as we shall see, it concerned the relationship between the provincial forces and the *limes*. On the Danube, old forts and fortresses were generally rehabilitated and converted into hard-point fortifications, but in the wake of Diocletian's victories over the Sarmatians—now the main enemy on this sector—a chain of bridgehead positions was also established on the far side of the river, in *Ripa Sarmatica*,[145] to facilite anticipatory attacks. In Egypt, the scene of a major revolt ca. 295 and a serious attempted usurpation ca. 296, the reorganized fortifications of the Nile valley and delta provided the storehouses for the food and fodder collected by the tetrarchic taxation-in-kind with the protection of *alae* and cohorts.[146]

Egypt retained a special role in the empire, and it had a peculiar geography (there could be no normal perimeter), but it is nevertheless significant that *alae* and cohorts were assigned to the defense of food and fodder; it was absolutely essential that supplies be denied to the enemy and assured to the *mobile* forces of the defense. Ultimately, the entire strategy of defense-in-depth rested on this logistic factor.[147]

The second element in the tetrarchic system of defense-in-depth was the new structure of forces. Aside from the border troops, frontier provinces were defended by legions and by cavalry units styled *vexillationes*, probably of roughly 500 men each.[148] Both were permanently deployed in their assigned sectors, but as in the past, they could also be temporarily redeployed elsewhere in whole or in part, to serve in *ad hoc* field armies.

Diocletian, who subordinated his entire policy to the pressing needs of imperial defense and who turned the entire empire into a regimented logistic base,[149] used much of the wealth extracted by a ruthless taxation-in-kind to rehabilitate and maintain the legionary forces. A century earlier, Septimius Severus had already done much to ease the conditions of service in order to improve recruitment and raise morale.[150] Diocletian followed the same policy and organized his fiscal system in order to supply the legions through payments in kind (though not without also attempting to preserve the much-diminished worth of money salaries).[151]

Of the thirty-four legions deployed until ca. 231,[152] most had survived the struggles of the mid-third century. It is possible that as many as thirty-five new legions might have been added by the time of Diocletian's abdication in 305, for a total of up to sixty-seven or sixty-eight legions. The minimum estimate is fifty-six[153] (thirty-three Severan legions, six more attested legions by 284, fourteen attested legions under Diocletian, and three more that are conjectural[154]). The growth in the legionary forces was thus very great, for the legions of Diocletian were definitely not the diminished 1,000-man battalions of the late empire. Whether the legionary soldier remained a heavy infantryman and combat engineer is unclear, though the great amount of military construction under Diocletian suggests that he did.

The role of the legions was central to Diocletian's defense-in-depth strategy. While the new cavalry *vexillationes* were deployed primarily in the interior, astride important roads, the legions—as before—remained concentrated in the major defense localities. In front of and next to them there were the *alae* and *cohortes*, by now probably indistinguishable from one another, and neither capable of executing offensive forward-defense tactics. It is, therefore, apparent that the intention was to meet the enemy *inside* the defended zone, with mobile interceptions by the cavalry *vexillationes* and with blocking positions formed by the legions, who were still mobile fighting units.

In Augusta Libanensis, for example, the defenders of the sector fronted by the *Strata Diocletiana* included, in addition to seven *alae* and five *cohortes* along the road itself, two legions and twelve *vexillationes* of cavalry (described as *equites* in the *Notitia*). The frontage held by the static border troops could obviously be penetrated by a mobile enemy, and the *equites* deployed on important routes would therefore have to intercept the intruders in the interior, with the legions (at Palmyra and Danaba) serving as pivots and support points of the system.[155] In Palestine, five *vexillationes* of high-grade cavalry (*equites Illyriciani*) and four of local cavalry (*equites indigenae*) were in similar sector-control positions, obviously constituting a mobile deployment. Here, too, the single legion holds a hinge position, at Aila (near Elat), while seventeen *alae* and *cohortes* in the Arava valley form a chain of static defended points across this major theater of migration and nomadic incursion.[156]

This, then, was the basic defensive scheme under Diocletian, as it can be deduced from the *Notitia*. It is authoritatively accepted[157] that the *alae* and *cohortes*, now immobile, manned a chain of self-contained strongholds; that the *equites* served as mobile forces for ready intervention; and that the legions were still concentrated to form the backbone of the defense and provide its ultimate guarantee. This defense-in-depth on a provincial scale was therefore quite shallow: the fighting was to be confined within the single cells of the frontier sectors and penetrations were to be dealt with by the local forces, since no large (empire-wide) field armies were ordinarily available. By containing the fighting to the narrowest band of frontier territory, the defenders would limit its ravages and the empire would be spared the highly damaging deep incursions entailed by the earlier (and later) strategy of elastic defense.

It was seemingly under Constantine (306–37) that this system gave way to another, in which powerful mobile field forces were concentrated for empire-wide service, and the provincial forces were correspondingly reduced. This Constantinian deployment has been reconstructed from the *Notitia* lists for the lower Danube sectors of Scythia, Dacia Ripensis, and the two Moesias.[158] In Scythia, for example, we find two legions, a Roman and an indigenous river flotilla, and neither *alae* nor *cohortes*. Legions now provided part of the border guard; they were divided into permanent detachments, each assigned to a specified stretch of the river under a local security officer, the *praefectus ripae*.[159] Close to the food storehouses, centerpiece of all late-Roman strategies, we find seven cavalry units listed as *cunei equitum*, and eight infantry units described as *auxilia*, both new types of combat formations.[160]

The cavalry *vexillationes* were no more, evidently having been transferred to the central field forces (or reorganized into *cunei*), and the legions were no longer deployed as concentrated striking forces. Their status had changed for the worse: in the hierarchy of forces of the mid-third century, the provincial legions were qualified as *ripenses*, holding an intermediate position between the low-status *alae* and *cohortes* and the first-class field forces, the *comitatenses*.[161] The sectoral commander (*dux limitis*) was no longer the commander of the sectoral slice of imperial forces but only a territorial commander.[162]

Since there was no increase in the overall resources of the empire, Constantine's creation of the field armies could only have resulted in a weakening of the provincial forces. There was both an attested qualitative decline (indicated by the relaxed physical standards of recruitment[163]) and most probably a numerical decline as well. Although Constantine did not strip the frontiers of their defenders,[164] it is obvious that the provincial forces had to be diminished if the field armies were to have food, money, and above all, men. There was thus a transition from the shallow defense-in-depth of Diocletian's time to a deeper system based on strong field armies and rather weaker sectoral forces. (In the *Notitia* we find legions designated as *pseudocomitatenses* under the control of field commanders: these units had quite obviously been transferred from the territorial to the mobile forces [*comitatenses*] without, however, attaining the full status of field units.)

The process continued after Constantine. In the *Notitia* lists for Upper Moesia we find, it seems, the depiction of a post-Constantinian state of deployment: three legionary detachments are listed (drawn from IV *Flavia* and VII *Claudia*); but there are also five units of *milites exploratores* (*milites* being a generic term like "unit"), all commanded by prefects. It seems that all eight units are remnants of the old legionary garrison.[165] Having broken all ties with their ancient mother units, the *milites*, like the "legions," are mere surveillance and scouting forces (*exploratores*), presumably acting in support of the eight *cunei* of cavalry and eight *auxilia* of infantry.[166] The *cunei* at least may have retained their cohesiveness (and therefore, their mobility) into the fifth century,[167] while the *auxilia*, for their part,

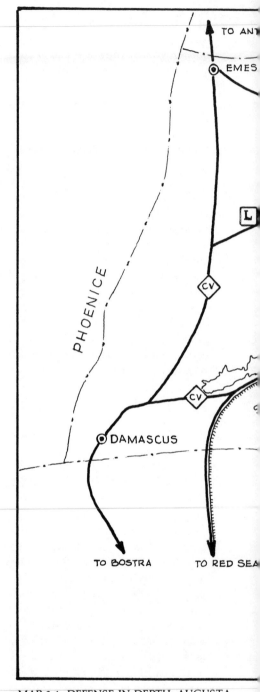

MAP 3.4. DEFENSE-IN-DEPTH: AUGUSTA
LIBANENSIS (ONLY ATTESTED UNITS SHOWN

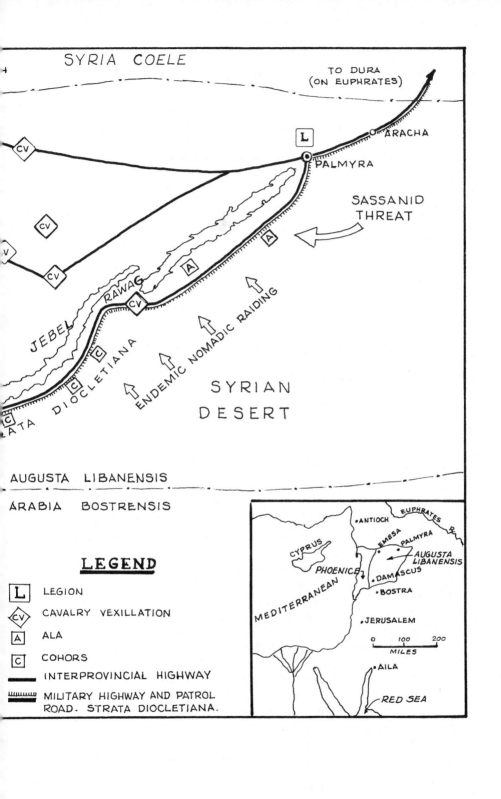

SYRIA COELE

TO DURA
(ON EUPHRATES)

ARACHA

L

PALMYRA

SASSANID
THREAT

JEBEL RAWAG

CV

A

A

ENDEMIC NOMADIC RAIDING

ATA DIOCLETIANA

C

C

C

C

SYRIAN
DESERT

AUGUSTA LIBANENSIS

ARABIA BOSTRENSIS

LEGEND

L	LEGION
CV	CAVALRY VEXILLATION
A	ALA
C	COHORS
▬▬	INTERPROVINCIAL HIGHWAY
▥▥▥	MILITARY HIGHWAY AND PATROL ROAD. STRATA DIOCLETIANA.

ANTIOCH

EUPHRATES

CYPRUS

EMESA

PALMYRA

PHOENICE

AUGUSTA
LIBANENSIS

DAMASCUS

BOSTRA

MEDITERRANEAN

JERUSALEM

0   100   200
MILES

AILA

RED SEA

may have assumed the backstop role of the legionary infantry, though of necessity in a much diminished form.

A still further stage of disintegration is recorded in the *Notitia* lists for the much-ravaged middle Rhine sector, where under the command of the Dux Mogontiacensis[168] we find eleven *praefecti* in charge of units that are mostly undifferentiated *milites*. One unit retains the mere memory of a legionary association (*Praefectus militum secundae Flaviae*); another unit's name recalls a function most probably defunct (*Praefectus militum balistariorum*). In the list it is clear that all are to be identified primarily by the place-names appended to the titulature—a symbol of the final localization of what had once been a purely mobile army.

VII
Central Field
Armies

If it were possible to create totally mobile military forces—that is, forces with a capacity for instant movement from place to place —then no part would ever have to be deployed forward at all. Instead, the entire force could be kept as a central reserve, without concern for ready availability and without regard for considerations of access or transit. On the other hand, if military forces are entirely immobile, the deployment scheme must make the best of individual unit locations in order to equalize the utility—tactical or political—of each forward deployment; and no forces should be kept in reserve at all, since immobile reserves can serve no purpose.

Not surprisingly, the strategy of imperial security that reached its culmination under Hadrian approximated the second of these two theoretical extremes. Even if their heavy equipment were carried by pack animals or in carts, the legions could not move any faster than a man could walk; in terms of the daily mileage of the Roman infantry, therefore, distances within the empire were immense. Since the frontiers *did* require the continuous presence of Roman forces to deter or defeat attacks, and since the enemies of the empire could not ordinarily coordinate their attacks, the deployment of a central reserve would have been a wasteful form of insurance: long delays would have intervened between the emergence of the threat and the arrival of redeployed forces. Better to keep all forces on the line and augment the defense of one sector by taking forces from another. Forces kept in reserve would serve no purpose and would cost as much as or more to maintain than forces in place and on duty. It is all very well to say that the Antonine deployment pattern was that of a thinly stretched line and to say that there was no mobile reserve

"*. . . prête à voler au secours des points menacés.*"[169] At the tactical level, auxiliary units and even legions could generally reach any threatened point of a provincial frontier in a matter of days, but a central reserve could hardly "fly"; it would have to march with agonizing slowness over a thousand miles or more to arrive at, say, the central Rhine sector from a central deployment point like Rome.

There is, nevertheless, one possible reason for the deployment of a centralized reserve even in a very low mobility environment: the protection of the central power itself. What might have been very inefficient from the point of view of the empire could have been very functional indeed for its ruler. Under the principate there was no central field force; there were only palace guards, private body-guards, officer cadets in retinue, and the like: Augustus had his picked men (*evocati*) and his Batavian slave-guards;[170] later, *speculatores* (select N.C.O.s) also appear in the retinue; and around the time of Domitian we find the *equites singulares*, a mounted force of perhaps 1,000 men.[171] By the later third century the retinue came to include the *protectores*, seemingly a combined elite guard force and officer nursery.[172] By 330 we find the *scholae*, an elite mounted force commanded, significantly, by the emperor rather than by the senior field officers (*magistri militum*), who controlled all the other central forces.[173] In the *Notitia*, five units of *scholae* are listed in the West and seven in the East, probably of 500 men each.[174] Private bodyguards often evolve into palace guards with official status, and there is a similar tendency on the part of elite military in the retinue to degenerate into ornamental palace guards. Another familiar pattern of evolution—palace guard to elite field force to field army—never developed in Rome, in spite of the fact that the Praetorian cohorts were from the beginning a much more substantial force than any bodyguard could be.

Formed in 27 B.C. at the very beginning of the principate,[175] the Praetorians were a privileged force receiving double the legionary salary, or 450 *denarii* per year.[176] In his survey of the imperial forces, Tacitus lists nine Praetorian cohorts, but their number had increased to twelve by A.D. 47;[177] one of the unsuccessful contenders of A.D. 69, Vitellius, further increased the number of cohorts to sixteen, but Vespasian reduced it again to nine. Finally, by 101 their number was increased once more to ten, resulting in a force of 5,000 troops, élite at least in status.[178] In addition to the Praetorian cohorts there were also the Urban cohorts, always four in number and each 500 strong, and the *vigiles*, 3,500 strong by the end of the second century. But the latter were freedmen who served as firemen and policemen, and they cannot be counted as soldiers.[179] Excluding the *vigiles*, there were thus a maximum of 8,000 men in organized units available as a central force. This was more than adequate to serve as a retinue to the emperor, but it certainly did not amount to a significant field force.

Even though there was a good deal of elasticity in the second-century system, it could not provide field armies for demanding campaigns. Hence, new legions had to be raised for major wars. Domitian raised the I *Minervia* for his war with the Chatti in 83, and Trajan had to raise the II *Traiana* and XXX *Ulpia* for his conquests; Antoninus Pius managed his not inconsiderable wars with expeditionary corps of auxiliary forces, but Marcus Aurelius was forced to form new legions (the II and III *Italicae*) to fight his northern wars.[180] Beginning in 193, Septimius Severus fought a civil war of major proportions; almost immediately afterward he began a major Parthian war. Like his predecessors, he did so with an *ad hoc* field army of legionary *vexillationes* and auxiliaries; but he found, as his predecessors had, that this was not enough: by 196 three new legions, the I, II, and III *Parthicae*, were raised.[181] No emperor since Augustus had raised as many.

Then came the major innovation: although the I and III *Parthicae* were duly posted on the newly conquered Mesopotamian frontier, in line with previous practice, the II *Parthica* was not. Instead, it was installed near Rome at Albanum, becoming the first legion to be regularly stationed anywhere in Italy since the inception of the principate. This, and the fact that all three Severan legions were placed under commanders of the equestrian class (*praefecti*) rather than of the senatorial class (*legati*), has suggested to both ancient and modern historians that the motive of the deployment of II *Parthica* was internal and political rather than external and military.[182] This may have been so; but it is equally evident that the II *Parthica* could also have served as the nucleus of a central field army. The new legion on its own was already a substantial force, more so than the total establishment of pre-Severan Praetorians, Urban cohorts, and *Equites Singulares*. But Severus increased substantially these forces: each Praetorian cohort was doubled in size to 1,000 men, for a total of 10,000; the Urban cohorts were tripled to 1,500 men each, for a total of 6,000; and even the number of *vigiles* was doubled to 7,000. Only the number of the *Equites Singulares* failed to increase.[183] There were, in addition, some troops, especially cavalry, attached to the obscure *Castra Peregrina*, an institution akin to an imperial G.H.Q.[184]

It is unfortunate that no coherent picture of the subsequent employment of these forces can be gleaned from the inadequate sources, but it is certain that out of the 30,000 men now permanently available in Rome and free of frontier-defense duties, a substantial central reserve could be extracted for actual campaigning, perhaps as many as 23,000 men—the equivalent of almost four legions.[185] This was a significant force: Marcus Aurelius took three legions with him to fight Parthia, and their absence from the frontiers may have triggered the dangerous northern wars of his reign.

It is in the most difficult years of the third century, under Gallienus (253–68), that we hear of a new central reserve, or rather, regional field reserves: these were cavalry forces deployed on major road axes such as Aquileia (controlling the major eastern gateway into Italy), Sirmium for the mid-Danube sector, Poetovio in the Drava valley, and Lychnidus on the major highway into Greece from the north.[186] On the basis of the scattered evidence we have, the outlines of a new strategy emerge: a defense-in-depth so deep that it is virtually an elastic defense in which nothing but the Italian core is securely held.[187]

The major instrument of this strategy was a wholly mobile cavalry corps, which appears to have been constituted by Gallienus, or at least increased by him. Aureolus served for ten years as its commander, fighting loyally against both internal and external enemies before finally turning against Gallienus in 268; the usurpation failed, but Gallienus was assassinated while besieging Milan, where the defeated Aureolus was seeking refuge. Significantly, his designated successor was another cavalry commander, Claudius, who was to rule for two years (268–70), winning great victories. Claudius, in turn, was succeeded by another and much greater cavalry commander, Aurelian, who ruled until his murder in 275.[188] Clearly, the existence of a mobile corps of cavalry unattached to any fixed position had great political significance: if its commander were not the emperor himself, he could become emperor, since there was no comparable force that could be brought to bear against a large, centralized cavalry corps.

Very little is known of the composition of this cavalry. It included units of *promoti* (which may have been the old 120-horse legionary cavalry contingents[189]), as well as units of native cavalry (*equites Dalmatae* and *equites Mauri*) and possibly some heavy cavalry (*Scutarii*).[190] It is also possible that under Gallienus the legions were given new cavalry contingents of 726 men in place of the original 120.[191] It was at this time that the term *vexillatio* underwent its change of meaning, for it appears in 269 with its original meaning of a legionary *infantry* detachment, but by 293 it denotes a cavalry unit.[192] The term must have initially connoted a mobile field unit *par excellence*, and it is easy to see the transformation taking place as the importance of the cavalry increases. In the celebrations of the tenth year of Gallienus's rule the new importance of the cavalry was given formal recognition: in the ritual hierarchy of the procession, it was given the same status as the Praetorian Guard.[193]

The cavalry doubled the strategic mobility of Roman expeditionary forces moving overland (ca. fifty miles per day against ca. twenty-five), but this strategic advantage entailed a tactical disadvantage: when the Roman soldier became a cavalryman he could retain no trace of his former tactical superiority. Roman cavalry fought the barbarians without the inherent advantage enjoyed by even a decadent legionary. Perhaps it is for this reason that the sources of the nostalgic Vegetius were hostile to the cavalry, arguing that the infantry was cheaper, more versatile, and more appropriate as a vehicle of legionary traditions.[194]

The history of the Roman cavalry records the consistent success of large bodies of light cavalry armed with missile weapons and the equally consistent failure of the heavy cavalry equipped with shock weapons.[195] Nevertheless, under Trajan a milliary unit of heavy lancers (*Ala I Ulpia Contariorum Miliaria*) had already appeared; and even earlier, Josephus had described a weapon of Vespasian's cavalry in Judea (ca. 68) as a *kontos*, i.e., a heavy lance, the characteristic weapon of the heavy cavalry.[196] This cavalry had no body armor; however, the first unit of *armored* cavalry appears in Hadrian's time, with an *Ala I Gallorum et Pannoniorum Catafractata*, a designation that describes mailed cavalry with little rigid armor.[197] The heavy cavalry had been the leading force of the Parthians, and it was also the leading force of the Sassanid armies. But their heavy cavalry was fully protected with rigid armor, and the horses were partly armored as well, in the familiar manner of late-medieval knights. Roman troops nicknamed them *clibanarii* (bread-ovens), and they certainly could not have had an easy time of it in the heat of the Syrian desert.[198]

Late in 271, Aurelian sailed east to destroy the power of Palmyra with a force of legionary detachments, Praetorian cohorts, and above all, light cavalry of Moorish and Dalmatian origin.[199] First by the Orontes River and then at Emesa,[200] Aurelian soundly defeated the Palmyrans, using the same tactic on both occasions: the light and unencumbered native horse retreated and the enemy *clibanarii* pursued—until they were exhausted. Then the real fighting began. Later, when Persian forces intervened to take the Romans besieging Palmyra in the flank, they were defeated in turn with the same tactics. In spite of this ample demonstration of the superiority of light cavalry over armored horsemen *if supported by steady infantry*, units of *clibanarii* began to appear in the Roman army: nine are listed in the

Notitia Dignitatum, including a unit described as *equites sagittarii clibanarii* (i.e., armored mounted archers)—most likely a decorative but ineffectual combination of light weaponry and heavy armor.[201] The combat record of this armored cavalry was dismal.[202]

There was no room for an unattached cavalry corps in Diocletian's scheme of shallow defense-in-depth. Strategically, it had been the natural instrument of an "elastic defense," while on the political level its very existence was destabilizing. But Diocletian did not need to dissolve the cavalry corps, for it had probably already disappeared.[203] It remains uncertain whether the Moorish and Dalmatian *equites* were disbanded by Aurelian after his victory over Palmyra in order to garrison the disorganized eastern frontiers—or whether Diocletian himself disbanded them.[204] The *promoti* may have been attached to the legions once again, though the link may have been only administrative.[205]

The question of the deployment of the cavalry under Diocletian is directly connected with a broader, more important, and much more controversial issue—the deployment of a field army as such. The orthodox view has been that Diocletian and his colleagues created or expanded the *sacer comitatus* (i.e., the field escort of the emperors), replacing the improvised field forces of their predecessors with standing field armies and creating the dual structure of static border troops (*limitanei*) and field forces (*comitatenses*) that characterized the army of the late empire. According to this approach, Constantine merely perfected the change by adding a command structure a generation later.[206] The *sacer comitatus* would thus have amounted to a field army and would have been much more than a bodyguard, since (1) it was of substantial size, and (2) it was not uniform in composition, as the old Praetorian cohorts had been. It included the latter, whose number was, however, reduced;[207] *lanciarii,* elite infantry selected from the legions;[208] cavalry units, called *comites*; the prestigious Moorish cavalry; select new legions (*Ioviani* and *Herculiani*); and possibly cavalry *promoti.*[209]

In the other, less traditional view, which was advanced earlier in the century and then rejected,[210] the argument was that the *sacer comitatus* was nothing more than the traditional escort of the emperors and not a field army or even the nucleus of one. It was held that Diocletian had expanded the army, doubling it in size, but it was Constantine who had removed large numbers of troops from the frontier sectors to form his central field force of *comitatenses*. Recently restated in a monographic study of considerable authority,[211] which has been criticized[212] but also authoritatively accepted, at least in great part,[213] this view now seems persuasive. The controversy over the authorship of the reform is still unresolved, for doubts on subordinate but important questions remain.[214] There is no doubt, however, that it was Constantine who created the new commands of the standing field army, the *magister peditum* of the infantry and the *magister equitum* of the cavalry.[215]

In any event, by the first decades of the fourth century the dual army structure was in existence, with *limitanei* and provincial troops on the border under the control of sector commanders (*duces*), and with centralized field forces under the emperor and his *magistri*. The subsequent evolution of the dual army structure was predictable. In the *Notitia*, there are forty-eight legions listed as *pseudocomitatenses*, indicating that they were transferred into the field army after having served as provincial forces.[216] When Constantine formed, or at least enlarged, his field army, he did raise some new units, including the *auxilia*,[217] but he must also have considerably weakened the provincial forces in order to augment his field forces. This was no doubt the transfer of troops from the frontiers to the cities that the fifth century historian, Zosimus, however prejudiced by his anti-Christian sentiments, rightly criticized.[218] It is probable that during the late fourth century the *comitatenses* grew steadily in size at the expense of the provincial forces (now all called *limitanei*), whose relative status and privileges continued to decline.[219]

VIII
Conclusion

It is apparent that reductions made in the provincial forces that guarded the frontiers in order to strengthen the central field armies would always serve to provide political security for the imperial power, but they must inevitably have downgraded the day-to-day security of the common people. In the very late stages of imperial devolution in the West, it is not unusual to find the frontiers stripped wholesale of their remaining garrisons to augment central field forces, as happened in 406 under Stilicho, who was engaging in internal warfare.[220] In such cases, the frontier was seemingly left to be "defended" by barbarian alliances,[221] which were hollow versions of the client relationships of the first century. Such alliances were rented, not bought; inducements could provide no security once the indispensable element of deterrence was gone.

The lists of the *Notitia Dignitatum*, whatever their exact date, give some notion of the distribution of forces between the frontier sectors and the field armies, and several attempts have been made to quantify the distribution on the basis of varying estimates of unit sizes.[222] (See Table 3.1.)

Table 3.1
Distribution of Troops: Frontiers and Field Armies in the East and West

Number of Troops

	(1)	(2)	(3)	(4)	(5)
Western *comitatus*	—	111,000	113,000	123,800	94,000
Eastern *comitatus*	—	94,500	104,000	96,300	79,000
Total *comitatenses*	194,500	205,500	217,000	220,100	173,000
Western *limitanei*	—	200,000	135,000	138,000	122,000/130,000
Eastern *limitanei*	—	332,000	248,000	165,700	201,500
Total *limitanei*	360,000	532,000	383,000	303,700	323,500/331,500
Total Western	—	311,000	248,000	261,800	226,000/224,000
Total Eastern	—	426,500	352,000	262,000	280,500
Percentage of *limitanei* in West	—	64%	54%	47%	56-58%
Percentage of *limitanei* in East	—	78%	70%	63%	72%
Total troops, East and West	554,500	737,500	600,000	523,800	496,500/504,500
Percentage of *limitanei* in total	65%	72%	64%	58%	65%–

Source: (1) T. Mommsen, "Das römische Militärwesen seit Diocletian," *Hermes* 24 (1889): 263 cited in Clemente, *La Notitia Dignitatum*, p. 156, n. 71; (2) Nischer, "Army Reforms of Diocletian and Constantine," p. 54; (3) Jones, *Later Roman Empire*, vol. 3, table 15, pp. 379–80; (4) Várady, "New Evidences on Some Problems of Late Roman Military Organization," p. 360; (5) J. Szilágyi, "Les Variations des centres de prépondérance militaire dans les provinces frontières de l'empire romain," *Acta Antiqua Academiae Scientarum Hungaricae* 2(1953): 217.

These estimates, so widely different in authority and reasoning (they reflect, *inter alia*, different datings of the *Notitia*) have one thing in common: in each case the percentage of *limitanei* is a substantially higher figure for the East, which survived the fifth century crisis, than for the West, which did not. The implication is obvious, and so is its relationship to the argument made here as to the strategic worth of reserve forces in a very low mobility environment. The fact that the enemies of the empire could not have been significantly more mobile is irrelevant. Since the external threat was uncoordinated, *relative* mobility was unimportant. What mattered was the *absolute* mobility of Roman forces deployed in the rear, which was much too low to justify the dual system on military grounds.

Septimius Severus commanded his armies against both internal and external enemies in both East and West once he became emperor, even though he had no experience of active duty until he came to power. Again the implication is clear: "The example of Severus became a rule to which there could be no exceptions. The emperor must command his armies in the field, whatever his age or his personal inclinations—and if he was unsuccessful, a better general would be put in his place."[223] The field armies of the later empire were much larger than those of the principate, but even when distributed in regional reserves the *comitatenses* could not hope to have adequate strategic mobility to defend imperial territory preclusively: the enemy could be intercepted and often defeated, but only after he had done his worst. On the other hand, the centralized field armies could serve to protect the power of the soldier-emperors who controlled them, and this was the one task that the field armies continued to perform effectively until the very end.

But the damage inflicted upon imperial territories, private lives, and private property was cumulative; it relentlessly eroded the logistic base of the empire and relentlessly diminished the worth of the imperial structure to its subjects.

EPILOGUE. *The Three Systems: An Evaluation.*

From the Constantinian version of defense-in-depth, with its dual structure of border troops and central field units, the stratification of the imperial army predictably evolved further. By the later fourth century,[1] we find new units, styled *palatini*, serving as the central field forces, under the direct command of the emperors of East and West; the *comitatenses* have become lower-status *regional* field armies, while the *limitanei* have sunk still lower in relative status. It may safely be assumed that this evolution caused a further reduction in the quality and quantity of the human and material resources available for territorial defense, both local and regional. Other things being equal, it must have entailed a further decline in territorial security, with all its logistic and societal consequences, manifest in the increasing weakness of the empire.

A triple deployment in depth would of course be much more resilient than any linear deployment, but this "resilience" could merely mean that the central power could thereby survive for another season of tax gathering from a population now constantly exposed to the violence of endemic warfare and the ravages of unopposed barbarian incursions. Finally, the situation could so deteriorate that in the fifth century an ordinary citizen of the empire, a merchant from Viminacium, could prefer life outside the empire, finding a desirable new home among a people no gentler than the Huns, in the very camp of Attila.[2]

Let us then reconsider the three systems of imperial security. First was the system described here as Julio-Claudian, but more properly perhaps to be thought of as the system of the republican empire. Around its core areas the empire was hegemonic in nature, with client states autonomously responsible for implementing Roman *desiderata* and providing out of their own resources, and through their obedience, for the territorial security of the core areas. No Roman troops are ordinarily deployed in the client states or with client tribes, but the stability of the system requires a constant diplomatic effort both to ensure that each client will be continually aware of the totality of Roman power (while being itself politically isolated) and to maintain the internal (e.g., dynastic) and regional (i.e., inter-client) equilibrium of the client structure. Client states great and small are thus kept in subjection by their own perceptions of Roman power, and this deterrent force was complemented by positive inducements, notably subsidies.

Under this system, the armed forces that the clients perceive as an undivided force of overwhelming strength are actually distributed in a vast circle around Rome. But these troops are still concentrated in multi-legion armies and are not committed to territorial defense, so they are inherently mobile and freely redeployable. The flexibility of the force structure is such that almost half the army can be sent to a single rebellious province (Illyricum in A.D. 6–9), without prejudicing the security of the rest of the empire. In the absence of such rebellions, this flexibility results in vast "disposable" military strength, which can be used for further expansion where the front remains "open," as in Germany before A.D. 9 or Britain under Claudius.

Owing to its hegemonic nature, the sphere of imperial control is limited only by the range at which others perceive Roman power as compelling obedience. The reach of Roman power and the costs of its military forces need not, therefore, be proportional. Further extensions of the empire, in a hegemonic mode, do not require increases in the military forces maintained. New clients added to the empire will respond to the same compulsion as have all the clients brought within the sphere of imperial control before them. Hence the economy of force of the Julio-Claudian system, and its efficiency. But this was a system whose goal was to enhance the security of Roman control rather than the security of the imperial territory and its populations.

The Antonine system, in use in one form or another from the Flavian era after A.D. 69 to the crisis of the mid-third century, reflects the territorialization of the empire and the reorientation of its priorities. Armed forces are now everywhere deployed to secure the tranquillity and, therefore, the prosperity of border lands and, *a fortiori*, of the interior. The military strength of the empire and its effective power are now rigidly proportional, since this strength is now largely used directly, not as a tool of political suasion. Clients remain, but they are much less useful than in the past: the task of maintaining territorial security is efficiently shifted from weak clients to widely distributed frontier forces, while strong clients can no longer be tolerated, since their strength may now dangerously exceed that of the adjacent imperial forces.

Nevertheless, the empire remains strong, and not the least of its strength is political. A real growing prosperity and a voluntary Romanization are eliminating the last vestiges of nativistic disaffection and creating a strong base of support for the unitary regime. Facing enemies widely separated from one another at the periphery, the empire can still send overwhelmingly powerful forces against them, since the tranquillity of the provinces—and, in places, elaborate border-defense infrastructures—allow peace to be temporarily maintained even with much-depleted frontier forces. This residual offensive capability is primarily useful as a diplomatic instrument, its latent threat serving to keep the neighbors of the empire divided—if not necessarily obedient.

Nevertheless, the cultural and economic influence of Rome on the lives of all the neighbors of the empire is itself creating a cultural and political basis for common action against it. Men who had nothing in common now acquire elements of a culture shared by all but belonging to none. Beyond the Rhine, the federation of border peoples that will turn them into formidable multi-tribal agglomerations is beginning. Opposed by the relentless force of cultural transformation, Roman diplomacy becomes less effective in keeping the enemies of the empire divided. And the system of perimeter defense, keyed to *low-intensity* threats, cannot adequately contend with their unity.

The third system arose in response to this intractable combination of diplomatic and military problems whose consequences became manifest in the great crisis of the third century. Under Diocletian, a shallow and structured defense-in-depth replaces the "elastic defense" of Gallienus and the previous generation, in which *ad hoc* field armies had fought agglomerations of barbarians deep within imperial territory.

Like the Antonine, the new system provides no disposable surplus of military power either for offensive use or for diplomatic coercion, deterrent, or compellent. The difference is that the third system no longer has a "surge" capability either, since the enemies of the empire are no longer kept on the defensive by forward defense tactics; instead, they are only contained. When the containment forces are reduced to muster *ad hoc* field forces, penetrations occur, and the Antonine remnants of a capacity to generate the image of power for the purposes of political suasion is irrevocably lost. It follows that diplomatic relationships with external powers must now reflect the local balance of forces—which cannot always favor the empire on every sector of the perimeter.

With this, the output and input of the system are finally equated. The level of security provided becomes directly proportional to the amount of the resources expended on the army and on frontier fortifications. The great economy of force that made the unitary empire a most efficient provider of security is lost. From now on it merely enjoys certain modest economies of scale over the alternative of independent regional states. And these economies of scale are not large enough to compensate for much administrative inefficiency or venality. In the end, the idea and the reality of the unitary empire is sustained no longer by the logic of collective security, but only by the will of those who control the imperial power, and by men's fear of the unknown.

APPENDIX. *Power and Force: Definitions and Implications.*

Military power is normally defined, in functional terms, more or less as ". . . the ability of states to affect the will and behavior of other states by armed coercion or the threat of armed coercion."[1] Such a definition clearly does not allow for any meaningful differentiation between power and force; indeed the quoted author immediately adds, "It [military power] is equivalent to 'force,' broadly defined."[2] It is apparent that the "power" manifest in the Roman security systems under consideration, as indeed in almost all other conceivable security systems, is a phenomenon much broader than force, even if force is "broadly defined."

Power itself, power *tout court* (but always as a relation rather than a unit of measurement), has been the subject of countless definitions,[3] including some so general as to define very little indeed (e.g., "man's control over the minds and actions of other men," in a popular textbook[4]). One modern definition analyzes the power relation in its components, treating power-in-action as a dynamic, manipulative relationship, of which power *tout court* is an instrumentality that includes diverse elements in a continuum from positive incentives to coercion.[5] In this fuller definition, voluntary compliance is attributed to "authority," while the absence of coercion or the threat thereof in *non-voluntary* compliance is said to reveal the working of "influence."[6]

Other modern definitions deliberately combine the notions of power and influence, treating both as actor-directed relationships,[7] whose nature can be viewed in terms of "intuitive notions very similar to those on which the idea of force rests in mechanics"[8]—Newtonian mechanics, that is. Not surprisingly, less formal definitions obscure entirely any distinction between power and force,[9] beginning (and sometimes ending) with some such phrase as "power is the ability to force. . . ."

Now these definitions may be adequate for a variety of analytical purposes, but not for our own. In seeking to evaluate the efficiency of the three systems of imperial security, we note first of all that in these, as in all comparable systems of security both ancient and modern, "power" as an aggregate of external action capabilities denotes the overall "output" of the system. (The output is power rather than security because the latter depends also on the level of the threat, a variable external to the system.)

Next, we observe that the efficiency of such systems is defined by the relationship between the power generated (output) and the costs to society[10] of operating the system (input). These costs are both the direct costs of force-deployments, of military infrastructures, and of subsidization, and the hidden costs that may be imputed to methods of *discretionary* defense (i.e., defense-in-depth and "elastic" defense), in which damage is inflicted on the society by enemy action that goes temporarily unopposed for strategic (i.e., systemic) reasons.

All else being equal, the efficiency of such systems must be inversely proportional to the degree of reliance on force, since the force generated will require a proportional input of human and material resources. In fact, the efficiency of the systems will reflect their "economy of force."

It follows that while in a static perspective, force is indeed a constituent of power, in *dynamic* terms force and power are not analogous at all, but they are rather, in a sense, opposites. One is an input and the other an output, and efficiency requires the minimization of the former and the maximization of the latter. Evidently we cannot rely on definitions that nullify the difference (in dynamic terms) between force and power, and must provide our own definitions instead.

Of course, the definition of force is by far the simpler. We know how force is constituted: in direct proportion to the quantity and quality of the inputs, whether these are legionary troops or armored divisions, auxiliary cavalry or helicopter squadrons or, at a different level of analysis, men and foodstuffs or equipment and fuels. We know how force "works": by direct application on the field of battle, or in active (non-combat) deployments. It is true that force also works indirectly (i.e., politically) since its mere presence—if recognized—may deter or compel. But the indirect suasion[11] of force, though undoubtedly a political rather than a physical phenomenon, occurs only in the narrowest "tactical" dimension.

Accordingly, while bearing in mind this qualification, we may treat force-in-operation as essentially analogous to a physical phenomenon, genuinely comparable to the concept of force in Newtonian mechanics. Both are consumed in application; both wane over distance to a degree that is dependent on the means of conveyance or the medium of transmission; both are characterized by perfect proportionality between qualitatively equal units. In other words, military force is indeed governed by constraints on accumulation, use, transmission, and dispersion akin to the physical laws that condition mechanical force.

How does power "work"? Very differently. First, it works not by causing effects directly, but by eliciting responses—if all goes well, the *desired* responses. The powerful issue an order, and those subject to their power obey. But in obeying, the latter are not the passive objects of the power relation (as are the objects of force). They are the *actors*, since those who obey carry out the required action themselves.

The powerful, who merely issue the order, only have a static attribute, i.e., "power"; it is the actor-objects of this power who supply the dynamic "energy" through their obedience.[12] It follows immediately that the physical constraints which impose a proportional relationship between the amount of force applied (and consumed in the process) and the results obtained does *not* apply to the power relation. One, two, or a thousand prisoners of war who walk to their place of internment in response to an order that they choose to obey do not *consume* the power to which their obedience is a response; in contrast, the physical removal of fifty demonstrators requires much less force than the removal of fifty thousand. In the latter case there is a rigid proportionality between the force-inputs and the output; in the former there is no such proportionality.

All this merely describes the power-relation without explaining it. Next we must ask why some men obey others, or, in other words, what the processes are whereby desired responses can be elicited in the minds of men, causing them to act in the manner required of them. Clearly, the actor objects of the power relation *decide* to obey; if we assume that they are rational,[13] their obedience or lack of it must reflect a comparison between the costs and benefits of obedience versus those of defiance. (This comparison may have been internalized into a mental habit, with obedience reflexive rather than deliberate. Such apparently instinctual processes merely reflect the ingrained results of *prior* comparisons of costs and benefits.)

At this point it would seem that power is easily defined as the ability to control the flows of costs and benefits to others, with force being merely a subordinate ability to impose a particular kind of cost through coercion or destruction. If this were indeed so, then our analysis would have fruitlessly returned to its starting point,[14] and the differentiation here being pursued between power and force would have to be abandoned. For it would appear that the "ability to control costs and benefits" must be subject to the same limiting proportionality between inputs and outputs as the ability to apply force, or force *tout court*.

But this is not so. The ability to elicit desired responses through the decisions of the actor/objects of the power relation is plainly *not* a function of the ability to control costs and benefits, but rather of the *perceived* ability to do so. In other words, the first stage of the power process is perceptual, and power is therefore initially a subjective phenomenon; it can only function through the medium of others' perceptions.

If power is in the first instance a perceptual process, then distance will not diminish it unless the means of perception are correspondingly degraded over the distance. A remote eastern client kingdom would normally be much closer to Roman realities in perceptual terms than would be the peoples beyond the Elbe, for in the East a Hellenistic civilization predisposed men to understand the meaning of imperial power, while no such cultural basis was to be found beyond the Elbe. It is true that repeated punitive actions (as well as positive inducements) could teach even the most primitive of men the meaning of Roman power, but in that case the "power" so validated would itself be a different sort of phenomenon: crucially, there *would be* a proportionality between inputs and outputs, at least as long as the process of education continued.

Perceived power does not diminish with distance, for it is not a physical (or quasi-physical) phenomenon. For the same reason, perceived power is not consumed by use. One client king or ten can perceive the same undivided power in the empire and can be influenced by it. Nor is the quantum of this power diminished when the obedience of a further dozen client kings is secured—by their own perception of this same power. Indeed, perception is one of the very few human activities (*pace* the romantics, love is another) that does not consume its objects, even imperceptibly. By contrast, force applied on one sector to impose tranquillity on one restless tribe is unavailable for simultaneous use against another, and any increase in the number of targets diminishes the amount of force that can be used against each. It is for this reason that the efficiency of systems of imperial security must depend on their economy of force. Or, to put it differently, their efficiency depends on the degree to which force is maintained as an inactive component of perceived power rather than used directly.

If one excludes for the moment consideration of all other components of power, that is, "static," perceived power, it may seem that once again the difference between the workings of power and those of force is inconsequential. For it is clear that in virtually all conceivable circumstances deployed military force will be the central ingredient of the overall power of states. Accordingly, it would appear that it hardly matters whether security is obtained by the static deployment of force-as-perceived power or by its direct use. Not so. Even if one does not take into account the actual wear and tear that force must suffer when actually used (casualties and matériel losses), force-as-power is inherently much more economical than force used directly, since it does not require proportionate inputs of force.

For example, a given perimeter may be secured by means of an active defense (in which case the forces deployed must suffice to defeat *all* threats on *every* segment of the perimeter) or else it may be secured by deterrence, for which one need only deploy a punitive striking force capable of inflicting greater damage on the values of potential attackers than the gains the latter may hope to make by attacking in the first place. Inevitably, an active defense requires altogether greater forces than does deterrence, for which credible retaliatory capabilities will suffice—assuming that one's opponents are rational *and* make predictable relative-value judgments.[15] In the first instance, security requires the protection of every single asset vulnerable to attack; in the second, it requires merely the *recognized* ability to destroy selected enemy assets and inflict unacceptable levels of damage. On the other hand, it must be pointed out that there is a qualitative difference between the security provided by deterrence and that provided by an active defense. The former, being the result of suasion, is subject to all the vagaries inherent in human perception and human decision; the latter, being physical, is definitive. Prudent men may well choose to pay the greater costs of an active defense for the sake of its reliability, which is independent of the decisions of other men.

This raises the entire broad question of error, beyond the specific case of cognitive time-lags. If power can only be manifest through the medium of others' perceptions, then the translation of the "objective" (and, by the same token, theoretical) ability to control costs and benefits into the perceived ability of doing so is subject to multiple errors: errors of physical perception, of the medium of communication, of cognitive processes, and also of communication between perceivers. A blind man will not be intimidated by the display of a gun, nor a bank clerk by a gun too well concealed, while cannibals ignorant of the chemistry of gunpowder may regard rifles as ineffectual clubs, or may at least fail to convey word of their lethality to other men who have never seen them. In such cases, it may suffice to kill one savage, blind man, or bank clerk to educate the rest, but the exercise of suasion will have been invalidated, since force had to be used instead. Nor will symbolic force suffice in every case.

Is power then merely a perceptual phenomenon, and politics nothing more than a particular psychological phenomenon—and a narrow one at that? Surely not. So far, we have implicitly treated the power relation as bilateral, with a single controller of costs and benefits facing—and being perceived by—a single actor/object of his power; even when groups were hypothesized, they were in fact treated as entirely monolithic, thus identical to individuals. But even if all politics could be treated as a sum of power relations, these relations would be for the most part not bilateral, but multilateral.

Returning to our example of the client kings who individually perceive Roman power and individually obey imperial commands, we note the implicit assumption that the client-kings do *not* also perceive the power of their fellow clients as being potentially additive and compare the sum total to the power of Rome. Had such a comparison been made, then the power of the empire would no longer have been seen as so totally superior.

It follows that the power relation between the empire and the single client king was only procedurally bilateral. In fact it depended on a variety of phenomena, most of them multi-lateral: the client's perception and calculation of his own power, of the power of other clients, of the possibilities of concerted action, of the risks, costs, and benefits of a joint defiance (versus the costs and benefits of obedience), and so on.

All these factors are conditioned by the perceptions of individuals and the decisions of (and between) groups—in other words, by all the processes of politics in their full diversity and inherent complexity. Politics in the round ultimately determines the relationship between client states and empires; most significantly, it determines the balance of power, which is a function not only of the perceived power of the individual units in the system but also of the degree of cohesion between the clients and within the empire. In spite of the importance of these complex relations, perception and the problems thereof remain central, and with it remains our distinction between power and force.

NOTES

Abbreviations Used in Notes

ANRW   *Aufsteig und Niedergang der Römischen Welt: Geschicte und Kultur Roms in Spiegel der neueren Forschung.* Hildegard Temporini, ed. Berlin and New York: Walter de Gruyter, 1974–.
BG   *Bellum Gallicum*
CAH   *Cambridge Ancient History.* Cambridge: At the University Press, 1923–39.
CW   *Transactions of the Cumberland and Westmoreland Antiquarian Society*
DE   *Dizionario epigrafico di antichità Romane.* Ettore di Ruggiero, ed. Rome: L. Pasqualucci, 1895.
JRS   *Journal of Roman Studies*
NH   *Naturalis Historia* of Pliny the Elder
REL   *Revue des Etudes Latines*
SHA   *Scriptores Historia Augustae*

CHAPTER ONE

1. Ronald Syme, "Some Notes on the Legions under Augustus," *JRS* 23 (1933): 14–33. See also H. M. D. Parker, *The Roman Legions* (Oxford: At the Clarendon Press, 1928), pp. 72–92. The major reference remains Ritterling's article, "*Legio*," in the Pauly-Wissowa *Real-Encyclopaedie der klassischen Altertumswissenschaft.*

2. For a brief summary of the evidence, see A. Passerini in *DE*, 4, fasc. 18, pp. 555–57, s.v. "Legio."

3. It is normally assumed that the legions of the principate had an establishment of 5,280 foot soldiers (nine standard cohorts of six centuries, with eighty men in each, and a first cohort with six double centuries, i.e., 960 men) as well as 120 mounted troops. (Ibid., p. 556.) A revised reading of *De Munitionibus Castrorum*, the prime source, yields a total of 5,120 combat foot soliders in nine standard cohorts and one first cohort consisting of five rather than six double centuries; see R. W. Davies, "Appendix," *Epigraphische Studien*, no. 4 (1957): 110–11. On headquarters' troops, see David

Breeze, "The Organization of the Legion: The First Cohort and the *Equites Legionis*," *JRS* 59 (1969): 50–55.

4. The basic work remains G. L. Cheesman, *The Auxilia of the Roman Imperial Army* (Oxford: At the Clarendon Press, 1914). A modern work by Professor J. F. Gilliam is eagerly awaited. See the recent survey by D. B. Saddington, "The Development of the Roman Auxiliary Forces from Augustus to Trajan," in *ANRW*, pt. 2, vol. 3, pp. 176–201.

5. *Annals*, IV, 5.

6. E.g., G. H. Stevenson in *CAH*, 10: 229; and Cheesman, *Auxilia*, p. 53.

7. Cf. J. Szilágyi, "Les Variations des centres de préponderance militaire dans les provinces frontières de l'empire romain," *Acta Antiqua Academiae Scientiarum Hungaricae* 2 (1953): 133, 147, 156. Szilágyi's sector analysis yields a total estimated force level of 325–356,000 men for A.D. 6. This decreases to 318–348,000 men in A.D. 20 and increases to 369–375,000 men in A.D. 46.

8. *Res Gestae*, 3.

9. *N.H.*, VII.149. See P. A. Brunt, *Italian Manpower 225 B.C.–A.D.14* (Oxford: At the Clarendon Press, 1971). According to Brunt, after the wars and colonization of Julius Caesar, the adult male citizen population in Italy amounted to roughly 1,200,000 men, of whom 900,000 would have been *iuniores*, i.e., the primary group of citizens of military age (p. 512). It is not surprising, therefore, that conscription was very unpopular (pp. 414–15); it was, in fact, abolished by Tiberius. As early as the first half of the first century A.D., one third of the legionary manpower may have been of provincial birth (though this would not exclude Roman origins and/or citizenship); see G. Forni, *Il Reclutamento delle legioni da Augusto à Diocleziano* (Milan-Rome: Fratelli Bocca, 1953), pp. 65–76, and Appendix B, pp. 159–68. Such conclusions are subject to the uncertainties inherent in very small samples; see, more recently, Forni, "Estrazione etnica e sociale dei soldati delle legioni nei primi tre secoli dell'impero," *ANRW*, pt. 2, vol. 1, p. 344.

10. See G. R. Watson, *The Roman Soldier* (London: Thames and Hudson, 1969), p. 92, for legionary pay and upkeep; on retirement grants (which could also be given in land), see ibid., pp. 147–53; on donatives, see ibid., pp. 108–14. For the pay of the *auxilia*, see Watson, "The Pay of the Roman Army: The Auxiliary Forces," *Historia* 8 (1959): 372–78.

11. Th. Pekáry, "Studien zur römischen Währungs und Finanzgeschichte von 161 bis 235 n. Chr.," *Historia* 8 (1959): 472–73.

12. *DE*, vol. 4, fasc. 18, p. 555, s.v. "Legio."

13. IV.5.

14. E.g., G. H. Stevenson in *CAH*, 10: 229; Parker, *Roman Legions*, p. 119, *et multi alii*.

15. E.g., H.-G. Pflaum, "Forces et faiblesses de l'armée romaine du Haut-Empire" in *Problèmes de la guerre à Rome*, ed. Jean-Paul Brisson (Paris and La Haye: Mouton & Co., 1969), p. 94. See also, retrospectively, D. van Berchem, *L'Armée de Dioclétien et la réforme Constantinienne*, Institut français d'archéologie de Beyrouth, Bibliothèque archéologique et historique 56 (Paris: Librairie orientaliste Paul Geuthner, 1952), pp. 103–4, whose argument, addressed at the army of the late Principate, applies *a fortiori* to the Julio-Claudian period.

16. G. H. Stevenson, *Roman Provincial Administration till the Age of the Antonines* (Oxford: Basil Blackwell, 1939), p. 102; F. E. Adcock in *CAH* 10: 598–99.

17. *Tiberius*, 16.

18. C. M. Wells, *The German Policy of Augustus: An Examination of the Archaeological Evidence* (Oxford: At the Clarendon Press, 1972). Wells's conclusions are summarized on pp. 237–46.

19. Tacitus (*Histories*, IV.23) makes this clear in describing the site of Vetera (Xanten), the camp in which part of one legion and the remnants of another came under attack during the revolt of Civilis (A.D. 69–70).

20. S. L. Dyson, "Native Revolts in the Roman Empire," *Historia* 20 (1971): 239–74, esp. pp. 264–67.

21. The characterization is that of G. Webster, *The Roman Imperial Army of the First and Second Century A.D.* (London: Adam & Charles Black, 1969), p. 52.

22. Wells, *German Policy*, p. 239. See also R. Chevallier, "Rome et la Germanie au Ier siècle de notre ère: Problèmes de colonisation," *Latomus* 20 (1961), p. 269.

23. See G. W. Bowersock, *Augustus and the Greek World* (Oxford: At the Clarendon Press, 1965), p. 66.

24. For the various meanings of *limes*, see G. Forni in *DE*, vol. 4, fasc. 34, s.v. "Limes," pp. 1076–83. For the meaning relevant to this period, see his heading "g" (p. 1080). For the transformation in the meaning of *limes*, see Henry F. Pelham, *Essays*, ed. F. Haverfield (Oxford: At the Clarendon Press, 1911), p. 168, and the discussion by A. Piganiol, "La notion de *limes*" in *Quintus Congressus Internationalis Limitis Romani Studiosorum* (Acta et Dissertationes Archaelogicae), *Arheološki Radovi i Rasprave*, III (Zagreb, 1963), pp. 119–22.

25. Legally, the constituted client states came under the *jus postliminii*, even though for most purposes they were treated as *de facto* extensions of imperial territory. See P. C. Sands, *The Client Princes of the Roman Empire under the Republic*, Cambridge Historical Essays no. 16 (Cambridge: At the University Press, 1908), p. 115.

26. Pliny, *N.H.*, V.81 f. Cited by M. P. Charlesworth in *CAH* 11: 616 n.

27. The phrase is Ernst Kornemann's, from the title of his lecture "Die unsichtbaren Grenzen des römischen Kaiserreichs," reprinted in *Staaten-Völker-Männer Aus der Geschichte des Altertums* (Leipzig: Dieterich, 1934), pp. 96–116.

28. For the motives of Tiberius's recall of Germanicus, see Tacitus, *Annals*, II.26; for the effect of relations between the Cherusci-based confederation of Arminius and the Marcomannic state of Maroboduus, see ibid., II.44. On the causes of the recall, see also Louis Harmand, *L'Occident romain: Gaule, Espagne, Bretagne, Afrique du Nord (31 av. J.C. à 235 ap. J.C.)* (Paris: Payot, 1960), pp. 106–8. See also Josef Dobiáš, "King Maroboduus as a Politician," *Klio* 38 (1960): 163.

29. On the Tiberian clients in general, see Ronald Syme in *CAH* 10: 781–83; Emilienne Demougeot, *La Formation de l'Europe et les invasions barbares: Des origines germaniques à l'avènement de Dioclétien* (Paris: Aubier, 1969), pp. 114–23. For Roman diplomacy with the Germanic peoples in general, see E. A. Thompson, *The Early Germans* (Oxford: Clarendon Press, 1965), pp. 72–108. On Maroboduus, see Dobiáš, "King Maroboduus," pp. 160–61. On the Sarmatian Iazyges, see John Harmatta, "The Sarmatians in Hungary," in *Studies in the History of the Sarmatians*, Magyar-Görök Tanulmányok, 30 (Budapest: Pázmány Péter Tudományegyetemi Görög Filológiai Intézet, 1950), pp. 45–46.

30. C. E. Stevens, "Britain between the Invasions (54 B.C.–A.D. 43)" in *Aspects of Archaeology in Britain and Beyond: Essays Presented to O. G. S. Crawford*, ed. W. F. Grimes (London: H. W. Edwards, 1951), pp. 322–44.

31. IV.5.3.

32. E. Badian, *Foreign Clientelae (264–70 B.C.)* (Oxford: At the Clarendon Press, 1958), especially pp. 1–14.

33. See Alban D. Winspear and Lenore K. Geweke, *Augustus and the Reconstruction of Roman Government and Society*, University of Wisconsin Studies in the Social Sciences and Philosophy no. 24 (Madison, Wis.: University of Wisconsin, 1935), p. 244.

34. See Sands, *Client Princes*, for a functional study of the spheres of Roman control. Page 77 deals with dynastic policy, and pp. 88–89 with foreign policy.

35. See David Magie, *Roman Rule in Asia Minor to the End of the Third Century after Christ*, 2 vols. (Princeton: Princeton University Press, 1950), vol. I, pp. 437, 476, 553–61.

36. Cheesman, *Auxilia*, pp. 15–16; and Sands, *Client Princes*, pp. 103–6.

37. Suetonius, *Augustus*, 23; idem, *Tiberius*, 17.

38. *Germania*, 37.

39. See Parker, *Roman Legions*, pp. 139–40, 162–63.

40. See, e.g., Stevenson, *Roman Provincial Administration*, pp. 47–50.

41. *Annals*, IV.24.

42. *Deiotarus*, 22.

43. See René Cagnat, *L'Armée romaine d'Afrique et l'occupation militaire de l'Afrique sous les empereurs*, 2d ed. (Paris: Ernest Leroux, 1913), pp. 7–24.

44. Ronald Syme, *CAH* 10: 356.

45. Perhaps the most striking instance of a seemingly disproportionate (though politically valid) investment of military effort was the siege of Masada. For the magnitude of the engineering effort, see I. A. Richmond, "The Roman Siege-Works of Masàda, Israel," *JRS* 52 (1962): 142–55.

46. See Sands, *Client Princes*, p. 155, n. 2, and Tacitus, *Annals*, Xii.29.

47. Mommsen (*Hist.*, III, pp. 234–36), cited by Stevenson, *Roman Provincial Administration*, p. 37.

48. In spite of a justly renowned road system, movements on land were of course very slow (3 mph for marching troops, then as now, or 24–30 miles a day at most). Inter-sector journeys (e.g., Pannonia to eastern Anatolia) would accordingly take up much of a campaigning season. Movements at sea could be much faster and often much more direct. See Lionel Casson, *Ships and Seamanship in the Ancient World* (Princeton: Princeton University Press, 1971). Casson cautions against taking instances of record-breaking journeys as indicative of normal seaborne mobility.

49. Bernard W. Henderson, *Five Roman Emperors: Vespasian, Titus, Domitian, Nerva, Trajan (A.D. 69–117)* (Cambridge: At the University Press, 1927), p. 60.

50. See Parker, *Roman Legions*, p. 148.

51. Parker, *Roman Legions*, pp. 89, 271.

52. Cheesman, *Auxilia*, p. 59.

53. Sands, *Client Princes*, p. 103.

54. *The Jewish War*, III.4.2. Cf. ibid., II.18.9.

55. Tacitus, *Germania*, 33.

56. See, e.g., E. Badian, *Roman Imperialism in the Late Republic*, 2d ed. (Oxford: Basil Blackwell, 1958), pp. 29–43.

57. *Annals*, IV.5.

58. Excerpts from A. H. M. Jones, ed., *A History of Rome Through the Fifth Century*, 2 vols. (New York: Harper & Row, 1970), vol. 2, pp. 148–49.

59. The distinction is considered in Badian, *Roman Imperialism*, p. 4.

60. See Bowersock, *Augustus and the Greek World*, pp. 42–61.

61. W. W. Tarn in *CAH* 10: 113–15.

62. Bowersock, *Augustus and the Greek World*, p. 46.

63. Josephus, *The Jewish War*, I.23.1, I.27.6.

64. On Eurycles and his removal, see Bowersock, *Augustus and the Greek World*, pp. 59–60; Josephus, *The Jewish War*, I.26.1–4.

65. Sands, *Client Princes*, p. 93.

66. Bowersock, *Augustus and the Greek World*, p. 56.

67. Sands, *Client Princes*, p. 93.

68. Tacitus, *Annals*, II.42. Ronald Syme, in *CAH* 11: 139, dismisses the accusation against Antiochus as a "flimsy pretext."

69. Badian, *Foreign Clientelae*, p. 12.

70. Bowersock, *Augustus and the Greek World*, p. 51, 53.

71. Josephus, *The Jewish War*, I.20.4.

72. Dobiáš, "King Maroboduus," p. 156.

73. See R. E. M. Wheeler, *Rome Beyond the Imperial Frontiers* (London: G. Bell and Sons, 1954), pp. 91–94, on the relationship between trade and migration routes.

74. Tacitus, *Agricola*, 21.

75. Dobiáš, "King Maroboduus," p. 161.

76. For an extended analysis of armed "suasion" (i.e., the political application of military force), see Edward N. Luttwak, *The Political Uses of Sea Power* (Baltimore: Johns Hopkins University Press, 1974), ch. 1.

77. For a narrative, see T. Rice Holmes, *The Architect of the Roman Empire, 27 B.C.-A.D. 14*, 2 vols. (Oxford: At the Clarendon Press, 1928–1931) vol. 2, pp. 116–21. For an analysis, see Dyson, "Native Revolts," pp. 253–258, and the reconstruction in Harmand, *L'Occident romain*, pp. 86–93.

78. See Chevallier, "Rome et la Germanie," pp. 271–73.

79. See Colin D. Gordon, "The Subsidization of Border Peoples as a Roman Policy of Imperial Defense" (Ph.D. diss., University of Michigan, 1948) (LC microfilm AC-1, no. 1105).

80. See Harmand, *L'Occident romain*, pp. 86–93.

81. Tacitus, *Annals*, XI.16.

82. This diplomacy cannot be faulted on moral grounds without reference to necessity. But see A. Alföldi, "The Moral Barrier on the Rhine and Danube" in *Congress of Roman Frontier Studies, 1949*, ed. E. B. Birley (Durham: Durham University, 1952), pp. 1–16, esp. p. 8.

83. See, e.g., Tacitus, *Germania*, 33.

84. See Thompson, *Early Germans*, pp. 93–99; and Dobiáš, "King Maroboduus," pp. 163–165.

85. *Germania*, 42.

86. Gordon, "Subsidization," pp. 11–34.

87. Tacitus, *Annals*, II.45, 46.

88. Ibid., II.46.

89. Ibid., II.62.

90. Ibid., II.63.

91. Gordon, "Subsidization," p. 23.

92. Tacitus, *Annals*, XII.29.

93. Suetonius, *Gaius*, 43–46.

94. Tacitus, *Annals*, XI.19.

95. Ibid., XII.27, 28.

96. J. G. C. Anderson in *CAH*, 10: 744–45.

97. Isoghli (near Melitene), where there was a bridge on the key highway to Nisibis, was in Cappadocia, but the crossing at Samosata, astride the road into Mesopotamia by way of Edessa and Carrhae, was in Commagene. The most important crossing was at Zeugma (Balkis) in N.E. Syria, linked to the Mediterranean by way of the Orontes valley. See Scramuzza, *Emperor Claudius*, pp. 193–95, and M. Cary, *The Geographic Background of Greek and Roman History* (Oxford: At the Clarendon Press, 1949), pp. 181–82.

98. J. G. C. Anderson, *CAH*, 10: 744–45.

99. Ibid., p. 750 (for Antiochus IV) and p. 751 (for Sohaemus and the sons of Cotys); see also M. P. Charlesworth in *CAH*, 10: 660–61.

100. Josephus, *The Jewish War*, II.9.6; Albino Garzetti, *L'Impero da Tiberio agli Antonini*, Istituto di Studi Romani, Storia di Roma, vol. 6 (Bologna: Licinio Cappelli, 1960), pp. 98–100. The characterization is Garzetti's ("*avventuriero orientale*"). See also Martin P. Charlesworth, *Five Men: Character Studies of the Roman Empire*, Martin Classical Lectures, vol. 6 (Cambridge, Mass.: Harvard University Press, 1936), pp. 3–30.

101. Cf. Duncan Fishwick, "The Annexation of Mauretania," *Historia* 20 (1971): 467–68.

102. J. G. C. Anderson, *CAH* 10: 752; Magie, *Roman Rule*, pp. 540–53.

103. J. G. C. Anderson, *CAH* 10: 752.

104. Scramuzza, *Emperor Claudius*, p. 185. Cf. Tacitus, *Annals*, XII.21.

105. See Donald Dudley and Graham Webster, *The Roman Conquest of Britain* (London: Dufour, 1965), p. 184.

106. Denis Van Berchem, "Conquête et organisation par Rome des districts Alpins," *REL* 11 (1962): 231.

107. M. P. Charlesworth in *CAH* 10:682.

108. See Parker, *Roman Legions*, pp. 9–20, and Webster, *Roman Army*, pp. 27–30, both based on the sixth book of Polybius.

109. Jacques Harmand, *L'Armée et le soldat à Rome (de 107 à 50 avant notre ère)* (Paris: A. et J. Picard et Cie., 1967), p. 39.

110. See Paul Coussin, *Les Armes romaines: Essai sur les origines et l'évolution des armes individuelles du légionnaire romain* (Paris: Librairie ancienne Honoré Champion, 1926), passim.

111. On the uncertain evidence on post-Marian legionary cavalry, see Harmand, *L'Armée et le soldat*, p. 46. Also Manuel Marin y Peña, *Instituciones militares romanas*, Enciclopedia Clasica, no. 2 (Madrid: Consejo Superior de Investigaciones Cientificas Patronato "Menendez y Pelayo," 1956), p. 74, para. 137.

112. Parker, *Roman Legions*, p. 43.

113. But the *hasta* did not disappear; see Coussin, *Les Armes*, pp. 359-60.

114. The sole evidence for the number is Josephus, *The Jewish War*, III.6.2.

115. See Eric William Marsden, *Greek and Roman Artillery: Historical Development* 2 vols. (Oxford: At the Clarendon Press, 1969), 1:183. The enthusiasm of Vegetius (*Epitoma rei militaris*, II.11) should perhaps be treated with some reserve.

116. When Claudius ordered Cn. Domitius Corbulo to disengage from his reprisal operations against the Chauci, Corbulo put his men to work digging a canal between the Maas and Rhine. (See Tacitus, *Annals*, XI.20.) After the battle of Bedriacum in the civil war of A.D. 69, Vitellius sent the legio XIII *Gemina* to build amphitheaters at Cremona and Bononia (Tacitus, *Histories*, II.67). All the roads were of course built by the legions, which included *mensores* (surveyors) in their headquarters.

117. Frontinus, *Strategemata*, IV.7.2. Cited in Marsden, *Greek and Roman Artillery*, p. 183, n. 3.

118. Harmand, *L'Armée et le soldat*, p. 62, citing a 19th century French army experiment.

119. Joachim Marquardt, *De l'Organisation militaire chez les Romains*, rev. ed. A. Von Domaszewski, trans. J. Brissaud, Manuel des antiquités romaines de J. Marquardt et Th. Mommsen, II (Paris: A. Fontemoing, 1891), pp. 156, 192.

120. On the notoriously poor performance of the Roman cavalry, beginning with the battles against Hannibal, see Paul Vigneron, *Le Cheval dans l'antiquité gréco-romaine; des guerres médiques aux grandes invasions: Contribution á l'histoire des techniques.* Annales de L'Est, Mémoire no. 35 (Nancy: Faculté des lettres *et de Sciences humaines* 1968), vol. 1, pp. 261-64.

121. The sling lost all military importance long ago, but see J. Harmand, *L'Armée et le soldat*, p. 77. On range comparability, see W. McLeod, "The Range of the Ancient Bow," *Phoenix* 19 (1965): 14. R. W. Davies, in the "The Romans at Burnswark," *Historia* 21 (1972): 105-6, has argued that slingers were never a regular element in the Roman army.

122. Tacitus, *Histories*, IV.12-80 and V.14-26. For the legions involved, see Parker, *Roman Legions*, pp. 143-45.

123. *Strategemata*, II.7.3,5.

124. *Crassus*, 27.6,7.

125. Tacitus, *Histories*, IV.71.

126. See below, chapter 3.

127. Tacitus, *Annals*, I.49.

128. Velleius Paterculus, II.117.

129. Harmand, *L'Armée et le soldat*, p. 46, n. 136.

130. After the "social war" (i.e., after 88 B.C.) the Italians, having all become citizens, no longer fought as auxiliaries, but as legionaries. (Ibid., p. 40 and n. 101.) On the role of the cavalry at that time, see pp. 46-51.

131. R. W. Davies, "Appendix" (cited in note 4, above). Davies suggests that there were 480 and 800 foot soldiers in the cohors *quingenaria* and *milliaria*, respectively.

132. They are not attested before the Flavian period; it is uncertain when they were first organized.

133. See the brief definitions in Vigneron, *Cheval*, p. 235.

134. See, e.g., Josephus, *The Jewish War*, III.5.5. Josephus's *kontus* is clearly a shock weapon, and the cavalry equipped with it is clearly that of the regular *auxilia* as opposed to client-state or irregular troops.

135. For the cavalry aspects of the battle, see Vigneron, *Cheval*, pp. 297-99.

136. XXII.37. Cited in Cheesman, *Auxilia*, p. 8.

137. *BG* II.7.1.

138. See note 118 above.

139. See the careful analysis in Marsden, *Greek and Roman Artillery*, p. 9 n. Marsden shows the composite nature of Odysseus's bow in his analysis of Homer's text (p. 10).

140. McLeod, "Range of the Ancient Bow," p. 8.

141. Ibid.

142. Tacitus, *Annals*, I.56 and II.20. Cf. Suetonius, Gaius, 46.

143. See Marsden, *Greek and Roman Artillery*, p. 184, who simply *assumes* it; but the presence of artillery among the often primitive troops of the auxilia would be surprising. When Civilis and his auxiliary troops besieged the camp at Vetera, they used siege engines built by Roman prisoners and deserters, i.e., legionary troops; Tacitus, *Histories*, IV.23

144. See the examples cited in Thompson, *Early Germans*, pp. 131–40.

145. Ibid., pp. 146–49.

146. Ronald Syme, *CAH II*: 146, based on Dio, LXVII.4.6.

147. Suetonius, *Domitian*, 7.

148. Syme, "Some Notes on the Legions", (n. 1) p. 33.

149. Ibid.

150. Tacitus, *Annals*, IV.5; the deployment structure did not change until two new legions were raised (XV *Primigenia* and XXII *Primigenia*) and preparations began for the invasion of Britain, c.a. A.D. 42–43; see Parker, *Roman Legions*, p. 129.

151. A letter of Pliny (LXXIV) has suggested the possibility of Daco-Parthian contacts; some scholars have taken the suggestion seriously, e.g., Henderson, *Five Roman Emperors*, pp. 273–74. For another view, see A. N. Sherwin-White, *The Letters of Pliny* (Oxford: At the Clarendon Press, 1966), p. 662.

152. Fifty km. east of Vienna. This was the southern pincer of the operation; a second pincer was to advance eastward from Mainz (on the Rhine), and the two armies were to meet on the Elbe. About 150,000 troops were involved in this vast operation. See Tacitus, *Annals*, II.46 and XI.16; and Velleius Paterculus, II.109.

153. See Syme, *CAH* 10:369–73; Holmes, *Architect of the Roman Empire*, vol. 2, pp. 111–15; and Dyson, "Native Revolts," pp. 250–52.

154. In A.D. 8 there may have been more than a hundred thousand troops engaged in suppressing the revolt: ten legions, seventy cohorts of auxiliary foot, ten cavalry *alae*, and large forces of irregulars, primarily Thracian cavalry supplied by Rhoemetalces I, client-king of Thrace; Syme, *CAH* 10:372.

155. The argument that follows is based on P.A. Brunt, *JRS* 53 (1963): 170–76 (review of Hans D. Meyer, *Die Aussenpolitik des Augustus und die Augusteische Dichtung*). For the injunction, see Tacitus, *Annals*, I.11. For the objection, see idem, *Agricola*, 13. Tacitus, of course, was writing at a time when conquest was in the air; see Ronald Syme, *Tacitus* 2 vols. (Oxford: At the Clarendon Press, 1958), vol. 1, pp. 10–29.

156. Tacitus, *Annals*, II.46. Cf. Parker, *Roman Legions*, pp. 82–85, passim.

157. See Syme, *CAH* 10:353.

158. This is an important subsidiary argument in Brunt's thesis, based on A. Klotz. Apparently in Augustan times the Romans thought that the distance from the Rhine to the Vistula, i.e., across the full width of "Germany," was less than the distance from the Pyrenees to the Rhine (636/686 miles vs. 920), the latter two being thought to be parallel. Similarly, the distance from the Vistula to the ocean on the far side of China was thought to be less than three times the distance from the Pyrenees to the Rhine (i.e., 2,560/2,660 miles). Since Julius Caesar had conquered Gaul in ten years with a force which never exceeded ten legions the conquest of all of Germany must have seemed a perfectly feasible proposition. A recent reexamination of the evidence endorses Klotz's conclusions and estimates; see J. J. Tierney, "The Map of Agrippa," *Proceedings of the Royal Irish Academy*, vol. 63, section C, no. 4 (1963), pp. 154–60.

CHAPTER TWO

1. Jacques Harmand, *L'Armée et le soldat à Rome (de 107 à 50 avant notre ère)* (Paris: A. et J. Picard et Cie., 1967), p. 132, n. 240.

2. Graham Webster, *The Roman Imperial Army of the First and Second Centuries A.D.* (London: Adam and Charles Black, 1969), pp. 170–71.

3. See, e.g., the camps described in I. A. Richmond, "The Romans in Redesdale, *History of Northumberland* 15 (1940): pp. 116–29.

4. Harmand, *L'Armée*, pp. 121–28. Harmand's survey of castrametation, pp. 99–135, is comprehensive.

5. E.g., Webster, *Roman Imperial Army*, p. 171: "This [the palisade] was merely a fence to keep out stray natives and wild animals." See also Harmand, *L'Armée*, pp. 129–34, where similar opinions are cited.

6. Roman troops seemingly marched from a "very early breakfast" (6 A.M.?) to midday (1 P.M.?), with the rest of the day given over to camp-building and rest; Frank E. Adcock, *The Roman Art of War Under the Republic*, Martin Classical Lectures 8 (Cambridge, Mass.: Harvard University Press, 1940), p. 13.

7. The figures are from the technical manual *Liber de munitionibus castrorum*, sect. 49 (trench) and sect. 50 (rampart).

8. Ibid.

9. From Albert Harkness, *The Military System of the Romans* (New York: D. Appleton and Company, 1887), p. xlix.

10. Adcock, *Roman Art of War*, pp. 13–15.

11. *Liber de munitionibus castrorum*, sect. 1.

12. Adcock, *Roman Art of War*, p. 15. Cf. Harmand, *L'Armée*, p. 129, n. 226, p. 130, n. 228, and generally pp. 129–34.

13. Adcock, *Roman Art of War*, p. 14.

14. *Res Gestae*, 31.

15. G. Forni in *DE*, vol. 4, fasc. 40, s.v. *"Limes,"* p. 1,280. See also Antonio Frova, "The Danubian *Limes* in Bulgaria, and Excavations at Oescus," *The Congress of Roman Frontier Studies 1949*, ed. E. B. Birley (Durham: Durham University, 1952), pp. 25–26. Frova cites and endorses D. Krandjalov's theory of a Domitianic date for the "Great Earthwork," as well as a pre-Roman dating for the "Small Earthwork" and a Constantinian dating for the stone wall. But cf., also Em. Condurachi, Ion Barnea, and Petre Diaconu, "Nouvelle recherches sur le *Limes* Byzantin au Bas-Danube aux X*ᵉ*-XI*ᵉ* siècles" in *Proceedings of the XIII International Congress of Byzantine Studies*, ed. J. M. Hussey, D. Obolensky, and S. Runciman (Oxford: At the Clarendon Press, 1967), p. 179, which casts doubts on the rest of Krandjalov's chronology.

16. A fifteen-mile double-ditch wall in northern Mesopotamia closes a gap between the natural defenses of the Khabur River to the west and the high ground of the Jebel Sinjar to the east, thus blocking off an otherwise easy access route to the key city of Nisibis from the south. See R. E. M. Wheeler, "The Roman Frontier in Mesopotamia," in *Congress of Roman Frontier Studies, 1949*, p. 126 and map, p. 115.

17. See the discussion of the various meanings of *limes* by G. Forni in *DE*, vol. 4, fasc. 34, pp. 1,075–83. The "horizontal" *limes* here discussed corresponds to Forni's type *h*, pp. 1,081–82.

18. Ibid., p. 1,084.

19. E.g., A. Alföldi in *CAH* 12: 213; H. C. Pflaum, "Forces et faiblesses de l'armée romaine du Haut-Empire," in *Problèmes de la guerre à Rome*, ed. Jean-Paul Brisson (Paris and The Hague: Mouton and Co., 1969), p. 96; Erich Swoboda, "Traian und der Pannonische *Limes*" in *Les Empereurs romains d'Espagne*, Colloques internationaux du centre national de la recherche scientifique (Paris: Centre national de la recherche scientifique, 1965), p. 197. Cf. Denis van Berchem, *L'Armée de Dioclétien et la réforme constantinienne*, Institut français d'archéologie de Beyrouth, Bibliothèque archéologique et historique, vol. 56 (Paris: Librairie orientaliste Paul Geuthner, 1952), p. 104.

20. E.g., Wilhelm Weber in *CAH* 11: 312–13; G. R. Watson, *The Roman Soldier* (London: Thames and Hudson, 1969), p. 67, commenting on Vegetius's "obsession" with defense; C. M. Wells, *The German Policy of Augustus: An Examination of the Archeological Evidence* (Oxford: At the Clarendon Press, 1972), p. 246, deprecating the "Maginot Line mentality" of the Flavians. In fact, it appears that a reference to the ill-fated Maginot Line is *de rigueur* in modern analyses of Roman frontiers.

21. On the turrets, see E. B. Birley, *Research on Hadrian's Wall* (Kendal: Titus Wilson and Son, 1961), pp. 103–10. For the latest survey of the state of research on Hadrian's

Wall, see David T. Breeze and Brian Dobson, "Hadrian's Wall: Some Problems," *Britannia:* 3 (1973): 182–208.

22. Birley, *Research,* pp. 227–33.

23. Jean Baradez, *Vue aérienne de l'organisation romaine dans le Sud-Algérien, Fossatum Africae* (Paris: Arts et métiers graphiques, 1949), p. 359. But see Denis van Berchem, *L'Armée de Dioclétien,* p. 44, where doubts are expressed as to the chronological coherence of the outposts and *fossatum* proper.

24. See Webster, *Roman Imperial Army,* pp. 246–48. For the shortcomings of such means of communication, see R. J. Forbes, *Studies in Ancient Technology* 6 (Leiden, 1967).

25. See Anne S. Robertson, "The Antonine Wall," in *Congress of Roman Frontier Studies, 1949,* p. 102.

26. I. A. Richmond, "Trajan's Army on Trajan's Column," *Papers of the British Shool at Rome* 13 (1935): 34–36.

27. Idem, "A Roman Arterial Signalling System in the Stainmore Pass," in *Aspects of Archeology in Britain and Beyond: Essays presented to O. G. S. Crawford,* ed. W. F. Grimes (London: H. W. Edwards, 1951), pp. 293–302.

28. See A. Poidebard, *La Trace de Rome dans le désert de Syrie: Le limes de Trajan à la conquête arabe, recherches aériennes (1925-1934)* (Paris: Librairie orientaliste Paul Geuthner, 1934); for other "open" *limites* see G. W. Bowersock, "A Report on *Arabia Provincia,*" *JRS* 61: (1971): 236–42; and Maurice Euzennat, "Le *Limes* de Volubilis" in *Studien zu den Militärgrenzen Roms,* Vorträge des 6, Internationalen Limes-Kongresses in Süddeutschland (Cologne and Graz: Bohlau, 1967), pp. 194–99.

29. See David Magie, *Roman Rule in Asia Minor to the End of the Third Century after Christ,* 2 vols. (Princeton: Princeton University Press, 1950), 1: 571.

30. F. A. Lepper, *Trajan's Parthian War* (London: Geoffrey Cumberledge, 1948), p. 108.

31. The thickness of the wall (and therefore the rampart walk—minus the parapet) varied from as little as five feet six inches to a maximum of ten feet; see Birley, *Research,* pp. 84–85.

32. E.g., Denis van Berchem, *L'Armée de Dioclétien,* p. 126; similarly, Wheeler, "Roman Frontier in Mesopotamia," p. 126.

33. See Jacques Harmand, *La Guerre antique, de Sumer à Rome* (Paris: Presses universitaires de France, 1973), pp. 177–78, for a list of pre-Roman linear barriers and their military function.

34. Birley, *Research,* p. 79.

35. Data of F. G. Simpson and Parker Brewis, cited in ibid., pp. 86–87.

36. See Jean Baradez, "Compléments inédits au 'Fossatum Africae,'" in *Studien zu den Militärgrenzen Roms,* p. 200.

37. S. A. M. [sic] Gichon, "Roman Frontier Cities in the Negev," *Quintus Congressus Internationalis Limitis Romani Studiosorum,* Acta et Dissertationes Archaeologicae (Zagreb), *Arheoloski Radovi i Rasprave* (1963: 201. Gichon draws attention to Sura 37 of the Koran, which alludes to the severe obstacle that even a simple ditch can constitute for desert raiders, whose tactics rely on speed and surprise.

38. F. G. Simpson and R. C. Shaw, "The Purpose and Date of the Vallum and Its Crossings," *C-W,* n.s. 27 (1922: 39. Cf. E. A. Thompson, *The Early Germans* (Oxford: Clarendon Press, 1965), pp. 114–15.

39. In the case of Hadrian's Wall, the barrier was much reinforced on the inward side by the so-called Vallum, a flat-bottomed trench twenty feet wide at the top, eight feet wide at the bottom and ten féet deep, the trench being set between six-foot-high ramparts formed by the upcast; together with the berms, the width of the earthwork amounted to 120 feet, a Roman *actus;* see I. A. Richmond, "Hadrian's Wall 1939-1949," *JRS* 40 (1950): 51–52. Until recently, the construction of this uniquely elaborate inward barrier was sometimes held to have preceded that of the wall; accordingly, its function could be explained as that of a wall-substitute. But new archeological evidence has shown that the construction of the Vallum was in fact concurrent with or even later than that of the wall; see ibid., pp. 51–52, and Birley, *Research,* pp. 118–25. Even before this evidence came to light, F. G. Simpson and R. C. Shaw had argued convincingly

that the Vallum could hardly have been used as a substitute outward barrier, while it was over-elaborate as a simple patrol track; Simpson and Shaw, "Purpose and Date of the Vallum," pp. 359–60, quoting T. H. Hodgson: "bar gunpowder, a party of schoolboys could stone the best troops of the world out of the Vallum." F. Haverfield hypothesized that owing to its obvious limitations *as a fighting rampart*, the Vallum marked the limit of civil jurisdiction as against the wall's military perimeter; R. G. Collingwood developed this theory further, suggesting that the Vallum was a customs barrier (under procuratorial control) while the wall was a military perimeter (under the control of the Legate). But since the Vallum is generally located so it can be observed from the wall turrets, and because of the implausibility of such a large construction effort for a minor jurisdictional purpose, these theories are no longer accepted; see John Morris, "The Vallum Again" *C-W*, n.s., 50, (1950): 43–53.

40. R. G. Collingwood theorized that the "curtain" could be used as a screen to mask the lateral approach of forces which could then emerge rapidly through the sally ports to intercept the enemy; see "The Purpose of the Roman Wall" in *Vasculum* 8 (1920): 4–9. This theory has been demolished by archeological evidence indicating that the road running parallel to the inner side of the wall was not built until a century after the rest of the wall complex; see Birley, *Research*, pp. 113–14. The second theory, which cannot be contradicted by archeological evidence but which is militarily implausible, is that of I. A. Richmond. It is explained most fully in John Collingwood Bruce, *Handbook to the Roman Wall*, 12th ed., ed. I. A. Richmond (Newcastle: H. Hill Hindson and A. Reid, 1966), pp. 25–26. In Richmond's view, Roman troops in their offensive sallies would use the curtain in order to corral the enemy, who would be squeezed between the defenders (now out in front of the wall) and the obstacle ditch behind them.

41. Baradez, *Fossatum Africae*, p. 359.

42. The structures of Hadrian's Wall as originally built are themselves eloquent testimony to the underlying tactical scheme; the forts built along the wall were provided with three twin portal gates, the last opening on the far side of the curtain. It is obvious that these gates were to serve as sally ports for a mobile and offensive defense. It is also apparent that the outpost forts were to provide early warning before, and base security during, these interception sallies, if a prolonged pursuit were necessary. But for a rebuttal of the general applicability of this scheme, see Swoboda, "Traian und der Pannonische *Limes*," pp. 195–208. Swoboda denies that the Romans at this time relied on mobile forward defense operations beyond the Danube in order to defend the Pannonian frontier; in particular, he maintains that the buildings of Roman construction (or rather, those incorporating Roman materials) found in a zone twenty to ninety kilometers beyond the river were *not* outposts.

43. Ibid, p. 197.

44. Eric B. Birley, "*Alae* and *Cohortes Milliariae*" in *Corolla Memoriae Erich Swoboda Dedicata*, Römische Forschungen in Niederösterreich V (Graz and Cologne: Hermann Böhlaus, 1966), p. 57; the unit establishments have been approximated at 1,000 and 500 for the milliary and quingenary units, respectively.

45. In Britain, for example, five of the seven attested milliary cohorts and thirty-one of the forty-six quingenary cohorts were *equitatae*; see R. W. Davies, "*Cohortes Equitatae*" *Historia* 20 (1971): 751, n. 1. But Britain was probably atypical. In Lower Germany there were six attested *cohortes equitatae* and as many infantry cohorts—all quingenary—during the period A.D. 104–20; earlier, when the sector had been more active, in A.D. 70–83, there is epigraphical evidence for eleven quingenary *cohortes equitatae* but only eight infantry cohorts, and there was also one milliary *cohors equitata* and two milliary infantry cohorts; Géza Alföldy, "Die Hilfstruppen der römischen Provinz Germania Inferior" in *Epigraphische Studien*, no. 6 (Düsseldorf: Rheinland Verlag, 1968), p. 151.

46. G. L. Cheesman, *The Auxilia of the Roman Imperial Army* (Oxford: At the Clarendon Press, 1914), p. 168.

47. Birley, *Research*, p. 272. Birley states that nearly one quarter of the infantry (13,000 men) was mounted, hence the "three thousand light cavalry" figure; but see note 55 below.

48. See G. Alföldy, "Die Hilfstruppen," p. 151.
49. Tacitus, *Histories*, I. 79. Note the number: 9,000 mounted Roxolani were involved, obviously a major attack.
50. Thompson, *Early Germans*, p. 116.
51. But see Watson, *Roman Soldier*, pp. 62–64, where doubts are cast on some estimates of the weight of individual kits.
52. *Tiberius*, 18.
53. H. M. D. Parker, *The Roman Legions* (1928; rpt. ed., with corrections and bibliography, Cambridge: W. Heffer and Sons, 1958), pp. 155, 162.
54. Wales required an active occupation force until the end of Roman rule and was never fully pacified. M. G. Jarrett, "The Roman Frontier in Wales" in *Studien zu den Militärgrenzen Roms*, pp. 21–31.
55. Birley, *Research*, p. 272. Birley gives a total of 13,000 infantry, but this appears to include 3,000 men assigned to guard duties in the milecastles; ibid., p. 271 (although Birley has also suggested that these troops may have belonged to separate units of *numeri*). Cf. Sheppard S. Frere, *Britannia: A History of Roman Britain* (London: Routledge and Kegan Paul, 1967), p. 137. Frere's figure of 9,500 men for the sixteen wall forts is not reconcilable with Birley's figures.
56. Richmond, "Hadrian's Wall 1939–1949," p. 47
57. Birley, *Research*, p. 271, opts for the higher figure. Frere, *Britannia*, p. 137, cites a range of 1,500 to 2,000 troops and points out that there is no evidence that these men belonged to *numeri* rather than regular *auxilia*, as Birley has suggested.
58. Birley, *Research*, pp. 106–9.
59. In addition to Birley's figures given in *Research*, p. 272, 11,000 legionary troops are assumed to have been on establishment and available.
60. G. Forni in *De*, vol. 4, fasc. 38, s.v. *"Limes,"* pp. 1212–13. This refers to the later Antonine period. The major fort of Aalen was built under Antoninun Pius, while Pfünz and Kösching were rebuilt, all being well behind the perimeter line; H. Schönberger, "The Roman Frontier in Germany: An Archaeological Survey," *JRS* 59 (1969): 170.
61. The trend seemed much clearer a generation ago than it is now; cf. Olwen Brogan, "The Roman *Limes* in Germany," *Archaeological Journal* 92 (1935): 17–18, with Schönberger, "Roman Frontier in Germany," pp. 164–65; see also Émilienne Demougeot, *La Formation de l'Europe et les invasions barbares: Des origines germaniques a l'avènement de Dioclétien* (Paris: Aubier, 1969), pp. 189–90. For Britain, see Richmond, "Hadrian's Wall 1939-1949," pp. 45–46, 55; see also Birley, *Research*, pp. 134–55, on the Stanegate, the line on which the original chain of forts was built.
62. As Alfoldi does in *CAH* 12:213.
63. See Thompson, *Early Germans*, pp. 146–49.
64. Suetonius, *Domitianus*, 7.
65. Morris, "Vallum Again," p. 50. The argument is developed further in Eric B. Birley, "Hadrianic Frontier Policy" in *Carnuntina, Vorträge beim internationalen Kongress der Altertumsforscher, Carnuntum, 1955*, ed. E. Swoboda, *Römische Forschungen in Niederösterreich*, 3 (Graz and Cologne, 1956), pp. 26–33.
66. Chester G. Starr, Jr., *The Roman Imperial Navy, 31 BC-AD 324*, Cornell Studies in Classic Philology, vol. 26 (Ithaca: Cornell University Press, 1941), pp. 135–37 (*Classis Moesica*); pp. 138–41 (*Classis Pannonica*); and pp. 144–52 (*Classis Germanica*). Between December and February the Danube freezes, and the river fleets could not operate. This was a recognized seasonal danger (ibid., pp. 138–41), since the land-based surveillance system was much less effective without the support of the river fleets.
67. Gichon, "Roman Frontier Cities," pp. 195–207; see also idem, "The Origin of the *Limes Palestinae* and the Major Phases of Its Development" in *Studien zu den Militärgrenzen Roms*, pp. 178, 184. See also the fuller account in Shimon Applebaum and Mordechai Gichon, *Israel and Her Vicinity in the Roman and Byzantine Periods* (Tel Aviv: Tel Aviv University Press, 1967), pp. 37–47. Cf. Euzennat, "Le *Limes* de Volubilis," pp. 194–99, for an open *limes* (in Mauretania) organized in a remarkably precise checkerboard pattern. On the *Limes* Tripolitanus as well, we know of no continuous linear barrier,

while road building began as early as A.D. 15–16. See R. G. Goodchild and J. B. Ward Perkins, "The *Limes Tripolitanus* in the Light of Recent Discoveries," *JRS* 39 (1949): 81–95.

68. Roads were always the primary infrastructures of the Syrian *limes*; see Raymond Chevallier, *Les Voies romaines* (Paris: Librairie Armand Colin, 1972), pp. 160–65.

69. Baradez, *Fossatum Africae*, pp. 163–208, esp. pp. 202–8, or idem, "Organization militaire romaine de l'Algérie antique et évolution du concept défensif de ses frontières," *Revue international d'histoire militaire* 13 (1953): 25–42.

70. Albino Garzetti, *L'Impero da Tiberio agli Antonini*, Istituto di Studi Romani, Storia di Roma, vol. 6 (Bologna: Licinio Capelli, 1960), p. 437.

71. It was only in the Black Sea that the *Classis Moesica* and the *Classis Pontica* had to deal with any seaborne opposition, and that was small scale, from pirates. Starr, *Roman Imperial Navy*, pp. 127–28.

72. See Lionel Casson, *Ships and Seamanship in the Ancient World* (Princeton: Princeton University Press, 1971), p. 270. Cf. Moché Amit in "Les Moyens de communication et la défense de l'empire romain" in *La Parola del Passato*, vol. 20, fasc. 102 (1965), p. 218. Casson cites the navigation season specified by Vegetius (IV.39), May 27 to September 14, with outer limits of March 10 to April 13. Cf. E. de Saint-Denis, "*Mare Clausum,*" *Revue des Études Latines* 25 (1947): pp. 200–203, where it is pointed out that there was some winter navigation, but passages were short and risks were much greater than normal.

73. Casson, *Ships and Seamanship*, p. 285.

74. Ibid., p. 293.

75. This corresponds to the *magnum iter* (with no day of rest) as opposed to the *justum iter* of 10,000 steps; see Chevallier, *Voies romaines*, pp. 224–25. Amit, "Moyens de communication," passim, calculates Roman strategic mobility on the basis of the twenty to twenty-four Roman miles claimed by Vegetius (I.9) for the "ancients," converted by Amit to thirty to thirty-six kilometers. This seems much too high; it is appropriate for a brisk exercise but not for long distance marching. Cf. Watson, *Roman Soldier*, p. 55.

76. E.g. Tacitus, *Histories*, I.31, re German troops sent to Alexandria and recalled. Nor is this detrimental effect surprising: the trip could be prolonged to fifty or seventy days; Casson, *Ships and Seamanship*, p. 289, n. 82.

77. Starr, *Roman Imperial Navy*, pp. 186–87. Sixty galleys sufficed to transport an entire legion. On the horses, see Albert Marin, *Dictionnaire des antiquités gregues et romaines*, ed. Charles Daremberg and Edm. Saglio, 9 vols. (Paris: Librairie Hachette, 1877–1919), vol. 3, pt. 2, s.v. "*Hippagogi.*"

78. See Parker, *Roman Legions* pp. 119, 158, 168—with minor adjustments. For A.D. 161 see Watson, *Roman Soldier*, pp. 15–16, based on ILS 2288 (= CIL VI 3492), reproduced on p. 160. Cf. J. Szilágy, "Les Variations des centres de prépondérance militaire dans les provinces frontières de l'empire romain," *Acta Antiqua Academiae Scientiarum Hungaricae* 2 (1953), fasc. 1–2, pp. 119–219, which is an attempt to estimate actual force levels at nine points in time between A.D. 6 and the *Notitia Dignitatum*, and between eight sectors covering the entire perimeter. In practice, Szilágy generally accounts for the *auxilia* by doubling the putative number of legionary troops, though he takes due notice of auxiliary deployments in the absence of legions, as in the provinces of Raetia, Noricum and, Mauretania.

79. Parker, *Roman Legions*, p. 167.

80. Ibid., pp. 156–58. According to Parker, Trajan had twelve legions on the Danube on the eve of the first Dacian war, and thirteen for the second.

81. Bowersock, "Report on *Arabia Provincia*," pp. 232–33.

82. It is generally assumed that the XXII *Deiotariana* was disgraced or destroyed in the Jewish revolt of A.D. 132–35, but not necessarily in Judea. See Parker, *Roman Legions*, pp. 162–63. In addition, the IX *Hispana* may also have been lost in the Jewish revolt.

83. *Annals*, IV, 5.

84. See Parker, *Roman Legions*, p. 135, where it is conjectured that the VII *Claudia pia fidelis* was redeployed to Moesia in A.D. 58, leaving only the XI *Claudia pia fidelis* in

Dalmatia. What is certain is that the VII *Claudia pia fidelis* was redeployed to Viminacium over the period A.D. 42–66; see J. J. Wilkes, *Dalmatia: History of the Provinces of the Roman Empire* (London: Routledge and Kegan Paul, 1969), p. 96.

85. Ibid.

86. Until A.D. 6 three legions of the original four remained in Egypt; see Ronald Syme, "Some Notes on the Legions under Augustus," *JRS* 23 (1933): 25. In Spain the number of legions decreased from an estimate six in 27 B.C. to four in 13 B.C. and three by A.D. 9; ibid., p. 22. Subsequently, one legion was removed under Claudius and a second during the civil war; Parker, *Roman Legions*, pp. 131, 144.

87. A total of eight new legions were raised and formed over the period spanned by the reigns of Gaius (A.D. 37–41) and Vespasian (A.D. 69–79), but four were disbanded in A.D. 70; see Gastone M. Bersanetti, *Vespasiano* (Rome: Edizioni Roma, 1941), pp. 75–79. This resulted in a total establishment of twenty-nine legions under Vespasian. Domitian created the legion I *Flavia Minerva* in A.D. 83 (see Parker, *Roman Legions*, p. 150), but the total declined to twenty-nine once more when the V *Alaudae* was lost in Domitian's Dacian war. The number only increased to thirty again with Trajan's formation of the XXX *Ulpia Victrix*; ibid., p. 156.

88. G. Alföldy, *Die Hilfstruppen*, p. 151, and (third century), p. 161.

89. Birley, "*Alae* and *Cohortes Milliariae*," p. 60.

90. See Michael G. Jarrett and John C. Mann, "Britain from Agricola to Gallienus," *Bonner Jahrbücher* 170 (1970): 179–81. In *Agricola*, 24, Tacitus records his hero's friendly detention of an exiled Irish chief against a possible conquest of Ireland, which would have served to surround Britain completely with Roman armies: this definitely suggests a scheme of total conquest. But on the significance of any scheme of Agricola's, see Eric B. Birley, "Britain under the Flavians: Agricola and His Predecessors" in idem, *Roman Britain and the Roman Army: Collected Papers* (Kendal: Titus Wilson and Son, 1953), pp. 10–19.

91. Jarrett and Mann, "Britain from Agricola to Gallienus," p. 180.

92. Kenneth A. Steer, "The Antonine Wall: A Reconsideration" in *Studien zu den Militärgrenzen Roms*, p. 36.

93. See Anne S. Robertson, "The Antonine Wall," for a description of the structures, especially pp. 100–103.

94. Jarrett and Mann, "Britain from Agricola to Gallienus," p. 189.

95. Steer, "Antonine Wall: A Reconsideration," p. 38.

96. See the summary calculation in Grace Simpson, "The Roman Forts in Wales: A Reassessment," in *Studien zu den Militärgrenzen Roms*, p. 33, where the number of attested auxiliary units in Britain during the Hadrianic period is estimated at sixty-four, compared to seventy-nine occupied forts, excluding fortlets, signal stations, etc. Simpson has suggested (p. 34) that the increased manpower requirements entailed by the advance of the frontier to the Antonine Wall (when the number of occupied forts increased to 114) were satisfied by several expedients: some forts (e.g., in Wales) were evacuated, some were short-manned, some were manned by *numeri* troops (see below, pp. 122–23), some by legionary *vexillationes*, and some by rapidly redeployed forces on a circulating basis. For the same argument in greater detail, see Grace Simpson, *Britons and the Roman Army: A Study of Wales and the Southern Pennines in the 1st–3rd Centuries* (London: The Gregg Press, 1964), pp. 119–21. Cf. Frere, *Britannia*, pp. 160–61.

97. See A. R. Birley, "Excavations at Carpow," in *Studien zu den Militärgrenzen Roms*, p. 4, for evidence that the Severan fort of Carpow on the Pertshire-Fife county border (in Scotland) was intended for permanent occupation. See Anthony R. Birley, *Septimius Severus: The African Emperor* (London: Eyre & Spottiswoode, 1971), pp. 258–61, for the Severan campaign in Britain and a discussion of his policy.

98. Starr, *Roman Imperial Navy*, pp. 144–52.

99. On specific instances, see Schönberger, "Roman Frontier in Germany," pp. 157–58, 164–65, though there were of course differences in emphasis and priority (as well as interpretation), as cited.

100. Ibid., p. 155. On the strategy in general, see also Ronald Syme in CAH 11: 160–61; and Louis Harmand, *L'Occident romain: Gaule, Espagne, Bretagne, Afrique du Nord(31 av. J.C. à 235 ap. J.C.)* (Paris: Payot, 1960), pp. 226–27.

101. Schönberger, "Roman Frontier in Germany," pp. 155-56.

102. Ibid., pp. 156-57.

103. *Strategemata*, I.3.10. On which, see G. Forni in *DE*, vol. 4, fasc. 34, s.v. *"Limes,"* p. 1,080; Frontinus wrote of roads cut into the territory of the Chatti for 120 Roman miles, but it is unclear whether this refers to a frontage, a linear penetration, or a set of separate penetration axes.

104. *Agricola*, 39. Ronald Syme in CAH 11: 162-63, takes exception to this negative view, as does Harmand, *L'Occident romain*, pp. 228-29. But cf. Schönberger, "Roman Frontier in Germany," p. 158, who describes the results as poor, viewing the establishment of the Taunus *limes* as the result of an abortive attempt to achieve greater goals; this is connected with his theory (p. 160) that A.D. 89-90 was the great turning point on this frontier, marking the abandonment of the last attempt at large-scale conquest. Troops, including two entire legions, were certainly redeployed to the Danube fronts; see ibid. Even so, there was a specific "tactical" reason for Tacitus's revival of the accusation that fake prisoners were produced for a sham triumph: in a slow moving, if relentless, engineering offensive very few prisoners would be taken. Tacitus obviously did not understand that the Roman Army could fight most effectively as a combat engineering force; cf. Frontinus, *Strategemata*, IV.7.2. on Corbulo's statement that wars are won with the *dolabra*, the multipurpose legionary pickax.

105. Schönberger, "Roman Frontier in Germany," pp. 158-59.

106. Tacitus, *Germania*, 29; Ronald Syme, CAH 11: 165; Demougeot, *La Formation*, p. 151.

107. Schönberger, "Roman Frontier in Germany," pp. 161-62.

108. Ibid., pp. 168-70. The straight line *limes* from Miltenberg-Ost to Welzheim is thought to be Antonine, but the Schirenhof-Bohming line may have been Hadrianic.

109. Ibid., pp. 174-75.

110. This is the argument of Syme in *CAH* 11: 165.

111. K. Stade, *CAH* 11: 528-29.

112. Except for the short perimeter cutoff across the Dobruja—if it was Domitianic. In any case Trajan's frontier certainly reached to the edge of the Danube delta; see R. P. Longden in *CAH* 11: 233 (The legionary base at Troesmis was less than ten miles south of the Danube bend.)

113. Constantin Daicoviciu, *La Transilvania nell' Antichitá* (Bucharest: n.p., 1943), pp. 41-64, and Emilienne Demougeot, *La Formation de l'Europe et les invasions barbares: Des origines germaniques à l'avènement de Dioclétien* (Paris: Anbier, 1969), pp. 156-60.

114. A Alföldi in *CAH* 11: 84-85.

115. Daicoviciu, *La Transilvania*, pp. 52-54.

116. See John Harmatta, "The Sarmatians in Hungary" in *Studies in the History of the Sarmatians*, Magyar-Görög Tanulmányok, 30 (Budapest: Pázmány Péter Tudományegyetemi Görög Filológiai Intézet, 1950), pp. 45-46.

117. *Histories*, I, 79.

118. Syme *CAH* 11: 168-72; and Demougeot, *La Formation*, pp. 162-64.

119. Syme, *CAH* 11: 175-76, based on fragmentary information (Dio LXVII.7.1).

120. Ibid., p. 176. Demougeot, *La Formation*, pp. 162-64.

121. Syme, *CAH* 11: 176-77. Demougeot, *La Formation*, pp. 162-64.

122. Jérôme Carcopino argues this, under the title "Un retour à l'impérialisme de conquête: L'Or des Daces" (1934), in *Les Etapes de l'imperialisme romain* (Paris: Hachette, 1961), pp. 106-17. See, *contra*, Lepper, *Trajan's Parthian War*, p. 107, in which he describes Trajan's Dacian policy as "Domitianic." The strength of Trajan's army (twelve to thirteen legions) in both wars, shows how powerful a state Decebalus had organized. An *economic* frontier strategy on that sector was incompatible with the survival of so strong a neighbor. There is also the evidence of Pliny's "Panegyric," which invokes no visions of grandiose conquest (*"non times bella nec provocas"*). Albino Garzetti, *Problemi dell'Eta Traianea: Sommario e testi* (Genova: Fratelli Bozzi, 1971), pp. 51-52, briefly states the arguments: that Trajan concluded his first Dacian war (A.D. 101-2) with another attempt to convert Dacia into a client state, refraining from conquest; that Decebalus himself provoked the second war (A.D. 105-6) by breaking

the terms of the treaty of A.D. 102; that the second war was not followed by total conquest, since only Transylvania was provincialized, while the lands on either side were left to the Sarmatians. See the recent survey of the debate in Kenneth Hugh Waters, "The Reign of Trajan and Its Place in Contemporary Scholarship," *ANRW*, pt. 2, vol. 2, pp. 417–22.

123. Szilágy, "Les Variations," p. 205, estimates the length of the imperial perimeter, including Dacia, at 10,200 kilometers, and without it, at 9,600 kilometers.

124. The *limes* is described in Daicoviciu, *La Transilvania*, pp. 89–99; for an updated account of the Trajanic settlement in Dacia, see idem, "Dacica" in *Hommages à Albert Grenier*, ed. Marcel Renard, 3 vols., Collection Latomus, vol. 58 (Brussels: Latomus, 1962), vol. 1, pp. 462–71.

125. For Dacia's role in the overall Danubian strategy, see Vasile Christescu, *Istoria Militară a Daciei Romane* (Bucharest: Fundația Regele Carol I, 1937), pp. 36–42. For a survey of the evidence, see Donald W. Wade, "The Roman Auxiliary Units and Camps in Dacia" (Ph.D. diss., University of North Carolina, 1969).

126. Frova, "The Danubian *Limes*," pp. 28–29.

127. Lepper, *Trajan's Parthian War*, pp. 109–10. For the subsidization of the Sarmatians, see Colin D. Gordon, "The Subsidization of Border Peoples as a Roman Policy of Imperial Defense" (Ph.D. diss., University of Michigan, 1948), p. 44.

128. Parker, *Roman Legions*, p. 157. On auxiliary units (including *numeri*) see Giovanni Forni, "Contributo alla storia della Dacia Romana," *Athenaeum*, n.s., vol. 36 (1958–59): 3–29 (fasc. 1–2) and 193–218 (fasc. 3), especially 206. See also Christescu, *Istoria Militară*, pp. 42–46 (on troops) and 47–52 (on fortifications).

129. The salient was used this way when the forces of C. Velius Rufus seemingly attacked the Iazyges in the rear after an advance north of the Danube and west across the river Tisza (Theiss), c.a. A.D. 89; R. P. Longden, *CAH* 11: pp. 176.

130. Numismatic evidence proves that Roman power was successfully maintained in the *Dacia Malvensis* until then (i.e., in Transylvania west of the river Olt); Eugenio Manni, *L'Impero di Gallieno: Contributo alla storia del III secolo* (Rome: Angelo Signorelli, 1949), p. 29.

131. Parker, *Roman Legions*, pp. 133–35.

132. This is the formulation of Garzetti, *Problemi dell'Età Traianea*, p. 53.

133. J. G. C. Anderson in *CAH* 10: 756–57. See also Magie, *Roman Rule*, pp. 551–53.

134. Until then Cappadocia had been ruled by a procurator supported only by *auxilia*; Parker, *Roman Legions*, p. 134.

135. Ibid., pp. 134–36; Anderson, *CAH* 10: 759–60.

136. There is a detailed account of the first stage of the conflict in Tacitus, *Annals* (XIII–XV); see Kristine Gilmartin, "Corbulo's Campaigns in the East," *Historia* 22 (1973): 583–626.

137. Anderson, *CAH* 10: 765–66.

138. Tacitus, *Annals*, XIII, 37–39.

139. Anderson, *CAH* 10: 768; Magie, *Roman Rule*, p. 558.

140. Magie, *Roman Rule*, pp. 558–60. On the XV *Apollinaris*, see Parker, *Roman Legions*, p. 137.

141. *Nero*, 13. On the diplomatic settlement, see Tacitus, *Annals*, XV, 27–30.

142. See, e.g., Webster, *Roman Imperial Army*, p. 63: "The prodigious efforts, losses and humiliation were all for nothing."

143. Cf. Henderson, *Five Roman Emperors*, p. 60, where the lack of Roman military deployments on the eastern Anatolian borders is called a "grave defect." Where would the legions needed for the job have come from?

144. Parker, *Roman Legions*, pp. 148–49; Syme, *CAH* 11: 141.

145. Lepper, *Trajan's Parthian War*, pp. 110–12. David Oates, *Studies in the Ancient History of Northern Iraq* (London: Oxford University Press for the British Academy, 1968), supports Lepper on the basis of a survey of climate, terrain (pp. 1–5), and strategic considerations (pp. 67–69). Cf. Waters, "The Reign of Trajan," pp. 422–28.

146. This is the major thesis of Lepper, *Trajan's Parthian War*, stated on pp. 112–22. Lepper is mindful of the objections to this thesis; see pp. 126–36; see also the review of M. I. Henderson in *JRS* 39 (1949): 125–26.

147. On the strategic advantages of the Khabur-Jebel Sinjar frontier, see Wheeler, "Mesopotamia," p. 127. On the rainfall levels, see Oates, *Studies in the Ancient History of Northern Iraq*, pp. 1–4 (and map, p. 2).

148. On the background and causes of the war, see R. P. Longden, *CAH* 11: 240; Magie, *Roman Rule*, p. 606 (the glory motive); Julien Guey, *Essai sur la guerre parthique de Trajan (114–117)*, Bibliothèque D "Istros", no. 2 (Bucharest: S. Lambrino, 1937), pp. 32–35; Lepper, *Trajan's Parthian War*, pp. 205–6 (summary), pp. 158–63 (rejects trade-route motive), and pp. 191–204 (critique of glory motive).

149. R. P. Longden, *CAH* 11: 241. In other words, Longden feels that Trajan, whatever his later aberrations, did not come east already in full pursuit of the Alexandrian dream.

150. Ibid. Osroes sent an ambassador to Athens to meet Trajan on his way east; but Trajan also seems to have offered an opening to a peaceful settlement by making himself available at Satala to an invited gathering of client kings from the Caucasus. Parthamasiris could have come to this meeting, but did not; ibid., p. 242. Cf. Guey, *Essai sur la guerre parthique*, pp. 140–41, who argues that Trajan was uninterested in a diplomatic settlement.

151. The sources for Trajan's Parthian war are exceedingly poor, and even the basic chronology is in doubt. R. P. Longden's chronology in *CAH* 11: 858–59 is as follows: A.D. 114, Armenia conquered and Northern Mesopotamia (i.e., north of the Jebel Sinjar line) annexed; 115, southern Mesopotamia and Adiabene annexed; winter 115, fall of Ctesiphon; 116, journey to the Persian Gulf and outbreak of the revolts (see note 152); 117, suppression of the revolt, withdrawal, and death of Trajan (firm date). Lepper's chronology, pp. 31–96, differs: A.D. 114, campaign in Armenia; 115, conquest of northern Mesopotamia and establishment of the putative Khabur-Jebel Sinjar frontier; 116, conquest of Adiabene and fall of Ctesiphon; 117, further conquests across the Tigris (Mesene) and outbreak of the revolt. Lepper exposes the limitations of his own chronology in careful detail. Cf. Henderson's review in *JRS* 39 (1949): 121–25. Guey, *Essai sur la guerre parthique*, p. 107, tabulates his chronology: A.D. 114, conquest of Armenia; September 114 to winter 115, conquest of northern Mesopotamia; spring 116, southern Mesopotamia, Adiabene and Ctesiphon conquered, and visit to the Persian Gulf; winter 116, trans-Tigris conquests, conquest of Babylon; 117, outbreak of the revolts, retreat, and death of Trajan. For attempted reconstructions of the campaigns, on the basis of the very fragmentary sources, see Longden, *CAH* 11: 243–51; Guey, *Essai sur la guerre parthique*, pp. 51–58, 66–77, 110–20, 122–25; and Lepper, *Trajan's Parthian War*, pp. 206–10. Lepper, on pp. 129–31, treats the campaigns of A.D. 116 as spoiling offensives, designed to enhance Roman diplomatic leverage, rather than as attempts at permanent conquest, and those of A.D. 117 as aberrations.

152. R. P. Longden, *CAH* 11: 248, holds that the revolts were triggered by the appearance of a Parthian army in Media; cf. Henderson in *JRS* 39 (1949): 127–28, who stresses that the Parthian counteroffensive is mentioned only by Malalas, a questionable sixth-century source. Lepper, *Trajan's Parthian War*, pp. 151–53, does not reject the possibility, and Guey, *Essai sur la guerre parthique*, pp. 123–25, accepts it. For the revolts themselves, under different chronologies, see Longden, *CAH* 11: 248–50; Lepper, *Trajan's Parthian War*, pp. 88–91; and Guey, *Essai sur la guerre parthique*, pp. 123–25. The role and timing of the Jewish revolts is unclear, as is their extent; see ibid., pp. 126–128 (Guey believes that the Jewish revolts were concurrent with localist revolts in Armenia, Mesopotamia, and Adiabene); Longden, *CAH* 11: 249–51.

153. Weber, in *CAH* 11: 301–2, follows tradition in making a sharp distinction between Trajan's expansionism and Hadrian's pacifism; accordingly, Hadrian is presented as effecting a sharp reversal of policy in making the withdrawal (while also contemplating the evacuation of Dacia). Magie, *Asia Minor*, pp. 609–11, does the same. Lepper, *Trajan's Parthian War*, pp. 212–13, holds that Trajan initiated a limited strategic withdrawal that Hadrian turned—for reasons of his own—into a total withdrawal. Guey, *Essai sur la guerre parthique*, pp. 133, 145–46, views the formation of client states (in A.D. 116–117) as a form of Trajanic withdrawal (c.f. Henderson, *JRS* 39 (1949): 126–27). For Hadrian's important role in the campaign, and his own position, see Louis Perret,

"Essai sur la carrière d'Hadrian jusqùa son avènement a l'empire (76–117)," in *Mémoires de la société nationale des antiquaires de France,* vol. 80, ser. 8, bk. 9 (Paris: G. Klincksieck, 1937).

154. See Dio, LXVIII.17.1, for Trajan's love of glory as the causal factor, and LXVIII.29.1, for his frustration at his inability to emulate Alexander's conquest of India. Quoted and translated in Garzetti, *Problemi dell'Età Traianea,* pp. 59, 62.

155. Magie, *Asia Monor,* pp. 606, 608; Wheeler, *Mesopotamia,* p. 116.

156. Guey, *Essai sur la guerre parthique,* rejects the glory motive (p. 19) but stresses the trade-route motive (pp. 20–22).

157. On the annexation of Nabatean Arabia, see Bowersock, "*Arabia Provincia,*" p. 229. Bowersock points out the significance of the official phraseology, "*Arabia adquisita*" as opposed to "*capta*"; in other words, the action was an administrative measure rather than a conquest. For the security arrangements, see ibid., pp. 232–40. For Vespasian's road building, see Syme, *CAH* 11: 130. Cf. Henderson, *JRS* 39 (1949): 128, who rejects the parallel with Flavian policy.

158. Josephus, *The Jewish War,* III.4.2.

159. Parker, *Roman Legions,* p. 138.

160. Ibid., p. 139. With the new legion I *Italica,* Nero's army comprised twenty-eight legions at this time; thus, counting the four legions in Syria, no less than one quarter of Rome's total legionary force was already engaged in this sector. It is doubtful whether any additional legionary forces could have been redeployed to the sector (e.g., to counter Parthian pressure) without dangerously unbalancing the legionary/auxiliary ratio elsewhere, risking internal civil disorders in less consolidated areas, or exposing frontiers to attack. The system was still highly elastic; but with the provision of the three legions for the Jewish War, this elasticity must have been heavily depleted.

161. Tacitus, *Annals,* XIII.35. This evaluation would not apply to the legion IV *Scythica,* drawn from Moesia. See Parker, *Roman Legions,* pp. 135, 138.

162. Bowersock, "*Arabia Provincia,*" pp. 219–29. On the limits of its usefulness, see Applebaum and Gichon, *Israel and Her Vicinity,* pp. 36–37.

163. Tacitus, *Annals,* XIII.7.

164. *Histories,* II.81.

165. Ibid., V.I.

166. Suetonius, *Nero,* 13; Magie, *Roman Rule,* p. 561.

167. Suetonius, *Vespasianus,* 8; Josephus, *The Jewish War,* VII.7.; Magie, *Roman Rule,* pp. 573–74. On Sophene, see Anderson in *CAH* 10: 758, n. 3.

168. On Agrippa II, see Thérèse Frankfort, "Le Royaume d'Agrippa II et son annexion par Domitien" in *Hommages à Albert Grenier,* vol. 2, pp. 665–66. For the Nabatean state, see Bowersock, "*Arabia Provincia,*" pp. 230–31. For the lesser Syrian states, see M. P. Charlesworth in *CAH* 11: 40.

169. Magie, *Roman Rule,* p. 607, n. 32.

170. See I. A. Richmond, "Palmyra under the Aegis of Rome," *JRS* 53 (1963): 42–43. On the Bosporan state, see Anderson, *CAH* 10: 265–66.

171. Magie, *Asia Minor,* pp. 569–70. Suetonius, in *Vespasianus* 8, mentions the annexation of Commagene and Cilicia Trachea together with the provincial reorganization of Achea, Lycia, Rhodes, Byzantium, and Samos.

172. George H. Stevenson, *Roman Provincial Administration till the Age of the Antonines* (Oxford: Basil Blackwell, 1939), pp. 50–51.

173. Guey, *Essai sur la guerre parthique,* pp. 145–46; M. Rostovtzeff in *CAH* 11: 119.

174. See Maxime Lemosse, *Le Régime des relationes internationales dans le haut-empire romain,* Publications de l'Institute de droit romain de l'Université de Paris, vol. 23 (Paris: Librairie Sirey, 1967), pp. 116–23.

175. Syme in *CAH* 11: 141.

176. Syme in *CAH* 11: 139. For Anatolia, see Magie, *Asia Minor,* pp. 570–73. Also, for the completed system, see Chevallier, *Voies romaines,* p. 161.

177. See Magie, *Asia Monor,* p. 574, p. 576; on Arabia, see Bowersock, "*Arabia Provincia,*" p. 230.

178. Cf. Tacitus, *Annals,* IV.5, with Parker, *Roman Legions,* p. 163: Cappadocia had two legions, Syria three, Judea two, and Arabia one. See also Syme in *CAH* 11: 140–41.

179. Suetonius, *Vesp.* 8; Magie, *Asia Minor*, p. 575 (and n. 24); ibid., p. 575 and n. 24, p. 1,438 (vol. II).

180. This "projection" was not costless in terms of fiscal exactions forgone, however. When Cappadocia was annexed, in A.D. 17, its revenue enabled Tiberius to reduce the auction tax by 50 per cent. Tacitus, *Annals*, II.42. Cf. ibid., I.78.

181. Lemosse, *Relationes internationales*, p. 117, n. 250.

182. Ibid., p. 119.

183. Domitian massed a force of nine legions against the Dacians in A.D. 87 (Parker, *Roman Legions*, p. 158), of which one, V *Alaudae*, may have been lost in the fighting; see Watson, *Roman Soldier*, p. 23, n. 43, for an abbreviated discussion of the issue. In his first Dacian war, Trajan had a force of twelve legions on the Danube (Parker, *Roman Legions*, p. 156), and he may have had a total of thirteen for the second war (ibid., p. 157). Cf. Longden, *CAH* 11: 231.

184. Ibid.; see also Gordon, "Subsidization of Border Peoples," p. 41.

185. Lemosse, *Relationes internationales*, p. 119.

186. I. A. Richmond, "Queen Cartimandua," *JRS* 44 (1954): 43–52; Jarrett and Mann, "Britain from Agricola to Gallienus," pp. 179–83; Eric B. Birley, "The Brigantian Problem and the First Roman Contact with Scotland" in *Roman Britain and the Roman Army*, pp. 31–47. Cf. Steer, "The Antonine Wall: A Reconsideration," p. 36.

187. On the Batavi, see Tacitus, *Germania*, 29; on the Frisii, ibid., 34; on the Tencteri and Usipetes, ibid., 32. See also Harmand, *L'Occident romain*, pp. 224–25, and Demougeot, *Formation*, p. 143.

188. Tacitus, *Histories*, I.67, with reference to the Helvetii.

189. As implied by the *Vita Hadriani*, of *SHA*, V.6.8; Gordan, "Subsidization of Border Peoples," p. 44.

190. Cf. Syme, *CAH* 11: 186.

191. S. N. Miller in *CAH* 12: 9. Also M. Rostovtzeff, *CAH* 11: 119 and Magie, *Roman Rule*, pp. 685–86.

192. Josephus, *The Jewish War*, trans. H. St. J. Thackeray, Loeb Classical Library, 3 vols. (London and New York: William Heinemann and G. P. Putnam, 1927–1929), III.5.

193. I. A. Richmond, "The Roman Siege-Works of Masàda, Israel," *JRS* 52 (1962): 154.

194. For a contrasting view, see Thompson, *Early Germans*, p. 150, on logistics.

195. The perimeter measured 9,600 kilometers (5,962 miles) without Dacia and 10,200 kilometers (6,334 miles) with Dacia; it also had 4,500 kilometers (2,794 miles) of coastline; Szilágyi, "Variations," p. 205.

196. Tacitus, *Annals*, XIII.35, 36.

197. Josephus, *The Jewish War*, II.18.9. Parker, *Roman Legions*, p. 138, interprets the passage as meaning that *vexillationes* of the IV *Scythica* and VI *Ferrata* were with Cestius Gallus.

198. Josephus, *The Jewish War*, II.19.7. Josephus implies that Cestius Gallus withdrew for no apparent reason. This is unlikely: Gallus was no coward (ibid., II.19.5), nor was he a fool. It may be conjectured that because the legionary troops had proved unsteady, the auxiliaries were affected, and the irregulars melted away.

199. Suetonius, *Vespasianus*, 4.

200. Josephus, *The Jewish War*, II.19.9. Josephus lists the casualties of the infantry and cavalry, but not of the irregulars.

201. Ramsay MacMullen, *Soldier and Civilian in the Later Roman Empire*, Harvard Historical Monographs 52 (Cambridge, Mass.: Harvard University Press, 1963), pp. 77–78.

202. G. Forni, "Estrazione etnica e sociale dei soldati delle legioni . . . " *ANWR*, pt. II, vol. 1, pp. 386–90.

203. Parker, *Roman Legions*, p. 145; Bersanetti, *Vespasiano*, pp. 75–79. See also, Eric B. Birley, "A Note on the Title 'Gemina'," *JRS* 18 (1928): 58.

204. G. E. F. Chilver, "The Army in Politics, A.D. 68–70," *JRS* 47 (1957): 35. Chilver points out that Vespasian did not feel compelled to purchase the loyalty of the army: his donatives were small, and there was no increase in pay.

205. Suetonius, *Domitianus*, 6, 7.

206. Ibid.

207. For the rebuilding of legionary bases in stone, see Schönberger, "Roman Frontier in Germany," p. 189 (nos. 38, 51, 21, 32).

208. When the British frontier was advanced, first to Hadrian's line and then to the still more remote Clyde-Forth line, the legions remained at York and Chester, in the deep rear. Legions also remained in Strasbourg, left almost eighty-seven miles behind the Antonine *limes* at its nearest point, Welzheim. But the fortress at Windisch was evacuated when the Lower German garrison was reduced, ca. A.D. 101; Schönberger, "Roman Frontier in Germany," p. 165.

209. R. W. Davies, "The Daily Life of the Roman Soldier under the Principate," *ANWR*, pt. II, vol. 1, p. 332.

210. Jean Baradez, "Les Thermes légionnaires de Gemellae," in *Corolla Memoriae Erich Swoboda Dedicata*, p. 16.

211. On hospitals and their arrangements, see Webster, *Roman Imperial Army*, pp. 195–96, 251, 254.

212. R. W. Davies, "The Medici of the Roman Armed Forces," in *Epigraphische Studien*, no. 8, (1969): 83–99; for standards, see p. 86.

213. R. W. Davies, "Joing the Roman Army," *Bonner Jahrbücher* 169 (1969): 208–13.

214. On basic training, see ibid., pp. 209–10, and Watson, *Roman Soldier*, pp. 54–72. Elaborate training methods were used, such as the construction of practice camps. One of these appears to have been used as an artillery range; see R. W. Davies, "The Romans at Burnswark," *Historia* 21 (1972): 107–8, 110.

215. David Breeze, in "The Organization of the Legion: The First Cohort and the *Equites Legionis,* " *JRS* 59 (1969): 50, n. 7, states that more than 154 different types of posts have been counted in the legionary establishment, excluding N.C.O.s in the centuries.

216. Cf. Ronald Syme, "Hadrian the Intellectual, "*Empereurs romains d'Espagne*, pp. 243–53.

217. ILS, *2487*, trans. Arnold H. M. Jones, in his *History of Rome Through the Fifth Century*, 2 vols. (New York: Harper and Row, 1970), vol. 2, *The Empire*, pp. 154–55.

218. He was, however, described as *armorum peritissimus et rei militaris scientissimus* in *The Vita Hadriani* of *SHA*; cited by Bernard W. Henderson, *The Life and Principate of the Emperor Hadrian* (London: Methuen & Co., 1923), pp. 171. See discussion, pp. 171–77, *contra* Marguardt et al.

219. E.g., Wilhel Weber, in *CAH* 11: 312–13.

220. *Strategemata*, IV.7.4.

221. On legionary pay from Augustus to Severus, see Watson, *Roman Soldier*, pp. 89–92. See also pp. 97–99, on pay of other citizen forces, pp. 102–4 on stoppages.

222. P. Coussin, *Les Armes romaines: Essai sur les origines et l'évolution des armes individuelles du légionnaire romain* (Paris: Librairie Ancienne Honoré Champion, 1926). The tendency was toward heavier and shorter *pila* (pp. 363–69); the replacement of the shorter *gladius*, legionary weapon *par excellence*, with the longer *spatha*, as always used by auxiliaries (p. 371); and the replacement of the heavy cylindrical shield with smaller and flatter shields (pp. 390–95). These tendencies had become general by the end of the period, under the Severi. Coussin sees all these changes in a negative light but does not argue the case.

223. Eric William Marsden, *Greek and Roman Artillery: Historical Development* (Oxford: At the Clarendon Press, 1969), p. 190.

224. Richmond, "Trajan's Army on Trajan's Column," p. 14.

225. This is the general assumption;see, e.g., G. L. Cheesman, *The Auxilia of the Roman Imperial Army* (Oxford: At the Clarendon Press, 1914), p. 168, where a total force of auxiliaries (including *numeri*) is estimated at 220,000, contrasted with c.a. 174,000 legionary troops.

226. Birley, "*Alae* and *Cohortes Milliariae*," pp. 55, 60.

227. The first is the general opinion; the second is that of Forni in "Contributo alla storia della Dacia Romana," p. 25. But the question may be moot; it has been claimed that

the very concept of the *"numeri"* is not merely artificial but misleading. See Michael P. Speidel, "The Rise of Ethnic Units in the Roman Imperial Army," *ANRW*, pt. 2, vol. 3, pp. 202–31.

228. J. C. Mann, "A Note on the Numeri," *Hermes* 82 (1954): 502.

229. In other words, the men were barbarians: ibid., pp. 505–6. For the *numeri* in general, see Chessman, *Auxilia of Roman Imperial Army,* pp. 85–90; Watson, *Roman Soldier,* p. 16; Webster, *Roman Imperial Army,* pp. 149–50; Syme in *CAH* 11: 132. For units in Britain, see Simpson, *Britons and the Roman Army,* pp. 131–35. Cf. note 227.

230. E.g., Watson, *Roman Soldier,* p. 16; the *élan* is presumably deduced from the war cries, mentioned by Arrian (*Tacita,* 44).

231. Watson, *Roman Soldier,* pp. 99–101. No data seem to be available for the *numeri,* but note the hierarchic pattern: legionary pay was 224 *denarii; ala* pay, 200; mounted *cohors equitata* pay, 150; and foot auxiliary pay, 100 *denarii.*

232. Troops of the *auxilia* were given the citizenship upon discharge, as had been the case since the time of Claudius; their sons could therefore aspire to legionary careers; A. N. Sherwin-White, *The Roman Citizenship* (Oxford: At the Clarendon Press, 1939), pp. 191–92. Under Antoninus Pius, however, sons born to auxiliaries prior to the grant of citizenship no longer received it with their fathers, and thus had to serve in the *auxilia* themselves in order to qualify; ibid., p. 215.

233. Mann, "A Note on the Numeri," p. 505.

234. See the map (no. 40) opposite p. 216 in Wilhelm Schleiermacher, *Der Römische Limes in Deutschland:Limesführer,* 3d ed. (Berlin: Gebr. Mann Verlag, 1967).

235. Garzetti, *L'Impero da Tiberio agli Antonini,* p. 439.

236. Forni, "Contributo," p. 214.

237. Birley, *"Alae* and Cohortes *Milliariae,"* p. 55.

238. Davies, *"Cohortes Equitatae,"* p. 752.

239. E.g., Cheesman, *Auxilia of the Roman Imperial Army,* p. 29.

240. Davies, *"Cohortes Equitatae,"* 754–63 *passim.* Davies argues that the horsemen of the *cohortes equitatae* were true cavalry and not mounted infantry, certainly not low-grade mounted troops. But he fails to draw the necessary distinction between light cavalry, suitable for scouting, "screening" patrols, and so on, and the heavy cavalry trained and equipped for high-intensity warfare; i.e., to charge *en masse* against enemy concentrations mounted or on foot. The cavalry of the *alae* was in fact dual purpose, trained to fight both with missile *and* shock weapons (the *contus*); the cavalry of the *cohortes equitatae* was only mounted and equipped for close contact and missile attack; as such it was limited-purpose light cavalry.

241. Marguerite Rachet, *Rome et les Berberes: Un problème militaire d'Auguste à Dioclétien,* Collection Latomus, vol. 110 (Brussels: Latomus, 1970), pp. 196–200.

242. Jean Baradez, "L'Enciente de Tipasa: Base d'operations de troupes venues de Pannonie sous Antonin Le Pieux" in *Quintus Congressus Internationalis Limitis Romani Studiosorum* (Zagreb: Arheoloski Radorii Rasprave III, 1963), pp. 75–77.

243. The evidence is reviewed in Anthony R. Birley, *Marcus Aurelius* (London: Eyre and Spottiswoode, 1966), p. 165.

244. Lucas de Regibus, *La Monarchia Militare di Gallieno* (Recco: Nicoloso da Recco, 1939), p. 108. There is a monographic study of the *vexillationes:* Robert Saxer, *Untersuchungen zu den vexillationen des römischen Kaiserheeres von Augustus bis Diokletian, Epigraphische Studien* Beihefte der Bonner Jahrbüchen, no. 18 (Cologne and Fraz: Böhlau, 1967).

245. Birley, *Marcus Aurelius,* p. 165. During the winter of A.D. 166/167 the northern frontiers were defended by mobile vexillation forces in anticipation of the return of the forces previously sent to the East. Major penetrations nevertheless took place; see Jenö Fitz, "Reorganisation militaire au début des guerres marcomanes," *Hommages à Marcel Renard,* ed. Jacqueline Bibaw, 3 vols., Collection Latomus, vol. 102. (Brussels: Latomus, 1969), vol. 1, pp. 262–74.

246. ILS 9200, cited by Syme in *CAH* 11: 163.

247. J. C. Mann, "The Raising of New Legions During the Principate," *Hermes* 91 (1963): 485.

CHAPTER THREE

1. The offense usually must accomplish this reduction because it needs the use of roads that are dominated by the strongholds of the defense, for logistic support.

2. H. M. D. Parker, *The Roman Legions* (Oxford: At the Clarendon Press, 1928), p. 167 On the deployment of the III *Italica* at Regensburg, see H. Schönberger, "The Roman Frontier in Germany: An Archaelogical Survey," *JRS* 59 (1969): 172.

3. See Lieut.-Col. Hamilton Tovey, *Elements of Strategy* (London: Eyre & Spottiswoode, 1887), pp. 133–34.

4. Tacitus had singled out the Chatti as an exception among the Germans in that they went ot war equipped with privisions; *Germania*, 33. See E. A. Thompson, *The Early Germans* (Oxford: At the Clarendon Press, 1965), pp. 140–49.

5. Mules, horses, and camels can, of course, move as fast or faster than men, but the logistic load was heavy, and *economical* support would require the use of carts pulled by oxen. Oxen require sixteen hours a day for rest and digestion, and are very slow. It has been calculated that a legion at full establishment needed 170 metric tons of wheat per month, and a quinquenary *ala* needed just under 53 tons of barley for its horses; R. W. Davies, "The Daily Life of the Roman Soldier under the Principate," in *ANRW*, pt. II, vol. 1, p. 318.

6. Until quite recently, in southeastern Europe the final segments of highway leading to international borders were frequently left unpaved as a counterinvasion measure. (This was true in Greece and Yugoslavia until well after the Second World War.)

7. For the skills of barbarians, see E. A. Thompson, *A Roman Reformer and Inventor: Being a new text of the treatise De Rebus Bellicis . . .* (Oxford: At the Clarendon Press, 1952), pp. 45–46.

8. For example, the legionary fortress of Eburacum, built ca. 107–8 under Trajan and rebuilt under Septimius Serverus had walls only 18 feet high and 5 3/4 feet wide; R. M. Butler, "The Defences of the Fourth Century Fortress at York" in *Soldier and Civilian in Rome Yorkshire* R. M. Butler ed. (Leicester: Leicester University Press, 1971), p. 97. The walls of post-third century fortifications, on the other hand, were generally 10 feet thick; see Harold von Petrikovits, "Fortifications in the North-Western Roman Empire from the Third to the Fifth Centuries A.D.," *JRS* 61 (1971): 197.

9. Von Petrikovits, "Fortifications in North-Western Roman Empire," pp. 194–95.

10. Butler, "Defenses of the Fourth Century Fortress at York," p. 97.

11. Von Petrikovits, "Fortifications in the North-Western Roman Empire," p. 193, attributed a purported improvement in Gothic siege technology to the capture of towns in Greece and Asia Monor. But these cities had been at peace for centuries, and there is no reason to believe that they contained equipment or men trained in siege warfare. Von Petrikovits adds (p. 193) that the Franks and Alamanni "very seldom tried a siege."

12. Thompson, *Early Germans*, pp. 133–34.

13. The sources on this subject are exceedingly poor; see the recent summary in Anthony R. Birley, *Marcus Aurelius* (London: Eyre and Spottiswoode, 1966), pp. 223–45, 283–86, and note 24, below.

14. E.g., Altenstadt; Schönberger, "Roman Frontier in Germany," pp. 171–72.

15. Birley, *Marcus Aurelius*, p. 165, based on S.H.A., *Vita Marci*, XII.13.

16. David Oates, *Studies in the Ancient History of Northern Iraq* (London: Oxford University Press for the British Academy, 1968), pp. 72–73. David Magie, *Roman Rule in Asia Minor to the End of the Third Century after Christ*, 2 vols. (Princeton: Princeton University Press, 1950), vol. 1, pp. 660–63.

17. Émilienne Demougeot, *La Formation de l'Europe et les invasions barbares: Des Origines germaniques à l'avènement de Dioclétien* (Paris: Aubier, 1969), pp. 215–29; J. Fitz, "A Military History of Pannonia from the Marcomann Wars to the Death of Alexander Serverus (180–235)," *Acta Archaeologica Academiae Scientiarum Hungaricae* 14 (1962): 32–36; Pavel Oliva, *Pannonia and the Onset of the Crisis in the Roman Empire* (Prague: Ceskoskovenské Akademie Věd, 1962), pp. 260–78.

18. *SHA, Vita Marci,* XXII.1.

19. Giovanni Brusin, "Le Difese della Romana Aquileia e la loro cronologia," *Corolla Memoriae Erich Swoboda Dedicata,* Römische Forschungen in Niederösterreich, 5 (Graz and Cologne: Hermann Bölaus Nachf., 1966), p. 87. Attilio Degrassi, *Il Confine nord-orientale dell'Italia romana: Ricerche storico-topografiche,* Dissertationes Bernenses ser. I. fasc. 6 (Bern: A. Grancke, 1954), p. 113.

20. Oliva, *Pannonia and the Onset of the Crisis,* 96-113; *Vita Marci,* XXI.6-8.

21. Parker, *Roman Legions,* pp. 116-17. See also J. C. Mann, "The Raising of New Legions during the Principate," *Hermes* 91 (1963): 486-89.

22. On the contemporary predominance of *vexillationes* as opposed to complete legions, see P. Romanelli, "L'esercito Romano nella rappresentazione della colonna," in *La Colonna di Marco Aurelio* (Rome: L"'Erma" di Bretschneider, 1955), p. 65; cf. Parker, *Roman Legions,* p. 168.

23. Ibid., p. 114.

24. Demougeot, *La Formation,* pp. 220-24; Birley, *Marcus Aurelius,* pp. 233-45.

25. Demougeot, *La Formation,* pp. 224-27; Birley, *Marcus Aurelius,* pp. 272-86, passim.

26. See Oliva, *Pannonia and the Onset of Crisis,* pp. 299-304. This contradicts sources as cited, including *SHA, Vita Marci,* XXIV.5; cf. Wilhelm Weber in *CAH* 11: 355, 362.

27. Demougeot, *La Formation,* p. 216, citing Dio, XLLII.3.1; Weber, *CAH* 11: 352, amends this to read 6,000 *survivors* of a larger initial force.

28. Demougeot, *La Formation,* p. 395. On Gothic attacks in general, see ibid., pp. 393-433, and John B. Bury, *The Invasion of Europe by the Barbarians* (1928); reprinted, (New York: Russel and Russel, 1963), pp. 3-22.

29. Schönberger, "Roman Frontier in Germany," pp. 176-77.

30. Demougeot, *La Formation,* pp. 521-32; Schönberger, "Roman Frontier in Germany," pp. 177-79.

31. Shappard S. Frere, *Britannia: A History of Roman Britain* (London: Routledge and Kegan Paul, 1967), pp. 188-89.

32. Demougeot, *La Formation,* pp. 419-28; A. Alföldi, *CAH* 11: pp. 147-50; Chester G. Starr, Jr., *The Roman Imperial Navy 31 B.C.-A.D. 324,* Cornell Studies in Classical Philology, vol. 26 (Ithaca: Cornell University Press, 1941), pp. 194-96.

33. Demougeot, *La Formation,* p. 419.

34. A. Alföldi, *CAH* 11: 148-49.

35. Fergus Millar, "P. Herennius Dexippus: The Greek World and the Third-Century Invasions" *JRS* 59 (1969): 26-27.

36. Homer A. Thompson, "Athenian Twilight: A.D. 267-600," *JRS* 49 (1959): 61-65.

37. This figure does not include insular and peninsular shorelines.

38. Frere, *Britannia,* pp. 188-89, 338 passim. On the *comes* and his command, see ibid., pp. 212, 229.

39. *SHA, Vita Claudii,* VIII.1 and VI.4.

40. A. Alföldi, *CAH* 12: 149. Bury, *The Invasions of Europe,* p. 22, merely remarks that the figures are grossly exaggerated.

41. See Arthur Christensen, *L'Iran sous les Sassanides,* 2d ed. (Copenhagen: Ejnar Munksgaard, 1944), pp. 84-96.

42. Oates, *Studies in the Ancient History of Northern Iraq,* p. 93; S. N. Miller, *CAH* 12: 16-17; Maurice Besnier, *L'Empire romain de l'avènement des Sévères au concile de Nicée,* Histoire ancienne, pt. 3; Histoire romaine, vol. 4 (Paris: Presses universitaires de France, 1937), pp. 24-25.

43. Christensen, *L'Iran sous les Sassanides,* pp. 97-98.

44. Ibid., p. 220.

45. Ibid., pp. 207-12.

46. Magie, *Roman Rule in Asia Monor,* pp. 695-96; Oates, *Studies in the Ancient History of Northern Iraq,* p. 74; Besnier, *L'Empire romain de l'avènement des Sévères,* pp. 105-7.

47. W. Esslin, *CAH* 12: 86-88; Christensen, *L'Iran sous les Sassanides,* pp. 130-31.

48. Besnier, *L'Empire romain de l'avènement des Sévères,* pp. 151, 153, 177-78.

49. See William Seston, *Dioclétien et la tétrarchie: Guerres et Réformes*, Bibliothèque des écoles françaises d'Athènes et de Rome, fasc. 162 (Paris: E. de Boccard, 1946), pp. 159–72. On the treaty of A.D. 298, see ibid., pp. 172–74. Cf. Ernst Stein, *Histoire du Bas-Empire: De l'étatromain à l'état byzantin*, ed. and trans. Jean-Remy Palanque, 2 vols. (Paris and The Hague: Desclée de Brouwer, 1959), vol. 1, pt. 1, pp. 79–80, where the date is given as A.D. 297. On the treaty of A.D. 363, see ibid., p. 171.

50. Schönberger, "Roman Frontier in Germany," p. 175, describes the attacks as "a decisive point in the history of Upper Germany and Raetia."

51. Ibid., p. 176.

52. On the Carpi, see Demougeot, *La Formation*, pp. 437–39. On the Goths in general, see the recent summary in Lucien Musset, *Les Invasions: Les vagues germaniques*, Nouvelle Clio no. 12 (Paris: Presses universitaires de France, 1965), pp. 80–82. On the sequence of events, see Demougeot, *La Formation*, pp. 409–11.

53. Demougeot, *La Formation*, p. 412.

54. On Dacia, see ibid., pp. 434–42; on Gothic victories and raids after 250, see ibid., pp. 416–25; on the emergence of the Frankish federation and its attacks until c.a. 260, see ibid., pp. 465–89 *passim*; on Shapur's threat to eastern Anatolia, see Besnier, *L'Empire romain de l'avènement des Sévères*, p. 178.

55. Demougeot, *La Formation*, p. 466.

56. Seston, *Dioclétien et la tétrarchie*, pp. 173–74. Cf. map, A.D. 309, in Stein, *Histoire du Bas-Empire*, vol. 1 book 2.

57. Cf. John C. Mann, "The Frontiers of the Principate," *ANWR* 2, vol. 1, pp. 524–25; his thesis is here controverted *in extenso* (chap. II).

58. The loss of Dacia was progressive, with the earlier abandonment of the Severan *Limes Transalutanus*. See Demougeot, *La Formation*, pp. 434–42, 452–57; and C. Daicoviciu, *La Transylvanie dans l'antiquité* (Bucharest: n.p., 1945), pp. 165–87. On the responsibility for the loss, see Eugenio Manni, *L'Impero di Gallieno: Contributo ala storia del III Secolo* (Rome: Angelo Signorelli, 1949), pp. 26–31, where each phase is distinguished.

59. Schönberger, "Roman Frontier in Germany," pp. 176–77.

60. Mann, "Frontiers of the Principate," p. 529.

61. Jean Lesquier, *L'Armée romaine d'Égypte d'Auguste à Dioclétien* (Cairo: Institut français d'archéologie orientale, 1918), pp. 474–77.

62. E. A. Thompson, *The Visigoths in the Time of Ulfila* (Oxford: At the Clarendon Press, 1966), pp. 3–6.

63. Under Constantine, who resumed an aggressive strategy of forward defense, a bridge across the Danube was built in 328 to provide access into the Olt valley. This trans-Danubian bridgehead was used, as Dacia as a whole had been used, as a base for lateral attacks. In 332, the Visigoths (then attacking the client Sarmatians in the Banat) were taken in the flank by a Roman force coming from the Olt valley and suffered a shattering defeat; see Thompson, *Visigoths*, pp. 10–12; on the strategy, see Stein, *Histoire du Bas-Empire*, pp. 128–29.

64. Marguerite Rachet, *Rome et les Berbères: Un problème militaire d'Auguste à Dioclétien*, Collection Latomus, vol. 110 (Brussels: Latomus, 1970), pp. 238–50; 252–54.

65. Seston, *Dioclétien*, p. 119, n. 1.

66. Ibid., pp. 117–20; Rachet, *Rome et les Berbères*, pp. 254–56.

67. Brian H. Warmington, *The North African Provinces from Diocletian to the Vandal Conquest* (Cambridge: Cambridge University Press, 1954), p. 8, for a brief overview; on the background, see Seston, *Dioclétien*, pp. 116–17.

68. See Rachet, *Rome et les Berbères*, p. 258; Maurice Euzennat, "Le Limes de Volubilis" in *Studien zu den Militärgrenzen Roms: Vorträge des 6 Internationalen Limes Kongress in Süddeutschland* (Cologne-Graz: Böhlau Verlag, 1967), pp. 198–99.

69. Lesquier, *L'Armée romaine d'Égypte*, pp. 474–77; Seston, *Dioclétien*, p. 158.

70. Seston, *Dioclétien*, pp. 168–74; Stein, *Histoire du Bas-Empire*, p. 80.

71. Mordechai Gichon, "The Negev Frontier," in Shimon Applebaum and Mordechai Gichon, *Israel and Her Vicinity in the Roman and Byzantine Periods* (Tel Aviv: Tel Aviv University Press, 1967), pp. 49–50.

72. Ibid., p. 52.

73. Ibid., pp. 52–54.

74. Davies, "Daily Life of the Roman Soldier," p. 326; Von Petrikovits, "Fortifications in the North-Western Roman Empire," p. 188.

75. Schönberger, "Roman Frontier in Germany," p. 178; J. Mertens and C. Leva, "Le Fortin de Braives et le *Limes Belgicus*" in R. Chevallier, ed., *Mélanges d'archéologie et d'histoire offerts à André Piganiol*, École Pratique des Hautes Études VIᵉ Section Centre de Recherches Historiques, 3 vols. (Paris: S.E.V.P.E.N., 1966), vol. 2, pp. 1063–74. The Cologne-Bavay road was not of course a *limes* in itself, for the frontier remained on the lower Rhine.

76. Von Petrikovits, "Fortifications in the North-Western Roman Empire," p. 188.

77. Ibid., p. 189.

78. Demougeot, *La Formation*, p. 497. These were also sea raids, however.

79. Ibid., p. 498.

80. The numbers given in the sources, 100,000 Alamanni versus 10,000 Romans, are almost certainly grossly exaggerated, but the food-gathering and loot-seeking dynamics of these raids would automatically lead to dispersion in the countryside and concentrations around target cities. See Besnier, *L'Empire romain de l'avènement des Sévères*, pp. 180–81, n. 234.

81. Clifford E. Minor, "Brigand, Insurrectionist and Separatist Movements in the Later Roman Empire" (Ph.D. diss., University of Washington, 1971), pp. 118–22.

82. Petrikovits, "Fortifications in the North-Western Roman Empire," p. 193.

83. Seston, *Dioclétien*, pp. 178–79; and map, opposite p. 374; but cf. map 1, opposite p. 130, in Denis van Berchem, *L'Armée de Dioclétien et la réforme Constantinienne*, Institut français d'archéologie de Beyrouth, Bibliothèque archéologique et historique 56 (Paris: Librairie orientaliste Paul Geuthner, 1952).

84. Von Petrikovits, "Fortifications in the North-Western Roman Empire," pp. 193–95.

85. Ibid., pp. 195–96.

86. This was the case of Dinogetia-Garvăn in Scythia; see Emil Condurachi, "Neue Probleme und Ergebnisse der *Limes*-forschung in Scythia Minor," *Studien zu den Militärgrenzen Roms*, pp. 165–66.

87. Von Petrikovits, "Fortifications in the North-Western Roman Empire," p. 197.

88. Ammianus Marcellinus (XX.6.5) writes of an *aries robustissimus* at the siege of Singara in A.D. 359; earlier, ironclad towers, firing platforms for artillery, had been unsuccessfully used by the forces of Shapur II at the siege of Amida. In any case, even the northern barbarians were not devoid of technical inventiveness; see Thompson, *Roman Reformer and Inventor*, pp. 44–50. Systematic siege technology, however, is another matter.

89. Von Petrikovits, "Fortifications in the North-Western Roman Empire," p. 197. This is a commonplace; see, e.g., the legionary fortresses at Strasbourg and the Constantinian fortress at Divitia (Deutz) opposite Cologne; Franz Oelmann, "The Rhine *Limes* in Late Roman Times," in [Third] *Congress of Roman Frontier Studies,1949*, ed. Eric Birley (Durham: Durham University Registrar, 1952), pp. 87, 95. But in Britain and elsewhere thin-walled structures remained in service (Frere, *Britannia*, pp. 342–59). And for a specific case, see Butler, "Defences of the Fourth Century Fortress at York," p. 97.

90. As in the case of the Rhine auxiliary fort at Remagen, where the existing structure dating from the principate was reconditioned in A.D. 275; Von Petrikovits, "Fortifications in the North-Western Roman Empire," p. 197. There is a graphic illustration of the process of successive changes in design in Radu Florescu, "Le Phases de construction du *castrum* Drobeta (Turnu Severin)," in *Studien zu den Militärgrenzen Roms*, pp. 144–51.

91. I. A. Richmond, *The City-Wall of Imperial Rome* . . . (Oxford: At the Clarendon Press, 1930), p. 243; Richmond calculated that the full complement of artillery would amount to 762 pieces (for 381 towers); Philip Corder, "The Reorganization of the

Defences of Romano-British Towns in the Fourth Century," *Archaeological Journal* 112 (1955): 34–35.

92. E. W. Marsden, *Greek and Roman Artillery: Historical Development*, 2 vols. (Oxford: At the Clarendon Press, 1969), 195–96.

93. Richmond, *City-Wall of Imperial Rome*, pp. 79–80; Corder, "Reorganization," pp. 34–36 (diagram). Under favorable conditions, the artillery could compensate for inadequate manpower, and this was an important consideration; see Thompson, *Roman Reformer and Inventor*, p. 49, on the author of the tract advocating a labor-saving weapon of his own design, described as a *ballista fulminalis*.

94. Von Petrikovits, "Fortifications in the North-Western Roman Empire," p. 197. The same technique was used in the twentieth-century police fortresses built in Palestine and India by the British.

95. R. Laur-Belart, "The Late *Limes* from Basel to the Lake of Constance," [Third] *Congress of Roman Frontier Studies, 1949*, p. 57; Florescu, "Le Phases de construction du *castrum* Drobeta," pp. 144–51; Oelmann, "The Rhine *Limes*," p. 87.

96. Von Petrikovits, "Fortifications in the North-Western Roman Empire," pp. 198–99. The Diocletianic *quadriburgium* had four square towers, in a pattern that varied little from province to province; Gichon, "The Negev Frontier," p. 52.

97. Petrikovits, "Fortifications in the North-Western Roman Empire," pp. 199–201.

98. Ibid., pp. 201–3; Schönberger, "Roman Frontier in Germany," p. 182; Laur-Belart, "Late *Limes* from Basel to Lake Constance," p. 58. Cf. Gichon, "The Origins of the *Limes Palestinae* and the Major Phases of Its Development," in *Studien zu den Militärgrenzen Roms*, pp. 180–81.

99. Schönberger, "Roman Frontier in Germany," p. 187, n. 346.

100. Some troops may have declined into parttime militias, but that is a very different thing from a *country-wide* system. There were exceptions: for example, *Collegia Iuventutis* may have manned road-forts; see Schönberger, "Roman Frontier in Germay," p. 178. The imperial authorities were reluctant to authorize the formation of voluntary militias (or even fire brigades). See Dio's third-century views, as reflected in the speech of Maecenas, translated in A. H. M. Jones, ed., *A History of Rome Through the Fifth Century*, 2 vols. (New York: Harper & Row, 1970) vol. 2, p. 58.

101. Marcianopolis and Philippopolis resisted Cniva successfully; so did Salonika in A.D. 256 and many other cities later.

102. E.g., the ancient walls of Aquileia, demolished by the late second century to accommodate the growth of the city; Brusin, "Le Difese della Romana Aquileia," p. 87.

103. R. M. Butler, "Late Roman Town Walls in Gaul," *Archaeological Journal* 116 (1959): 26; see his list of pre-third-century walled towns.

104. Ibid.; Von Petrikovits, "Fortifications in the North-Western Roman Empire," p. 189.

105. Butler, "Late Roman Town Walls in Gaul," p. 26.

106. See Demougeot, *La Formation*, pp. 485–88, on the Alamannic attack of A.D. 254; pp. 488–90 on the Frankish attacks; pp. 496–98 on the incursions of A.D. 259–60.

107. Butler, "Late Roman Town Walls in Gaul," p. 40. But some fairly large cities remained, e.g., Toulouse, whose 3,000 meters of enceinte enclosed 90 hectares; Michel Labrousse, "Recherches et hypothèses sur l'enceinte romaine de Toulouse," in *Hommages à Albert Grenier*, ed., Marcel Renard, vol. I, p. 925.

108. Homer A. Thompson, "Athenian Twilight," p. 63.

109. Butler, "Late Roman Town Walls in Gaul," p. 40.

110. Laur-Belart, *"Limes* from Basel to the Lake of Constance," p. 56.

111. Schönberger, "Roman Frontier in Germany," p. 178, n. 286.

112. Von Petrikovits, "Fortifications in the North-Western Roman Empire," n. 30 p. 192.

113. Renato Bartolucci, "Il porto di Leptis Magna nella sua vita economica e sociale," in *Hommages à Albert Grenier*, ed. Michel Renard, vol. 1, pp. 241–43.

114. Cf. Ramsay MacMullen, *Soldier and Civilian in the Later Roman Empire*, Harvard Historical Monographs 52 (Cambridge, Mass.: Harvard University Press, 1963), pp. 79–80.

115. R. G. Goodchild and J. B. Ward-Perkins, "The Limes Tripolitanus in the Light of Recent Discoveries," JRS 39 (1949): 84.

116. Von Petrikovits, "Fortifications in the North-Western Roman Empire," p. 191. Its purpose is irrelevant—it could be done.

117. MacMullen, Soldier and Civilian, pp. 138-51.

118. Van Berchem, L'Armée de Dioclétien, pp. 19-24, argues that the limitanei were generally the former alae and cohortes in a new and more localized guise, and dismisses the evidence of SHA Severus Alexander, 58.4, as being an anachronistic transposition of fourth-century notions. In so doing, he refects a traditional view, maintained by Stein, Histoire du Bas-Empire, p. 62, among others. W. Seston, in "Du comitatus de Dioclétien aux comitatenses de Constantin," Historia 4 (1955): 289, argues that the farmer-soldiers were not alares and cohortales transformed, but were rather barbarians enrolled for local, parttime military service (gentiles); MacMullen, Soldier and Civilian, on the other hand, questions the rejection of the SHA Severus Alexander as evidence (p. 13, n. 34). A. H. M. Jones, The Later Roman Empire (284-602: A social and administrative survey, 3 vols. (Oxford: Basil Blackwell, 1964), vol. 2, p. 649, concurs with Van Berchem's rejection of the early dating but stresses the evidence from North Africa where the militia were gentiles, while static troops, i.e., limitanei proper (ex-alares and cohortales), remained full-time garrison troops (pp. 650, 652-53). See also Guido Clemente, La "Notitia Dignitatum," Saggi di storia e letteratura, no. 4 (Cagliari: Editrice Sarda Fossataro, 1968), pp. 319-42.

119. Jones, Later Roman Empire, p. 649, insists on the military status of the limitanei proper (as opposed to barbarian farmer-soldiers), and hence on their likely efficiency, subject to contrary proof. Jones and others point out that full rations in kind were supplied to them all year until A.D. 364 and thereafter for nine months a year, which shows, he says (p. 651), that they did not grow their own food (and drilled instead?). Earlier, Santo Mazzarino, Aspetti Sociali del Quarto Secolo: Richerche di storia tardo-romana (Rome: L'Erma di Bretschneider, 1951), pp. 314-30 and passim, had argued that only in Africa were the limitanei peasants. For the more widespread view that the limitanei, whatever their origins, were a degraded peasant militia, see MacMullen, Soldier and Civilian, pp. 1-22 and 151-53.

120. SHA Severus Alexander cannot be accepted as evidence. "It is completely worthless and has no support whatever in our substantial evidence from the Severan period." [J. F. G.]

121. The limitanei were front-line defenders, even if both groups coexisted, as they seem to have done in the case of North Africa, at least; Jones, Later Roman Empire, p. 643. Cf. Van Berchem, L'Armée de Dioclétien, pp. 37-49.

122. Cf. MacMullen, Soldier and Civlian, pp. 155-56. Both Eric B. Birley, "Septimius Severus and the Roman Army," Epigraphische Studien, no. 8 (1969): 63-82, and R. E. Smith, "The Army Reforms of Septimius Severus," Historia 12 (1972): 489-500, argue against the tradition of the narrative sources, which is maintained by some modern historians; in their view, the pay increases, the permission given soldiers to cultivate the legionary lands, and all other privileges (gold ring, clubs, etc.) were intended to improve recruitment and to raise morale, not to bribe the army to support the dynasty.

123. Van Berchem, L'Armée de Dioclétien, pp. 21-24, followed in part by Jones, Later Roman Empire, vol. 2, p. 608, and formalized by Roger Rémondon, La Crise de l'empire romaine de Marc-Aurèle à Anastase, Nouvelle Clio, no. 11 (Paris: Presses universitaires de France, 1964), diagram, p. 126.

124. Seston, "Du Comitatus de Dioclétien," pp. 285-88. In any case, Van Berchem sees the dux limitis as becoming a purely territorial commander, in charge of limes and limitanei, in the wake of the Constantinian reforms; see L'Armée de Dioclétien, pp. 100-1.

125. Van Berchem, L'Armée de Dioclétien, pp. 100-2.

126. MacMullen, Soldier and Civilian, p. 153.

127. Ibid.; paraphrased but reversed. Based on Goodchild and Ward-Perkins, "The limes Tripolitanus," pp. 94-95. They resisted until 363 at least, and on their own.

128. Ibid., p. 43, citing a Theodosian constitution [Cod. Theod. VII, 15, 1].

129. Jones, Later Roman Empire, vol. 1, p. 274; vol. 2, p. 663, based on Cod. Just. I.xxvii.2 (vol. 3, p. 205, n. 130).

130. Schönberger, "Roman Frontier in Germany," p. 187.

131. Van Berchem, *L'Armée de Dioclétien*, pp. 91–92. For example the V *Macedonica* and XIII *Gemina* along the Danube in Dacia Ripensis and Upper Moesia were divided into five and four detachments, respectively, and the division had a permanent character, each detachment coming under the command of a separate *praefectus legionis* (Ibid., p. 93). The evidence dates from the *Notitia Dignitatum*, but in Van Berchem's "stratigraphic" analysis it is given a Constantinian dating.

132. These are the generally accepted figures; see Clemente, *La "Notitia Dignitatum,"* pp. 146–51, where the authoritative views are stated. But it also has been suggested that the *auxilia* were smaller (300 men), while the *cunei* were much larger (1,200 men); L. Várady, "New evidences on some problems of Late Roman military organization," *Acta Antiqua Academiae Scientiarum Hungaricae* 9 (1961): 360, and also as cited in Clemente, *La "Notitia Dignitatum,"* p. 151, n. 58.

133. Van Berchem, *L'Armée de Dioclétien*, pp. 85, 89, 101. Van Berchem distinguishes between the *limitanei* proper and the *ripenses,* a category that now comprised the provincial forces.

134. *"Le legioni di frontiera avevano assunto tutti i peggiori atteggiamenti degli imboscati d'ogni tempo . . . Vicini al nemico senza combatterlo, sedentari, oziosi, politicanti. . . ."* This is said of the third-century legions prior to the reforms of Gallienus; Luca de Regibus, *La Monarchia Militare di Gallieno* (Recco: Nicoloso da Recco, 1939), p. 63.

135. For the Severan list, see Jones, *Later Roman Empire*, vol. 3, table 9, pp. 368–74. The last mention of VI *Ferrata* is in Dio, LV.23; cited in Léon P. Homo, *Essai sur le règne de l'empereur Aurélien (270–275)*, Bibliothèque des écoles françaises d'Athènes et de Rome, fasc. 89 (Paris: Albert Fontemoing, 1904), p. 201, n. 9; the III *Parthica* is not listed in the *Notitia*, but internal evidence suggests that this may have been due to a clerical error; ibid., n. 2. The *Notitia* lists for the Rhine have been lost, but only one of the Rhine legions, the XXII *Primigenia*, is totally unattested in contingents of the field forces, as are I *Minervia* (*Minervii or.ix.37*), XXX *Ulpia* (*Truncensimani occ.vii.108*), and VIII *Augusta* (*Octaviani occ.vii.28*), and the XXII *Primigenia is* mentioned in the coins of Carausius in the Tetrarchic period; ibid., p. 202, n. 1. The only other legion not recorded in the *Notitia*, the XX *Valeria Victrix*, is also last mentioned in the coinage of Carausius; ibid., p. 203, n. 2. On the III *Augusta*, disbanded after 238 and reconstituted in 253, see René Cagnat, *L'Armée romaine d'Afrique et l'occupation militaire de l'Afrique sous les empereurs* (Paris: Ernest Leroux, 1913), pp. 159–61. Forty-four legions are listed in the *Notitia* as *limitanei* (meaning territorial forces) of which twenty-nine were in the East (on the Libya-Dacia circuit) and fifteen in the West; this excludes four detachments of legions also listed elsewhere as well as four detachments of Egyptian legions listed twice. In the eastern field army (*comitatus*) there are thirteen higher-grade palatine legions and thirty-eight regular field legions (*comitatenses*) as well as twenty transferred border legions (*pseudocomitatenses*); in the western field army, there are twelve palatine legions and thirty-three regular legions, as well as twenty-eight *pseudocomitatenses*. The grand total comes to 188 legions, which would be equivalent to 1,128,000 men under the old level of legionary unit manpower, a totally impossible number; Jones, *Later Roman Empire*, vol. 3, table 15, pp. 379–80.

136. Jones, *Later Roman Empire*, vol. 2, pp. 681–82. See Clemente, *"Notitia Dignitatum,"* pp. 146–56, on the question of unit numbers. There is some circumstantial archaeological evidence that the tetrarchic centuries were reduced to sixty men; E. B. Birley, "Hadrian's Wall and Its Neighbourhood" in *Studien zu den militärgrenzen roms*, p. 7.

137. Vegetius, I.20, 21. See François Paschoud, *Roma Aeterna: Études sur le patriotisme dans l'occident latin à l'époque des grandes invasions*, Bibliotheca Helvetica Romana, no. 7 (Rome: Institut Suisse de Rome, 1967), pp. 110–18.

138. Marsden, *Greek and Roman Artillery*, p. 195. There were separate legions instead, it seems; p. 196. The implication of Ammianus Marcellinus, XIX.5.2, is that normal legions were no longer trained to handle artillery or to build fortifications.

139. Paul Coussin, *Les Armes romaines: Essai sur les origines et l'évolution des armes individuelles du légionnaire romain* (Paris: Librarie Ancienne Honoré Champion, 1926), pp. 480–92.

140. Van Berchem, *L'Armée de Dioclétien*, p. 52; Von Petrikovits, "Fortifications in the North-Western Roman Empire," p. 181. The policy was continued by Constantine; see ibid., p. 182, and Thompson, *Visigoths in the Time of Ulfila*, pp. 10–12.

141. Paneg. Lat. IX, 18, 4, as cited in Van Berchem, *L'Armée de Dioclétien*, p. 89. For Malalas, see ibid., p. 17.

142. Lactantius naturally preferred to denounce his "building mania"; *De mortibus persecutorum*, 7. On Diocletian's personal role, see Seston, *Dioclétien et la tétrarchie*, pp. 297–98.

143. Ibid., pp. 177–78; cf. Van Berchem, *L'Armée de Dioclétien*, pp. 3–6.

144. Ibid., pp. 26–27, and map, following p. 130.

145. Seston, *Dioclétien et al tétrarchie*, pp. 131–32.

146. Van Berchem, *L'Armée de Dioclétien*, pp. 69–71.

147. Except for a single *numerus barcariorum* in Raetia, the only *numeri* surviving in the *Notitia* were ten units on Hadrian's Wall and another four under the *Comes Litoris Saxonici*, in charge of British coast defenses; eventually the term *numeri* become generic, but perhaps in tetrarchic times it still distinguished an ethnic unit. Ibid., pp. 57–58.

148. Jones, *Later Roman Empire*, vol. 1, p. 56.

149. This transformation is a large subject: see the summaries in Jones, *Later Roman Empire*, pp. 61–68; Seston, *Dioclétien et la tétrarchie*, pp. 261–94, and Denis van Berchem, "*L'Annone militaire dans l'empire romain au IIIème siècle*," *Mémoires de la société nationale des antiquaires de France*, vol. 80, ser. 8, bk. 10 (Paris: G. Klincksieck, 1937).

150. He granted the right to marry, surely a case of *ex post facto* recognition, raised pay (for the first time since Domitian) from 300 to 450 *denarii*, allowed the formation of social clubs, and facilitated promotions (the gold rings); Smith, "Army Reforms of Septimius Severus," pp. 492–96, and Birley, "Septimius Severus and the Roman Army," pp. 63–65.

151. See the preamble to the celebrated edict on prices translated in Jones, *History of Rome*, vol. 2, pp. 308–12. "Sometimes the single purchase of a soldier deprives him of his bonus and salary."

152. This figure includes the uncertain IV *Italica* supposedly raised by Alexander Severus; Mann, "The Raising of New Legions during the Principate," p. 484.

153. Rather schematically, E. Nischer, "The Army Reforms of Diocletian and Constantine and Their Modifications up to the Time of the *Notitia Dignitatum*," *JRS* 13 (1923): 1–55, had estimated a 100 percent increase in the legionary force, from thirty-four to sixty-eight units; for this he was criticized in detail by H. M. D. Parker, "The Legions of Diocletian and Constantine," *JRS* 23, pt. 2 (1933): 177–80. However, Besnier, *L'Empire romain de l'avènement des Severes*, p. 304 and nn. 160, 164, endorsed Nischer's figure, and Jones, *Later Roman Empire*, vol. 1, pp. 59–60, arrives at the same result.

154. Parker, "The Legions of Diocletian and Constantine," p. 80.

155. Van Berchem, "*L'Armée de Dioclétien*, pp. 15–17 and map, opposite p. 130.

156. Ibid., pp. 24–26.

157. Jones, *Later Roman Empire*, vol. 1, p. 57.

158. Van Berchem, *L'Armée de Dioclétien*, pp. 90–93, endorsed by Jones, *Later Roman Empire*, vol. 1, p. 99.

159. Van Berchem, *L'Armée de Dioclétien*, pp. 90–91.

160. On the *cunei* and *auxilia* at the time of Constantine, see Jones, *Later Roman Empire*, vol. 1, pp. 99–100.

161. Van Berchem, *L'Armée de Dioclétien*, p. 85.

162. Ibid., pp. 101–2.

163. If an inference can be drawn from a constitution of 372, *Cod. Theod.* VII, 22, 8 (372) as cited; ibid., p. 102, n. 1.

164. Zosimus charged that he had done so; Jones, *Later Roman Empire*, vol. 2, p. 609.

165. Van Berchem, *L'Armée de Dioclétien*, p. 93.

166. Jones, *Later Roman Empire*, vol. 3, table 12, p. 378.

167. L. Várady, "Additional Notes on the Problem of Late-Roman Dalmatian *Cunei*," *Acta Antiqua Academiae Scientarum Hungaricae* 11 (1963): 391–406.

168. Clemente, *"Notitia Dignitatum,"* p. 299, reproduces the list.

169. André Alföldi, "La Grande Crise du monde romain au IIIe siècle," *L'Antiquité Classique* 7 (1938): 7.

170. Richard I. Frank, *Scholae Palatinae: The Palace Guards of the Later Roman Empire,* Papers and Monographs of the American Academy in Rome, vol. 23 (Rome: American Academy in Rome, 1969), pp. 17–26.

171. M. Speidel, *Die Equites Singulares Augusti* (Bonn, 1965).

172. Stein, *Histoire du Bas-Empire,* vol. 1, pp. 57–58. Jones *Later Roman Empire,* vol. 1, pp. 53–54; vol. 2, pp. 636–40. Frank, *Scholae Palatinae,* pp. 33–41.

173. Frank, *Scholae Palatinae,* pp. 47–49. Cf. Jones, *Later Roman Empire,* vol. 2, p. 613. The *Scholae* were actually under the Master of Offices, but the latter would be an administrative supervisor, and not an operational commander; ibid.

174. Ibid., pp. 52–53.

175. On these beginnings, see Marcel Durry, *Les Cohortes Prétoriennes.* Bibliothèque des écoles françaises d'Athènes et de Rome, fasc. 146 (Paris: E. de Boccard, 1938), and Alfredo Passerini, *Le Coorti Pretorie* (1939); rpt. ed. (Rome: Centro Editoriale Internazionale, 1969), pp. 1–53, for origins and early history.

176. Ibid., p. 44.

177. *Annals,* IV.5; Passerini, *Coorti Pretorie,* p. 53.

178. Ibid., pp. 54–55, 61.

179. On the *Vigiles,* see P. K. B. Reynolds, *The Vigiles of Ancient Rome* (Oxford: At the Clarendon Press, 1926).

180. Mann, "Raising of New Legions" (n. 27); Birley, *Marcus Aurelius,* p. 217.

181. Smith, "Army Reforms of Septimius Severus," p. 486, n. 28.

182. Ibid., n. 1, for detailed citations of ancients, and n. 33 (p. 487) for some moderns.

183. These numerical comparisons are summarized in Durry, *Les Cohortes Prétoriennes,* pp. 81–87, and table, p. 89, n. 4.

184. Birley, "Septimius Severus and the Roman Army," p. 65.

185. Maurice Platnauer, *The Life and Reign of the Emperor Lucius Septimius Severus* (London and Bombay: Humphrey Milford, 1918), called it a "halfway house" to the field armies of Diocletian and Constantine (pp. 162–63).

186. A. Alföldi, *CAH* 12: 213.

187. Manni, *L'Impero di Gallieno,* pp. 58–59 and notes; De Regibus, *La Monarchia Militare di Gallieno,* pp. 78–79; Alföldi, *CAH* 12: 216–18; Besnier, *L'Empire romain de l'avènement des Sévères,* p. 190.

188. Ibid., p. 185, 225, 232.

189. Parker, "Legions of Diocletian and Constantine," p. 188.

190. Besnier, *L'Empire romain de l'avènement des Sévères,* p. 190.

191. Stein, *Histoire du Bas-Empire,* p. 55 and n. 216 (vol. 2, p. 430), based on the number in Vegetius, II.6, and on the dating of Stein's source to the period 260–90. Cf. H. M. D. Parker, "The *Antiqua Legio* of Vegetius," *Classical Quarterly* 26 (1932): 137–49 *passim,* for dating.

192. Alföldi, *CAH* 12: 217.

193. Ibid., p. 216.

194. Cited in Paschoud, *Études sur le partriotisme romain,* p. 117.

195. The conclusion of John W. Eadie, "The Development of the Roman Mailed Cavalry," *JRS* 57 (1967): 161–73.

196. Ibid., pp. 166 (Josephus, B. J. III.5.5) and 167. The *contus* is the standard cavalry weapon in Vegetius; Coussin, *Armes romaines,* p. 479.

197. Ibid., p. 167.

198. Ibid., pp. 169–70.

199. Homo, *Essai sur le règne de l'empereur Aurélien,* p. 88.

200. Ibid., pp. 94, 99.

201. Eadie, "Development of Roman Mailed Cavalry," p. 170. Listed in the *Nortitia* are a *schola,* a *cuneus* and five *equites* of *clibanarii,* in the East, as well as one *equites* and the *sagittarii* in the West.

202. See ibid., p. 172, for some examples.

203. Seston, *Dioclétien et la tétrarchie,* pp. 52–53. The date 298 in Seston is a misprint. Read 285. Cf. Besnier, *L'Empire romain de l'avènement des Sévères,* pp. 277–78.

204. Jones, *Later Roman Empire,* vol. 1, p. 55; there are certainly many *equites* in the *Notitia* for Palestine. It was garrisoned by twelve *equites,* Arabia by eight, Phoenice by twelve, Syria by ten, Osrhöene by nine, and Mesopotamia by nine; ibid., vol. 3, table 10, p. 376.

205. Seston, *Dioclétien et la tétrarchie,* p. 299. Note, however, that in the *Notitia* lists for the eastern frontiers (Jones, *Later Roman Empire,* vol. 3, table 10, p. 376), there is no numerical correlation between the number of legions and the number of *equites promoti.* Cf. Jones, *Later Roman Empire,* vol. 1, p. 53.

206. This is a view held by Mommsen, Seeck, and Grosse, and reiterated by Stein, *Histoire du Bas-Empire,* vol. 1, pp. 72–73, among others. Seston, *Dioclétien et la tétrarchie,* pp. 302–7, presents a modified orthodox view, concluding, "L'armée des comitatenses du Bas-Empire est donc née d'une conception stratégique de Gallien, dont le danger politique a èté supprimé par Dioclétien et dont Constantin a perfectionné l'organization technique."

207. Passerini, *Coorti Pretorie,* p. 57. For example, some Praetorians went to Mauretania with the Augustus Maximian in 296; cited by Seston, *Dioclétien et la Tétrarchie,* p. 119, n. 1.

208. On the *lanciarii* as troops of the *comitatus,* see Parker, "Legions of Diocletian and Constantine," p. 186. Jones, *Later Roman Empire,* vol. 1, pp. 55, suggests that the *lanciarii* were probably assigned to the frontier sectors under Diocletian. and that they were not part of the *comitatus.* Van Berchem, *L'Armée de Dioclétien,* p. 107, suggests that they were, in any case, few in number. But in the *Notitia* there are several legions of *lanciarii;* see S. Mazzarino, *DE,* vol. 4 s.v. *"Lanciarii";* and Seston, "Du *Comitatus* de Dioclétien aux *Comitatenses* de Constantin," pp. 293–94. Both reiterate the role of the *lanciarii* in the *comitatus.*

209. As members of the *comitatus* (therefore made larger), see ibid.; as normal cavalry, which had once been attached temporarily to the imperial retinue but not permanently of it, van Berchem, *L'Armée de Dioclétien,* pp. 107–8. In contrast, see Jones, *Later Roman Empire,* vol. 1, p. 52, 53. Nevertheless, Jones (vol. 2, p. 608) describes the *comitatus* as "small."

210. By Nischer, "Army Reforms of Diocletian and Constantine." Cf. N. H. Baynes' rebuke: "Three Notes on the Reforms of Diocletian and Constantine," *JRS* 15 (1925): 201–8, and Parker's detailed refutation, "Legions of Diocletian and Constantine."

211. Van Berchem, *L'Armée de Dioclétien,* whose conclusions are stated in pp. 113–18. In his conclusion, van Berchem finds that the narrative sources, the *Suda,* Aurelius Victor (cited n. 3 and 4, p. 115), and especially Zosimus II.34, confirm his argument, which is, however, independent of them; Nischer too had found corroborative support in the narrative sources, but Parker had rejected their value. Seston, in his review of van Berchem (n. 246), insists on the prejudiced mendacity of Zosimus. It is interesting to note that in any case the passage in dispute, II.34, exemplifies the inability of Zosimus, and doubtless many others with him, to understand the military logic of a deep defense-in-depth strategy.

212. Seston, "Du *Comitatus* de Dioclétien aux *comitatenses* de Constantin" (n. 246). Seston praises Van Berchem's method but does not accept his conclusions. Várady, "New Evidences on Some Problems of Late Roman Military Organization" (n. 158), rejects the method also, since he does not believe that the *Notitia* has ordered strata.

213. Jones, *Later Roman Empire,* vol. 1, pp. 54–55, 97; vol. 2, p. 608.

214. Denis Van Berchem, "On Some Chapters of the *Notitia Dignitatum* Relating to the Defense of Gaul and Northern Britain," *American Journal of Philology* 76 (1955): 147.

215. Jones, *Later Roman Empire,* vol. 1, p. 97. Seston, *Dioclétien et la tétrarchie,* p. 307, describes them as *techniciens.*

216. Total figure is from Jones, *Later Roman Empire,* vol. 3, table 15, p. 379.

217. Ibid., vol. 1, p. 98. Cf. Stein, *Histoire du Bas-Empire,* vol. 1, p. 73, where the *auxilia* are attributed to Diocletian.

218. Zosimus, *Historia Nova,* trans. James J. Buchanan and Harold T. Davis (San Antonio: Trinity University Press, 1967), II. 34.

219. Jones, *Later Roman Empire,* vol. 2, pp. 649–54. From 325 on, the sectoral forces (*ripenses*) were given a status lower than the *comitatenses* though higher than the *alares* and *cohortales,* according to Van Berchem, *L'Armée de Dioclétien,* p. 85.

220. Émilienne Demougeot, *De L'Unité à la division de l'empire romain 395–410: Essai sur le gouvernement imperial* (Paris: Librairie d'Amerique et d'Orient, 1951), p. 511.

221. Santo Mazzarino *Stilicone: La crisi imperiale dopo Teodosio* (Rome: Angelo Signorelli, 1942), pp. 128–29.

222. The figures in Table 3.1 may be contrasted to the data cited by Arthur E. R. Boak in *Manpower Shortage: And the Fall of the Roman Empire in the West,* Jerome Lectures, 3d ser. (Ann Arbor: The University of Michigan Press, 1955), p. 91, estimates of the fourth-century army by Piaganiol (under 400,000), Seeck (400–600,000), Lot (450–471,000), Cary, Grosse, Stein and Segrè (ca. 500,000), and J. B. Bury (600–650,000), in all of which the field army is estimated at ca. 200,000.

223. Birley, "Septimius Severus and the Roman Army," p. 78.

EPILOGUE

1. The *palatini* are first recorded in a constitution of 365, *C.Th.* VIII.i.10; cited by Jones, *Later Roman Empire,* vol. 3, n. 28, pp. 21–22.

2. Related by Priscus, quoted, with comments, in E. A. Thompson, *A History of Attila and the Huns* (Oxford: At the Clarendon Press, 1948), pp. 113, 185–86. But others thought otherwise; see, among others, Adrian N. Sherwin-White, *The Roman Citizenship,* 2d ed. (Oxford: At the Clarendon Press, 1973), pp. 425–68 passim.

APPENDIX

1. Robert E. Osgood, in Robert E. Osgood and Robert W. Tucker, *Force, Order and Justice* (Baltimore: Johns Hopkins Press, 1967), p. 3

2. Ibid.

3. See, for example, Roderick Bell, David V. Edwards, and R. Harrison Wagner, eds. *Political Power: A Reader in Theory and Research* (New York: The Free Press, 1969), a compendium of definitions in modern American political science. Also, for a phenomenological study in historical perspective, see Bertrand de Jouvenel, *Power: Its Nature and the History of Its Growth* (Boston: Beacon Press, 1967). For a sociological orientation, see Dorothy Emmet, *Function, Purpose and Powers* (London: MacMillan and Co. 1958). For an anthropological perspective, see Eugene V. Walter, *Terror and Resistance: A Study of Political Violence* (New York: Oxford University Press, 1969), which is a study of Zulu political life under the kings.

4. Hans J. Morgenthau, *Politics Among Nations,* 3d. ed. (New York: Alfred A. Knopf, 1962), p. 26.

5. Peter Bachrach and Morton S. Baratz, *Power and Poverty* (New York: Oxford University Press, 1970), pp. 17–38.

6. Ibid.

7. E.g., Robert A. Dahl, *Modern Political Analysis* (Englewood Cliffs, N.J.: Prentice-Hall, Inc., 1963), pp. 39–54; J. David Singer, "Inter-Nation Influence: A Formal Model," *American Political Science Review* 57 (1963): 420–30; K. J. Holsti, *International Politics,* 2d ed. (Englewood Cliffs, N.J.: Prentice-Hall, Inc., 1972), pp. 154–58, and many others.

8. Dahl, *Modern Political Analysis,* p. 41.

9. For a notable exception, see P. Bachrach and M. S. Baratz, "Decision and Nondecision: An Analytical Framework," *American Political Science Review* 57 (1963): 632–42, where the distinction is made clear, and where it is pointed out that it is noncompliance with the orders of the powerful that imposes on the latter the costs of using force.

10. It does not matter to whom, or to what groups, the "ownership" of the means of security (and the burden of providing the inputs) is attributed. Given full internal control, *all* the resources of society are available for appropriation by the ruling power,

so that societal costs not borne directly by the latter are still costs to it, at least in possible exactions forgone.

11. For the development of the concept of "suasion," descriptive of the actual process resulting from the presence, display, or symbolic application of force, see Edward N. Luttwak, *The Political Uses of Sea Power* (Baltimore: John Hopkins University Press, 1974). The context is naval but the theory is generally applicable.

12. Peter Blau, *Exchange and Power in Social Life* (New York: John Wiley, 1964), compares power to status but then goes on to treat it as capital—expendable capital. Cf. Talcott Parsons, "On the Concept of Political Power" in *Political Power: A Reader in Theory and Research,* pp. 256–57, where power is defined in terms comparable to money, this also suggesting its exhaustion by use.

13. I mean "rational" in the value-free sense of an ability to align ends and means in a way intended to optimize the former, whatever they may be.

14. I.e., to the Bachrach-Baratz definition; see note 12, above.

15. This admittedly excludes from consideration cases in which the opponents seek negative values, e.g., glorious martyrdom, as well as cases in which the opponents have no values vulnerable to attack, or at least no values that are attack-worthy.

LIST OF WORKS CITED

I
Articles and Contributions to Collective Works

Alföldi, Andrés. "La Grande Crise du monde romain au IIIe siècle." *L'Antiquite classique* 7 (1938): 5–18.
——. "The Moral Barrier on Rhine and Danube." In [Third] *Congress of Roman Frontier Studies, 1949*, pp. 1–16.
Alföldy, Géza. "Die Hilfstruppen der römischen Provinz Germania Inferior." *Epigraphische Studien*, no. 6.
Amit, Moché. "Les Moyens de communication et la défense de l'empire romain." *La Parola del Passato*, vol. 20, fasc. 102 (1965), pp. 207–22.
Bachrach, Peter, and Baratz, Morton S. "Two Faces of Power." *American Political Science Review* 56 (December 1962): 947–52.
——. "Decisions and Non-Decisions: An Analytical Framework." *American Political Science Review* 57 (September 1963): 632–43.
Baradez, Jean L. "Organisation militaire romaine de l'Algérie antique et l'evolution du concept défensif de ses frontières." *Revue internationale d'histoire militaire*, no. 13 (1953), pp. 24–42.
——. "L'Enceinte de Tipasa: Base d'opérations des troupes venues de Pannonie sous Antonin Le Pieux." In *Quintus Congressus Internationalis Limitis Romani Studiosorum*. pp. 75–82.
——. "Les Thermes légionnaires de Gemellae." In *Corolla Memoriae Erich Swoboda Dedicata*, pp. 14–22.
——. "L'Enceinte de Tipasa et ses portes." In *Mélanges Piganiol* [ed. Chevallier], vol. 2, pp. 1133–52.
——. "Compléments inédits au 'Fossatum Africae.'" In *Studien zu den Militärgrenzen Roms*, pp. 200–10.

Bartoccini, Renato. "Il Porto di Leptis Magna nella sua vita economica e sociale." In *Hommages à Albert Grenier* [ed. Renard], vol. 1, pp. 228–42.

Baynes, N.H. "Three Notes on the Reforms of Diocletian and Constantine." *Journal of Roman Studies* 15 (1925): 195–208.

Berchem, Denis van. "L'Annone militaire dans l'empire romain au IIIème siècle." In *Mémoires de la société nationale des antiquaires de France*, vol. 80, ser. 8, bk. 10, pp. 117–202. Paris: G. Klinckseick, 1937.

———. "Aspects de la domination romaine en Suisse." *Schweizerische Zeitschrift für Geschichte* 5 (1955): 145–75.

———. "On Some Chapters of the *Notitia Dignitatum* Relating to the Defense of Gaul and Britain." *American Journal of Philology*, vol. 76, no. 302 (1955), pp. 138–47.

———. "Conquête et organisation par Rome des districts alpins." *Revue des études latines* 11 (1962):228–35.

Betz, A. "Zur Dislokation der Legionen in der Zeit vom Tode des Augustus bis zum Ende der Prinzipatsepoche." In *Carnuntina* [ed. Swoboda], pp. 17–24.

Birley, Anthony R. "Excavations at Carpow." *Studien zu den Militärgrenzen Roms*, pp. 1–5.

Birley, Eric B. "A Note on the title 'Gemina.'"*Journal of Roman Studies* 18 (1928): 56–60.

———. "The Brigantian Problem and the First Roman Contact with Scotland." In *Roman Britain and the Roman Army*, pp. 31–47.

———. "Britain after Agricola and the End of the Ninth Legion." In idem, *Roman Britain and the Roman Army*, pp. 25–28.

———. "Britain under the Flavians: Agricola and His Predecessors." In idem, *Roman Britain and the Roman Army*, pp. 10–19.

———. "Hadrianic Frontier Policy." In *Carnuntina* [ed. Swoboda], pp. 26–33.

———. "*Alae* and *Cohortes Milliariae*." In *Corolla Memoriae Erich Swoboda Dedicata*, pp. 54–67.

———. "Hadrian's Wall and Its Neighbourhood." *Studien zu den Militärgrenzen Roms*, pp. 6–14.

———. "Septimius Severus and the Roman Army." *Epigraphische Studien*, no. 8 (1969), pp. 63–82.

———. "The Fate of the Ninth Legion." In *Soldier and Civilian in Roman Yorkshire* [ed. Butler], pp. 71–80.

Bowersock, G. W. "A Report on *Arabia Provincia*." *Journal of Roman Studies* 61 (1971): 219–42.

Breeze, D. J. "The Organization of the Legion: The First Cohort and the *Equites Legionis*." *Journal of Roman Studies* 59 (1969): 50–55.

Breeze, D. J., and Dobson, Brian. "Hadrian's Wall: Some Problems." *Britannia* 3 (1972): 182–208.

Brogan, Olwen. "The Roman *Limes* in Germany." *Archaeological Journal* 92 (1935): 1–41.

Brunt, P. A. Review of *Die Aussenpolitik des Augustus und die augusteische Dichtung*, by Hans D. Meyer. *Journal of Roman Studies* 53 (1963): 170–76.

Brusin, Giovanni. "Le Difese della romana Aquileia e la loro cronologia." In *Corolla Memoriae Erich Swoboda Dedicata*, pp. 84–94.

Burns, T. S. "The Battle of Adrianople: A Reconsideration." *Historia* 23 (1973): 336–45.

Butler, R. M. "The Roman Walls of Le Mans." *Journal of Roman Studies* 48 (1958): 33–39.

———. "Late Roman Town Walls in Gaul." *Archaeological Journal* 116 (1959): 25–50.

———. "The Defences of the Fourth-Century Fortress at York." In *Soldier and Civilian in Roman Yorkshire* [ed. Butler], pp. 97–106.

Cagnat, R. "Les Frontières militaires de l'empire romain." *Journal des savants*, January 1901, pp. 29–40.

Cavaignac, E. "Les Effectifs de l'armée d'Auguste." *Revue des études latines* 30 (1952): 285–96.

Chevallier, Raymond. "Rome et la Germanie au 1er siècle: Problèmes de colonisation." *Latomus* 20 (1961), fasc. i, pp. 33–51, fasc. ii, pp. 266–80.

Chilver, G. E. F. "The Army in Politics A.D. 68-70." *Journal of Roman Studies* 47 (1957): 29–35.

Collingwood, R. G. "The Purpose of the Roman Wall." *Vasculum* 8 (1920): 4–9.

Condurachi, E. "Neue Probleme und Ergebnisse der Limes-forschung in Scythia. Minor." *Studien zu den Militärgrenzen Roms*, pp. 162–74.

Corder, Philip. "The Reorganization of the Defences of Romano-British Towns in the Fourth Century." *Archaeological Journal*, 112 (1955): 20–42.

Crump, G. A. "Ammianus and the Late Roman Army." *Historia* 23 (1973): 91–103.

Daicoviciu, Constantin. "Dacica." In *Hommages à Albert Grenier* [ed. Renard], vol. 1, pp. 462–73.

Davies, R. W. "The 'Abortive Invasion' of Britain by Gaius." *Historia* 15 (1966): 124–28.

——. "A Note on a Recently Discovered Inscription in Carrawburgh. Appendix." *Epigraphische Studien*, no. 4 (1967), pp. 108–11.

——. "Joining the Roman Army." *Bonner Jahrbücher* 169 (1969): 208–32.

——. "The Medici of the Roman Armed Forces." *Epigraphische Studien*, no. 8 (1969), pp. 83–99.

——. "Cohortes Equitatae." *Historia* 20 (1971): 751–63.

——. "The Romans at Burnswark." *Historia* 21 (1972): 98–113.

——. "The Daily Life of the Roman Soldier under the Principate." *Aufstieg und Niedergang der Römischen Welt* [ed. Temporini], pt. 2, Vol. 1, pp. 299–338.

Dobiáš, J. "King Maroboduus as a Politician." *Klio* 38 (1960): 155–66.

Dobson, Brian, and Breeze, D. J. "Hadrian's Wall: Some Problems." *Britannia* 3 (1972): 182–208.

Doise, J. "Le Commandement de l'armée romaine sous Theodose et les débuts des règnes d'Arcadius et d'Honorius." *Mélanges d'archéologie et d'histoire*, École française de Rome, vol. 61 (1949), pp. 183–94.

Dyson, L. "Native Revolts in the Roman Empire." *Historia* 20 (1971): 239–74.

Eadie, John W. "The Development of Roman Mailed Cavalry." *Journal of Roman Studies* 57 (1967): 161–73.

Euzennat, Maurice. "Le *Limes* de Volubilis." In *Studien zu den Militärgrenzen Roms*, pp. 194–99.

Finley, M. I. Review of *Manpower Shortage*, by A. E. R. Boak. *Journal of Roman Studies* 48 (1958): 156–64.

Fishwick, D. "The Annexation of Mauretania." *Historia* 20 (1971): 467–87.

Fitz, J. "A Military History of Pannonia from the Marcomann Wars to the Death of Alexander Severus (180-235)." *Acta Archaeologica Academiae Scientiarum Hungaricae* 14 (1962): 25–112.

——. "Réorganization militaire au début des guerres marcomannes." *Hommages à Marcel Renard* [ed. Bibaw], vol. I, pp. 262–74.

Florescu, Radu. "Les Phases de construction du *castrum* Drobeta (Turnu Severin)." *Studien zu den Militärgrenzen Roms*, pp. 144–51.

Forni, Giovanni. "Contributo alla storia della Dacia romana." *Athenaeum* n.s., vol. 36 (1958-59): 3–29 (fasc. 1-2), 193–218 (fasc. 3).

——. "Limes," in *Dizionario Epigrafico*," vol. 4, fasc. 34–40, pp. 1,074–280.

——. "Estrazione etnica e sociale dei soldati delle legioni nei primi tre secoli dell'impero." *Aufstieg und Niedergang der Römischen Welt* [ed. Temporini] pt. 2, vol. 1, pp. 339–91.

Frankfort, Thérèse. "Le Royaume d'Agrippa II et son annexion par Domitien." In *Hommages à Albert Grenier* [ed. Renard], vol. 2, pp. 659–72.

Frova, Antonio. "The Danubian *Limes* in Bulgaria and Excavations at Oescus," [Third] *Congress of Roman Frontier Studies*, 1949, pp. 23–30.

Gichon, M. [S.A.M.] "Roman Frontier Cities in the Negev." *Quintus Congressus Internationalis Limitis Romani Studiosorum*, pp. 195–207.

——. "The Origin of the *Limes Palestinae* and the Major Phases of Its Development." *Studien zu den Militärgrenzen Roms*, pp. 175–93.

——. "The Negev Frontier." In *Israel and Her Vicinity in the Roman and Byzantine Periods* [ed. Applebaum], pp. 35–61.

Gigli, G. "Forme di reclutamento militare durante il basso impero." *Rendiconti della classe di scienze morali, storiche e filologiche dell'Accademia dei Lincei*, vol. 8, ser. 2 (1947), pp. 268–89.

Gilmartin, Kristine. "Corbulo's Campaigns in the East." *Historia* 23 (1973): 583–626.

Goodchild, R. G. "The *Limes Tripolitanus* II." *Journal of Roman Studies* 40 (1950): 30–38.

——. "The Roman and Byzantine *Limes* in Cyrenaica." *Journal of Roman Studies* 43 (1953): 65–76.

Goodchild, R. G., and Ward-Perkins, J. B. "The Limes Tripolitanus in the Light of Recent discoveries." Journal of Roman Studies 39 (1949): 81-95.

Gray, W. D. "A Politcal Ideal of the Emperor Hadrian." Annual Report of the American Historical Association for the Year 1914, vol. 1, pp. 113-24.

Hardy, E. G. "Augustus and his Legionaires." Classical Quarterly 14 (1921): 187-194.

Harmand, Jaques. "Les Origines de l'armée impériale: Un Témoignage sur la réalité du pseudo-principat et sur l'évolution militaire de l'Occident." Aufstieg und Niedergang der Römischen Welt [ed. Temporini], part 2, vol. 1, pp. 263-98.

Haverfield, F. "Some Roman Conceptions of Empire." Occasional Publications of the Classical Association Cambridge , no. 4 (ca. 1916).

Henderson, M. I. Review of Trajan's Persian War, by F. A. Lepper. Journal of Roman Studies 39 (1949): 121-32.

Jarrett, Michael G. "The Roman Frontier in Wales." Studien zu den Militärgrenzen Roms. pp. 21-31.

Jarrett, Michael G., and Mann, John C. "Britain from Agricola to Gallienus." Bonner Jahrbücher 170 (1970): 178-210

Kornemann, E. "Die unsichtbaren Grenzen des römischen Kaiserreichs." In Staaten-Männer-Völker; Aus der geschichte des altertums. Leipzig: Deiterich, 1934. Pp. 96-116.

Laet, S. J. de. "Claude et la romanisation de la Gaule septentrionale." Mélanges Piganiol [Chevallier], vol. 2, pp. 951-62.

Laur-Belart, R. "The Late Limes from Basel to the Lake of Constance." [Third] Congress of Roman Frontier Studies, 1949, pp. 55-67.

Leva, C., and Mertens, J. "Le fortin de Braives et le limes belgicus." Mélanges Piganiol [Chevallier], vol. 2, pp. 1,063-74.

McLeod, W. "The Range of the Ancient Bow." Phoenix 19, no. 1 (1965): 1-14.

Mann, John C. "A Note on the Numeri." Hermes 82 (1954): 501-6.

――. "The Raising of New Legions during the Principate." Hermes 91 (1963): 483-89.

――. "The Role of the Frontier Zone in Army Recruitment." Quintus Congressus Internationalis Limitis Romani Studiosorum, pp. 145-50.

Mann, John C., and Jarrett, M. G. "Britain from Agricola to Gallienus." Bonner Jahrbücher 170 (1970): 178-210.

――. "The Frontiers of the Principate." Aufstieg und Niedergang der Römischen Welt [ed. Temporini], part 2, vol. 1, pp. 508-33.

Marin, A. "Hippagogi." In Dictionnaire des antiquités greques et romaines [Daremberg-Saglio], vol. 4, pp. 183-86.

Mertens, J. "Oudenburg, camp du Litus Saxonicum en Belgique?" In Quintus Congressus Internationalis Limitis Romani Studiosorum, pp. 123-31.

Mertens, J., and Leva, C. "Le Fortin de Braives et le Limes Belgicus." Mélanges Piganiol [Chevallier], vol. 2, pp. 1,063-74.

Millar, Fergus. "P. Herennius Dexippus: The Greek World and the Third-Century Invasions." Journal of Roman Studies, 59 (1969): 12-29.

Morris, John. "The Vallum Again." Transactions of the Cumberland and Westmoreland Antiquarian and Archaeological Society, n.s. 50 (1951): 43-53.

Moss, J. R. "The Effects of the Policies of Aetius on the History of the Western Empire." Historia 23 (1973): 711-31.

Nischer, E. "The Army Reforms of Diocletian and Constantine and Their Modifications up to the Time of the Notitia Dignitatum." Journal of Roman Studies 13 (1923): 1-55.

Nock, A. D. "The Roman Army and the Roman Religious Year." Harvard Theological Review 45 (1952): 187-252.

Oelmann, F. "The Rhine Limes in Late Roman Times." [Third] Congress of Roman Frontier Studies, 1949, pp. 81-99.

O'Neill, R. J. "Doctrine and Training in the German Army 1919-1939." The Theory and Practice of War [ed. Howard], pp. 145-65.

Parker, H. M. D. "The Antiqua Legio of Vegetius." Classical Quarterly 26 (1932): 137-49.

――. "The Legions of Diocletian and Constantine." Journal of Roman Studies 23 (1933): 175-89.

Parsons, T. "On the Concept of Political Power." In Political Power [Bell et al.], pp. 251-84.

Passerini, A. "Gli Aumenti del soldo militare da Commodo a Massimino." *Athenaeum* 24 (1946): 145–59.

———. "*Legio*." In *Dizionario Epigrafico*, vol. 4, fasc. 18–20, pp. 549–627.

Pekáry, Th. "Studien zur römischen Währungs und Finanzgeschichte von 161 bis 235 n. Ch." *Historia* 8 (1959): 443–89.

Perret, Louis. "Essai sur la carrière d'Hadrien jusqu'a son avènement a l'empire (76–117)." *Mémoires de la société nationale des antiquaires de France*, vol. 80, ser. 8, bk. 9. Paris: G. Klincksieck, 1937.

Petrikovits, Harald von. "Fortifications in the North-Western Roman Empire from the Third to the Fifth Centuries A.D." *Journal of Roman Studies* 61 (1971): 178–218.

Pflaum, H-C. "Forces et faiblesses de l'armée romaine du Haut-Empire." *Problèmes de la guerre à Rome* [Brisson], pp. 85–98.

Piganiol, A. "La Notion de *Limes*." *Quintus Congressus Internationalis Limitis Romani Studiosorum*, pp. 119–22.

Ramsay, A. M. "The Speed of the Roman Imperial Post." *Journal of Roman Studies* 15 (1925): 60–74.

Rémondon, Roger. "Problèmes militaires en Egypte et dans l'empire à la fin du IV siècle." *Revue historique* 213 (1955): 21–38.

Richmond, Sir Ian A. "Trajan's Army on Trajan's Column." *Papers of the British School at Rome* 13 (1935): 1–40.

———. "The Romans in Redesdale." *History of Northumberland* 15 (1940): 116–29.

———. "Hadrian's Wall 1939–1949." *Journal of Roman Studies* 40 (1950): 43–56.

———. "A Roman Arterial Signalling System in the Stainmore Pass." *Aspects of Archaeology* [ed. Grimes], pp. 293–302.

———. "Queen Cartimandua." *Journal of Roman Studies* 44 (1954): 43–52.

———. "The Roman Frontier Land." *History* [U.K.], vol. 44, no. 150 (February 1959), pp. 1–15.

———. "The Roman Siege-Works of Masàda, Israel." *Journal of Roman Studies* 52 (1962): 142–55.

———. "Palmyra under the Aegis of Rome." *Journal of Roman Studies* 53 (1963): 43–54.

Robertson, Anne S. "The Antonine Wall." *Congress of Roman Frontier Studies, 1949*, pp. 99–111.

Robinson, H. R. "Problems in Reconstructing Roman Armour." *Bonner Jahrbücher* 172 (1972): 24–35.

Rowell, H. T. "The *Honesta Missio* from the *Numeri* of the Roman Imperial Army." *Yale Classical Studies* 6 (1939): 73–108.

Saddington, D. B. "Roman Attitudes to the *Externae Gentes* of the North." *Acta Classica* [S.A.] 4 (1961): 90–102.

———. "The Development of Roman Auxiliary Forces from Augustus to Trajan." *Aufstieg und Niedergang der Römischen Welt* [ed. Temporini], pt. 2, vol. 3, pp. 176–201.

Salama, Pierre. "Occupation de la Maurétanie césarienne occidentale sous les Bas-Empire romain." *Mélanges Piganiol* [Chevallier], vol. 3, pp. 1,291–311.

Salmon, E. T. "The Roman Army and the Disintegration of the Roman Empire." *Proceedings and Transactions of the Royal Society of Canada*, 3d series, vol. 52 (1958), sect. 2, pp. 43–60.

Saint-Denis, E. de. "*Mare Clausum*." *Revue des études latines*, 25 (1947): 200–203.

Schönberger, H. "The Roman Frontier in Germany: An Archaeological Survey." *Journal of Roman Studies* 59 (1969): pp. 144–97.

Seston, William. "Du *Comitatus* de Dioclétien aux *comitatenses* de Constantin." *Historia* 4 (1955): 284–96.

Shaw, R. C., and Simpson, F. G. "The Purpose and Date of the Vallum and Its Crossings." *Transactions of the Cumberland and Westmoreland Antiquarian and Archaeological Society*, n.s. 27 (1922): 40–100.

Sherwin-White, A. N. "Geographical Factors in Roman Algeria." *Journal of Roman Studies* 34 (1944): 1–10.

Simpson, F. G., and Shaw, R. C. "The Purpose and Date of the Vallum and Its Crossings." *Transactions of the Cumberland and Westmoreland Antiquarian and Archaeological Society*, n.s. 27 (1922): 40–100.

Simpson, Grace. "The Roman Forts in Wales: A Reassessment." *Studien zu den Militär-grenzen Roms*, pp. 32–34.
Smallwood, E. Mary. "Palestine c. A.D. 115–118." *Historia* 11 (1962): 502–5.
Smith, R. E. "The Army Reforms of Septimius Severus." *Historia* 12 (1972): 481–500.
Steer, Kenneth A. "The Antonine Wall: A Reconsideration." *Studien zu den Militärgrenzen Roms*, pp. 35–41.
Stevens, C. E. "The British Sections of the *Notitia Dignitatum*." *Archaeological Journal* 97 (1940): 125–54.
———. "Britain between the Invasions (54 B.C.-A.D. 43): A Study of Ancient Diplomacy." In *Aspects of Archaeology* [ed. Grimes], pp. 332–44.
Swoboda, E. "Traian und der Pannonische *Limes*." *Empereurs romains d'Espagne* [Centre nationale de la recherche scientifique], pp. 195–208.
Syme, R. "Rhine and Danube Legions under Domitian." *Journal of Roman Studies* 18 (1928): 41–55.
———. "Some Notes on the Legions under Augustus." *Journal of Roman Studies* 23 (1933): 14–33.
———. "The Lower Danube under Trajan." *Journal of Roman Studies* 49 (1959): 26–33.
———. "Hadrian the Intellectual." *Empereurs romains d'Espagne* [Centre nationale de la recherche scientifique], pp. 243–53.
Szilágyi, J. "Roman Garrisons Stationed at the Northern Pannonia-Quad Frontier-Sectors of the Empire." *Acta Archaeologica Academiae Scientiarum Hungaricae* 2 (1952): 189–220.
———. "Les Variations des centres de prépondérance militaire dans les provinces frontières de l'empire romain." *Acta Antiqua Academiae Scientiarum Hungaricae* 2(1953): fasc. 1–2, pp. 119–219.
Thompson, E. A. "The Foreign Policies of Theodosius II and Marcian." *Hermathena*, no. 76 (1950), pp. 58–75.
———. "The Settlement of the Barbarians in Southern Gaul." *Journal of Roman Studies* 46 (1956): 65–75.
Thompson, Homer A. "Athenian Twilight: A.D. 267–600." *Journal of Roman Studies* 49 (1959): 61–72.
Tierney, J. J. "The Map of Agrippa." *Proceedings of the Royal Irish Academy*, vol. 63, sect. C, no. 4 (1963), pp. 151–66.
Vannérus, Jules. "Le *Limes* et le fortifications gallo-romaines de Belgique: Enquête toponymique." Académie royale de Belgique, *Mémoires*, coll. 4, 2ᵉ ser., vol 9, fasc. 2.
Várady, L. "New Evidences on Some Problems of Late Roman Military Organization." *Acta Antiqua Academiae Scientiarum Hungaricae* 9 (1961): 333–96.
———. "Additional Notes on the Problem of Late-Roman Dalmatian *Cunei*." *Acta Antiqua Academiae Scientiarum Hungaricae* 11 (1963): 333–96.
Vita, A. Di. "Il *Limes* romano di Tripolitania nella sua concretezza archeologica e nella sua realtá storica." *Libya Antiqua* 1 (1964): 65–98.
Ward-Perkins, J. B., and Goodchild, R. G. "The *Limes Tripolitanus* in the Light of Recent Discoveries." *Journal of Roman Studies* 39 (1949): 81–95.
Waters, Kenneth Hugh. "The Reign of Trajan in Contemporary Scholarship." *ANRW*, pt. 2, vol. 2, pp. 381–430.
Watson, G. R. "The Pay of the Roman Army: The Auxiliary Forces." *Historia* 8 (1959): 372–78.
Webster, G. "The Legionary Fortress at Lincon." *Journal of Roman Studies* 39 (1949): 57–78.
———. "The Claudian Frontier in Britain." *Studien zu den Militärgrenzen Roms*, pp. 42–53.
Wells, C. M. "The Augustan Penetration of Germany, Dates and Destinations." *Roman Frontier Studies 1967*, pp. 1–6.
Wheeler, [Sir] R. E. M. "The Roman Frontier in Mesopotamia." *Congress of Roman Studies, 1949*, pp. 112–29.
Wilkes, J. J. "A Note on the Mutiny of the Pannonian Legions in A.D. 14." *Classical Quarterly*, n.s., vol. 13, no. 2 (November 1963), pp. 268–71.
Will, E. "Les Enceintes du bas-empire à Bavay." *Quintus Congressus Internationalis Limitis Romani Studiosorum*, pp. 99–110.

II
Books and Monographs

Adcock, Frank Ezra. *The Roman Art of War under the Republic*. Martin Classical Lectures, vol. 8. Cambridge, Mass.: Harvard University Press, 1940.

Alföldi, Andreas. *A Conflict of Ideas in the Late Roman Empire: The Clash between the Senate and Valentinian I*. Oxford: At the Clarendon Press, 1952.

Andreotti, R. *Il Regno dell'imperatore Giuliano*. Bologna: N. Zanichelli, 1936.

Applebaum, Shimon, and Gichon, Mordechai. *Israel and Her Vicinity in the Roman and Byzantine Periods*. Tel Aviv: Tel Aviv University Press, 1967.

Arias, Paolo E. *Domiziano: Saggi e ricerche*. No. 9. Catania (Sicily): G. Crisafulli, 1945.

Aussaresses, F. *L'Armée byzantine à la fin du VIe siècle: d'après le strategicon de l'empereur Maurice*. Bibliothèque des universités du midi. Fasc. 14. Bordeaux: Feret and fils, 1909.

Badian, Ernst. *Foreign Clientelae (264–70 B.C.)*. Oxford: At the Clarendon Press, 1958.

———. *Roman Imperialism in the Late Republic*. 1965. Reprint. Oxford: Basil Blackwell, 1968.

———. *Publicans and Sinners: Private Enterprise in the Service of the Roman Republic*. Ithaca: Cornell University Press, 1972.

Balsdon, J. P. V. D. *The Emperor Gaius (Caligula)*. Oxford: At the Clarendon Press, 1934.

Baradez, Jean Lucien. *Vue-Aerienne de l'organisation romaine dans le Sud-Algérien, fossatum Africae*. Paris: Arts et métiers graphiques, 1949.

Bell, Roderick; Edwards, David V.; Wagner, R. Harrison, eds. *Political Power: A Reader in Theory and Research*. New York: The Free Press, 1969.

Berchem, Denis van. *L'Armée de Dioclétien et la réforme constantinienne*. Institut français d'archéologie de Beyrouth, Bibliothèque archéologique et historique 56. Paris: Librairie orientaliste Paul Geuthner, 1952.

Bersanetti, Gastone M. *Vespasiano*. Rome: Edizioni Roma, 1941.

Besnier, Maurice. *L'Empire romain de l'avènement des Sévères au concile de Nicée*. Histoire générale I; Histoire ancienne, pt. 3; Histoire romaine, vol. 4. Paris: Presses universitaires de France, 1937.

Birley, Anthony R. *Hadrian's Wall: An Illustrated Guide*. Ministry of Public Building and Works. London: H. M. Stationery Office, 1963.

———. *Marcus Aurelius*. London: Eyre and Spottiswoode, 1966.

———. *Septimius Severus: The African Emperor*. London: Eyre and Spottiswoode, 1971.

Birley, Eric B. *Roman Britain and the Roman Army: Collected Papers*. Kendal: Titus Wilson and Son, 1953.

———. *Research on Hadrian's Wall*. Kendal: Titus Wilson and Son, 1961.

Blau, Peter. *Exchange and Power in Social Life*. New York: John Wiley, 1964.

Boak, Arthur Edward Romilly. *The Master of Offices in the Later Roman and Byzantine Empires*. University of Michigan Studies. Humanistic Series, vol. 14. London: Macmillan and Co., 1919.

———. *Manpower Shortage: And the Fall of the Roman Empire in the West*. The Jerome Lectures, third series. Ann Arbor: The University of Michigan Press, 1955.

Bowersock, Glen W. *Augustus and the Greek World*. Oxford: At the Clarendon Press, 1965.

Braithwaite, A. W. C. *Suetoni Tranquilli Divus Vespasianus*. Oxford: At the Clarendon Press, 1927.

Brand, Clarence Eugene. *Roman Military Law*. Austin: University of Texas Press, 1968.

Bréhier, Louis. *Les Institutions de l'empire byzantin*. L'évolution de l'humanité, vol. 32, bis. Paris: Éditions Albin Michel, 1949.

Bruce, John Collingwood. *Handbook to the Roman Wall*. 12th ed. by [Sir] Ian A. Richmond. Newcastle: H. Hill Hindson and A. Reid, 1966.

Brunt, P. A. *Italian Manpower 225 BC-AD 14*. Oxford: At the Clarendon Press, 1971.

Bury, John Bagnell. *A History of the Later Roman Empire: From Arcadius to Irene (395 A.D. to 800 A.D.)*. Reprint. 2 vols. 1889. Amsterdam: Adolf M. Hakkert, 1966.

———. *The Invasion of Europe by the Barbarians*. 1928. Reprint. New York: Russell and Russell, Inc., 1963.

Cagnat, René. *L'Armée romaine d'Afrique et l'occupation militaire de l'Afrique sous les empereurs*. Ministère de l'instruction publique. 2d ed. Paris: Ernest Leroux, 1913.

Calderini, Aristide. *I Severi: La crisi dell'impero nel III secolo*. Istituto di studi romani, Storia di Roma, no. 7. Bologna: Licinio Cappelli Editore, 1940.

Carcopino, Jérôme. *Les étapes de l'impérialisme romain*. 1934. Reprint. Paris: Hachette, 1961.

Cary, Max. *The Geographic Background of Greek and Roman History*. Oxford: At the Clarendon Press, 1949.

Casson, Lionel. *Ships and Seamanship in the Ancient World*. Princeton: Princeton University Press, 1971.

Chapot, Victor. *La Frontière de l'Euphrate: De Pompée à la conquête arabe*. Paris: A. Fontemoing, 1907.

Charlesworth, Martin Percival. *Trade Routes and the Commerce of the Roman Empire*. 2d rev. ed. Cambridge: At the University Press, 1926.

———. *Five Men: Character Studies from the Roman Empire*. Martin Classical Lectures, no. 6. Cambridge, Mass.: Harvard University Press, 1936.

———. *The Lost Province, or the Worth of Britain*. Cardiff: University of Wales Press, 1949.

Chastagnol, André. *Les Bas Empire*. Texts. Paris: Librairie Armand Colin, 1969.

Cheesman, George Leonard. *The Auxilia of the Roman Imperial Army*. 1914. Reprint. Hildesheim: George Olms, 1971.

Chevallier, Raymond. *Les Voies romaines*. Paris: Librairie Armand Colin, 1972.

Chilver, Guy Edward F. *Cisalpine Gaul: Social and Economic History from 49 B.C. to the Death of Trajan*. Oxford: At the Clarendon Press, 1941.

Christensen, Arthur. *L'Iran sous les Sassanides*. 2d ed. Copenhagen: Ejnar Munksgaard, 1944.

Christescu, Vasile. *Istoria militară a Daciei Romane*. Bucharest: Fundatia Regele Carol I, 1937.

Clemente, Guido. *La "Notitia Dignitatum."* Saggi di storia e letteratura, no. 4. Cagliari, Sardinia: Editrice Sarda Fossataro, 1968.

Courcelle, Pierre Paul. *Histoire littéraire des grandes invasions germaniques*. 3d ed. Paris: Etudes Augustinnienes, 1964.

Coussin, Paul. *Les Armes romaines: Essai sur les origines et l'evolution des armes individuelles du légionnaire romain*. Paris: Librairie ancienne Honoré Champion, 1926.

Curzon, George Nathan, Lord Kedleston. *Frontiers*. Romanes Lecture Series. Oxford: At the Clarendon Press, 1907.

Dahl, Robert A. *Modern Political Analysis*. Englewood Cliffs, N.J.: Prentice-Hall, 1963.

Daicoviciu, Constantin. *La Transilvania nell'antichità*. Rev. ed. of 1938 essay. Bucharest: n.p., 1943.

———. *La Transylvanie dans l'antiquité*. Bucharest: n.p., 1945.

Daicoviciu, Constantin, and Daicoviciu, Hadrain. *Columna lui Traian*. Bucharest: Editura Meridiane, 1968.

Degrassi, Attilio. *Il Confine nord-orientale dell'Italia romana: Ricerche storico-topografiche*. Dissertationes Bernenses, ser. I, fasc. 6. Bern: A. Francke, 1954.

Demougeot, Émilienne. *De l'Unité à la division de l'empire romain 395–410: Essai sur le gouvernement imperial*. Paris: Librairie d'Amerique et d'Orient, 1951.

———. *La Formation de l'Europe et les invasions barbares: Des origines germaniques à l'avènement de Dioclétien*. Paris: Aubier, 1969.

Dudley, Donald Reynolds, and Webster, Graham. *The Roman Conquest of Britain A.D. 43–57*. London: Dufour Éditions, 1965.

Durry, Marcel. *Les Cohortes Prétoriennes*. Bibliothèque des écoles françaises d'Athènes et de Rome, fasc. 146. Paris: E. de Boccard, 1938.

Emmet, Dorothy. *Function, Purpose and Powers*. London: Macmillan and Co., 1958.

Fink, Robert O. *Roman Military Records on Papyrus*. Texts, Varia. Philological Monographs of the American Philological Association, no. 26. Cleveland: Case Western Reserve University, 1971.

Forni, Giovanni. *Il Reclutamento delle legioni da Augusto a Diocleziano*. Pubblicazioni della facolta di filosofia e lettere della Università di Pavia, 5. Milan and Rome: Fratelli Bocca, 1953.

Frank, Richard Ira. *Scholae Palatinae: The Palace Guards of the Later Roman Empire*. Papers and Monographs of the American Academy in Rome, vol. 23. Rome: American Academy in Rome, 1969.

Frere, Sheppard S. *Britannia: A History of Roman Britain.* London: Routledge and Kegan Paul, 1967.

Garbsch, Jochen G. *Der Spätrömische Donau-Iller Rhein Limes.* Stuttgart: A. W. Gentner, 1970.

Garzetti, Albino. *L'Impero da Tiberio agli Antonini.* Instituto di studi romani, Storia di Roma, vol. 6. Bologna: Licinio Cappelli, 1960.

——. *Problemi dell'eta traianea: Sommario e testi.* Genova: Fratelli Bozzi, 1971.

Geweke, Lenore K., and Winspear, Alban D. *Augustus and the Reconstruction of Roman Government and Society.* University of Wisconsin Studies in the Social Sciences and Philosophy, no. 24. Madison: University of Wisconsin, 1935.

Ghirshman, R. *Les Chionites-Hephtalites.* Mémoires de l'institut français d'archéologie orientale du Caire, vol. 53. Mémoires de la délégation archéologique française en Afghanistan, vol. 13. Cairo: Institut français d'archéologie orientale, 1948.

Gianelli, Giulio. *Trattato di storia romana.* 2 vols. Rev. ed. by Santo Mazzarino. Rome: Tumminelli, 1953-1956.

Gitti, A. *Ricerche sui rapporti tra i vandali e l'impero romano.* Bari: Laterza, 1953.

Gonella, Guido. *Pace romana e pace cartaginese.* Quaderni di studi romani, serie seconda, no. 1. Rome: Istituto di studi romani, 1947.

Goodyear, Francis Richard D. *The Annals of Tacitus.* Vol. 1, Annals I.1–54. Cambridge: At the University Press, 1972.

Guey, Julien. *Essai sur la guerre parthique de Trajan (114–117).* Bibliothèque d'Istros, no. 2. Bucharest: S. Lambrino, 1937.

Hammond, Mason. *The Antonine Monarchy.* American Academy in Rome, Papers and Monographs, no. 19. Rome: American Academy in Rome, 1959.

——. *The Augustan Principate: In Theory and Practice During the Julio-Claudian Period.* Enlarged edition. New York: Russel and Russel, 1968.

Hardy, Ernest George. *Studies in Roman History.* 2d ser. London: S. Sonnenschein and Co., 1909.

Harkness, Albert. *The Military System of the Romans.* New York: D. Appleton and Company, 1887.

Harmand, Jacques. *L'Armée et le soldat à Rome (de 107 à 50 avant notre ère).* Paris: Ed. A. et J. Picard et Cie., 1967

——. *La Guerre antique, de Sumer á Rome.* Paris: Presses universitaires de France, 1973.

Harmand, Louis. *L'Occident romain: Gaule, Espagne, Bretagne, Afrique du Nord (31 av. J. C. à 235 ap. J. C.).* Paris: Payot, 1960.

Harmatta, John. *Studies in the History of the Sarmatians.* Magyar-Görög Tanulmányok, 30. Budapest: Pázamány Péter Tumányegyetemi Görög Filológiai Intézet, 1950.

Hatt, Jean-Jacques. *Histoire de la Gaule romaine (120 avant J-C 451 après J-C): Colonisation ou colonialisme.* Paris: Payot, 1966.

Henderson, Bernard W. *The Life and Principate of the Emperor Hadrian A.D. 76–138.* London: Methuen and Co., 1923.

——. *Five Roman Emperors: Vespasian, Titus, Domitian, Nerva, Trajan (69–117).* 1927. Reprint. New York: Barnes and Noble, 1969.

Holmes, T. Rice. *The Architect of the Roman Empire 27 B.C.-A.D. 14.* 2 vols. Oxford: At the Clarendon Press, 1928-1931.

Holsti, K. J. *International Politics: A Framework for Analysis.* 2d ed. Englewood Cliffs, N.J.: Prentice-Hall, 1972.

Homo, Léon P. *Essai sur le règne de l'empereur Aurélien (270–275).* Bibliothèque des écoles françaises d'Athènes et de Rome, fasc. 89. Paris: A. Fontemoing, 1904.

——. *Le Siècle d'or de l'empire romain.* Paris: A. Fayard, 1947.

——. *Vespasien l'empereur du bon sens (69-79 ap. J-C).* Paris: Albin Michel, 1949.

Jones, Arnold Hugh Martin. *The Later Roman Empire (284–602): A Social and Economic Survey.* 3 vols. Oxford: Basil Blackwell, 1964. [3 vols. in 2: Oklahoma University Press, 1964.]

——. ed. Texts, varia *A History of Rome Through the Fifth Century.* 2 vols. New York: Harper and Row, 1970.

——. *Augustus*. London: Chatto and Windus, 1970; New York: W. W. Norton, 1970.

Jouvenel, Bertrand de. *Power: Its Nature and the History of Its Growth*. Boston: Beacon Press, 1967.

Kaegi, Walter Emil, Jr. *Byzantium and the Decline of Rome*. Princeton: Princeton University Press, 1968.

Katz, Solomon. *The Decline of Rome and the Rise of Mediaeval Europe*. Ithaca: Cornell University Press, 1955.

La Penna, Antonio. *Orazio e l'ideologia del principato*. Saggi no. 332. Turin: Giulio Einaudi, 1963.

Lemosse, Maxime. *Le Régime des relationes internationales dans le haut-empire romain*. Publications de l'Institut de droit romain de l'Université de Paris, vol. 23. Paris: Librairie Sirey, 1967.

Lepper, F. A. *Trajan's Parthian War*. London: Geoffrey Cumberlege, 1948.

Lesquier, Jean. *L'Armée romaine d'Égypte d'Auguste à Dioclétien*. Cairo: Institut français d'archéologie orientale, 1918.

Levi, M. A. [Canavesi, M.] *La Politica estera di Roma antica*. Manuali di politica internazionale 34. 2 vols. Milan: Instituto per gli studi di politica internazionale, 1942.

Levick, Barbara Mary. *Roman Colonies in Southern Asia Minor*. Oxford: At the Clarendon Press, 1967.

Lot, Ferdinand. *Les Invasions Germaniques: La pénétration mutuelle du monde barbare et du monde romain*. Paris: Payot, 1935.

——. *L'Art militaire et les armées au Moyen Age en Europe et dans le Proche Orient*. 2 vols. Paris: Payot, 1946.

——. *Nouvelle recherches sur l'impot foncier et la capitation personelle sous le Bas-Empire*. Bibliothèque de l'école des hautes études, fasc. 304. Paris: Librairie ancienne Honoré Champion, 1955.

MacMullen, Ramsay. *Soldier and Civilian in the Later Roman Empire*. Harvard Historical Monographs, vol. 52. Cambridge, Mass.: Harvard University Press, 1963.

Magie, David. *Roman Rule in Asia Minor to the End of the Third Century after Christ*. 2 vols. Princeton: Princeton University Press, 1950.

Manni, Eugenio. *L'Impero di Gallieno: Contributo alla storia del III secolo*. Rome: Angelo Signorelli, 1949.

Marichal, Robert. *L'Occupation romaine de la Basse Égypte: Le statut des auxilia*. Paris: E. Droz, 1945.

Marin y Peña, Manuel. *Instituciones militares romanas*. Enciclopedia Clasica no. 2. Madrid: Consejo Superior de Investigaciones Cientificas Patronato "Menendez y Pelayo," 1956.

Marquardt, Joachim. *De l'Organisation militaire chez les Romains*. Rev. ed. A. Von Domaszewski. Trans. J. Brissaud. Manuel des antiquités romaines de Joachim Marquardt et Théodore Mommsen, vol. 11. Paris: A Fontemoing, 1891.

Marsden, Eric William. *Greek and Roman Artillery: Historical Development*. 2 vols. Oxford: At the Clarendon Press, 1969.

Marsh, Frank Burr, *The Reign of Tiberius*. London: Oxford University Press, 1931.

Maspero, Jean. *Organisation militaire de l'Égypte Byzantine*. Bibliothèque de l'école des hautes etudes, fasc. 201. Paris: Librairie ancienne Honoré Champion, 1912.

Mazzarino, Santo. *Stilicone: La crisi imperiale dopo Teodosio*. Studi pubblicati dal R. istituto italiano per la storia antica, fasc. 3. Rome: Angelo Signorelli, 1942.

——. *Aspetti sociali del quarto secolo: Ricerche di storia tardo-romana*. Rome: L'Erma di Bretschneider, 1951.

Mazzarino, Santo, and Gianelli, Giulio. *Trattato di storia romana*. Rev. ed. 2 vols. Rome: Tumminelli, 1953–1956.

Momigliano, Arnaldo. *Contributo alla storia degli studi classici*. Rome: Edizioni di Storia e Letteratura, 1955.

——. *Terzo Contributo alla storia degli studi classici e del mondo antico*. Rome: Edizioni di Storia e Letteratura, 1966.

——. *Ricerche sull'organizzazione della Giudea sotto il dominio romano (63 a.C-70 d.C)*. Amsterdam: A. M. Hakkert, 1967.

——. *Quarto Contributo alla storia degli studi classici e del mondo antico.* Rome: Edizioni di Storia e Letteratura, 1969.

Morgenthau, Hans J. *Politics Among Nations.* 3d ed. New York: Alfred A. Knopf, 1962.

Murphy, Gerard James. *The Reign of the Emperor L. Septimius Severus from the Evidence of the Inscriptions.* Philadelphia: n.p., 1945.

Musset, Lucien. *Les Invasions: Les vagues germaniques.* Nouvelle Clio, no. 12. Paris: Presses universitaires de France, 1965.

Oates, David. *Studies in the Ancient History of Northern Iraq.* London: Oxford University Press for the British Academy, 1968.

Oliva, Pavel. *Pannonia and the Onset of the Crisis in the Roman Empire.* Prague: Československé Akademie Věd, 1962.

Oman, Charles W. C. *A History of the Art of War in the Middle Ages.* 2d rev. ed. 2 vols. London: Methuen and Co., 1924.

Ondrouch, Vojtěch. *Limes Romanus na Slovensku (il limes romano in Slovacchia).* Bratislava: Práce Učene Společnosti Šafarikovy v Bratislavě, 1938.

Orgeval, Bernard d'. *L'empereur Hadrien: Oeuvre législative et administrative.* Paris: Editions Domat Montchrestien, 1950.

Osgood, Robert E., and Tucker, Robert W. *Force, Order, and Justice.* Baltimore: The Johns Hopkins Press, 1967.

Parker, Henry Michael Denne. *The Roman Legions.* 1928. Reprinted, with corrections and bibliography. Cambridge: W. Heffer and Sons, 1958.

Paschoud, François. *Roma aeterna: Études sur le patriotisme romain dans l'occident latin á l'époque des grandes invasions.* Bibliotheca Helvetica Romana, no. 7. Rome: Institut Suisse de Rome, 1967.

Passerini, Alfredo. *Le Coorti Pretorie.* 1939. Reprint. Rome: Centro Editoriale Internazionale, 1969.

——. *Linee di storia romana in etá imperiale.* 2d ed. Revised by Nicola Criniti. Milan: Celuc, 1972.

Pelham, Henry Francis. *Essays.* Edited by F. Haverfield. Oxford: At the Clarendon Press, 1911.

Piganiol, André. *L'Empire Chrétien 325–395.* 2d ed. Revised by A. Chastagnol. 1948. Reprint. Paris: Presses universitaires de France, 1972.

——. *Scripta Varia.* Edited by R. Bloch. et al. 3 vols. Collection Latomus, nos. 131–33. Brussels: Latomus, 1973.

Platnauer, Maurice. *The Life and Reign of the Emperor Lucius Septimius Severus.* London and Bombay: Humphrey Milford, 1918.

Poidebard, A. *La Trace de Rome dans le désert de Syrie: Le limes de Trajan à la conquête arabe, recherches aériennes, (1925–1934).* Paris: Librairie orientaliste Paul Geuthner, 1934.

Pugliese, Carratelli. *L'età di Valeriano e Gallieno: Appunti di storia romana.* Pisa: Libreria Goliardica, 1950.

Rachet, Marguerite. *Rome et les Berbères: Un Problème militaire d'Auguste à Dioclétien.* Collection Latomus, vol. 110. Brussels: Latomus, 1970.

Regibus, Luca de. *La Monarchia militare di Gallieno.* Recco, Italy: Editrice Nicoloso da Recco, 1939.

Rémondon, Roger. *La Crise de l'empire romain de Marc Aurèle à Anastase.* Nouvelle Clio, no. 11. Paris: Presses universitaires de France. 1964.

Reynolds, P. K. B. *The Vigiles of Ancient Rome.* Oxford: At the Clarendon Press, 1926.

Richmond, Sir Ian A. *The City Wall of Imperial Rome: An Account of its Architectural Development from Aurelian to Narses.* Oxford: At the Clarendon Press, 1930.

Romanelli, Pietro. *La Cirenaica Romana 96 A.C.-642 D.C.* Verbania: A. Airoldi, 1943.

Rossi, Lino. *Trajan's Column and the Dacian Wars.* Edited and translated by J. M. C. Toynbee. London: Thames and Hudson, 1971.

Rougé, Jean. *Les Institutions romaines: De la Rome royale à la Rome chrétienne.* Paris: Librairie Armand Colin, 1969.

Rowell, Henry T. *Ammianus Marcellinus, Soldier-Historian of the Late Roman Empire.* Cincinnati: University of Cincinnati Press, 1964.

Salway, Peter. *The Frontier People of Roman Britain.* Cambridge: At the University Press, 1965.

Sands, P.C. *The Client Princes of the Roman Empire under the Republic.* Cambridge Historical Essays, no. 16. Cambridge: At the University Press, 1908.

Saxer, Robert. *Untersuchungen zu den vexillationen des römischen Kaiserreichs von Augustus bis Diokletian.* Epigraphische Studien, no. 1. Beihefte der Bonner Jahrbücher, no. 18. Cologne and Graz: Böhlau, 1967.

Schleiermacher, Wilhelm. *Der römische Limes in Deutschland. Limesführer.* 3d ed. Berlin: Gebr. Mann, 1967.

Scramuzza, Vincent M. *The Emperor Claudius.* Cambridge, Mass.: Harvard University Press, 1940.

Seager, Robin, *Tiberius.* London: Eyre Methuen, 1972.

Seston, William. *Dioclétien et la tétrarchie.* vol. 1. *Guerres et réformes (284–300).* Bibliothèque des Écoles françaises d'Athènes et de Rome, fasc. 162. Paris: E. de Boccard, 1946.

Sherwin-White, Adrian N. *The Roman Citizenship.* 2d ed. Oxford: At the Clarendon Press, 1973.

———. *The Letters of Pliny: A Historical and Social Commentary.* Oxford: At the Clarendon Press, 1966.

Simpson, Grace. *Britons and the Roman Army: A Study of Wales and the Southern Pennines in the 1st-3d Centuries.* London: The Gregg Press, 1964.

Sirago, Vito Antonio. *Galla Placidia e la trasformazione politica dell'occidente.* Université de Louvain. Recueil des travaux d'histoire et de philologie. 4e série, fasc. 25. Louvain: Publications universitaires, 1961.

Smith, Richard Edwin. *Service in the Post-Marian Roman Army.* Manchester: Manchester University Press, 1958.

Solari, Arturo. *La Crisi dell'impero romano.* 2 vols. Milan: Soc. Ed. Dante Alighieri, 1933.

———. *Il Rinnovamento dell'impero romano.* Milan: Soc. Ed. Dante Alighieri, 1938.

Starr, Chester G., Jr. *The Roman Imperial Navy, 31 B.C.-A.D. 324.* Cornell Studies in Classical Philology, vol. 26. Ithaca: Cornell University Press, 1941.

Stein, Ernst. *Histoire du Bas-Empire: De l'état romain à l'état byzantin (284–476).* Vol. I [two parts]. Edited and translated by Jean-Remy Palanque. Paris: Desclée de Brouwer, 1959.

———. *Opera Minora Selecta.* Amsterdam: A. M. Hakkert, 1968.

Stevenson, George Hope. *Roman Provincial Administration Till the Age of the Severi.* Oxford: Basil Blackwell, 1930.

Syme, Ronald. *The Roman Revolution.* Oxford: At the Clarendon Press, 1939.

Syme, Sir Ronald. *Tacitus.* 2 vols. Oxford: At the Clarendon Press, 1958.

Thompson, E. A. *The Historical Work of Ammianus Marcellinus.* Cambridge: At the University Press, 1947.

———. *A History of Attila and the Huns.* Oxford: At the Clarendon Press, 1948.

———. *A Roman Reformer and Inventor: Being a New Text of the Treatise De Rebus Bellicis with a Translation and Introduction.* Oxford: At the Clarendon Press, 1952.

———. *The Early Germans.* Oxford: Clarendon Press, 1965.

———. *The Visigoths in the Time of Ulfila.* Oxford: At the Clarendon Press, 1966.

Tovey, Lieut.-Col. Hamilton. *Elements of Strategy.* London: Eyre and Spottiswoode, 1887.

Vigneron, Paul. *Le Cheval dans l'antiquité gréco-romaine, de guerres médiques aux grandes invasions: Contribution à l'histoire des techniques.* Annales de l'Est, mémoires no. 35. Nancy: Faculté des lettres et de sciences humaines, 1968.

Walter, Eugene Victor. *Terror and Resistance: A Study of Political Violence.* New York: Oxford University Press, 1969.

Warmington, Brian H. *The North African Provinces from Diocletian to the Vandal Conquest.* Cambridge: Cambridge University Press, 1954.

Watson, G. R. *The Roman Soldier.* London: Thames and Hudson, 1969.

Webster, Graham. *The Roman Imperial Army of the First and Second Centuries A.D.* London: Adam and Charles Black, 1969.

Wells, Colin Michael. *The German Policy of Augustus: An Examination of the Archaeological Evidence.* Oxford: At the Clarendon Press, 1972.

Wheeler, Sir R. E. Mortimer. *Rome Beyond the Imperial Frontiers.* London: G. Bell and Sons, 1954.

White, Donald A. *Litus Saxonicum: The British Saxon Shore in Scholarship and History.* Madison: University of Wisconsin Press, 1961.
White, Lynn Townsend, ed. *The Transformation of the Roman World: Gibbon's Problems after Two Centuries.* Berkeley: University of California Press, 1966.
Wilkes, J. J. *Dalmatia: History of the Provinces of the Roman Empire.* London: Routledge and Kegan Paul, 1969.
Winspear, Alban D., and Geweke, Lenore K. *Augustus and the Reconstruction of Roman Government and Society.* University of Wisconsin Studies in the Social Sciences and Philosophy, no. 24. Madison: University of Wisconsin Press, 1935.
Zancan, Paola. *La Crisi del Principato nell'anno 69 D.C.* R. Universita di Padova. Pubblicazioni della Facultà di Lettere e Filosofia, vol. 16. Padova: Dott. Antonio Milani, 1939.

III
Unpublished Works
Gordon, Colin D. "The Subsidization of Border Peoples as a Roman Policy of Imperial Defense." Ph.D. diss., University of Michigan, 1948. (LC microfilm AC-1, no. 1105.)
Kaltenbach, Philip E. "Non-Citizen Troops in the 'Roman Army.' " Ph.D. diss., Johns Hopkins University, 1948.
Minor, Clifford E. "Brigand, Insurrectionist and Separatist Movements in the Later Roman Empire." Ph.D. diss., University of Washington, 1971.
Moscovich, Maurice James. "The Role of Hostages in Roman Foreign Policy." Ph.D. diss., McMaster University (Canada), 1972.
Petersen, Hans E. "Governorship and Military Command in the Roman Empire." Ph.D. diss., Harvard University, 1953.
Wade, Donald W. "The Roman Auxiliary Units and Camps in Dacia." Ph.D. diss., University of North Carolina, 1969.
Uspensky, Th. I. "Military Organization of the Byzantine Empire." Typescript. Translated by J. Krenov, from Bulletin of the Russian Archaeological Institute at Constantinople, vol. 6. Sophia [Bulgaria], 1900. W.P.A. No. 3888, 1941. O.P. 165-1-93-11. [L. of C.].

IV
Collective Works
1. Congresses of Roman Frontier Studies (in chronological order).
[Third] *Congress of Roman Frontier Studies, 1949.* Edited by Eric B. Birley. Durham: Durham University Registrar, 1952.
Carnuntina: Ergebnisse der Forschung über die Grenzprovinzen des römischen Reiches, Vorträge beim internationalen Kongress der Altertumsforscher Carnuntum, 1955. Edited by Erich Swoboda. Römische Forschungen in Niederösterreich, vol. 3. Graz and Cologne: Hermann Böhlaus Nachf., 1956.
Limes Romanus Konferenz, Nitra. Slovenskej Akadémie vied Bratislava. Bratislava: Slovenskej Akadémie, 1959.
Quintus Congressus Internationalis Limitis Romani Studiosorum [Fifth Congress]. Acta et Dissertationes Archaeologicae. Zagreb: Arheološki Radovi i Rasprave III, 1963.
Corolla Memoriae Erich Swoboda Dedicata. Römische Forschungen in Niederösterreich, vol. 5. Graz and Cologne: Hermann Böhlaus Nachf., 1966.
Studien zu den Militärgrenzen Roms: Vorträge des 6. Internationalen Limes Kongresses in Süddeutschland. Beihefte der Bonner Jahrbücher, vol. 19. Cologne and Graz: Böhlau, 1967.
Roman Frontier Studies, 1967 [7th Congress]. Tel Aviv: Students' Organization, 1971.

2. Others (by editor or title).
Applebaum, Shimon, and Gichon, Mordechai. *Israel and Her Vicinity in the Roman and Byzantine Periods.* Tel Aviv: Tel Aviv University Press, 1967.
Bell, Roderick; Edwards, David V.; Wagner, Harrison. *Political Power: A Reader in Theory and Research.* New York: The Free Press, 1969.

Bibaw, Jacqueline, ed. *Hommages à Marcel Renard.* 3 vols. Collection Latomus, vol. 102. Brussels: Latomus, 1969.

Brisson, Jean-Paul, ed. *Problèmes de la guerre à Rome.* École pratique des hautes études-Sorbonne 6 section: Sciences économiques et sociales. Centre de recherches historiques civilisations et sociétés. 12. Paris and The Hague: Mouton and Co., 1969.

Butler, Ronald M., ed. *Soldier and Civilian in Roman Yorkshire: Essays to Commemorate the Nineteenth Centenary of the Foundation of York.* Leicester: Leicester University Press, 1971.

Cambridge Ancient History. Gen. ed. John B. Bury. Vols. 10, 11, 12. Cambridge: At the University Press, 1934–1939.

Caprino, C.; Colini, A. M.; Gatti, G.; Pallottino, M.; Romanelli, P. *La Colonna di Marco Aurelio.* Rome: L'"Erma" di Bretschneider, 1955.

Centre national de la recherche scientifique. *Les Empereurs romains d'Espagne.* Colloques internationaux du centre national de la recherche scientifique. Paris: Éditions du centre national de la recherche scientifique, 1965.

Chevallier, Raymond, ed. *Mélanges d'archéologie et d'histoire offerts à André Piganiol.* École pratique des hautes études—VIe Section Centre de recherches historiques. 3 vols. Paris: S.E.V.P.E.N., 1966.

Grimes, W. F., ed. *Aspects of Archaeology in Britain and Beyond: Essays Presented to O. G. S. Crawford.* London: H. W. Edwards, 1951.

Howard, M., ed. *The Theory and Practice of War: Essays Presented to Captain B. H. Liddel Hart.* London: Cassell, 1965.

Proceedings of the XIII International Congress of Byzantine Studies. Edited by J. M. Hussey, D. Obolensky, and S. Runciman. Oxford: At the Clarendon Press, 1967.

Mélanges Marcel Durry: Revue des études latines. Vol. 47 bis. Paris: Soc. d'édition "Les Belles Lettres," 1969.

Millar, Fergus; Berciu, D.; Frye, Richard N.; Kossack, Georg; Talbot, Rice Tamara. *The Roman Empire and its Neighbours.* London: Weidenfeld and Nicolson, 1967.

Renard, Marcel, ed. *Hommages à Albert Grenier.* 3 vols. Collection Latomus, vol. 58. Brussels: Latomus, 1962.

Temporini, Hildegard, ed. *Aufstieg und Niedergang der Römischen Welt: Geschichte und Kultur Roms in Spiegel der neueren Forschung* [A.N.R.W.] Berlin and New York: Walter de Gruyter, 1974.

INDEX

THE JOHNS HOPKINS UNIVERSITY PRESS

This book was composed in Andover text and display type by Jones Composition Company from a design by Susan Bishop. It was printed on 50-lb. Publishers Eggshell Wove and bound by The Maple Press Company.

Library of Congress Cataloging in Publication Data

Luttwak, Edward.
　The grand strategy of the Roman Empire from the first century
A.D. to the third.

　Bibliography: p. 233
　Includes index.
　1. Rome—Army. 2. Strategy. 3. Military history, Ancient. I.
Title.

U35.L8　355.03′303′7　76–17232
ISBN 0–8018–1863–X